LIBRARY OF NEW TESTAMENT STUDIES

467

*Formerly Journal for the Study of the New Testament Supplement Series*

Editor
Mark Goodacre

*Editorial Board*
John M. G. Barclay, Craig Blomberg,
R. Alan Culpepper, James D. G. Dunn, Craig A. Evans, Stephen Fowl,
Robert Fowler, Simon J. Gathercole, John S. Kloppenborg, Michael Labahn,
Robert Wall, Steve Walton, Robert L. Webb, Catrin H. Williams

# IS PAUL ALSO AMONG THE PROPHETS?

An Examination of the Relationship between Paul and the Old Testament Prophetic Tradition in 2 Corinthians

Jeffrey W. Aernie

t&t clark

Published by T&T Clark International
*A Continuum imprint*
The Tower Building, 11 York Road, London SE1 7NX
80 Maiden Lane, New York, NY 10038

www.continuumbooks.com

All rights reserved. No part of this publication may be reproduced or transmitted in any form or by any means, electronic or mechanical, including photocopying, recording or any information storage or retrieval system, without permission in writing from the publishers.

© Jeffrey W. Aernie, 2012

Jeffrey W. Aernie has asserted his right under the Copyright, Designs and Patents Act, 1988, to be identified as the Author of this work.

**British Library Cataloguing-in-Publication Data**
A catalogue record for this book is available from the British Library

ISBN: HB: 978-0-567-17572-4

**Library of Congress Cataloging-in-Publication Data**
A catalog record for this book is available from the Library of Congress.

Typeset and copy-edited by Forthcoming Publications Ltd. (www.forthpub.com)
Printed and bound in Great Britain

## Contents

| | |
|---|---|
| Acknowledgments | ix |
| Abbreviations | xi |

**Chapter 1**
INTRODUCTION — 1
1. The Object of the Study — 1
2. The Parameters of the Study — 2
3. The Position of the Study — 3

**Chapter 2**
THE DEVELOPMENT OF THE PROPHETIC TRADITION — 8
1. Introduction — 8
2. The Prophetic Tradition in the Old Testament — 10
   a. Prophetic Material in the Pentateuch and Historical Books — 10
   b. The Prophetic Literature — 19
   c. Conclusions — 27
3. The Prophetic Tradition in Second Temple Judaism — 28
   a. The Potential Cessation of Prophecy — 29
   b. Prophetic Activity in the Second Temple Period — 36
   c. Conclusions — 50
4. Hellenistic Prophetic Traditions — 51
5. The Prophetic Tradition in the Gospel Traditions — 61
6. Conclusion — 70

**Chapter 3**
THE PROPHETIC TRADITION IN 1 CORINTHIANS — 72
1. Introduction — 72
2. Prophetic Persona (1 Corinthians 9.15-18) — 73
   a. Renunciation of Rights (1 Corinthians 9.15) — 76
   b. Prophetic Constraint (1 Corinthians 9.16-17) — 78
   c. Free Proclamation (1 Corinthians 9.18) — 87
   d. Conclusions — 89

    3.  Prophetic Rhetoric (1 Corinthians 14.20-25)                 90
        a.  Exhortation (1 Corinthians 14.20)                       92
        b.  Scriptural Quotation (1 Corinthians 14.21)              93
        c.  Inspired Speech in the Assembly
            (1 Corinthians 14.22-25)                              102
        d.  Conclusions                                            111
    4.  Conclusion

## Chapter 4
### PAUL'S PROPHETIC SELF-PRESENTATION IN 2 CORINTHIANS   113
    1.  Introduction                                                  113
    2.  The Relationship between Paul and Moses                  114
        a.  The Ministerial Call of Paul                          116
        b.  The Nature of Paul's Ministry                       120
        c.  The Function of Paul's Ministry                     130
        d.  Conclusions                                            132
    3.  The Relationship between Paul and the Isaianic Servant   133
        a.  Paul and the Servant Outside of 2 Corinthians      135
        b.  Paul and the Servant Within 2 Corinthians           139
        c.  Conclusions                                            157
    4.  The Relationship between Paul and Jeremiah               158
        a.  The Call of Paul in Relation to Jeremiah              159
        b.  Paul as a Minister of the New Covenant             161
        c.  Jeremiah's Mission and Paul's Authority             166
        d.  Paul's Act of Boasting in the Lord                  175
        e.  Conclusions                                            183
    5.  Conclusion                                                 184

## Chapter 5
### PAUL'S PROPHETIC RHETORIC IN 2 CORINTHIANS   185
    1.  Introduction                                                  185
    2.  Prophetic Triumph in 2 Corinthians 2.14-16               186
        a.  Paul's Apostleship as Defeated Sacrifice             186
        b.  Paul's Prophetic Framework                         192
        c.  Conclusions                                            195
    3.  Prophetic Proclamation in 2 Corinthians 4.1-6           195
        a.  Paul's Apostolic Character (2 Corinthians 4.1-2)    196
        b.  Christocentric Proclamation (2 Corinthians 4.3-4)   199
        c.  Prophetic Light (2 Corinthians 4.5-6)               202
        d.  Conclusions                                            214

|    |    | Contents | vii |
|---|---|---|---|

4. Prophetic Exhortation in 2 Corinthians 6.14–7.1   215
    a. Initial Exhortation (2 Corinthians 6.14)   217
    b. Rhetorical Antitheses (2 Corinthians 6.14-16)   219
    c. Scriptural Substantiation (2 Corinthians 6.16-18)   223
    d. Final Exhortation (2 Corinthians 7.1)   231
    e. Conclusions   233
5. Prophetic Ascent in 2 Corinthians 12.1-10   233
    a. Paul's Failed Heavenly Ascent   234
    b. Paul's Prophetic Framework   239
    c. Conclusions   243
6. Conclusion   244

## Chapter 6
### CONCLUSION   245
1. Summary and Implications   245
2. Further Research   250

Bibliography   251
Index of References   278
Index of Authors   291

## Acknowledgments

The present study constitutes a slightly revised version of my doctoral thesis, submitted to the University of Aberdeen in 2011. The completion of such a project is rarely done in isolation and I am grateful for the numerous contributions of time, effort, and encouragement offered throughout the course of that unique academic pilgrimage. Special acknowledgment is due especially to Dr. Andrew Clarke for his patient and attentive supervision of the project. His own measured approach to biblical and theological studies is an admirable example of scholarship.

The examiners of the original thesis, Dr. Jutta Leonhardt-Balzer and Prof. Karl Olav Sandnes, offered invaluable insights and sharpened the work at numerous points. Thanks are also due to Dr. Eckhard Schnabel, who first introduced me to the depths of the argument in 2 Corinthians, and to Dr. Robert Yarbrough, who provided continual scholarly wisdom and support. Likewise, the faculty and postgraduate students at the University of Aberdeen created a constructive academic community within which to develop the study. Sincere thanks are also due to Dr. Mark Goodacre and the editorial staff at T&T Clark International for accepting the volume as part of the Library of New Testament Studies.

Gratitude must also be expressed to my extended family. My parents, Debra Hansen and Robert Aernie, supplied constant love and encouragement. Michael, Nicole, Haley, and Bonnie Aernie, as well as Randy, Norma, Andrea, and Arica Coleman, took great interest in the project and offered support in more ways than can be counted. My late maternal grandparents, George and Jean Pirtle, were in many ways the catalyst for the project. I am particularly indebted to my brother, Dr. Matthew Aernie, who read the entire work and contributed sage insights at a number of points. I am especially grateful for his encouragement throughout the process.

Above all, I am indebted to my immediate family, all of whom graciously sacrificed in many ways to ensure that this study came to fruition. My daughters, Abigail Jean and Chloe Anne, who both arrived during the course of the project, provided constant joy and refreshment. My wife and best friend, Allison, supplied both editorial insight and loving support. No aspect of this study was completed without her wisdom and encouragement, and so I dedicate it to her.

# ABBREVIATIONS

| | |
|---|---|
| AB | Anchor Bible |
| *ABD* | *Anchor Bible Dictionary*. Edited by D.N. Freedman. 6 vols. New York, 1992 |
| ABRL | Anchor Bible Reference Library |
| ACNT | Augsburg Commentaries on the New Testament |
| AGJU | Arbeiten zur Geschichte des antiken Judentums und des Urchristentums |
| AnBib | Analecta biblica |
| *ANRW* | *Aufstieg und Niedergang der römischen Welt: Geschichte und Kultur Roms im Spiegel der neueren Forschung*. Edited by H. Temporini and W. Haase. Berlin, 1972– |
| ATANT | Abhandlungen zur Theologie des Alten und Neuen Testaments |
| AUM | Andrews University Monographs |
| *AUSS* | *Andrews University Seminary Studies* |
| BA | *Biblical Archaeologist* |
| BBB | Bonner biblische Beiträge |
| *BBR* | *Bulletin for Biblical Research* |
| BDAG | Bauer, W., F.W. Danker, W.F. Arndt, and F.W. Gingrich. *Greek–English Lexicon of the New Testament and Other Early Christian Literature*. 3d ed. Chicago, 1999 |
| BEATAJ | Beiträge zur Erforschung des Alten Testaments und des antiken Judentum |
| BECNT | Baker Exegetical Commentary on the New Testament |
| BETL | Bibliotheca ephemeridum theologicarum lovaniensium |
| BDF | Blass, F., A. Debrunner, and R.W. Funk. *A Greek Grammar of the New Testament and Other Early Christian Literature*. Chicago, 1961 |
| BFT | Biblical Foundations in Theology |
| BHT | Beiträge zur historischen Theologie |
| *Bib* | *Biblica* |
| BJS | Brown Judaic Studies |
| BNTC | Black's New Testament Commentaries |
| *BSac* | *Bibliotheca sacra* |
| BST | Basel Studies of Theology |
| BT | *Bible Translator* |
| BTB | *Biblical Theology Bulletin* |
| BTS | Biblical Tools and Studies |
| *BTZ* | *Berliner Theologische Zeitschrift* |
| BZAW | Beihefte zur Zeitschrift für die alttestamentliche Wissenschaft |

| | |
|---|---|
| CahT | Cahiers Théologiques de l'Actualité Protestante |
| CBET | Contributions to Biblical Exegesis and Theology |
| *CBQ* | *Catholic Biblical Quarterly* |
| CEB | Commentaire Evangélique de la Bible |
| CGTC | Cambridge Greek Testament Commentary |
| CNT | Commentaire du Nouveau Testament |
| CNTC | Calvin's New Testament Commentaries |
| CRINT | Compendia rerum iudaicarum ad Novum Testamentum |
| *CTJ* | *Calvin Theological Journal* |
| *CTR* | *Criswell Theological Review* |
| *DJG* | *Dictionary of Jesus and the Gospels*. Edited by J.B. Green and S. McKnight. Downers Grove, 1992 |
| *DNTB* | *Dictionary of New Testament Background*. Edited by Craig A. Evans and Stanley E. Porter. Downers Grove, 2000 |
| *DPL* | *Dictionary of Paul and His Letters*. Edited by G.F. Hawthorne and R.P. Martin. Downers Grove, 1993 |
| Ebib | Études biblique |
| EDNT | *Exegetical Dictionary of the New Testament*. Edited by H. Balz, G. Schneider. ET. Grand Rapids, 1990–93 |
| *EgT* | *Église et théologie* |
| EKKNT | Evangelisch-katholischer Kommentar zum Neuen Testament |
| ESEC | Emory Studies in Early Christianity |
| *ETR* | *Etudes théologiques et religieuses* |
| *EvQ* | *Evangelical Quarterly* |
| *ExpTim* | *Expository Times* |
| FAT | Forschungen zum Alten Testament |
| FRLANT | Forschungen zur Religion und Literatur des Alten und Neuen Testaments |
| FzB | Forschung zur Bibel |
| GBS | Guides to Biblical Scholarship |
| GTA | Göttinger theologische Arbeiten |
| *HBT* | *Horizons in Biblical Theology* |
| HKAT | Handkommentar zum Alten Testament |
| HNT | Handbuch zum Neuen Testament |
| HSM | Harvard Semitic Monographs |
| HTA | Historisch Theologische Auslegung |
| *HTR* | *Harvard Theological Review* |
| *HUCA* | *Hebrew Union College Annual* |
| IBC | Interpretation: A Bible Commentary for Teaching and Preaching |
| ICC | International Critical Commentary |
| *Int* | *Interpretation* |
| IRT | Issues in Religion and Theology |
| *JAAR* | *Journal of the American Academy of Religion* |
| *JBL* | *Journal of Biblical Literature* |
| JBLMS | Journal of Biblical Literature Monograph Series |
| JDDS | Jian Dao Dissertation Series |
| *JETS* | *Journal of the Evangelical Theological Society* |

| | |
|---|---|
| *JHS* | *Journal of Hellenic Studies* |
| *JJS* | *Journal of Jewish Studies* |
| *JPT* | *Journal of Pentecostal Theology* |
| *JSNT* | *Journal for the Study of the New Testament* |
| JSNTSup | Journal for the Study of the New Testament: Supplement Series |
| *JSOT* | *Journal for the Study of the Old Testament* |
| JSOTSup | Journal for the Study of the Old Testament: Supplement Series |
| *JSP* | *Journal for the Study of the Pseudepigrapha* |
| JSPSup | Journal for the Study of the Pseudepigrapha: Supplement Series |
| *JTS* | *Journal of Theological Studies* |
| KD | *Kerygma und Dogma* |
| KEK | Kritisch-exegetischer Kommentar über das Neue Testament (Meyer-Kommentar) |
| LBS | Library of Biblical Studies |
| LCL | Loeb Classical Library |
| LHBOTS | Library of Hebrew Bible/Old Testament Studies |
| LNTS | Library of New Testament Studies |
| *LS* | *Louvain Studies* |
| LSJ | Liddell, H.G., R. Scott, H.S. Jones, *A Greek–English Lexicon*. 9th ed. with revised supplement. Oxford, 1996 |
| MNTC | Moffatt New Testament Commentary |
| NAC | New American Commentary |
| NACSBT | New American Commentary Studies in Bible and Theology |
| NEchtB | Neue Echter Bibel |
| *Neot* | *Neotestamentica* |
| NewDocs | *New Documents Illustrating Early Christianity*. Edited by G.H.R. Horsley and S. Llewelyn. North Ryde, N.S.W., 1981– |
| *NIB* | *The New Interpreter's Bible* |
| NIBCNT | New International Bible Commentary on the New Testament |
| NICNT | New International Commentary on the New Testament |
| NICOT | New International Commentary on the Old Testament |
| *NIDNTT* | *New International Dictionary of New Testament Theology*. Edited by C. Brown. 4 vols. Grand Rapids, 1975–1985 |
| *NIDOTTE* | *New International Dictionary of Old Testament Theology and Exegesis*. Edited by W.A. VanGemeren. 5 vols. Grand Rapids, 1997 |
| NIGTC | New International Greek Testament Commentary |
| NIVAC | The New International Version Application Commentary |
| *NovT* | *Novum Testamentum* |
| NovTSup | Supplements to Novum Testamentum |
| NSBT | New Studies in Biblical Theology |
| NTD | Das Neue Testament Deutsch |
| *NTS* | *New Testament Studies* |
| NTTS | New Testament Tools and Studies |
| OBO | Orbis biblicus et orientalis |
| ÖTK | Ökumenischer Taschenbuch-Kommentar |
| OTL | Old Testament Library |
| PBM | Paternoster Biblical Monographs |

| | |
|---|---|
| PNTC | Pillar New Testament Commentary |
| POut | De Prediking van het Oude Testament |
| *RB* | *Revue biblique* |
| RechBib | Recherches bibliques |
| *RevExp* | *Review and Expositor* |
| RHPR | *Revue d'histoire et de philosophie religieuses* |
| *RSR* | *Recherches de science religieuse* |
| *RTR* | *Reformed Theological Review* |
| SAA | State Archives of Assyria |
| SANT | Studien zum Alten und Neuen Testament |
| SBAB | Stuttgarter biblische Aufsatzbände |
| SBLDS | Society of Biblical Literature Dissertation Series |
| SBLMS | Society of Biblical Literature Monograph Series |
| SBLSBL | Society of Biblical Literature Studies in Biblical Literature |
| SBLSCS | Society of Biblical Literature Septuagint and Cognate Studies |
| SBLSP | Society of Biblical Literature Seminar Papers |
| SBLSymS | Society of Biblical Literature Symposium Series |
| SBLWAW | Society of Biblical Literature Writings from the Ancient World |
| SBT | Studies in Biblical Theology |
| SFEG | Schriften der Finnischen Exegetischen Gesellschaft |
| *SJOT* | *Scandinavian Journal of the Old Testament* |
| SMBen | Série monographique de Benedictina |
| SNT | Studien zum Neuen Testament |
| SNTSMS | Society for New Testament Studies Monograph Series |
| SNTW | Studies of the New Testament and Its World |
| SP | Sacra Pagina |
| *SPhilo* | *Studia Philonica Annual* |
| STDJ | Studies on the Texts of the Desert of Judah |
| SUNT | Studien zur Umwelt des Neuen Testaments |
| TBü | Theologische Bücherei: Neudrucke und Berichte aus dem 20. Jahrhundert |
| TCT | Textual Criticism and the Translator |
| *TDNT* | *Theological Dictionary of the New Testament*. Edited by G. Kittel and G. Friedrich. Translated by G.W. Bromiley. 10 vols. Grand Rapids, 1964–76 |
| *Text* | *Textus* |
| THKNT | Theologischer Handkommentar zum Neuen Testament |
| ThSt | Theologische Studien |
| *TS* | *Theological Studies* |
| TSAJ | Texte und Studien zum antiken Judentum |
| TUGAL | Texte und Untersuchungen zur Geschichte der altchristlichen Literatur |
| *TynBul* | *Tyndale Bulletin* |
| *TZ* | *Theologische Zeitschrift* |
| *TZT* | *Tübingen Zeitschrift für Theologie* |
| UNT | Untersuchungen zum Neuen Testament |
| *VT* | *Vetus Testamentum* |

| | |
|---|---|
| VTSup | Supplements to Vetus Testamentum |
| WBC | Word Biblical Commentary |
| WC | Westminster Commentaries |
| WMANT | Wissenschaftliche Monographien zum Alten und Neuen Testament |
| *WTJ* | *Westminster Theological Journal* |
| WUNT | Wissenschaftliche Untersuchungen zum Neuen Testament |
| *ZAW* | *Zeitschrift für die alttestamentliche Wissenschaft* |
| *ZNW* | *Zeitschrift für die neutestamentliche Wissenschaft und die Kunde der älteren Kirche* |

Chapter 1

## INTRODUCTION

### 1. *The Object of the Study*

In light of its overtly autobiographical nature, 2 Corinthians may offer a unique window through which to view the way Paul presents his apostolic ministry and forms his rhetorical argument. The present study seeks to examine in particular the ways in which 2 Corinthians, particularly the material developed 2 Cor. 2.14–7.4 and 2 Corinthians 10–13, reflects the prophetic dimension(s) of Paul's apostolic self-presentation and rhetoric. The primary argument is that these portions of 2 Corinthians further substantiate the notion that at least certain aspects of Paul's construction of his apostolic identity and argument are influenced by the prophetic tradition of the Old Testament.[1]

This thesis is developed through: (1) an analysis of the shape and influence of the prophetic material of the Old Testament that defines the parameters of the Old Testament prophetic tradition and examines its relationship with prophetic material in Second Temple Judaism, Hellenistic prophetic traditions, and the prophetic dimensions of the Gospel traditions; (2) a survey of material in 1 Corinthians (i.e. 1 Cor. 9.15-18 and 14.20-25) that provides evidence for the prophetic nature of Paul's self-presentation and rhetoric; (3) an extended examination of the material in 2 Corinthians in which Paul presents various dimensions of his apostolic self-understanding in terms of particular prophetic figures

---

1. The potentially ambiguous phrase 'prophetic tradition' is discussed in the next chapter. Briefly, in the present work the phrase refers to the broad progression of prophetic history developed in the Old Testament, which, as will be argued, provides a substructure for prophetic material in both the Second Temple period and the early Christian movement. The singular use of the phrase is not meant to deny the existence of a plurality of prophetic traditions in the Old Testament, but to emphasize the (canonical) unity of those traditions within the prophetic history of the Old Testament.

(i.e. Moses [2 Cor. 2.16–3.18], the Isaianic servant [2 Cor. 5.14–6.2], and Jeremiah [2 Cor. 3.1-6; 10.8, 17; 13.10]), and (4) an investigation of the prophetic influence on Paul's development of certain portions of his rhetorical argument in the epistle (i.e. 2 Cor. 2.14-16; 4.1-6; 6.14–7.1; 12.1-10).

## 2. The Parameters of the Study

The inherent limitations in the present study require a specific description of its parameters. The present argument works under the assumption that canonical 2 Corinthians is one piece of correspondence written by Paul himself. The specific arguments concerning 2 Corinthians within the present work, however, are not directly dependent upon this assumption. In contrast, the text of 2 Corinthians functions as the source upon which the analysis is based.[2] Consequently, the study seeks to examine a number of sections within canonical 2 Corinthians in order to analyse the potential influence of the Old Testament prophetic tradition on both Paul's presentation of his apostolic identity and the formation of his rhetorical framework at certain points of the epistle.

In view of the particular focus on the Old Testament prophetic tradition in the present study, those aspects of Paul's self-presentation and rhetoric derived from other resources, such as Graeco-Roman traditions or the social history of Corinth, constitute only a limited component of the subsequent argument. The intent of this work, however, is not to argue that the Old Testament prophetic material provides the sole basis upon which Paul constructs either his own self-presentation as an apostle or his particular rhetorical arguments in 2 Corinthians. Rather, the argument developed in the following chapters represents one dimension of the broader discussion concerning the narrative and rhetorical framework upon which Paul constructs, explains, and asserts his apostolic

---

2. For an extensive summary of the history of discussion concerning the integrity of 2 Corinthians, see Reimund Bieringer, 'Teilungshypothesen zum 2 Korintherbrief: Ein Forschungsüberblick', in *Studies on 2 Corinthians* (ed. Reimund Bieringer and Jan Lambrecht; BETL 112; Leuven: Leuven University Press, 1994), 67-105; Steven S.H. Chang, 'The Integrity of 2 Corinthians: 1980–2000', *Torch Trinity Journal* 5 (2002): 167-202; Fredrik Lindgård, *Paul's Line of Thought in 2 Corinthians 4:16–5:10* (WUNT 2/189; Tübingen: Mohr Siebeck, 2005), 28-62; Frederick J. Long, *Ancient Rhetoric and Paul's Apology: The Compositional Unity of 2 Corinthians* (SNTSMS 131; Cambridge: Cambridge University Press, 2004), 1-14; Udo Schnelle, *Apostle Paul: His Life and Theology* (trans. M. Eugene Boring; Grand Rapids: Baker, 2005), 237-45.

ministry. The specifically prophetic dimensions of Paul's persona and rhetoric, therefore, comprise only one facet of his presentation of his apostolic identity.³

## 3. The Position of the Study

Paul's relationship with the prophetic tradition of the Old Testament has been viewed through both literary and theological lenses, with attempts to correlate the apostle's ministry with the Old Testament prophets on a number of different planes, including ministerial call, apostolic function, and theological agenda. Perhaps the most influential work with regard to this aspect of Pauline studies is that of Sandnes, whose thorough analysis provides a sustained depiction of the way in which Paul's apostolic self-understanding developed with respect to the prophetic tradition manifest in the Old Testament.⁴ In particular, Sandnes attempts to expand on the notion that there are general similarities between Paul and the Old Testament prophets by contending that the existence of a number of 'prophetic features' in the Pauline literature evinces a more systematic association, with the result that Paul's self-conception and apostolic ministry are rooted in the prophetic framework outlined in the Old Testament.⁵ Sandnes develops this thesis initially from Paul's reliance on prophetic material in his autobiographical statement in Gal. 1.15-16 and then attempts to substantiate the argument through an analysis of several

---

3. Cf. David G. Horrell, 'Paul's Narratives or Narrative Substructure? The Significance of "Paul's Story"', in *Narrative Dynamics in Paul: A Critical Assessment* (ed. Bruce W. Longenecker; Louisville: Westminster John Knox, 2002), 167 n. 20, who notes, in relation to a somewhat different methodological question, that certain dimensions of Paul's narrative and rhetorical background have meaning only with respect to their relationship to the apostle's broader theological agenda.

4. Karl Olav Sandnes, *Paul—One of the Prophets? A Contribution to the Apostle's Self-Understanding* (WUNT 2/43; Tübingen: Mohr Siebeck, 1991).

5. Sandnes, *Paul—One of the Prophets?*, 5-20, particularly highlights several works which identify certain prophetic elements in the Pauline corpus, but do not provide an analysis of the way in which those prophetic elements function in the development of Paul's apostolic self-understanding (e.g. Scott J. Hafemann, *Suffering and the Spirit: An Exegetical Study of II Cor. 2:14–3:3 within the Context of the Corinthian Correspondence* [WUNT 2/19; Tübingen: Mohr Siebeck, 1986]; Johannes Munck, *Paul and the Salvation of Mankind* [trans. Frank Clarke; London: SCM, 1959]; Jacob M. Myers and Edwin D. Freed, 'Is Paul also among the Prophets?', *Int* 20 [1966]: 40-53; Peter Stuhlmacher, *Das paulinische Evangelium* [FRLANT 95; Göttingen: Vandenhoeck & Ruprecht, 1968]; Hans Windisch, *Paulus und Christus: Ein biblisch-religionsgeschichtlicher Vergleich* [UNT 24; Leipzig: J.C. Hinrichs, 1934]).

other portions of the Pauline corpus (i.e. Rom. 1.1-5; 10.14-18; 11.25-36; 1 Cor. 2.6-16; 9.15-18; 2 Cor. 4.6; Eph. 2.19–3.7; 1 Thess. 2.3-8), which he believes provide both quantitative and qualitative evidence for the prophetic nature of Paul's apostolic self-understanding. In broad terms, Sandnes asserts that Paul's apostleship coordinates with various contours of the Old Testament prophetic tradition even though certain aspects of his ministry reflect a distinctly different position from that of the prophets with respect to salvation history.[6]

In spite of disagreements with particular exegetical and methodological aspects of Sandnes' work, his assessment of the prophetic dimension of Paul's apostolic ministry has generally been regarded as a useful depiction of Paul's relationship with the Old Testament prophetic tradition. In the wake of Sandnes' study, however, there have been relatively few attempts at a systematic exploration of the way in which the prophetic tradition shaped Paul's apostolic self-understanding.[7] One notable exception at this point is Wilk's comprehensive analysis of the way in which the book of Isaiah functions in Paul's (undisputed) epistles.[8] Wilk argues

---

6. Sandnes, *Paul—One of the Prophets?*, 18, 243-44.

7. There have, however, been a variety of studies on the way in which Paul's prophetic self-understanding may affect certain aspects of his theology. See, for example, Craig A. Evans, 'Paul and the Prophets: Prophetic Criticism in the Epistle to the Romans (with Special Reference to Romans 9–11)', in *Romans and the People of God* (Festschrift Gordon D. Fee; ed. Sven K. Soderlund and N.T. Wright; Grand Rapids: Eerdmans, 1999), 115-28; Mark Gignilliat, *Paul and Isaiah's Servants: Paul's Theological Reading of Isaiah 40–66 in 2 Corinthians 5.14–6.10* (LNTS 330; London: T&T Clark International, 2007); Sigurd Grindheim, 'Apostate Turned Prophet: Paul's Prophetic Self-Understanding and Prophetic Hermeneutic with Special Reference to Galatians 3.10-12', *NTS* 53 (2007): 545-65; Grindheim, *The Crux of Election: Paul's Critique of the Jewish Confidence in the Election of Israel* (WUNT 2/202; Tübingen: Mohr Siebeck, 2005); Scott J. Hafemann, *Paul, Moses, and the History of Israel: The Letter/Spirit Contrast and the Argument from Scripture in 2 Corinthians 3* (PBM; Milton Keynes: Paternoster, 2005); Winfield Scott Hall II, 'Paul as a Christian Prophet in His Interpretation of the Old Testament in Romans 9–11' (Th.D. diss., Lutheran School of Theology at Chicago, 1982); Frank Thielman, *From Plight to Solution: A Jewish Framework for Understanding Paul's View of the Law* (NovTSup 61; Leiden: Brill, 1989); Ulrich B. Müller, *Prophetie und Predigt im Neuen Testament, Formgeschichtliche Untersuchung zu urchristliche Prophetie* (SNT 10; Gütersloh: Gütersloher Verlagshaus, 1972); Andrzej Jacek Najda, *Der Apostel als Prophet: Zur prophetischen Dimension des paulinischen Apostolats* (Europäische Hochschulschriften 784; Frankfurt: Peter Lang, 2004).

8. Florian Wilk, *Die Bedeutung des Jesajabuches für Paulus* (FRLANT 179; Göttingen: Vandenhoeck & Ruprecht, 1998), and Florian Wilk, 'Paulus als Interpret der prophetischen Schriften', *KD* 45 (1999): 284-306, which is a condensed discussion of the major tenets of Wilk's thesis.

1. *Introduction* 5

specifically that the 'Botschaft' of the prophetic material, particularly that developed in the Isaianic tradition, constitutes the basis upon which Paul constructs his own self-understanding and theology.[9] The prophetic material of the Old Testament then becomes in Wilk's view the central aspect of Scripture ('Zentrum der Schrift') from which the rest of the Pauline material radiates.[10] In somewhat of a contrast to the emphasis of Sandnes, however, Wilk's more narrow methodological focus on the book of Isaiah leads him to contend that the connection between Paul and the Old Testament prophetic material is particularly rooted in Paul's conception of his apostolic ministry as an extension of the message developed in Isaiah:

> Der Kern des paulinischen Selbstverständnisses liegt demnach nicht in der Entsprechung zwischen ihm, dem Apostel, und den Propheten, sondern darin, daß der Prophet Jesaja ihn als den Apostel für die Heiden angekündigt hat. Auf dieser Basis gewinnt dann das Jesajabuch im Werdegang des Paulus zunehmend Bedeutung für sein Theologie.[11]

In general terms, therefore, Wilk asserts that the Isaianic material provides the primary rhetorical and theological foundation upon which Paul constructs his apostolic identity.

The broader approach to the relationship between Paul and the prophetic tradition developed in Sandnes' monograph is also reflected in a recent essay by Nicklas that seeks to renew the discussion of the prophetic influence on Paul's construction of both his apostolic self-understanding and his epistolary material.[12] In specific terms, Nicklas' thesis is that 'Der Apostel Paulus verstand seine Berufung und das damit verbundene Handeln und Argumentieren auch als prophetisches Handeln im Anschluss an Israels Prophetie'.[13] In support of this overarching thesis he provides an analysis of a number of texts from the Pauline corpus under the general headings of 'Berufung und Selbstverständnis' and 'Argumentationsformen' in order to explore the ways in which the prophetic material shapes both Paul's identity and rhetoric. Consequently, despite the relative brevity of his essay, Nicklas is able to account for the methodological implications of both Sandnes and Wilk, as he discusses the influence of the prophetic material on both Paul's

---

9. Wilk, 'Paul als Interpret', 286.
10. Wilk, 'Paul als Interpret', 290-91.
11. Wilk, 'Paul als Interpret', 300.
12. Tobias Nicklas, 'Paulus—der Apostel als Prophet', in *Prophets and Prophecy in Jewish and Early Christian Literature* (ed. Joseph Verheyden, Korinna Zamfir, and Tobias Nicklas; WUNT 2/286; Tübingen: Mohr Siebeck, 2010), 77-104.
13. Nicklas, 'Paulus—der Apostel als Prophet', 78.

apostolic self-conception and his theological argumentation. Nicklas provides a cautious assessment of his analysis in light of Paul's apparent reluctance to identify himself as a προφήτης in his extant letters, but notes that the various ways in which the prophetic material influences Paul's presentation of his ministry and formation of his epistolary arguments suggest that this is an important part of Paul's apostolic self-conception.[14] Consequently, Nicklas concludes his essay by noting the importance of further study into the prophetic dimensions of Paul's apostolic ministry:

> Trotzdem zeigt sich, dass die hier diskutierte Dimension des paulinischen Selbstverständnisses nicht vernachlässigt werden sollte, ja dass auch die weitergehende Frage, inwiefern der *paulinische* Begriff des Apostolats von Ideen der Sendung alttestamentlicher Propheten abhängig ist, noch einmal systematisch untersucht werden sollte. Das weitere Suchen entlang dieser Fragestellung könnte mithelfen, Paulus von Tarsus noch stärker als bisher als charismatischen Juden seiner Zeit verstehen zu lernen.[15]

The present work aims to analyse Paul's relationship to the prophetic tradition in 2 Corinthians along similar methodological lines to those drawn by Nicklas, examining the influence of the prophetic tradition on both Paul's presentation of his apostolic self-understanding ('Berufung und Selbstverständnis') and the formation of his rhetoric ('Argumentationsformen') in the epistle.[16] The selection of 2 Corinthians as the primary textual basis for the present study stems from the relatively minimal amount of material on this portion of the Pauline corpus with respect to a systematic examination of Paul's relationship with the Old Testament prophetic tradition. For example, Sandnes provides a contextual analysis of only 2 Cor. 4.6,[17] Wilk, in light of his stated methodology,

---

14. Nicklas, 'Paulus—der Apostel als Prophet', 100-104; cf. Grindheim, 'Apostate Turned Prophet', 556-57. Luke, however, groups Paul among the Antiochene προφῆται καὶ διδάσκαλοι in Acts 13.1.

15. Nicklas, 'Paulus—der Apostel als Prophet', 104. Original emphasis.

16. In contrast to Nicklas, however, the present work is less concerned with the categories of form criticism that Nicklas implies with his use of the term 'Argumentationsformen'. With regard to the argument of the present work the term rhetoric and its derivates are used as broad references to Paul's development of his argument with respect to the Corinthians. The intent of the terminology, therefore, is neither to allude to particular formal prophetic categories nor to reference specific rhetorical styles or forms inherent, for example, in the formal study of Graeco-Roman rhetorical categories. That the term rhetoric and its derivates can function in this broader sense is confirmed by Dale Patrick and Allen Scult, *Rhetoric and Biblical Interpretation* (JSOTSup 82; Sheffield: Almond, 1990), 12, who define the term '*as the means by which a text establishes and manages its relationship to its audience in order to achieve a particular effect*' (original emphasis).

17. Sandnes, *Paul—One of the Prophets?*, 131-45.

refers extensively only to the Isaianic quotation in 2 Cor. 6.2,[18] and Nicklas, potentially due to space limitations, offers no analysis of material in 2 Corinthians. There have, however, been several studies that have attempted to analyse specific sections of 2 Corinthians with a view to the way in which the apostle's argument is representative of a scriptural substructure. In general terms, the present study seeks to examine a broader range of material in 2 Corinthians in order to develop a more extensive portrait of Paul's relationship with the prophetic tradition of the Old Testament. In a similar fashion to the preceding studies, the present work is dependent on an exegetical analysis of the relevant sections of 2 Corinthians as the primary means of elucidating the meaning of Paul's argument. The analysis on the development of the prophetic tradition and its potential influence on certain sections of Paul's argument in 1 Corinthians is meant to provide a contextual and methodological introduction for the examination of the material in 2 Corinthians.

---

18. Wilk, *Die Bedeutung des Jesajabuches*, 96-101. Wilk also provides a more limited analysis of several texts in 2 Corinthians (i.e. 2 Cor. 4.6, 11; 5.17; 7.6; 9.10) that may contain allusions to (or echoes of) the Isaianic material. Throughout this work the terms 'allusion' and 'echo' will be used as functional synonyms. For a concise analysis of the relationship between the two terms, see Stanley E. Porter, 'Allusions and Echoes', in *As It Is Written: Studying Paul's Use of Scripture* (ed. Stanley E. Porter and Christopher D. Stanley; SBLSymS 50; Atlanta: Society of Biblical Literature, 2008), 29-40.

Chapter 2

THE DEVELOPMENT OF THE PROPHETIC TRADITION

1. *Introduction*

In order to analyse Paul's relationship with the Old Testament prophetic tradition in 2 Corinthians it will be helpful to delineate what is meant by the phrase 'the prophetic tradition'. Previous discussion concerning the development of the prophetic tradition has been thoroughly multifaceted, dealing with linguistic, exegetical, theological, historical, cultural, and even psychological concerns.[1] The variegated nature of this discussion is due in part to the complex picture of prophecy and prophesying that develops in the Old Testament. This lack of uniformity in the presentation of the Old Testament prophetic material derives, at least partially, from the wide variety of phenomena which constituted prophetic activity, as well as the distinction between those persons who are referred to as prophets in the text and those who themselves contributed to it, the so-called writing prophets.[2] In addition to the internal complexity of the Old Testament with regard to the prophetic material, there is discrepancy with regard to the state of prophetic activity after the ministry of the writing prophets seemingly ended in the fifth century B.C.E.[3] That is, uncertainty remains with regard to whether prophetic

---

1. For an introduction to these dimensions of the prophetic tradition, see David L. Petersen (ed.), *Prophecy in Israel: Search for an Identity* (IRT 10; Philadelphia: Fortress, 1987).
2. H. Krämer et al., 'προφήτης, κτλ.', *TDNT* 6:796.
3. It is generally agreed that the ministry of the canonical prophets ceased by the end of the fifth century B.C.E. However, there is less agreement on the specific dating of the prophetic material, particularly with regard to the Minor Prophets; see David L. Petersen, *The Prophetic Literature: An Introduction* (Louisville: Westminster John Knox, 2002), 171-74; Christopher R. Seitz, *Prophecy and Hermeneutics: Toward a New Introduction to the Prophets* (Grand Rapids: Baker, 2007), 130-46; Hans Walter Wolff, 'Prophecy from the Eighth Through the Fifth Century', in *Interpreting the Prophets* (ed. James Luther Mays and Paul J. Achtemeier; Philadelphia: Fortress, 1987), 15.

## 2. The Development of the Prophetic Tradition

activity was stagnant during the Second Temple period or whether certain strands of the prophetic material continued to persist. Further difficulty emerges in light of the rising influence of additional prophetic categories in the ancient Mediterranean world, specifically those stemming from aspects of Hellenistic society.[4] Thus, in addition to the potential Old Testament background of the prophetic material discussed in the Pauline epistles, both Paul and the recipients of his letters may have been influenced by their surrounding Hellenistic culture in this regard.[5] For this reason, while it may be valid simply to associate Paul with portions of the Old Testament prophetic material in light of autobiographical texts such as Gal. 1.15-16, it is necessary to clarify which aspects of that material might be associated with Paul's presentation of his own apostolic ministry.

The purpose of the present chapter will be to outline the basic parameters of the prophetic material in the Old Testament in order to establish a framework for understanding Paul's presentation of his connection with the prophetic tradition in 2 Corinthians. Attention will be focused on the portrait of the prophetic tradition that develops in the Old Testament. Additionally, discussion will surround the potential influence of Hellenistic categories on the Old Testament prophetic tradition, since this may have influenced both the Corinthians' understanding of prophecy and Paul's pragmatic exhortations concerning prophecy in the Corinthian correspondence. Primarily, however, this chapter will seek to show that while it may be possible to argue that there are a variety of unrelated prophetic traditions encompassed in the Old Testament, it is also possible to assert that there is a general, though not monolithic, prophetic tradition in the Old Testament, which develops in part from the internal progression of the Old Testament itself. The argument will proceed, therefore, by discussing the progression of the prophetic material within the Old Testament, evaluating the state and function of the prophetic material within the intertestamental period,

---

4. For example, the possible semantic overlap of the terms προφήτης and μάντις in this period may have resulted in a modified understanding of προφῆται in the early Christian period.

5. For the view that early Christian prophecy was in some way conditioned by Hellenistic categories, see T.M. Crone, *Early Christian Prophecy: A Study of Its Origin and Function* (Baltimore: St. Mary's University, 1973), and Erich Fascher, *ΠΡΟΦΗΤΗΣ: Eine sprach- und religionsgeschichtliche Untersuchung* (Giessen: Töpelmann, 1927). For a consistent refutation of this view, see Christopher Forbes, *Prophecy and Inspired Speech in Early Christianity and Its Hellenistic Environment* (WUNT 2/75; Tübingen: Mohr Siebeck, 1995).

and analysing the form and function of the prophetic material in the Gospel traditions in light of the numerous historical and cultural influences that may have shaped the material in that period.

## 2. The Prophetic Tradition in the Old Testament

In light of the variegated nature of the prophetic material within the Old Testament it is difficult to ascertain whether there is an internal, unified prophetic tradition or merely a conglomeration of prophetic events and writings that constitute a multiplicity of prophetic traditions. One of the most distinct issues in tracing the prophetic tradition of the Old Testament is the scholarly divide over what material actually constitutes prophetic literature.[6] At a basic level this divide stems from the literary division between the so-called former prophets, comprising material found in the Deuteronomistic history, and the so-called latter prophets, comprising the material found in the works attributed to the Major and Minor Prophets. This potential distinction, though not the sole difficulty in a discussion of the prophetic tradition, provides a helpful starting point for an analysis of the Old Testament prophetic material since it highlights the complexity involved in attempting to group all of the prophetic material under one heading. The intention within this section, therefore, is to survey the image of the prophetic material developed in the Pentateuch and Historical books as well as the Prophetic literature in order to help determine the nature of the prophetic tradition that emerges.

### a. *Prophetic Material in the Pentateuch and Historical Books*

While there are numerous figures that are described with prophetic terminology and associated with prophetic actions outside the ministry of the writing prophets, the Old Testament does not always present a clear picture of either their identity or their function within Israelite society.[7] Confusion also arises as to whether any of the material in the Pentateuch or Historical books can legitimately be referred to as prophetic literature. In other words, while it is ostensible that prophets and prophecy are presented in the development of Hebrew and Israelite society, it is not clear how this material might coordinate with that developed in the Prophetic literature. However, prior to discussing the

---

6. Petersen, *Prophetic Literature*, 1-4.
7. Robert R. Wilson, 'Early Israelite Prophecy', in Mays and Achtemeier (eds.), *Interpreting the Prophets*, 1-2.

possible connection between the distinct Old Testament literary corpora, it will be helpful to provide an overview of the shape of prophecy presented in the Deuteronomistic history.

In comparison with the material found in certain Historical books, the Pentateuch, Joshua, and Judges, appear fairly silent with regard to the shape and function of prophecy among the Hebrew and Israelite people. These books, however, are not devoid of material dealing with prophetic figures and themes. In the Pentateuch Abraham (Gen. 20.7), Aaron (Exod. 7.1), and Miriam (Exod. 15.20) are labeled as prophets. Likewise, the book of Judges refers to Deborah as a נביאה (Judg. 4.4). While the term prophet, understood through the lens of the Prophetic literature, may not define these figures precisely, it is difficult to assert that these formulations simply represent the work of a later redactor.[8] A potentially more likely hypothesis is that the prophetic label within these texts functions primarily as a reference to the close relationship between these figures and the Lord.[9] Evidence of this relational aspect is found in the description of Moses presented in Numbers 12. Through the means of a theophany Miriam and Aaron are rebuked for speaking against Moses, who is established as distinct from other 'prophets of the Lord' because of the direct nature of his communication with YHWH (Num. 12.8).[10] One of the purposes of the passage appears to be to portray Moses as a unique prophetic figure within Israel's history.[11] This affirmation of Moses' unique prophetic authority, however, serves neither to negate the existence of the prophets mentioned in Num. 12.6 nor to invalidate their prophetic message.[12] Rather, since the passage functions as a rebuke of

---

8. Contra some strands of earlier scholarship which claimed that prophecy commenced in Israel with the rise of the kingly office (e.g. William F. Albright, 'Samuel and the Beginnings of the Prophetic Movement', in *Interpreting the Prophetic Tradition: The Goldenson Lectures, 1955–1966* [ed. Harry Orlinsky; LBS; Cincinnati: Hebrew Union College Press, 1969], 149-76, and Frank Moore Cross, *Canaanite Myth and Hebrew Epic: Essays in the History of the Religion of Israel* [Cambridge, Mass.: Harvard University Press, 1973], 223-29).

9. Johannes Lindblom, *Prophecy in Ancient Israel* (Oxford: Blackwell, 1962), 99-100. As with descriptions of Moses, this close relationship often pertains to particular notions of communication with the Lord, as well as communication of the Lord's words to others; cf. Petersen, *Prophetic Literature*, 216-17.

10. Baruch A. Levine, *Numbers 1–20* (AB 4A; New York: Doubleday, 1993), 341-42. Levine notes that the phrase 'face-to-face' is an idiom for direct communication: 'There is nothing intervening between God and Moses in the transmission of God's voice' (341).

11. Levine, *Numbers 1–20*, 338-43.

12. Wilson, 'Prophecy', 9-10.

Miriam and Aaron, who are not in this instance the 'prophets of the Lord', the passage actually serves as evidence for the existence of prophetic figures among the Hebrew people within this textual context.

In addition to the material on the close relationship between Moses and the Lord in Numbers 12, the book of Deuteronomy contains several passages that portray Moses in a distinct position with respect to Israel's prophetic tradition. The discussion of Moses' ministry in Deut. 34.10-12 again describes the unique nature of Moses' face-to-face relationship with the Lord and also emphasizes the qualitative and quantitative superiority of his work *vis-à-vis* his prophetic contemporaries.[13] Along with this prophetic epitaph, Moses' ministry is given primary importance for the course of the prophetic material in Deut. 18.14-22. Although the precise meaning of the prepositional phrase כמוך in this context is somewhat ambiguous, one of the purposes of the passage seems to be to signify that Moses was to have an important function in shaping the nature of future prophetic material, particularly with regard to the prophet's function as a divine intermediary.[14] In at least this sense, therefore, Moses serves as a paradigm for a general prophetic tradition.[15] That Moses has a paradigmatic function with regard to the prophetic material, however, is not an affirmation that Moses was first among the prophets in terms of chronology; rather, Moses is seen as a paradigm because of the importance of his communication with the Lord and the nature of the material that came out of that unique relationship. More specifically, the 'prophetic tradition had its origin in the Mosaic revelation'.[16] In other words, both the person of Moses and the ministry associated with him in the Deuteronomistic history are seemingly foundational for understanding the course of the prophetic material in the Old Testament.[17]

---

13. Willem A. VanGemeren, *Interpreting the Prophetic Word: An Introduction to the Prophetic Literature of the Old Testament* (Grand Rapids: Zondervan, 1990), 30.

14. Richard Coggins, 'An Alternative Prophetic Tradition?', in *Israel's Prophetic Tradition* (Festschrift Peter R. Ackroyd; ed. Richard Coggins, Anthony Phillips, and Michael Knibb; Cambridge: Cambridge University Press, 1982), 91.

15. Walter Brueggemann, *The Prophetic Imagination* (2d ed.; Minneapolis: Fortress, 2001), 5, 131-32; cf. Niels Christian Hvidt, *Christian Prophecy: The Post-Biblical Tradition* (Oxford: Oxford University Press, 2007), 39.

16. VanGemeren, *Prophetic Word*, 34.

17. This hypothesis stands against Petersen, *Prophetic Literature*, 220-26, who argues that understanding Moses as a prophet is merely a polemical affirmation that diminishes the message of subsequent prophetic material. Hans M. Barstad, 'The Understanding of the Prophets in Deuteronomy', *SJOT* 8 (1994): 236-51 (249-50), argues that the author(s) of Deuteronomy understood Moses as a prophetic figure, but concurs with Petersen that this affirmation diminishes the usefulness of the latter prophets. These contentions, however, are based on arguments from silence. Barstad

## 2. The Development of the Prophetic Tradition

In spite of the information concerning prophecy derived from the Pentateuch and portions of the Deuteronomistic history, the brevity of this material makes it difficult to formulate any precise affirmation concerning the development of a particular prophetic tradition within Israel.[18] Further difficulty emerges when one attempts to determine the level of correlation between prophecy within Israel and prophetic figures and prophetic material derived from other cultures in the ancient Near East. It is likely that nearly all of Israel's cultural counterparts sought to acquire the same type of divine knowledge found in the Old Testament through persons functioning as divine intermediaries in their own setting.[19] Indeed, the Old Testament itself affirms the existence of external prophetic figures and actions (e.g. Num. 22–24; Deut. 13.1-2; 1 Kgs 18.20-40). Thus, in addition to the foundation established in the person and ministry of Moses, the form and function of Israel's prophetic material may have been shaped by external sources.

In conjunction with the Old Testament texts that acknowledge the existence of non-Israelite prophecy there are numerous extra-biblical sources that provide insight into the nature of prophecy in the ancient Near East.[20] For example, a plaster inscription from Tell Deir 'Alla, located in an area that would have comprised part of ancient Amnon, dates from the eighth century B.C.E. and appears to discuss part of the ministry of Balaam (cf. Num. 22–24).[21] Although the inscription is not

---

attempts to argue that the lack of quotations or allusions to the writing prophets in the Deuteronomistic history is evidence that the author(s) of these books 'were not especially interested in prophecy' and desired 'to downplay the role of the prophets' (250). Petersen, on the other hand, argues from the opposite direction, asserting that since Moses' name is only mentioned in four prophetic texts (i.e. Isa. 63.11-12; Jer. 15.1; Mic. 6.4; Mal. 4.4) it is untenable that Moses was an influential figure in prophetic history (220-21).

18. J.R. Porter, 'The Origins of Prophecy in Israel', in Coggins, Phillips, and Knibb (eds.), *Israel's Prophetic Tradition*, 17.

19. Harry A. Hoffner, Jr., 'Ancient Views of Prophecy and Fulfillment: Mesopotamia and Asia Minor', *JETS* 30 (1987): 257-65.

20. For a survey of prophetic material outside of Israel, see Herbert Huffmon, 'Prophecy (ANE)', *ABD* 5:477-82; cf. Martti Nissinen, *Prophets and Prophecy in the Ancient Near East* (ed. Peter Machinist; SBLWAW 12; Atlanta: Society of Biblical Literature, 2003); Simo Parpola, *Assyrian Prophecies* (SAA 9; Helsinki: Helsinki University Press, 1997).

21. For a complete analysis of this inscription, see Jo Ann Hackett, *The Balaam Text from Deir 'Alla* (HSM 31; Chico, Calif.: Scholars Press, 1980), and Jacob Hoftijzer and Gerrit van der Kooij (eds.), *The Balaam Text from Deir 'Alla Reevaluated: Proceedings of the International Symposium Held at Leiden, 21-24 August 1989* (Leiden: Brill, 1991).

entirely intact, its relation of the Balaam account seems to corroborate some of the narrative of Numbers 22-24, while also providing additional material that contains characteristics of other prophetic narratives in the Old Testament.[22] Potentially more important for determining the nature of prophecy outside of the Israelite context, however, are a group of clay tablets from the city of Mari which contain a number of texts pertaining to the activity of non-Israelite prophets.[23] These inscriptions, though brief, contain several characteristics that are similar to prophetic material in the Old Testament, including the use of consistent introductory formulas, the importance of the monarch in the content of the prophecy, and the apparent divine source of the material.[24] In addition to these earlier sources there are several texts from the Neo-Assyrian period that provide a picture of non-Israelite prophecy during the eighth and seventh centuries B.C.E.[25]

Although portions of this extra-biblical evidence resemble prophetic material in the Old Testament, there are at least three differences between them. First, a significant portion of the prophetic material derived from the ancient Near East consists primarily of divination, including forms of extispicy, astrology, augury, kleromancy, and oneiromancy.[26] Although there are some forms of divination that were accepted in the course of Israel's history, divination itself was often seen as evidence that the purveyor of the prophecy did not have true knowledge of YHWH and, consequently, acts of divination were regarded as false prophecy.[27] Secondly, while there are certain similar formulaic characteristics between Israelite

22. Petersen, *Prophetic Literature*, 15.
23. For the text of the Mari documents, see Nissinen, *Prophets*, 13-91.
24. For further parallels between the Mari documents and Israel's prophetic texts, see Simon B. Parker, 'Official Attitudes Toward Prophecy at Mari and in Israel', *VT* 43 (1993): 50-68, and Robert Gordon, 'From Mari to Moses: Prophecy at Mari and in Ancient Israel', in *Of Prophets' Visions and the Wisdom of Sages* (Festschrift R. Norman Whybray; ed. Heather A. McKay and David J.A. Clines; JSOTSup 162; Sheffield: JSOT, 1993), 63-79.
25. Petersen, *Prophetic Literature*, 17.
26. Hoffner, 'Prophecy', 258-62.
27. The use of the Urim and Thummim may serve as an example of an accepted practice of kleromancy within Israel. In addition, the practice of oneiromancy is exhibited in the narratives of Jacob (Gen. 28.10-22), Joseph (Gen. 35.7-11; 40.1-23; 41.1-40), and Daniel (Dan. 2; 4; 7-12). However, for the general view that divination was evidence of false prophecy, see Num. 22.1-7; Deut. 18.10-13; 2 Kgs 21.1-6; 2 Chron. 33.1-6; Isa. 44.24-26; 47.13-15. Cf. David E. Aune, *Prophecy in Early Christianity and the Ancient Mediterranean World* (Grand Rapids: Eerdmans, 1983), 82; Hoffner, 'Prophecy', 258.

and non-Israelite prophecy, there is a significant difference in the progression of those two prophetic strands. This difference in progression may be seen primarily in the extensive literary creations that were generated from prophetic activity in Israel and which have no literary parallel in the ancient Near East.[28] Thirdly, the non-Israelite prophetic figures seen within the Mari texts appear to function less prominently within their particular cultural setting.[29] These differences point to the notion that the prophetic activity of Israel was in some way distinct from prophetic activities that were practised in surrounding cultures. In light of these differences, as well as the particular nature of Israel's covenant relationship with YHWH, it may be appropriate to state that Israel's prophetic tradition stems from its own internal development.[30]

The claim that Israel's prophetic literature is distinct from other material in the ancient Near East is not, however, an affirmation that the prophetic tradition in Israel is itself 'a homogenous phenomenon'.[31] It would be more accurate to assert that the prophetic material in Israel is comprised of distinct figures, purposes, messages, and forms that are part of a singular progression in Israel's history. That is, while there are various features that comprise the Old Testament prophetic material, it is possible to see those features as comprising a single, albeit developing, tradition. Evidence of this progression can be seen in the figure of Samuel, whose ministry, like that of Moses, seemingly served to define the shape and nature of Israel's prophetic tradition in certain respects.[32] While the ministry of Samuel is later linked with that of Moses (cf. Jer. 15.1), their ministries remain distinct from one another due to their separate contextual settings. Samuel's prophetic ministry is particularly important for understanding the development of the prophetic tradition

---

28. Petersen, *Prophetic Literature*, 18; cf. Abraham Malamat, 'A Forerunner of Biblical Prophecy: The Mari Documents', in *Ancient Israelite Religion* (Festschrift Frank Moore Cross; ed. Patrick D. Miller, Jr., Paul D. Hanson, and S. Dean McBride; Philadelphia: Fortress, 1987), 35.

29. Malamat, 'Forerunner', 35-36. Malamat rightly notes, however, that 'this distinction may be merely an illusion deriving from the nature of the sources at our disposal' (36). This caution also applies to the previous distinction, namely the lack of extensive prophetic literary creations in the ancient Near East.

30. Gene M. Tucker, 'Prophecy and the Prophetic Literature', in *The Hebrew Bible and Its Modern Interpreters* (ed. Douglas A. Knight and Gene M. Tucker; Chico, Calif.: Scholars Press, 1985), 348; cf. Lindblom, *Prophecy*, 66; Paul L. Redditt, *Introduction to the Prophets* (Grand Rapids: Eerdmans, 2008), 3-4.

31. Helmer Ringgren, 'Prophecy in the Ancient Near East', in Coggins, Phillips, and Knibb (eds.), *Israel's Prophetic Tradition*, 11.

32. VanGemeren, *Prophetic Word*, 35.

in light of the prophet's relationship with Israel's monarchy. This distinct association between Samuel and the monarchy seemingly provides insight into this dimension of Israel's prophetic tradition, since a significant amount of Israel's prophetic activity is placed in either direct or indirect correlation with the monarchy.[33] While other prophets were known during Samuel's ministry (cf. 1 Sam. 19.18-24), Samuel functioned to legitimize the monarchy and to explain the characteristics and duties of the monarch (1 Sam. 10.17-27).[34] Even after the establishment of the monarchy Samuel remained a significant leader among the Israelites, functioning as a 'guardian of the theocracy'.[35] In other words, part of Samuel's prophetic function was to remind both the monarch and the Israelites that YHWH was the true ruler of Israel (e.g. 1 Sam. 12.1-25; 13.1-4; 15.22-26).

The connection between Israel's prophetic history and the monarchy led to the rise of a number of prophetic persons who worked closely with the monarchs of Israel. While these figures, normally referred to as court prophets, were not uncommon, the precise nature of their relationship with the monarch and his court is not clear. Additionally, it is not transparent whether that relationship involved any consistent function or role.[36] A portion of this ambiguity stems from the lack of uniformity in the terminology used to describe these prophets.[37] Further complexity arises from the fact that the close relationship between prophets and monarchs was not unique to Israel's experience. For example, Ahab and Jezebel are closely connected with the prophets of Baal in 1 Kgs 18.16-19. Likewise, a significant portion of the prophetic material from the Mari documents exhibits communication between monarchs and intermediaries.[38] However, while there are formulaic similarities between the texts of Mari and those of the Old Testament, there appears to be a distinction between them with regard to the particular covenantal function of Israel's court prophets. That is, at least one of the functions of Israel's court prophets was to recognize and affirm the covenantal relationship between the monarch, the people, and the Lord.[39]

---

33. Joseph Blenkinsopp, *A History of Prophecy in Israel* (rev. and enl. ed.; Louisville: Westminster John Knox, 1996), 47-48.
34. Wilson, 'Prophecy', 11.
35. VanGemeren, *Prophetic Word*, 35.
36. Aune, *Prophecy*, 85.
37. Aune, *Prophecy*, 85.
38. Petersen, *Prophetic Literature*, 16.
39. VanGemeren, *Prophetic Word*, 46-47. This was not, however, their only function. For a concise survey of Israel's court prophets, see Aune, *Prophecy*, 84-85.

## 2. The Development of the Prophetic Tradition

In addition to the significance of Samuel's prophetic ministry in relation to the establishment of Israel's monarchy, the prophet is also associated with aspects of Israel's religious existence. Of particular importance is the combination of Samuel's prophetic ministry with locations and actions normally associated with the priestly office in Israel (e.g. 1 Sam. 2.18-21; 3.19-20; 9.11-14). This combination of the priestly and prophetic traditions, however, is not unique to the ministry of Samuel. Both Jeremiah and Ezekiel, for example, appear to have familial ties to the priestly tradition (Jer. 1.1; Ezek. 1.1). Moreover, there are several other instances of association between the prophetic and the priestly tradition (e.g. Ezra 5.1-2; Isa. 6.1-13; Jer. 29.26-27; Amos 7.10-13).[40] The existence of these associations, however, is not necessarily evidence that the prophetic tradition was always characterized by a relationship with the priestly office. On the other hand, their existence at multiple stages of Israel's history makes it difficult to posit any artificial historical distinction between different stages of Israelite prophecy based solely on the relationship between the prophetic and priestly traditions.[41] Conversely, it seems possible to assert that Samuel's relationship with the priestly office served as a paradigm for a portion of the prophetic material. Thus, as with Moses' prophetic ministry, it appears that Samuel's ministry served to shape a particular portion of the prophetic tradition rather than defining it in its entirety.

In terms of the significance of the literary presentation of the Deuteronomistic history, the figure of Elijah may arguably stand in the most important position.[42] As with Moses and Samuel, Elijah is portrayed as having a close relationship with the Lord. Indeed, certain narratives describing the life of Elijah seem to show that his prophetic ministry was part of a particular Mosaic succession.[43] For example, the background of Elijah's interaction with the Lord at Horeb in 1 Kings 19 likely reflects Moses' similar encounter with the Lord in Exodus 24. However, while the accounts are similar, the differences between them highlight the distinct functions that the two figures serve within Israel's history generally, and

---

40. Aune, *Prophecy*, 84.
41. Wilson, 'Prophecy', 4-5.
42. Wilson, 'Prophecy', 11-12, argues that that this distinction belongs to Ahijah of Shiloh because of his role in the division of the northern and southern kingdoms (1 Kgs 11.29-39). Although the prophetic and monarchial histories are closely intertwined, it seems that Ahijah is distinct primarily for political reasons and not for his contribution to prophetic history.
43. See Robert P. Carroll, 'The Elijah–Elisha Sagas: Some Remarks on Prophetic Succession in Ancient Israel', *VT* 19 (1969): 400-415.

the course of the prophetic tradition particularly.[44] These differences, such as the way in which the Lord manifests himself to Elijah in 1 Kgs 19.11-13, may point to a particular development in Israel's prophetic tradition. While nearly all of the prophetic material presented as being prior to Elijah's ministry served the positive function of communicating divine information to the people and to the monarch, Elijah's ministry, and that of his contemporaries, is characterized by a more distinctly negative message (e.g. 1 Kgs 13; 14.1-18; 16.1-4; 22). Indeed, material concerning prophetic history within the narrative of 1–2 Kings is almost entirely shaped by the confrontational style of prophecy developed in the ministry of Elijah.[45] Thus, the more acutely negative ministry of Elijah can be seen as a shaping force on the prophetic material, so that, as VanGemeren notes,

> Elijah is the beginning of a long line of prophets who charged God's people with breaking the covenant and pronounced God's judgment on them... He was God's first covenant prosecutor, for he charged Israel with its failures to conform to the covenantal expectations (1 Kings 18:21)... The prophet no longer warns and threatens; he proclaims judgment and the reality of the covenantal curses.[46]

It is as a prosecutor of the covenant that Elijah functions as a paradigm for the prophetic tradition since a significant portion of Israel's prophetic material, such as that developed in the Prophetic literature, focused on rebuking the people for neglecting their covenantal obligations, as well as reminding them of the consequences of that disobedience.

The multiplicity of figures, forms, and messages that comprise the prophetic material in the Pentateuch and Historical books stand as evidence of the thoroughly complex nature of this segment of Israel's prophetic tradition. Thus, whether an analysis of this prophetic material is completed through the lens of particular literary forms or through a description of certain figures presented as having shaped the course of prophetic history, care must be taken to understand the unique association between the prophetic tradition and the development of Israel's society.[47] In light

---

44. Brevard S. Childs, 'On Reading the Elijah Narratives', *Int* 34 (1980): 128-37.

45. Robert R. Wilson, 'The Former Prophets: Reading the Book of Kings', in *Old Testament Interpretation: Past, Present, and Future* (Festschrift Gene M. Tucker; ed. James Luther Mays, David L. Petersen, and Kent Harold Richards; Edinburgh: T. & T. Clark, 1995), 86.

46. VanGemeren, *Prophetic Word*, 37.

47. Porter, 'Origins', 28. For an extended discussion of the development of Israel's distinct social and political categories, see Morton Smith, *Palestinian Parties and Politics that Shaped the Old Testament* (New York: Columbia University Press, 1971).

of this potential connection, it seems helpful to observe that much of the prophetic material presented in this portion of the Old Testament appears to pertain primarily to the development of a society that understood itself to have a unique covenantal relationship with YHWH.[48] This is not meant to affirm that all of the prophetic material contained within the Pentateuch and the Historical books pertains only to the religious development of Israel; rather, it is an affirmation that these literary sections of the Old Testament present a distinction between prophetic material that is intertwined with the covenant and material which represents non-covenantal, or non-Israelite, prophecy.[49] Similarly, the notion that this literary material was focused on covenant traditions is not an affirmation that the prophetic material of the Old Testament was neither aware of culturally external prophetic activities nor influenced by them. Instead, the import of the assertion is that, despite its complexity, this portrait of the Old Testament prophetic tradition manifests its own internal progression. In other words, the prophetic material in these literary corpora may point to the notion that Israel's prophetic tradition is an organic entity that expands and contracts in conjunction with Israel's own historical, political, and national identity.

b. *The Prophetic Literature*
While it may be possible that the material in the Pentateuch and Historical books presents a relatively unified prophetic tradition, there is a transparent shift in the nature and form of the prophetic material present in the Prophetic literature. In order to formulate the concept of a unified prophetic tradition within the Old Testament, therefore, it is necessary to determine if there is a connection between these apparently distinct literary corpora. The emergence of the writing prophets may serve as further evidence for the organic nature of the prophetic material present in the Pentateuch and Historical books. Although the literary

48. Wilson, 'Prophecy', 13; cf. Brueggemann, *Prophetic Imagination*, 5.
49. While this distinction is present, it is not always transparent. Determination of what constitutes 'true' or 'false' prophecy requires a careful exegetical and historical analysis of particular texts; cf. Lindblom, *Prophecy*, 210-15. The contention of Aune, *Prophecy*, 87, however, that '[n]o distinction between 'true' and 'false' prophets can be made on the basis of objective, historical criteria', is somewhat overstated. For example, the author of 1 Kings appears to establish that the actions of the prophets of Baal in 1 Kgs 18.16-29 are a form of false prophecy. Thus, the internal argument of the Old Testament, at least at this point, seems to show that there is a distinction between prophetic acts associated with YHWH and his covenant and those acts that are not. Cf. D.A. Carson, review of *Prophecy in Early Christianity and the Ancient Mediterranean World*, by David E. Aune, *JETS* 28 (1985): 236-38.

shape of the prophetic writings differs dramatically from the predominantly narrative content of the prophetic material within the Deuteronomistic history, their connection with this material may be seen in certain formulaic parallels (e.g. prophetic call structures), as well as in particular aspects of their message (e.g. the place and function of the covenant). In other words, it seems likely that the prophetic material developed within the Prophetic literature is not entirely distinct from that contained in either the Pentateuch or the Historical books, in spite of the fact that much of the material is seemingly representative of a different dimension of Israel's prophetic tradition.[50] Conversely, the material associated with each of the writing prophets may serve as evidence that no single prophetic tradition can be delineated within the Old Testament. For, at one level, every prophetic book could simply represent its own prophetic tradition. The material comprised in the final canonical form of Isaiah, for example, may correspond only to the work of a particular prophetic tradition stemming from Isaiah, son of Amoz, and his prophetic followers.[51] Because of these possibilities, the formulation of the development of a prophetic tradition within the Old Testament will require an analysis of both the historical circumstances surrounding the writing prophets and the particular message (or messages) developed in their individual writings.

The movement toward a more culturally negative prophetic ministry, evidenced in the ministry of Elijah, likely stands at the background of the ministry of the writing prophets, who, in contrast with those prophets who served in the royal court, ministered primarily from a position that was external to societal institutions.[52] The writing prophets and their prophetic material, however, did not develop in a manner irrespective of Israel's political and social history. Indeed, it is probably accurate to state that the message of the writing prophets is 'only intelligible in the context of an understanding of the social, political, and religious conditions and circumstances of their prophecy'.[53] The tumultuous nature of Israel's history from the eighth to the fifth century B.C.E., therefore, likely provided a significant catalyst for development within the prophetic material.[54] More specifically, it is possible to argue that the

---

50. Ronald E. Clements, *Prophecy and Tradition* (Oxford: Blackwell, 1975), 39.
51. Petersen, *Prophetic Literature*, 4.
52. Aune, *Prophecy*, 85; cf. VanGemeren, *Prophetic Word*, 37.
53. Patrick D. Miller, Jr., 'The World and Message of the Prophets: Biblical Prophecy in Its Context', in Mays, Petersen, and Richards (eds.), *Old Testament Interpretation*, 97.
54. Aune, *Prophecy*, 85.

prophetic material comprised in the works attributed to the Major and Minor Prophets primarily revolves around three historical events: (1) the destruction of Israel's northern kingdom manifested in the fall of Samaria in 722 B.C.E., (2) the destruction of Israel's southern kingdom manifested in the fall of Jerusalem in 587 B.C.E., and (3) the restoration of power in Jerusalem in 538 B.C.E.[55] Thus, in spite of the primarily external position that the writing prophets held with regard to societal institutions, the shape and content of their message also pertains generally to the development of Israel's society, and particularly to the shape and function of the monarchy. In terms of its historical and societal situations, therefore, the material attributed to the writing prophets appears to represent concerns similar to those associated within prophetic figures in the Pentateuch and Historical books.

The historical purview of the writing prophets, however, cannot be constructed in precise terms due to the complexity involved in the extensive theories concerning the collection and redaction of this portion of the prophetic material.[56] For example, it may be possible to identify at least five different stages in the production of a particular prophetic book: (1) the initial prophetic speech, (2) a pre-exilic redaction, (3) a Deuteronomistic redaction, (4) later prophetic additions, and (5) a final redaction of the material.[57] This complexity becomes particularly transparent when one attempts to identify the character and personality of the prophets to whom the prophetic books are attributed. Apart from biographical material in the prescripts of the prophetic books and other limited instances of biographical material, such as Jeremiah's so-called confessions and the more overtly biographical portions of Hosea and Jonah, a particular prophetic figure may be nearly impossible to locate in the actual course of the prophetic work attributed to him.[58] The hidden nature of the prophet in this regard makes it difficult to formulate either a precise understanding of the identity of the prophet or of the material which comprised his initial oral presentation.[59]

---

55. Ronald E. Clements, *Old Testament Prophecy: From Oracles to Canon* (Louisville: Westminster John Knox, 1996), 197-98.

56. For a representative example of the critical understanding of the historical process involved in the creation and transmission of the prophetic texts, see Lindblom, *Prophecy*, 220-91.

57. Aune, *Prophecy*, 101.

58. Seitz, *Prophecy and Hermeneutics*, 88.

59. Odil Hannes Steck, *The Prophetic Books and Their Theological Witness* (trans. James D. Nogalski; St. Louis: Chalice, 2000), 7, 128.

Similarly, the stark literary differences between the material in the Pentateuch and Historical books and that in the Prophetic literature may function to complicate one's understanding of the relationship between the prophetic material present in each. While prophetic material in the Pentateuch and the Historical books primarily consists of narrative, the Prophetic literature contains a wide variety of genres and forms. The Prophetic literature also appears to be more overtly negative and unsolicited. These factors likely stem from the unique historical and societal settings of the individual writing prophets. However, due to the disparity between the amount of prophetic material found in these distinct literary corpora, it is difficult to claim that the material found in the writing prophets is representative of all prophetic activity within Israel's history.[60] That is, while the prophetic material attributed to the writing prophets is expansive *vis-à-vis* non-Israelite prophetic material from the same historical period, the writing prophets themselves represent only a small portion of the prophetic activity that took place in the course of Israel's history.[61] Moreover, the complex historical process of the transmission of the Old Testament prophetic corpus testifies to the fluidity of the form and content which comprise the material attributed to the individual writing prophets.[62]

Despite this complexity, however, it is possible to delineate several specific formulaic features that are consistently featured in the prophetic writings.[63] For example, oracles of judgment and salvation function prominently throughout the Old Testament (e.g. 1 Kgs 11.31; 21.17-19; 2 Kgs 1.3-4, 6; 20.5-6; Isa. 3.12; 29.13-14; Jer. 16.11-13; 27.9, 16; 28.2-4;

---

60. Aune, *Prophecy*, 88-89.
61. Cf. Lindblom, *Prophecy*, 202.
62. Lindblom, *Prophecy*, 279.
63. Numerous studies have focused on identifying particular forms of speech and literature within the prophetic writings; e.g. Aune, *Prophecy*, 88-101; Katheryn Pfisterer Darr, 'Literary Perspectives on Prophetic Literature', in Mays, Petersen, and Richards (eds.), *Old Testament Interpretation*, 127-43; John H. Hayes, 'The History of the Form-Critical Study of Prophecy', in *SBL Seminar Papers, 1973* (ed. George W. MacRae; 2 vols.; SBLSP 12; Missoula, Mont.: Scholars Press, 1973), 1:60-99; W. Eugene March, 'Prophecy', in *Old Testament Form Criticism* (ed. John H. Hayes; San Antonio: Trinity University Press, 1974), 141-77; Alexander Rofé, 'The Classification of the Prophetical Stories', *JBL* 89 (1970): 427-40; Gene M. Tucker, *Form Criticism of the Old Testament* (GBS; Philadelphia: Fortress, 1971); Gene M. Tucker, 'Prophetic Speech', *Int* 32 (1978): 31-45; Tucker, 'Prophecy', 335-45; Claus Westermann, *Basic Forms of Prophetic Speech* (trans. Hugh Clayton White; Philadelphia: Westminster, 1967); Robert R. Wilson, 'Form-Critical Investigation of the Prophetic Literature: The Present Situation', in MacRae (ed.), *SBL Seminar Papers, 1973*, 1:100-27.

29.10-11; 32.37; 33.6; Amos 2.6-8; 3.2; 4.1-2; 6.11-12; 7.16-17; 8.4-8; Mic. 3.9-12; 7.13).⁶⁴ Yet, even with respect to these two identifiable forms there may be evidence of development within the prophetic history, as material from the post-exilic period appears to demonstrate that these two forms were later merged together (e.g. Isa. 56.12–57.1; 65.7-8, 13-15).⁶⁵ The fluidity of these forms, however, may actually establish the organic nature of the prophetic material. In other words, the continued and fluid transmission of the prophetic material may be representative of God's own continued interaction with humanity through the course of history.⁶⁶ It may be more appropriate, therefore, to define prophetic literature not simply through an analysis of particular forms, but through a generative approach, in which prophetic literature is defined more broadly as that material which generates from, and is associated with, prophetic figures.⁶⁷ An oversimplified divide between the prophetic material presented in the various Old Testament literary corpora centred on particular differences in terms of genre likely fails to account for the changing nature of prophecy in light of particular historical circumstances, and appears to neglect the prophets' own understanding of God's ability to express himself in multiple ways.

Furthermore, there are textual connections between the literary corpora. Both Amos and Hosea exhibit knowledge of prophetic history outside of their own ministries (e.g. Hos. 6.5; 9.7-8; 12.10, 13; Amos 2.11-12).⁶⁸ More specifically, the text of Hos. 12.13 establishes a connection with the prophetic ministry of Moses. The function of the allusion to Moses in this passage is likely to reemphasize the central nature of the Mosaic covenant for the life of the community.⁶⁹ Further mention of prophetic figures potentially portrayed in the Pentateuch and Historical books is made in the writing prophets. Jeremiah 7.25 affirms that prophets were sent by the Lord למן־היום אשר אבותיכם מארץ מצרים עד היום הזה (cf. Jer. 11.7), while the author of Zechariah references potentially earlier prophetic material on several occasions in order to

64. Aune, *Prophecy*, 92-94; VanGemeren, *Prophetic Word*, 78-79.
65. Aune, *Prophecy*, 93.
66. Steck, *Prophetic Books*, 167.
67. Petersen, *Prophetic Literature*, 4, 44.
68. Blenkinsopp, *Prophecy*, 20, 62.
69. Douglas Stuart, *Hosea–Jonah* (WBC 31; Waco: Word, 1987), 195. Petersen, *Prophetic Literature*, 221, however, claims that the antecedent of נביא in Hos. 12.13 is ambiguous. Nevertheless, the mention of Egypt and the parallel nature of the second line of the verse make it unlikely that anyone but Moses is in view at this point; cf. Stuart, *Hosea–Jonah*, 195, who affirms that both occurrences of the noun represent an 'obvious reference to Moses'.

substantiate the importance and reliability of his own message (e.g. Zech. 1.4-6; 7.4-12; 8.9). The writing prophets also refer to prophetic figures whose messages did not appear to align with their own. Jeremiah's confrontation with Hananiah in Jeremiah 28, for example, highlights the existence of competing prophetic activity within this portion of Israel's history. Similarly, Amos' confrontation with Amaziah, the priest of Bethel, in Amos 7, appears to show that Amos was aware of a professional prophetic tradition with which he was unwilling to associate.[70] It may also be possible to affirm connections between the writing prophets themselves. For example, Amos and Hosea may have influenced certain portions of the material in Isaiah and Jeremiah, respectively.[71] Thus, while the material found within the Prophetic literature does not always parallel that within the Deuteronomistic history precisely, there is at least some evidence that the writing prophets were cognizant of other prophetic material.

The connection between the prophetic material in the Old Testament corpora may also be seen in the themes developed within the Prophetic literature itself. This connection is particularly evident in the plurality of references to the covenant within the writing prophets. For example, the curses and blessings of the Mosaic covenant provide a significant background for the thematic structure of the Minor Prophets (e.g. Hos. 1.9; 2.14-15; 3.4-5; 4.6; 5.7, 14; 7.16; 8.13-14; 9.3, 17; 10.15; 11.5-6; Joel 1.1–2.27; Obad. 1-21).[72] The material in the prophetic corpus also focuses uniquely on YHWH's importance within the community, a theme reflected in material pertaining to Moses, Samuel, and Elijah. Likewise, Wilson notes the close relationship between the prophetic

---

70. It is unlikely that Amos' statement in Amos 7.14 that he was 'neither a prophet nor the son of a prophet', is an affirmation of complete separation between himself and other prophetic persons. Amos describes his own activity with the verb נבא in the following verse (Amos 7.15). More probable is the notion that Amos was denying a connection with a strand of professional prophetic activity that he perceived to be unfaithful to YHWH; Stuart, *Hosea–Jonah*, 376-77; cf. Lindblom, *Prophecy*, 107-9.

71. Clements, *Prophecy and Tradition*, 91.

72. Stuart, *Hosea–Jonah*, xxxi-ii. Although Stuart is correct to see a connection between the writing prophets and the Mosaic covenant, he likely goes too far in his assertion that the 'prophets had not the slightest sense that they were creating any new doctrine but considered themselves spokespersons for Yahweh, who through them called his people *back* to obedience to the covenant' (xxxii). The development of the prophetic message from the exilic to the postexilic era, for example, provides evidence of new, or developing, themes within the prophetic literature; cf. VanGemeren, *Prophetic Tradition*, 57-59.

message presented in the narrative of 1–2 Kings and that of Isaiah, both of which deny the validity of foreign alliances and call on the people to serve YHWH alone.[73] The overall shape and transmission of the writing prophets may also contain a unified message that is consistent with the notion of an internal development within the prophetic material. That is, the distinct messages of the individual prophetic writings can also be seen within the framework of a singular message concerning YHWH's interaction with Israel and the nations in the course of history.[74] For example, Seitz contends that 'the canonical form of the twelve Minor Prophets is concerned both to protect the original witness and to comprehend how that witness is meant to speak meaningfully across the ages, through time'.[75] The final shape of the prophetic texts, therefore, provides insight into the message of both the individual prophet and the entire prophetic corpus. In this view, the final form of the writing prophets serves an important function with regard to the development of their uniquely prophetic message.

The existence of this uniquely prophetic message, however, continues to be somewhat enigmatic. While certain historical and societal situations may explain the shape and form of the material that constitutes the prophetic corpus, the cause of the initial recording and subsequent development of this material remains to be explored. Although the political and social circumstances of the writing prophets may provide insight into the nature of their particular prophetic messages, the reason for the origin and preservation of the prophetic material may prove to be more inherently theological. That is, if the prophetic material was merely meant to reflect the historical situations of particular prophetic figures, then it becomes difficult to explain the contrast between the genres exhibited in the Deuteronomistic history and the Prophetic literature. However, it is possible to argue that the prophetic figures believed that their particular oracles were representative of the very words of YHWH.[76] This notion, that the writing prophets were sources of divine discourse, may also serve as an explanation for the creation and transmission of the material historically associated with them. In other words, the history of the prophetic corpus may also represent the notion that the prophetic material is to be viewed as a divine message to the covenant community.[77]

73. Wilson, 'Former Prophets', 95.
74. Steck, *Prophetic Books*, 162-63.
75. Seitz, *Prophecy and Hermeneutics*, 150.
76. This seems to be at least one of the purposes of the common phrase in the MT: כה־אמר יהוה.
77. Clements, *Old Testament Prophecy*, 206; Steck, *Prophetic Books*, 134.

Even more, however, it could be argued that the prophetic message does not merely represent a divine word or message, but evinces an understanding of reality that is thoroughly intertwined with the divine economy. Thus, as Miller helpfully asserts:

> Both formally and conceptually, the prophetic oracle is a message, not simply from the deity but from the divine world, from the divine assembly where the decrees of God are set forth and transmitted as a divine proclamation or message by the prophetic herald: 'Thus says the Lord.' Prophetic activity, therefore, cannot be understood simply in terms of its social, religious or political world. It has to be understood from a frame of reference outside the realia of social existence though never separated from them. Prophetic oracles and prophetic narratives attest to a starting point for prophetic activity in a transcendent world identified by the image of the council of the Lord, the heavenly assembly (e.g., 1 Kngs 22:19-23; Isaiah 6; and Jer 23:16-22)… The social world of the prophet is to be found in heaven as much as on earth.[78]

In this view, the prophetic material is conditioned primarily by its divine source so that it might be more effective in shaping, or re-shaping, the community to which it was addressed. Thus, the prophetic material is not merely a spoken word; rather, it is the spoken (or written) and effective word of the Lord, which is able to interpret past events, describe how the Lord is currently operating, and explain (or cause) future events. The prophetic material, therefore, is 'the word of God [that] reveals and effects'.[79] This close relationship between the message of the writing prophets and this transcendent reality may function as additional evidence for a connection between the prophetic material present in the different corpora. For example, the relational nature of Moses' prophetic activity may have been a catalyst for the development of an understanding that prophetic material was to be uniquely related to the message of YHWH (cf. Num. 12.7-8; Deut. 34.10). Consequently, it may be possible to argue that the function of the prophetic material throughout the Old Testament was, at a basic level, to provide the covenant community with an additional means of receiving divine information and communication.

As with the material in the Deuteronomistic history, the multiplicity of figures, forms, and messages that can be delineated within the writing prophets highlight the complex nature of Israel's prophetic history. Amidst this complexity, however, there are several important connections between the different Old Testament literary corpora, including the

78. Miller, 'World and Message of the Prophets', 101.
79. Steck, *Prophetic Books*, 134-35.

close relationship between prophecy and the monarchy, the use of particular literary constructions, thematic connections, such as an emphasis on the Mosaic covenant, and in the internal presentation of their particular messages as representative of the divine word. Moreover, several inter-textual connections can be identified in the material. Thus, although the Prophetic literature develops a variety of themes and emphases, it is possible to see at least some level of connection between its material and that present in the Pentateuch and Historical books, as well as parallels to the continued internal progression of Israel's own societal development. Because of this it seems reasonable to argue that the Prophetic literature exhibits similar organic categories of expansion and contraction in conjunction with Israel's history to those present in the Pentateuch and Historical books.

c. *Conclusions*

The Old Testament provides variegated evidence for the shape of the prophetic tradition. Ambiguity surrounds the task of determining the role and purpose of particular prophetic figures, as well as the process of delineating what material can be accurately labeled as prophetic literature. In light of the multifaceted nature of prophets, prophetic activity, and prophetic material presented in the Old Testament it is necessary to avoid the affirmation that the prophetic history developed in the Old Testament is a uniform phenomenon.[80] However, in spite of the complex nature of the prophetic material, it is possible to see the development of a prophetic tradition within the Old Testament. In other words, although certain aspects of the prophetic material are both multifaceted and equivocal, there is evidence of an internal progression within the material. This progression can be seen in the influence of particular prophetic figures, such as Moses, Samuel, and Elijah, on the shape of the prophetic tradition and in particular historical, textual, and thematic connections between the prophetic material present in the different Old Testament corpora. Furthermore, that this progression was unique to Israel is manifest in several differences between Old Testament prophetic material and the extant prophetic material derived from historically contemporary cultures. Thus, while the prophetic material of Israel is not a completely unique phenomenon, it is reasonable to assert that it underwent a unique development in light of the political, social, and religious history of Israel. It seems, therefore, that the prophetic tradition of the Old Testament is not a monolith, but an organic entity that grows in conjunction with the community to which it pertains.

80. Ringgren, 'Prophecy', 11.

The notion that the Old Testament prophetic tradition can expand and contract may suggest that it is possible that the nature, form, and function of the prophetic material changed significantly prior to the commencement of Paul's relationship with the Corinthian community. Thus, while it may be possible to identify a unified prophetic tradition within the Old Testament, Paul's presentation of his ministry may have been shaped by subsequent alterations of that tradition. It will be helpful, therefore, to analyse the course of the prophetic material through both the Second Temple period and the early development of the Christian movement.

## 3. *The Prophetic Tradition in Second Temple Judaism*

Similar to the complex prophetic tradition developed in the Old Testament, the nature of prophetic material and activity that originates in the Second Temple period does not attest to the existence of an entirely monolithic prophetic tradition. Rather, the nature, form, and function of the prophetic material that stems from the Second Temple period exhibit both similarities and differences with respect to the prophetic material of the Old Testament. Although the prophetic material of the Old Testament functions in a variety of ways in the literary corpora of the Second Temple period, the differences between the material composed in the two eras led an earlier generation of scholars to argue, in a variety of forms, that prophecy was non-existent during at least a significant portion of the Second Temple period.[81] Apart from debate concerning the existence or

---

81. E.g. C.K. Barrett, *The Holy Spirit and the Gospel Tradition* (London: SPCK, 1947), 108-9; Cross, *Canaanite Myth*, 223; Jean Giblet, 'Prophétisme et attente d'un messie prophète dans l'ancien Judaïsme', in *L'attente d'un Messie* (ed. Lucien Cerfaux; RechBib 1; Paris: Desclée de Brouwer, 1954), 91; Paul D. Hanson, *The Dawn of the Apocalyptic* (Philadelphia: Fortress, 1975), 16; David Hill, *New Testament Prophecy* (London: Marshall, Morgan & Scott, 1979), 21; Friedrich Wilhelm Horn, *Das Angeld des Geistes: Studien zur paulinischen Pneumatologie* (FRLANT 154; Göttingen: Vandenhoeck & Ruprecht, 1992), 31; Joachim Jeremias, *New Testament Theology* (New York: Scribner's, 1971), 81; Yehezkel Kaufmann, *Toldot ha-'Emunah ha-Yis-ra'elit* (4 vols.; Jerusalem: Bialik Institute, 1955), 4:378-403; Rex Mason, 'The Prophets of the Restoration', in Coggins, Phillips, and Knibb (eds.), *Israel's Prophetic Tradition*, 140-42; Erik Sjöberg, 'πνεῦμα, πνευματικός', *TDNT* 6:385; Julius Wellhausen, *Prolegomena to the History of Israel* (Atlanta: Scholars Press, 1994), 401-4; repr. of *Prolegomena to the History of Israel* (trans. J. Sutherland Black and Allan Enzies, with preface by W. Robertson Smith; Edinburgh: Black, 1885); trans. of *Prolegomean zur Geschichte Israels* (2d ed.; Berlin: Reimer, 1883); Robert R. Wilson, *Prophecy and Society in Ancient Israel* (Philadelphia: Fortress, 1980), 306-7.

viability of original prophetic activity after the apparent end of the ministry of Israel's writing prophets in the fifth century B.C.E., questions remain with regard to the function of the Old Testament prophetic material in the Second Temple period. That is, the assertion that the Second Temple period is devoid of prophetic activity does not prevent the prophetic history of the Old Testament from impacting the historical, social, and religious dimensions of the period. It is the intention within this section, therefore, to analyse questions regarding the potential cessation of prophetic activity within Second Temple Judaism and to examine how the prophetic history of the Old Testament expands or contracts in the intertestamental period in order to determine the nature of the prophetic tradition (or traditions) that may have influenced early Christianity.

a. *The Potential Cessation of Prophecy*
The view that the Second Temple period is devoid of original prophetic activity is based primarily on the apparent content of several influential texts (e.g. Zech. 13.2-3; 1 Macc. 4.46; 9.27; 14.41; Bar. 1.21; Pr Azar 15; Josephus, *Ag. Ap.* 1.41; *2 Bar.* 85.1, 3; cf. Ps. 74.9; Ezek. 13.9). Although the individual passages ostensibly have different situations in view, their seemingly negative assertions concerning the present or future existence of prophetic activity make it likely that at least certain 'segments of Second Temple Judaism questioned the continued viability of prophecy after the biblical period'.[82] Although certain individuals or groups within the Second Temple period may have denied the existence of contemporary prophetic material, this denial does not necessarily eliminate the possibility that prophecy existed within a more expansive social setting. In other words, while prophetic activity may have been seen as non-existent in some settings, this may not have been a universal reality.[83]

More recent examples of this claim include Gordon D. Fee, *God's Empowering Presence: The Holy Spirit in the Letters of Paul* (Peabody, Mass.: Hendrickson, 1994), 914, and Benjamin D. Sommer, 'Did Prophecy Cease? Evaluating a Reevaluation', *JBL* 115 (1996): 31-47.

82. Alex P. Jassen, *Mediating the Divine: Prophecy and Revelation in the Dead Sea Scrolls and Second Temple Judaism* (STDJ 68; Leiden: Brill, 2007), 14.

83. One of the primary difficulties at this point is the lack of consensus on the definition of prophecy and the consequent issues thereby created with regard to a determination of how 'prophetic' texts from different periods might relate to one another. For the purpose of the present work, the term prophecy is understood in generative terms as representing revelatory material that develops out of the social and literary portrayal of prophetic figures. On the difficulty of defining prophecy see Lester L. Grabbe, 'Poets, Scribes, or Preachers: The Reality of Prophecy in the

Prior to examining the evidence for contemporary prophetic activity in the Second Temple period, however, it will be helpful to analyse a portion of the textual evidence put forth in defence of the argument against the continued existence of prophets and prophecy.

Initially, the scriptural evidence cited for the non-existence of prophecy does not prove to be overtly clear in its understanding of the nature of prophetic traditions during the intertestamental period. Zechariah 13.1-6, for example, does not claim that prophets and prophecy would cease to exist entirely; rather, the text affirms only that certain forms of prophetic activity would not be compatible with the people of Israel due to their unique relationship with YHWH. Furthermore, a theologically conservative dating schema would locate the ministry of Zechariah in the last decades of the sixth century B.C.E., making his prophetic ministry contemporaneous with the construction of the post-exilic temple.[84] Yet, in light of the complex process involved in the formulation of the prophetic books of the Old Testament, it is likely that the textual tradition represented in the canonical form of Zechariah is representative of at least some later editorial work. For example, the book may be comprised of two separate traditions, with Zechariah 9–14 representing a later prophetic composition.[85] The book of Zechariah itself, therefore, may serve as an early witness for the continued development of prophetic material within the nation of Israel during the Second Temple period.[86] Thus, instead of attesting to a decline in prophetic activity, the compositions attributed to the post-exilic writing prophets appear to provide insight into the way in which Second Temple Judaism viewed the development of Israel's prophetic history, as well as the significance of that development for their own setting within the Second Temple period.[87] In addition, while Ps. 74.9 and Ezek. 13.9 may discuss a decline in prophecy, or at least in its political importance, the primary emphasis of these texts

Second Temple Period', in *Knowing the End from the Beginning: The Prophetic, the Apocalyptic, and Their Relationships* (ed. Lester L. Grabbe and Robert D. Haak; JSPSup 46; London: T&T Clark, 2003), 193-97.

84. VanGemeren, *Prophetic Word*, 193.

85. For a discussion of the historical context of Zechariah and the divide between chs. 1–8 and 9–14, see Carol L. Meyers and Eric M. Meyers, *Zechariah 9–14* (AB 25C; New York: Doubleday, 1993), 15-69.

86. Matthias Henze, 'Invoking the Prophets in Zechariah and Ben Sira', in *Prophets, Prophecy, and Prophetic Texts in Second Temple Judaism* (ed. Michael H. Floyd and Robert D. Haak; LHBOTS 427; London: T&T Clark International, 2006), 129.

87. Michael H. Floyd, 'Introduction', in Floyd and Haak (eds.), *Prophets, Prophecy, and Prophetic Texts*, 2.

appears to be the sovereignty of the Lord over all prophetic activity.[88] Thus, discussion of a decline in prophecy within the Old Testament often stems primarily from a particular ideological concern, namely the determination of what prophetic forms are compatible with the covenant relationship formed between YHWH and his people. The biblical evidence, therefore, does not seem to establish the cessation of prophecy in the Second Temple period; rather, it highlights that the Old Testament itself was concerned with determining the viability of certain forms of prophetic activity with respect to its own social, political, and religious history.

Similarly, the non-biblical material put forth for the notion that prophecy ceased within the Second Temple period does not provide consistent evidence for this claim. The clearest example of the cessation of prophetic activity stems from 1 Macc. 9.27, which refers to a level of distress ἥτις οὐκ ἐγένετο ἀφ' ἧς ἡμέρας οὐκ ὤφθη προφήτης αὐτοῖς. Although it could be argued that this verse merely refers to the absence of prophets during this particular period of distress, the temporal and historical emphasis of the phrase seems to suggest that it refers to a more extended period of time.[89] Read in isolation, therefore, this text may point to a lack of prophetic activity in the Maccabaean period. Two additional texts, 1 Macc. 4.44-46 and 14.41, however, are also used as evidence for a void in the prophetic tradition. While both texts acknowledge that no prophet is available to guide the community, they also look forward to the rise of an eschatological prophet who would fulfill this function.[90] In contrast with the purview of 1 Macc. 9.27, these two passages do not seem to affirm that prophetic activity had ceased, but only that a suitable prophetic figure was not present at that point.[91] If both 1 Macc. 4.44-46 and 14.41 assume that it was possible that a suitable prophet would come forth, then it is difficult to affirm that they are representative examples of the cessation of prophetic activity. Rather, they appear to serve as evidence that a certain form of prophetic activity was expected, even if no prophet arose within that particular setting.[92] At most, therefore, the material in 1 Maccabees presents a multifaceted picture of the state of prophecy in the Second Temple period.

---

88. Aune, *Prophecy*, 105.
89. Contra Frederick E. Greenspahn, 'Why Prophecy Ceased', *JBL* 108 (1989): 37-49 (40).
90. For further information on the identity and function of the prophet in 1 Maccabees, see Jassen, *Mediating the Divine*, 149-54.
91. Grabbe, 'Poets', 198.
92. Aune, *Prophecy*, 105.

Material from Josephus' writings is also used to support the position that prophetic activity ceased after the ministry of the writing prophets seemingly ended in the fifth century B.C.E. The following portion of *Against Apion* is often cited as the primary evidence for this position:

ἀπὸ δὲ Ἀρταξέρξου μέχρι τοῦ καθ' ἡμᾶς χρόνου γέγραπται μὲν ἕκαστα, πίστεως δ'οὐχ ὁμοίας ἠξίωται τοῖς πρὸ αὐτῶν διὰ τὸ μὴ γενέσθαι τὴν τῶν προφητῶν ἀκριβῆ διαδοχήν. (1.41)

It is difficult, however, to maintain that this brief statement implies that Josephus believes that prophecy had ceased completely during the Second Temple period. Rather than affirming the cessation of all prophetic activity, the import of Josephus' argument in this portion of the treatise seems to be that the twenty-two books which he affirms as Scripture, thirteen of which he attributes to prophetic writers, all represent material composed before the end of the Persian period.[93] Thus, the previous discussion concerning the nature and composition of Josephus' own scriptural canon (e.g. *Ag. Ap.* 1.37-40) may point to the idea that only a certain form of prophetic activity, namely that which resulted in the creation of authoritative historical works, ceased to exist at some point after the reign of Artaxerxes.[94] Yet, this possibility is merely an inference from the fact that Josephus closely relates earlier prophetic activity to the creation of certain portions of the Old Testament, and may go too far in determining how Josephus defines particular prophetic functions. In other words, to combine definitions of canon with elements of prophecy in Josephus may result in anachronistic definitions of the form and function of prophecy in the Second Temple period. At most, therefore, it seems that Josephus is aware of some form of distinction between prophetic activity before and after the reign of Artaxerxes, whether it be genealogical, functional, or qualitative.

In further opposition to the argument that Josephus affirms the cessation of prophecy, it may be possible to assert that the material in *Against Apion* actually points to the reality of later prophetic activity, since it focuses not on the existence of individual prophetic figures, but on their exact succession.[95] In other words, it might have been necessary for Josephus to know of Second Temple prophets who could not be

---

93. Greenspahn, 'Prophecy', 40 n. 18.
94. Rebecca Gray, *Prophetic Figures in Late Second Temple Jewish Palestine: The Evidence from Josephus* (Oxford: Oxford University Press, 1993), 8-16; cf. Louis H. Feldman, 'Prophets and Prophecy in Josephus', *JTS* 41 (1990): 386-422.
95. Lester L. Grabbe, 'Thus Spake the Prophet Josephus…': The Jewish Historian on Prophets and Prophecy', in Floyd and Haak (eds.), *Prophets, Prophecy, and Prophetic Texts*, 242.

associated with Old Testament prophets in order to assert that the exact succession of prophets did not continue. On the other hand, it may be that Josephus derives his understanding of the lack of a prophetic succession from his view that no later work πίστεως δ'οὐχ ὁμοίας ἠξίωται τοῖς πρὸ αὐτῶν (*Ag. Ap.* 1.41).⁹⁶ The potential for variations in prophetic activity, however, was a reality witnessed to even in the material which Josephus likely viewed as Scripture (e.g. 1 Sam. 3.1). Thus, although it may be impossible to determine the precise meaning of Josephus' discussion of the succession of the prophets, it does not appear that the statement itself can support the burden of proving that prophecy ceased to exist.

Rabbinic material is also advanced to support the cessation of prophecy after the ministry of the writing prophets. *Tosephta Soṭa* 13.2 is prominent in this regard due to its claim that the activity of the Holy Spirit ceased in Israel when the ministries of Haggai, Zechariah, and Malachi ended.⁹⁷ However, *t. Soṭa* 13.2b-4 affirms the continued existence of divine communication through means of the בת קול. This distinction between means of receiving divine communication in this segment of the rabbinic literature likely points to 'a qualitative distinction between canonical prophecy and that which has succeeded it'.⁹⁸ In addition, Sommer rightly points to further instances in the rabbinic literature that claim that the Holy Spirit had departed, a parallel way of stating that prophetic activity had ceased (e.g. *b. Yoma* 9b, *b. Soṭa* 48b, *y. Soṭa* 9.13), and that the בת קול was less authoritative than the Holy Spirit (e.g. *Cant. Rab.* 8.11).⁹⁹ However, despite this evidence, there are separate portions of the rabbinic literature that attest to continued prophetic activity (e.g. *m. Sanh.* 1.5; 11.1; *b. Sanh.* 90a; *b. Ber.* 55b).¹⁰⁰ Moreover, as Aune points out, some of the rabbinic material that makes negative statements with regard to the continued existence of prophetic activity may be intended to legitimate particular rabbinic sages over against their opponents, or possibly over against early Christians.¹⁰¹ Similar to the material derived from 1 Maccabees, therefore, it seems that the rabbinic literature witnesses, at most, to competing views concerning prophetic activity in the Second Temple period.

---

96. Gray, *Prophetic Figures*, 13.
97. On this text, see especially John R. Levison, 'Did the Spirit Withdraw from Israel? An Evaluation of the Earliest Jewish Data', *NTS* 43 (1997): 46-56.
98. Aune, *Prophecy*, 104.
99. Sommer, 'Prophecy', 33-34, 39-40.
100. Greenspahn, 'Prophecy', 44.
101. Aune, *Prophecy*, 104; cf. Ephraim E. Urbach, 'Matai Pasqa ha-Nevuah?', *Tarbiz* 17 (1945–46): 2-3, 9-11.

Additionally, the claim that prophecy ceased within the Second Temple period is sometimes put forth in conjunction with the argument that prophetic activity was eclipsed by the rise of apocalyptic material. Although certain portions of the Old Testament may represent examples of apocalyptic literature (e.g. Dan. 8–12; Zech. 9–14), the intertestamental period witnessed a significant increase in the writing of apocalypses and additional apocalyptic literature.[102] It would be inaccurate, however, to assert that apocalyptic material simply represents a progressive step in a trajectory created by earlier prophetic activity. Both prophetic and apocalyptic works result from a wide variety of social and cultural circumstances, as well as from multiple historical periods.[103] In addition, the development of prophecy and prophetic material does not necessarily provide a helpful basis for understanding the categories developed within apocalyptic material, making it difficult to assert either a sequential or chronological correlation between the two phenomena.[104] Conversely, it would also be inaccurate to assert that prophetic material and apocalyptic literature are not closely related. Apart from possible distinctions between the two phenomena, such as their mode of revelation or expressed eschatology, both serve as examples of revelatory material within Israelite (and non-Israelite) history.[105] In the sense that apocalyptic literature mirrors the concerns and themes of prophetic material, it seems reasonable to argue that the apocalyptic material represents an additional form of prophetic activity or a continuation of it in some sense.[106] If apocalyptic

---

102. For an extensive overview of apocalyptic literature from the Second Temple period, see Richard Bauckham, 'Apocalypses', in *The Complexities of Second Temple Judaism* (vol. 1 of *Justification and Variegated Nomism*; ed. D.A. Carson, Peter T. O'Brien, and Mark A. Seifrid; WUNT 2/140; Tübingen: Mohr Siebeck, 2001), 135-87; cf. Jonathan M. Knight, 'Apocalyptic and Prophetic Literature', in *Handbook of Classical Rhetoric in the Hellenistic Period (330 B.C.–A.D. 400)* (ed. Stanley E. Porter; Leiden: Brill, 1997), 467-88.

103. Lester L. Grabbe, 'Prophetic and Apocalyptic: Time for New Definitions—And New Thinking', in Grabbe and Haak (eds.), *Knowing the End from the Beginning*, 130; cf. Ben Witherington III, *Jesus the Seer: The Progress of Prophecy* (Peabody, Mass.: Hendrickson, 1999), 217.

104. Michael H. Floyd, 'The Production of Prophetic Books in the Early Second Temple Period', in Floyd and Haak (eds.), *Prophets, Prophecy, and Prophetic Texts*, 278.

105. Aune, *Prophecy*, 114.

106. Michael A. Knibb, 'Prophecy and the Emergence of the Jewish Apocalypses', in Coggins, Phillips, and Knibb (eds.), *Israel's Prophetic Tradition*, 176; cf. James C. VanderKam, 'The Prophetic-Sapiential Origins of Apocalyptic Thought', in *A Word in Season* (Festschrift William McKane; ed. James D. Martin and Philip R. Davies; JSOTSup 42; Sheffield: JSOT, 1986), 163-76. Additionally, Grabbe argues

literature is parallel to prophetic material in certain regards, then the existence of apocalyptic material in the Second Temple period may provide evidence for the continuation of prophetic activity. In other words, the increased amount of apocalyptic material in the intertestamental period may serve as an additional witness for the notion that revelatory practices were an accepted part of the social, cultural, and religious experience of at least certain segments of Second Temple Judaism.

Based on this brief analysis of both biblical and non-biblical evidence it seems that the assertion that prophecy ceased after the ministry of the writing prophets ended is untenable for several reasons. First, the discussion of the cessation of prophecy does not provide a consistent definition of prophecy. Generally, it seems that what is meant is that prophetic activity which resulted in canonical material was no longer present. This argument, however, suffers both from a potentially anachronistic understanding of canon and a narrowly defined understanding of the purpose and function of prophetic activity. Based on its organic development, it seems unlikely that even the creation of the prophetic material in the Old Testament could be defined in terms of its eventual inscripturation. Secondly, the various arguments against the continuation of prophecy do not provide a consistent terminus for prophetic activity. For example, the material from the post-exilic writing prophets provides evidence for prophetic activity at the beginning of the Second Temple period, while the material in 1 Maccabees may witness to the expectation of prophetic activity nearly three centuries later. At one level, therefore, the Second Temple period is simply too broad to make a single assertion concerning the existence, or lack thereof, of prophetic activity. Thirdly, the textual evidence paints a diverse picture of prophetic activity in the Second Temple period, with different segments affirming different viewpoints. The previous two points, therefore, do not dismiss the reality that certain authors argued for some type of distinction between the prophetic

---

extensively that apocalyptic material should be understood as a sub-division or subgenre of prophecy (see, e.g., Lester L. Grabbe, *Judaic Religion in the Second Temple Period: Belief and Practice from the Exile to Yavneh* [London: Routledge, 2000], 235). Inasmuch as Grabbe's concern is to highlight both the continuity and discontinuity between prophetic and apocalyptic materials then this is a helpful consideration. However, John J. Collins, 'Prophecy, Apocalypse and Eschatology: Reflections on the Proposals of Lester Grabbe', in Grabbe and Haak (eds.), *Knowing the End from the Beginning*, 50-52, contends that the same distinctions and parallels can be drawn if prophecy and apocalyptic literature (as well as phenomena such as divination and mantic wisdom) are simply grouped within the larger category of revelatory experience or literature, and that Grabbe is merely 'obliterating useful distinctions' (51).

activity of the Old Testament and that seen within Second Temple Judaism. As a matter of conjecture, it may be that the language of certain authors was merely meant to stress, hyperbolically for instance, that certain forms of prophetic activity had changed from the author's contextual point of reference. In that regard, their statements concerning prophecy primarily represent their own viewpoints concerning YHWH's interaction with his people through prophetic means during this portion of Israel's history. Nevertheless, while prophecy undoubtedly transformed and developed in many ways after the composition of the material attributed to the Old Testament writing prophets was completed, it does not seem that the textual history of the period uniformly supports the cessation of prophetic activity. Rather, it reflects a diversity of opinion concerning the prevalence, function, and form of prophetic activity within Second Temple Judaism.

b. *Prophetic Activity in the Second Temple Period*
In addition to surveying the material used to argue for the decline of prophetic activity in the Second Temple period, it may also be possible to highlight examples of continued prophetic activity within this portion of history. If it can be shown that certain segments of Second Temple Judaism were aware of contemporary prophetic activity, then claims in favour of the cessation of prophecy would likely prove invalid. Within this section, four sources of material will be analysed in order to determine the significance of the Old Testament prophetic tradition in the Second Temple period and the shape of any contemporary prophetic material. These sources—the material from Qumran, Josephus, Philo, and Ben Sira—provide a number of reference points for examining the nature and form of prophetic activity within the intertestamental period. In spite of their different contexts and forms, however, each source provides a window into worldviews that existed within Second Temple Judaism.

(1) *Prophecy at Qumran.* One of the most useful sources for understanding the shape of prophetic activity in the Second Temple period is the extensive material derived from the caves at Qumran. The Qumran material is particularly important for its ability to highlight the sectarian community's understanding of prophecy, as well as its ability to provide insight into a larger segment of Second Temple Judaism by means of the non-sectarian documents. However, in spite of the potential usefulness of the Qumran material for developing an understanding of prophetic activity in the Second Temple period, the use of 'prophetic' vocabulary at Qumran is both infrequent and varied. The verb נבא occurs ten times in

## 2. The Development of the Prophetic Tradition

the literature (CD 6.1; 3Q4 3; 4Q385-386 [×8]; cf. PAM 44.102 66 4), while the noun נבואה occurs only once (11Q5 27.11).[107] The noun נביא is somewhat more prominent, occurring fifty-seven times.[108] The term, however, is used with a number of different referents.[109] Generally, the material pertaining to prophetic activity within the Qumran literature is directly related to the Old Testament prophetic material. There appears, therefore, to have been a significant interest in the prophetic history of the Old Testament within both the sectarian and non-sectarian communities.

However, apart from the general connection between the Qumran material and the Old Testament prophetic material, neither the sectarian nor non-sectarian material ever clearly refers to a member of the community with prophetic terminology.[110] This void is particularly transparent with regard to the Teacher of Righteousness. There are several references in the literature to the divine inspiration and authority that were attributed to the Teacher of Righteousness (e.g. 1QH$^a$ 10.10-18; 12.27-28; 15.26-27; 16.16-19; 23.10-14; 1QpHab 2.8-9), and, in some respects, the Teacher may have functioned within the paradigm established by the Mosaic tradition.[111] The contrast between the Teacher of Righteousness and a group of נביאי כזב in 1QH$^a$ 12.5-17 likely also functions to stress the Teacher's ability to mediate the divine will accurately in his role as a biblical exegete. That the Teacher of Righteousness is not labeled as a נביא in the hymn may actually serve as an additional means for asserting his superiority over his perceived opponents.[112]

---

107. The noun also appears in two fragments (4Q165 1-2.1; 4Q458 15.2), but neither has a discernable context. In addition, there is some discrepancy as to whether 4Q458 15.2 should read הנביאה or הנבואה. See Jassen, *Mediating the Divine*, 27-28 n. 6.

108. Cf. Jassen, *Mediating the Divine*, 27-28.

109. At least seven different referents can be identified: (1) individual biblical prophets (e.g. CD 4.13), (2) the prophets generally (e.g. 1QS 8.15-16), (3) God's 'servants' (e.g. 1QS 1.2-3), (4) the prophetic books (e.g. CD 7.17), (5) an eschatological prophet (e.g. 1QS 9.11), (6) a new Mosaic prophet (e.g. 4Q175 1.5), and (7) modern-day prophets (e.g. 1QH$^a$ 12.16). See Peter W. Flint, 'The Prophet David at Qumran', in *Biblical Interpretation at Qumran* (ed. Matthias Henze; Grand Rapids: Eerdmans, 2005), 161-62.

110. Cf. James E. Bowley, 'Prophets and Prophecy at Qumran', in *The Dead Sea Scrolls After Fifty Years: A Comprehensive Assessment* (ed. Peter W. Flint and James C. VanderKam; 2 vols.; Leiden: Brill, 1998–99), 2:371.

111. Bowley, 'Prophets and Prophecy', 2:371. For a discussion of the relationship between the Teacher of Righteousness and the Mosaic tradition, see Chapter 4.

112. Bowley, 'Prophets and Prophecy', 2:372-73. It is generally assumed, following Gert Jeremias, *Der Lehrer der Gerechtigkeit* (SUNT 2; Göttingen: Vandenhoeck

Furthermore, the Teacher of Righteousness also shares some similarities with the eschatological prophetic figure described in the *Rule of the Community*, the *Testimonia*, and *Melchizedek*. Particularly, both figures are associated with the Mosaic prophetic tradition. However, the two figures are never explicitly linked and the distinct functions attributed to each figure make it difficult to correlate them outside of their connection to previous prophetic traditions.[113] Although the Teacher of Righteousness is never explicitly identified as a נביא, it may be possible to assert that he 'achieved a quasi-prophetic status'[114] in light of both claims to his divinely appointed authority and to his role as an interpreter of the prophetic material. Thus, while the Teacher of Righteousness may not have been understood, within either the sectarian or non-sectarian material, as a prophetic figure, it is relatively clear that his role within the community was indebted to the prophetic history of the Old Testament.

Apart from the fact that no member of the sectarian community is referred to as a prophet within the Qumran literature, it remains difficult to affirm the notion that the community denied the existence of prophetic activity altogether. This difficulty stems from the realization that the literature at Qumran affirms the presence and activity of the Spirit among the community (e.g. 1QS 3.6-7; 9.3-4; 4Q248 1.5; 4Q301 1.1), as well as access to special divine revelation (e.g. 1QH$^a$ 4.26; 6.25; 9.21; 12.23; 17.32).[115] Additionally, while there do not appear to be any formulaic prophetic oracles in the literature at Qumran, several of the documents may be accurately labeled as oracular (e.g. 4Q370; 11QT),

---

& Ruprecht, 1963), 168-267, that the Teacher of Righteousness himself is the author of 1QH$^a$ 10-17. The material in 1QH$^a$ 12.5-17, therefore, may represent the Teacher's own 'prophetic' self-understanding in relation to other contemporary prophetic figures. For an extended discussion of 1QH$^a$ 12.5-17, see Jassen, *Mediating the Divine*, 280-90. Furthermore, *Pesher Habakkuk* (1QpHab 4.3-8) illustrates the perceived superiority of the Teacher over against the biblical prophets because of his complete knowledge of God's plan (so Jutta Leonhardt-Balzer, 'The Minor Prophets in the Judaism of the Second Temple Period', in *The Minor Prophets in the New Testament* [ed. Maarten J.J. Menken and Steve Moyise; LNTS 377; London: T&T Clark International, 2009], 11).

113. Jassen, *Mediating the Divine*, 190.

114. David L. Petersen, *Late Israelite Prophecy: Studies in Deutero-Prophetic Literature and in Chronicles* (SBLMS 23; Missoula, Mont.: Scholars Press, 1977), 101-2. See also the analysis in George J. Brooke, 'Was the Teacher of Righteousness Considered a Prophet?', in *Prophecy After the Prophets? The Contribution of the Dead Sea Scrolls to the Understanding of Biblical and Extra-Biblical Prophecy* (ed. Kristin De Troyer and Armin Lange; CBET 52; Leuven: Peeters, 2009), 77-98.

115. Bowley, 'Prophets and Prophecy', 2:373-75.

## 2. The Development of the Prophetic Tradition 39

and there is some evidence of visionary experiences in the material (e.g. 4Q286 1.ii.1-8; 4Q417 1.7-10; 2.i.16; cf. 4Q300 1.ii.3).[116] More broadly, the actual origin of the community at Qumran may represent a type of prophetic activity, with their exodus to the wilderness serving as a parallel to prophetic signs exhibited by some Old Testament prophetic figures.[117] There may also be external evidence for prophetic activity at Qumran if Josephus' statements regarding the predictive practices of the Essenes can properly be understood as referring to any portion of the Qumran community, or to any of the interpretative methodologies exhibited in the Qumran literature.[118] Thus, while it may be argued that a segment of the community represented by the documents at Qumran believed that original prophetic activity was no longer possible, this view does not appear to represent a consensus within the literature.[119]

Furthermore, several Qumran texts appear to establish the existence of prophecy that was contrary to the community's own belief system, thereby providing evidence for contemporary prophetic activity within the larger stream of the Second Temple period. In this regard, Jassen's study is particularly useful in identifying texts within the scrolls that point to ongoing prophetic activity.[120] Jassen highlights five texts that contribute to an understanding of prophetic activity in the period (i.e. 1QH[a] 12.5-17; CD 5.20–6.2; 11Q19 54.8-18; 4Q375; 4Q339). All five texts are concerned in some fashion with prophetic conflict. The first two examples from the *Hoyadot* and the *Damascus Document* are polemical texts and in both instances prophetic terminology is applied to opponents of the sectarian community. In 1QH[a] 12.16 the opponents are described as נביאי כזב and in CD 6.1 the 'movers of the boundary' are said to have ינבאו שקר. As Jassen notes, if one is able to move temporarily beyond the

---

116. George J. Brooke, 'Prophecy', in *Encyclopedia of the Dead Sea Scrolls* (ed. Lawrence H. Schiffman and James C. VanderKam; 2 vols.; Oxford: Oxford University Press, 2000), 2:697-98.

117. Richard A. Horsley and John S. Hanson, *Bandits, Prophets, and Messiahs: Popular Movements in the Time of Jesus* (San Francisco: Harper & Row, 1988), 157.

118. E.g. Josephus, *J.W.* 2.159 (cf. *J.W.* 1.78; 2.113; *Ant.* 15.373-79). It is unlikely, however, that Josephus' discussion of the Essene prophetic activity should be understood as a discussion of the method of pesher exegesis in particular; cf. Gray, *Prophetic Figures*, 105-7.

119. Contra Millar Burrows, 'Prophecy and Prophets at Qumran', in *Israel's Prophetic Heritage: Essays in Honor of James Muilenburg* (ed. Bernhard W. Anderson and Walter Harrelson; New York: Harper, 1962), 224-26, and Howard M. Teeple, *The Mosaic Eschatological Prophet* (JBLMS 10; Philadelphia: Society of Biblical Literature, 1957), 52.

120. Jassen, *Mediating the Divine*, 279-308.

polemical nature of these texts, they can be seen to relate the existence of certain forms of prophetic activity within the Second Temple period. More specifically, both texts represent a 'heightened portrait of prophetic conflict' and an 'increased concern with true and false prophecy'.[121] Thus, although both texts condemn the actions of those to whom prophetic terminology is attributed, they provide evidence for a contemporary concern about the nature of prophecy and prophets, much in the same way that questions of prophetic legitimacy were addressed in Jeremiah.

Similarly, the final three texts that Jassen identifies (i.e. 11Q19 54.8-18; 4Q375; 4Q339) are all non-sectarian documents which provide evidence for the same heightened interest in discussions of true and false prophecy within the larger stream of Second Temple Judaism. The first two texts, 11Q19 54.8-19 and 4Q375, both consist of rewritten versions of the material in the Deuteronomic law code that pertains to false prophets (i.e. Deut. 13.2-6; 18.18-22). While the material in the *Temple Scroll* may simply be a re-presentation of the biblical material, Jassen argues that the detailed reformulation of Deuteronomy 13 in 4Q375 'suggests that this was a genuine and tangible concern' in the contemporary period.[122] The final text, 4Q399, may also provide evidence for prophetic activity in the Second Temple period. The fragment contains a list of false prophets ([נביאי] [ש]קרא די קמו ב[ישראל]), the first seven of which are all biblical figures.[123] The final line appears to mention an additional name, but due to the incomplete nature of the fragment only three letters (עון) are recognizable. Qimron, however, contends that the final line contains the name of a contemporary figure and that the entire list was created to damage the reputation of this particular figure, since placement alongside the preceding names would likely damage the perception of his (or her) prophetic abilities.[124] If Qimron and Jassen are correct that the final line

---

121. Jassen, *Mediating the Divine*, 298.
122. Jassen, *Mediating the Divine*, 304.
123. The seven figures are Balaam son of Beor (Num. 22–24), the Old Man from Bethel (1 Kgs 13.11-31); Zedekiah son of Chenaanah (1 Kgs 22.1-28), Ahab son of Koliath (Jer. 29.21-24), Zedekiah son of Maaseiah (Jer. 29.21-24), Shemaiah the Nehlemite (Jer. 29.24-32), and Hananiah son of Azur (Jer. 28).
124. Elisha Qimron, 'Le-Pišrah šel Rešimat Nevi'e ha-Šeqer', *Tarbiz* 63 (1993): 273-75. Assuming that the three letters עון comprise the final portion of a patronymic, Qimron speculates that the final person referenced is John Hyrcanus I. For a reconstruction of the line that does not refer to a Second Temple figure, see Florentino García Martínez and Eibert J.C. Tigchelaar, *The Dead Sea Scrolls Study Edition* (2 vols.; Leiden: Brill, 1997–98), 2:708, which renders the final line as a further description of Hananiah. However, see Jassen, *Mediating the Divine*, 305-6, for a critique of this alternative rendering.

refers to a post-biblical figure, then this fragment also attests to the existence of prophetic activity in the Second Temple period. It appears, therefore, that there is at least a small amount of textual evidence at Qumran that supports the existence of original prophetic activity within Second Temple Judaism, even if certain segments of the sectarian or non-sectarian communities perceived this activity to be illegitimate.

Potentially more important for the present study is the way in which the prophetic material of the Old Testament is handled within the Qumran literature. A significant portion of the biblical material found at Qumran stems from the writing prophets.[125] This textual evidence may add further support to the notion that the Qumran community was itself a type of prophetic community. In other words, the discussion of the prophetic material in the *pesharim* at Qumran and the use of portions of the prophetic material in other writings may show that the Qumran community viewed itself as a further extension of the prophetic tradition developed in the Old Testament, with their own experiences being seen as the actualization of prior prophetic material (e.g. 1QpHab 7.4-5).[126] Moreover, the sectarian community's thematic commentaries on the Old Testament prophetic texts contain a particular emphasis on the eschatological aspect of the Old Testament material. Within the commentaries this eschatological emphasis is directed toward the community, presumably in an effort to explain that the life of the community itself was in some sense a fulfillment of the original prophetic proclamation.[127] Thus, it appears that the Qumran community was interested in the prophetic material of the Old Testament because at least some of the community believed that the prophetic material was being fulfilled among them.

In addition to the sectarian material at Qumran that points to a connection between the community and the Old Testament prophetic tradition, there is a significant amount of non-sectarian, parabiblical material that pertains to the canonical writing prophets, as well as other biblical figures commonly understood as prophets in the Qumran literature (e.g. Moses, David, and Daniel).[128] In Brooke's view these parabiblical documents serve as evidence 'that many Jews in the Second Temple

---

125. Cf. James C. VanderKam, *The Dead Sea Scrolls Today* (Grand Rapids: Eerdmans, 1994), 30.

126. George J. Brooke, 'Parabiblical Prophetic Narratives', in Flint and VanderKam (eds.), *The Dead Sea Scrolls After Fifty Years*, 1:271, 298.

127. George J. Brooke, 'Thematic Commentaries on Prophetic Scriptures', in Henze (ed.), *Biblical Interpretation at Qumran*, 156-57.

128. For an overview of all the extant parabiblical prophetic material at Qumran, see Brooke, 'Parabiblical Prophetic Narratives', 1:271-301.

period had an intense interest in the prophets of old and sought to identify themselves as the heirs of what God had promised through them'.[129] This affirmation stems from the argument that the presentation of the prophetic material in a new form in the parabiblical material is itself an example of ongoing prophetic activity in the Second Temple period.[130] In other words, works such as *Pseudo-Daniel*, the *Apocryphon of Jeremiah*, *Pseudo-Ezekiel*, and the *Temple Scroll*, all represent a re-presentation of Old Testament prophetic material meant to highlight a connection between the community and earlier prophetic history. Indeed, the 'inspired interpretation of Scripture began to be understood in direct continuity with the world of the ancient prophets'.[131] It is important, however, to understand that this re-presentation of the Old Testament prophetic material in both the *pesharim* and the parabiblical writings was meant neither to replace nor to diminish the authority or intention of the original material. Rather, it appears that the intent of these writings was to apply the earlier tradition to the present context of the Second Temple period and to serve as a contemporary extension of the prophetic tradition of the Old Testament.[132] It seems, therefore, that the material from Qumran provides evidence both for continued prophetic activity and for the importance of the Old Testament prophetic material in the Second Temple period.

(2) *Prophecy in Josephus*. Apart from the possible evidence for the cessation of prophecy in *Ag. Ap.* 1.41, Josephus serves as an additional source for analysing prophetic activity after the ministry of the Old Testament writing prophets ended.[133] It may even be possible to claim that '[Josephus]

129. Brooke, 'Parabiblical Prophetic Narratives', 1:298.
130. George J. Brooke, 'Prophecy and Prophets in the Dead Sea Scrolls: Looking Backwards and Forwards', in Floyd and Haak (eds.), *Prophets, Prophecy, and Prophetic Texts*, 156.
131. Jassen, *Mediating the Divine*, 240. Jassen's argument concerning 'revelatory exegesis' (see esp. 213-40) develops the notion that certain segments within Second Temple Judaism viewed their own *written* material as divine revelation. While Aune, *Prophecy*, 339-40, believes that this form of exegesis is defined more helpfully as divination, Jassen points out that the Qumran exegetes also attributed this exegetical practice to the biblical prophets in order to create continuity with the earlier tradition (240).
132. Brooke, 'Prophecy and Prophets', 156-57.
133. The most extensive survey of prophetic material in Josephus is Gray, *Prophetic Figures*. In addition, see Joseph Blenkinsopp, 'Prophecy and Priesthood in Josephus', *JJS* 25 (1974): 239-62; Feldman, 'Prophets', 386-422; Robert K. Gnuse, *Dreams and Dream Reports in the Writings of Josephus: A Traditio-Critical Analysis* (AGJU 36; Leiden: Brill, 1996), 22-24; Grabbe, 'Thus Spake', 240-47; Jean-Claude

## 2. The Development of the Prophetic Tradition

is the fullest source for the reality of ongoing prophetic activity in the Second Temple period'.[134] As in the Qumran literature, much of the prophetic terminology that Josephus employs is directly related to his interpretation of biblical texts. In light of the biblical source material for the *Jewish Antiquities*, Josephus primarily uses prophetic terminology to refer to biblical figures, such as Moses (*Ant*. 2.327; 4.329), Samuel (5.341), Nathan (7.91), Elijah (8.319-62), Elisha (8.352), Jonah (9.280), Isaiah (9.276), Jeremiah (10.78), Ezekiel (10.79), and Daniel (10.245-49, 267-69; 11.322).[135] More generally, in terms of biblical prophecy as a whole, it seems that 'Josephus consistently holds the view that the Biblical prophets spoke by a binding, overriding divine inspiration' (cf. *Ant*. 6.56, 76; 8.346; 9.35; *J.W*. 4.388).[136] That is, Josephus is interested in highlighting the mediatory function of the biblical prophets as they served as divine representatives for the community (e.g. *Ant*. 4.329; 10.267).[137] In addition, although Josephus never presents a systematic definition of prophecy, it appears that another of its primary characteristics was the act of prediction (e.g. *Ant*. 8.418). This emphasis on prediction may serve a particularly apologetic purpose for Josephus. As Bockmuehl notes:

> Josephus shows a recurring interest in the specific intervals which elapsed between a prophet's prediction and its fulfilment. This seems to be motivated primarily by an apologetic desire to stress the antiquity and continuity of the Jewish faith (e.g. *Ap* 1:1ff.; *Ant* 1:5 ff.) as well as God's providence in history (esp. *Ant* 10:277, 280). Perhaps for similar reasons men like Moses, Isaiah, and Daniel seem to assume the familiar Hellenistic guise of θεῖοι ἄνδρες: men privileged to converse with God, and endowed with divine qualities. Through them God spoke His Word to His people, and by fulfilling their predictions He manifests His providential sovereignty in history.[138]

---

Ingelaere, 'L'Inspiration Prophétique dans le Judaïsme: Le Témoignage de Flavius Josèphe', *ETR* 62 (1987): 236-45; Sid Z. Leiman, 'Josephus and the Canon of the Bible', in *Josephus, the Bible, and History* (ed. Louis H. Feldman and G. Hata; Detroit: Wayne State University Press, 1989), 55-56.

134. Jassen, *Mediating the Divine*, 13 n. 30, 17.

135. In addition, Feldman, 'Prophets', 389-91, identifies 169 instances in which Josephus inserts prophetic terminology into biblical references where it was not originally present. The majority of the examples constitute Josephus inserting the title προφήτης as a further identification of a biblical figure.

136. Markus N.A. Bockmuehl, *Revelation and Mystery in Ancient Judaism and Pauline Christianity* (WUNT 2/36; Tübingen: Mohr Siebeck, 1990), 83.

137. Gray, *Prophetic Figures*, 34.

138. Bockmuehl, *Revelation*, 84.

However, Josephus recognizes accurate predictions made by both prophetic and non-prophetic figures. Thus, while prediction serves as an important aspect of prophetic activity for Josephus, it is not accurate to assert that prediction constituted prophecy in its entirety.[139] Additionally, Josephus argues that the prophets were crucial for the composition of Israel's history after Moses (e.g. *Ag. Ap.* 1.37-41). It seems reasonable to conclude that Josephus' understanding of ancient and contemporary prophecy was shaped by his awareness of both particular prophetic figures and the overarching functions of prophecy within the history of the Old Testament.

Josephus also labels several non-biblical figures with prophetic terminology. Of primary importance is his affirmation of the prophetic activity associated with John Hyrcanus I. Specifically, Josephus claims that Hyrcanus was uniquely privileged to serve in three distinct capacities: τὴν...ἀρχὴν τοῦ ἔθνους καὶ τὴν ἀρχιερωσύνην καὶ προφητείαν (*J.W.* 1.68-69; cf. *Ant.* 13.299-300).[140] Feldman posits that his high view of Hyrcanus may stem either from a Hasmonean source or from Josephus' own pride in his Hasmonean ancestry.[141] Contrary to Feldman, however, it is not transparent that Josephus differentiates Hyrcanus' prophetic ability with that of the biblical prophets. Rather, Josephus' emphasis in *Ant.* 13.300 on Hyrcanus' ability to foresee (πρόγνωσιν) and to foretell the future (προλέγειν) appears to correlate well with Josephus' statements regarding biblical prophetic figures (e.g. *Ant.* 4.320; 6.344; 7.334; 10.92, 267-68).[142] In light of this correlation Gray argues that Josephus understood the decline of prophecy to have started not in the beginning of the post-exilic period, but after Hyrcanus' lifetime.[143] However, whether or not Josephus believes Hyrcanus to be associated in kind with the biblical prophets, the terminology and abilities that he attributes to Hyrcanus stand as evidence of continued prophetic activity during at least a portion of the Second Temple period.

Along with the prophetic terminology linked with John Hyrcanus I, Josephus labels a number of figures as ψευδοπροφῆται (e.g. *Ant.* 8.236-42; 20.169; *J.W.* 6.285-87; cf. *J.W.* 7.438; *Life* 424-25).[144] Two further

---

139. Grabbe, 'Thus Spake', 243. See Feldman, 'Prophets', 394-95, for the argument that Josephus believed that prophecy also had functions corresponding to the past and the present.

140. Philo uses similar language to describe 'the perfect ruler' Moses (cf. Philo, *Moses* 2.187).

141. Feldman, 'Prophets', 402.

142. Contra Feldman, 'Prophets', 402; cf. Grabbe, 'Thus Spake', 241-43.

143. Gray, *Prophetic Figures*, 16-23.

144. Grabbe, 'Thus Spake', 241.

examples are of particular importance. First, although Theudas presents himself as a προφήτης (*Ant.* 20.97), Josephus' description of him in the same passage as a γόης likely establishes that Josephus does not regard Theudas in the same manner. Secondly, a man from Egypt who declares himself to be a προφήτης (*Ag. Ap.* 1.312; *Ant.* 20.169) and, apparently, convinced others of his prophetic ability (*J.W.* 2.261) is explicitly referred to by Josephus as a ψευδοπροφήτης (*J.W.* 2.261). In both instances, however, it seems that the two men are deemed to be false prophets not because of their self-designation, but because of the nature of their messages and activities.¹⁴⁵ Thus, in addition to the prophetic ability of Hyrcanus, the existence of certain ψευδοπροφῆται in Josephus' writings may provide evidence for the reality of prophetic activity in the Second Temple period. It seems clear at this point, however, that Josephus is willing to refer to figures within the Second Temple period with prophetic terminology.

While it is possible to show that Josephus is capable of referring to figures within the Second Temple period with prophetic terminology, it also seems that Josephus recognizes a distinction between the Old Testament prophetic material and prophetic activity in the Second Temple period. In fact, this distinction may be the reason for Josephus' discussion of the lack of τὴν τῶν προφητῶν ἀκριβῆ διαδοχήν in *Ag. Ap.* 1.41. In other words, Josephus does not assert that all prophetic activity ceased; rather, he claims that there is a distinct difference between prophetic activity prior to and after the reign of Artaxerxes.¹⁴⁶ Josephus' use of particular vocabulary may serve as evidence for some form of distinction in his thought between the biblical prophets and figures within the Second Temple period. More specifically, Josephus normally reserves the term προφήτης for biblical figures, while later figures are most often labeled with the term μάντις and its cognates (e.g. *Ant.* 13.311-13; *J.W.* 1.78-80).¹⁴⁷ This is not, however, a uniform practice within Josephus' writings. In addition to the self-designations of Theudas and the man from Egypt, several men are referred to by the term προφῆται in *J.W.* 6.285-87 and *Ant.* 1.240 contains a quotation from Alexander Polyhistor concerning a προφήτης named Kleodemos.¹⁴⁸ Although several

---

145. Jassen, *Mediating the Divine*, 290 n. 41.

146. Leiman, 'Josephus', 56; cf. Gray, *Prophetic Figures*, 23-26.

147. Jassen, *Mediating the Divine*, 17; Jannes Reiling, 'The Use of ΨΕΥΔΟΠΡΟΦΗΤΗΣ in the Septuagint, Philo and Josephus', *NovT* 13 (1971): 147-56.

148. Cf. David E. Aune, 'The Use of ΠΡΟΦΗΤΗΣ in Josephus', *JBL* 101 (1981): 419-21. Bockmuehl, *Revelation*, 85 nn. 23-24, contends that the examples of Theudas and the man from Egypt are exceptions due to the polemical contexts in which they

of these examples occur within a polemical framework, their existence prevents the creation of a strict terminological distinction between biblical and Second Temple figures. It is also difficult to delineate a clear distinction between the actions performed by persons in either category.[149] Nevertheless, these few examples do not preclude the possibility that there may be some type of distinction within Josephus' writings between the Old Testament prophetic material and that of the Second Temple period. Thus, although there is not a consistent terminological or functional distinction between the two groups, it may be possible to argue that Josephus recognizes a qualitative distinction between them. In other words, while Josephus is willing to recognize prophetic activity within the Second Temple period, this prophetic activity may be inferior to that of the biblical prophets in terms of inspiration, function, and effect.[150] Similar to the material at Qumran, therefore, Josephus appears to witness to the reality that although prophetic activity did not cease during the Second Temple period, it did begin to transform in various ways *vis-à-vis* the prophetic material in the Old Testament.

In addition to Josephus' discussion of prophecy and prophetic figures, there is some evidence to suggest that Josephus conceives of his own position in prophetic terms. For example, he claims that the Lord informed him of the Roman conquest (*J.W.* 3.351-53) and states that Vespasian verified his predictive abilities after consulting with prisoners who were aware of Josephus' prior claims (*J.W.* 3.399-408). Furthermore, on several occasions Josephus may implicitly compare his own life and ministry with several of the biblical prophets, including Elijah, Jeremiah, Ezekiel, and Daniel (e.g. *Ant.* 10.79, 275; *J.W.* 3.340).[151] It is also likely that Josephus understands his work as a historian to be an extension of the work of the biblical prophets (*J.W.* 1.18).[152] As with the community

---

stand. Similarly, Sommer, 'Prophecy', 40 n. 36, argues that the example of προφῆται in *J.W.* 6.285-87 is an exception due to its polemical nature, and that Josephus is merely quoting Alexander in *Ant.* 1.240, not affirming the prophetic ability of Kleodemos (contra Aune, 'ΠΡΟΦΗΤΗΣ', 419-21). Sommer, however, acknowledges that Josephus applies the cognate term προφητείαν to John Hyrcanus I (40 n. 36). In addition, the biblical figure Balaam is referred to only with the word μάντις (cf. *Ant.* 4.104, 112), but this may simply be due to the fact that Balaam was not an Israelite prophet.

149. Grabbe, 'Thus Spake', 243-44.
150. Gray, *Prophetic Figures*, 34.
151. Bockmuehl, *Revelation*, 88.
152. Cf. Feldman, 'Prophets', 397. Feldman also argues, however, that although prophets and historians are related, Josephus 'does not regard himself as being in the former category' (406).

at Qumran, however, Josephus never explicitly identifies himself as a prophet. Grabbe conjectures that this lack of personal identification pertains to Josephus' belief that his prophetic abilities derived from his role as a priest, as well as the potential fear that claiming to be a prophet would incite a negative reaction against him.[153] Neither of these suggestions, however, prevents Grabbe from asserting that 'it is clear that [Josephus] regards himself as [a prophet]'.[154] It may be more accurate, however, to affirm that Josephus' presentation of his own activity reflects the position that the Old Testament prophetic material continued to influence the course of Israel's history throughout the Second Temple period so that its categories were still recognizable in Josephus' own context.

(3) *Prophecy in Philo.* Philo's material on prophecy derives most readily from the prophetic history of the Old Testament, with a particular emphasis on the Mosaic tradition.[155] In general terms, Philo seems to equate prophetic activity with divine possession and inspiration. More specifically, prophetic figures are completely under the control of God during their prophetic performance and do not use any of their own faculties in order to fulfill their prophetic function (e.g. *Heir* 259-66; *Spec. Laws* 1.65). It would likely be an overstatement, however, to say that Philo's understanding of prophecy could be understood solely in terms of ecstatic activity. This caution stems from the realization that Philo's ecstatic vocabulary primarily deals with the mental capacities of the individual and not with other aspects of their physical existence.[156] Yet, at a basic level it seems that Philo conceives of prophets simply as those who were responsible for mediating divine oracles.

Philo offers several further considerations concerning prophecy with regard to Moses, whom he presents as the prophet *par excellence* (*Moses* 2.187). While prophecy was normally defined by divine possession, Philo claims that Moses prophesied both ἐκ προσώπου and ἐξ αὐτοῦ κατασχεθέντος (*Moses* 2.188-89). Thus, it seems that Philo is affirming both Moses' human insight and prophetic ability.[157] Moreover, Moses experienced

153. Grabbe, 'Poets', 203-4; cf. Grabbe, *Judaic Religion*, 239.
154. Grabbe, 'Thus Spake', 247.
155. Cf. David M. Hay, 'Philo's View of Himself as an Exegete: Inspired, But Not Authoritative', *SPhilo* 3 (1991): 40-52; John R. Levison, 'Philo's Personal Experience and the Persistence of Prophecy', in Floyd and Haak (eds.), *Prophets, Prophecy, and Prophetic Texts*, 194-209; David Winston, 'Two Types of Mosaic Prophecy According to Philo', *JSP* 2 (1989): 49-67.
156. Forbes, *Prophecy*, 144.
157. Levison, 'Philo's Personal Experience', 206.

both divine possession and the ability to retain control of his mental faculties while making prophetic proclamations (*Moses* 2.188-90). Consequently, Moses is an important prophetic figure at this point due especially to the close association between his own reason and the divine plan.[158] Moses' composition of the Torah, therefore, becomes a particular expression of his prophetic relevance as it evinces the rational nature of his prophetic activity. This combination of human insight and prophetic proclamation may also result in a close connection between prophecy and the inspired interpretation of Scripture. For example, Philo's discussion of the origin of the Sabbath seems to highlight the close relationship between interpretation and prophecy (cf. *Moses* 2.264-69).[159] For this reason, Levison is able to argue that '[Philo] regarded the inspired interpretation of scripture as the rightful expression of prophecy rather than its inferior surrogate'.[160]

As with the material derived from Josephus, it is also likely that Philo considers himself to be a prophet in some sense. Philo's autobiographical description in *Migration* 34-35 is parallel to a number of other passages concerning divine inspiration (e.g. *Heir* 264-65; *QG* 3.9; *Spec. Laws* 1.65; 4.49) and shows that Philo believes he was privileged with a type of divine possession similar to that of other prophetic figures. Furthermore, statements in *Dreams* 2.252 and *Cherubim* 27-29 witness to the idea that Philo thinks he was privy to the same type of prophetic inspiration seen in the life of Moses.[161] Philo's personal claims concerning divine possessions and divine inspiration likely serve as the background for his understanding of the importance of his own allegorical insights. In light of this connection, Philo's understanding of this dimension of prophecy may manifest a connection to his broader philosophical concerns.[162] This possible connection between prophetic and philosophical categories may serve as additional evidence that Philo perceives his own exegetical material to be an extension of the prophetic tradition. That is, Philo seems to understand his own allegorical material as the result of divine possession and inspiration, which he experiences in a manner similar to the biblical prophets.[163] Thus, while the exegetical practices exhibited in the Qumran material differ widely from the allegorical exegetical

158. See Helmut Burkhardt, *Die Inspiration heiliger Schriften bei Philo von Alexandrien* (Monographien und Studienbücher 340; Giessen: Brunnen Verlag, 1988).
159. Cf. Grabbe, 'Poets', 201.
160. Levison, 'Philo's Personal Experience', 196.
161. Levison, 'Philo's Personal Experience', 201-3.
162. Bockmuehl, *Revelation*, 73.
163. Levison, 'Philo's Personal Experience', 207.

practices of Philo, it seems that both were seen as a continuation of earlier prophetic activities. As with the Qumran material, therefore, it would seem that Philo views his own experience as an extension of the prophetic tradition of the Old Testament.[164]

(4) *Prophecy in Ben Sira*. Prophetic terminology occurs at a number of points within Sirach, but textual and linguistic concerns serve to make the overall picture of prophecy in the book somewhat opaque.[165] Yet, as with the other source material examined from the Second Temple period, nearly all of Ben Sira's references to prophetic activity pertain to the former and latter prophets of the Old Testament. The *Laus Patrum* (Sir. 44.1–50.24), for example, uses prophetic terminology entirely in connection with biblical prophets.[166] There are, however, several occurrences of prophetic language that may be associated uniquely with Ben Sira himself (e.g. Sir. 24.32-34; 36.20-21; 38.34–39.3). Of primary significance is Ben Sira's autobiographical claim that ἔτι διδασκαλίαν ὡς προφητείαν ἐκχεῶ

---

164. Levison, 'Philo's Personal Experience', 209, goes so far as to argue that Philo understood himself as having the same authority as the Old Testament prophets and that he is their 'rightful heir'. It may be more accurate, however, to argue that Philo understood prophetic ability as a divine gift given to the ἀστεῖος, σοφός, and δίκαιος (*Heir* 259-60; cf. Forbes, *Prophecy*, 144). Thus, although Philo's implicit connection with Moses may serve to justify his own activity, his superlative claims about Moses (e.g. *Moses* 2.187) make it difficult to affirm that Philo understood himself as equal to Moses (cf. Jutta Leonhardt-Balzer, 'Philo und die Septuaginta', in *Die Septuaginta—Texte, Kontexte, Lebenswelten: Internationale Fachtagung veranstaltet von Septuaginta Deutsch [LXX.D], Wuppertal 20.-23. Juli 2006* [ed. Martin Karrer and Wolfgang Kraus; WUNT 219; Tübingen: Mohr Siebeck, 2008], 623-37).

165. In terms of textual concerns, there is evidence of prophetic language in both the extant Hebrew portions of the book, as well as its Greek translation (cf. Benjamin G. Wright, *No Small Differences: Sirach's Relationship to Its Parent Text* [SBLSCS 26; Atlanta: Scholars Press, 1989]). Linguistically, Greek prophetic terminology is used to translate a number of different terms, several of which are not normally associated with the prophecy, such as נדרש in Sir. 46.20 and התיצב in Sir. 47.1 (Pancratius C. Beentjes, 'Prophets and Prophecy in the Book of Ben Sira', in Floyd and Haak [eds.], *Prophets, Prophecy, and Prophetic Texts*, 137). For a succinct introduction to the history of Sirach's textual transmission, see Beenjtes, 'Prophets', 135-36.

166. There is a small minority, however, that regards the term נבואה in Sir. 44.3 as a reference to Hellenistic officials; see, e.g., Martin Hengel, *Judentum und Hellenismus* (WUNT 10; Tübingen: Mohr Siebeck, 1969), 249. Hengel points to Israel Lévi, *L'Ecclésiastique* (2 vols.; Paris: Ernest Lerous, 1898), 1:82, for the origination of this theory. For a complete analysis of all of the prophetic terminology in the *Laus Patrum*, see Beentjes, 'Prophets', 137-45.

καὶ καταλείψω αὐτὴν εἰς γενεὰς αἰώνων in Sir. 24.33. This phrase seemingly parallels the preceding statement in Sir. 24.32: ἔτι παιδείαν ὡς ὄρθρον φωτιῶ καὶ ἐκφανῶ αὐτὰ ἕως εἰς μακράν. As noted by Beentjes, the final portions of the two verses, read consecutively, pertain first to the extent (either spatial or temporal) of wisdom and then to its permanence.[167] In general, therefore, the passage seems simply to highlight the didactic nature of the wisdom Ben Sira derives from his study of the Law and the wisdom tradition.[168] Precisely what is meant by Ben Sira's use of the term προφητείαν at this point, however, is somewhat less transparent. Jassen asserts that the phrase ὡς προφητείαν 'can refer to either the process of "pouring out" or the content of the "instruction"'.[169] In light of the parallel nature of Sir. 24.32-33, it seems reasonable that the phrase refers to the content of Ben Sira's instruction as opposed to the act of pouring out, since the preceding ὡς ὄρθρον is most readily connected with παιδεία in Sir. 24.32. In other words, Ben Sira's understanding of his own sapiential teaching is related to the nature of prophetic instruction, particularly, in terms of Sir. 24.33b, with regard to its reliability and future significance. Thus, although Ben Sira does not explicitly identify himself as a προφήτης, it seems likely that he perceives his teaching to be parallel to the divine proclamation of the Old Testament prophets and that he considers himself to be a type of 'inspired mediator'.[170] However, there does appear to be a development in the prophetic tradition within Ben Sira. While the discussion of prophecy stands in continuity with the earlier prophetic tradition, there is a movement in the locus of divine revelation from the prophet to the sage.[171] Thus, while Sirach can be used to affirm the continued viability of the Old Testament prophetic tradition in the Second Temple period, the work may also serve as evidence for the continued development of that tradition.

c. *Conclusions*

The material from the Second Temple period provides evidence for a multiplicity of views concerning the existence of prophetic activity and the continued relevance of the Old Testament prophetic material.

---

167. Beenjtes, 'Prophets', 149.
168. Eckhard J. Schnabel, *Law and Wisdom from Ben Sira to Paul: A Tradition-Historical Enquiry into the Relation of Law, Wisdom, and Ethics* (WUNT 2/16; Tübingen: Mohr Siebeck, 1985), 76.
169. Jassen, *Mediating the Divine*, 312.
170. Beentjes, 'Prophets', 149; cf. Anthony R. Ceresko, *Prophets and Proverbs: More Studies in Old Testament Poetry and Biblical Religion* (Quezon City: Claretian, 2002), 53-71; Henze, 'Invoking the Prophets', 133.
171. Jassen, *Mediating the Divine*, 313-14.

Although certain texts have been put forth as evidence that prophetic activity ceased when the ministry of the writing prophets concluded, this position appears to apply only to a relatively small segment of Second Temple Judaism. Conversely, several additional literary sources from the Second Temple period provide evidence for both original prophetic activity and the continued importance of the prophetic tradition developed within the Old Testament. Moreover, it appears that the continued prophetic activity of the Second Temple period correlates with the Old Testament prophetic material in two ways. First, there is a tendency to relate, either implicitly or explicitly, leaders or other prominent figures within the Second Temple period with earlier prophetic figures in order to establish the authority of the former. Secondly, the prophetic material of the Old Testament itself is used as source material for new prophetic activity, either through literary re-presentations or exegetical practices. Thus, while the material from the Second Temple period witnesses in some ways to distinctions between its own prophetic activity and that described in the Old Testament, it seems that the organic prophetic tradition continued to exist in its own right and was applied in a variety of ways to the social and religious circumstances of the Second Temple period.

The continued existence and influence of the Old Testament prophetic tradition within Second Temple Judaism provides support for the notion that Paul's own understanding of prophecy was shaped primarily by that tradition. It is possible, however, that Paul's presentation was influenced by prophetic material in the larger stream of Hellenistic culture, as well as prophetic developments stemming from the early development of Christianity, particularly the relationship between the Old Testament prophetic tradition and Jesus. In order to elucidate further the background for Paul's relationship to the prophetic tradition in 2 Corinthians it will be helpful to discuss both prophetic material from non-Jewish Hellenistic materials and that contained with the Gospel traditions.

## 4. *Hellenistic Prophetic Traditions*

In addition to the organic prophetic tradition developed in the Old Testament and fostered in the Second Temple period, Hellenistic prophetic traditions may form at least a portion of the background for Paul's understanding of his relationship to the prophetic tradition as expressed in 2 Corinthians. Although it is difficult to establish any direct connection between Paul's presentation of prophetic categories and those developed within the Hellenistic material, it seems possible that the social and cultural background of the Corinthian community provides at least an indirect connection between the apostle and Graeco-Roman prophetic traditions. It will be helpful, therefore, to outline the shape and function of prophetic activity in the Hellenistic world in order to establish a basis for determining the relationship between Graeco-Roman prophetic categories and the Old Testament prophetic tradition, and whether Paul's relationship to the prophetic tradition was influenced by material external to the biblical tradition.

As with the prophetic material derived from the Old Testament and the intertestamental literature, there is a significant amount of information that relates to the nature and function of prophetic activity within Graeco-Roman literature. In general, the prophetic material derived from the Hellenistic period is thoroughly multifaceted, containing material associated with numerous revelatory practices that were used in an attempt to receive information from the divine world concerning both public and private matters. Furthermore, as with the prophetic material of the Old Testament, the Graeco-Roman material exhibits evidence of a progression of prophetic categories and activity.[172] More specifically, it is possible that at least a portion of the prophetic categories present in the Hellenistic period were shaped by material stemming from the earlier, classical period of Greek history. This influence can be seen both in the use of parallel prophetic terminology and in the presence of similar literary forms.[173] Thus, despite the political, religious, and social changes that took place between the classical and Hellenistic eras, material from both periods attests to the viability and validity of revelatory activity.[174] Prophetic material derived from the Hellenistic setting, therefore, provides a window into the development of prophetic categories within the Greek-speaking world, as well as insight into the form and function of non-Jewish prophetic material that was contemporaneous with the rise of Christianity.

The potential correlation between the classical and Hellenistic periods manifests itself most clearly with regard to the use and meaning of

172. Aune, *Prophecy*, 23. For the continued function of Graeco-Roman prophetic categories in the Roman Empire from the first to the fourth century C.E., see David Potter, *Prophets and Emperors: Human and Divine Authority from Augustus to Theodosius* (Cambridge, Mass.: Harvard University Press, 1994).

173. See, e.g., John S. Hanson, 'Dreams and Visions in the Graeco-Roman World and Early Christianity', *ANRW* 23.2:1395. Although Hanson's argument pertains primarily to dream-vision reports, his discussion of the parallels between the two eras functions usefully with regard to a broader picture of prophetic material. See also Porter (ed.), *Handbook of Classical Rhetoric*, especially the essays in 'Part I: Rhetoric Defined' (3-167).

174. Aune, *Prophecy*, 24.

## 2. The Development of the Prophetic Tradition 53

prophetic terminology. Throughout the classical period the term προφή-της was customarily used to emphasize the oracular function of the individual being described as opposed to their possession, or lack, of divine inspiration. This point is illustrated, for example, in the material attributed to both Herodotus and Plato. Although Herodotus makes numerous references to material stemming from the oracle at Delphi, only two passages, *Hist.* 8.36-37 and 9.93, refer specifically to the προφήτης. As Forbes notes, these two references serve only to show that the prophet served an official role, but give no specific evidence concerning the character or function of the position.[175] Two additional references in Herodotus, *Hist.* 7.111 and 8.135, discuss prophetic figures from other shrines and provide evidence that the term προφήτης was not always applied to the figure responsible for mediating between the god and the human audience. In these instances the inspired mediatory work was accomplished by an additional figure, the πρόμαντις.[176] Similarly, Plato uses different terminology in order to refer to those who are characterized by divine inspiration (e.g. θεομάντεις or χρησμῳδοί).[177] Additionally, within Plato's writings the function of the prophet is not usually defined in terms of inspiration; rather, the prophet is characterized most frequently as a general spokesman. For example, in *Charm.* 173c, those described as the ἀληθῶς μάντεις are apparently only referred to as προφή-τας because of their ability to speak about the future.[178] In light of this material, it seems that within the classical period the term μάντις and its cognates were predominant in emphasizing that a particular individual was the recipient of divine inspiration, while προφήτης and its cognates dealt primarily with the act of proclamation. In those instances where inspired individuals were also labeled as προφῆται (e.g. the προφῆτις at Delphi), the label likely pertained only to the oracular function of the individual.[179] This practice stands in apparent contrast with much of the prophetic material in the LXX, where figures are seemingly labeled with προφητ-terminology primarily in light of the notion that they received divine inspiration and then, consequently, for the pronouncements which they made.

175. Forbes, *Prophecy*, 196-97.
176. Forbes, *Prophecy*, 197. However, in Herodotus, *Hist.* 8.135 the πρόμαντις is labeled as a προφήτης in the same context (cf. Plutarch, *Mor.* 412A; *Arist.* 19.1-2; Pausanias, *Descr.* 9.23.6).
177. Aune, *Prophecy*, 38.
178. See also Plato, *[Alc. maj.]* II.148d-150b; *Phileb.* 28b. In *Tim.* 71e-72b, however, Plato attributes the activity of discernment to the prophets, a role more closely related to the activity of mediation. Cf. Krämer et al., *TDNT* 6:790.
179. Krämer et al., *TDNT* 6:790; contra Aune, *Prophecy*, 28-29.

The importance of this contrast is clarified further when the LXX tradition is considered alongside the use of prophetic terminology in the larger context of the Hellenistic period. As with the material from the classical period, references to prophetic figures in Hellenistic literature appear to centre either on the oracular function of certain individuals or upon their particular political or religious position within the community, not on notions of inspiration.[180] This perception is supported, for example, by the epigraphic evidence which pertains to prophetic figures associated with the oracular centre at Didyma, which was located in southwestern Turkey.[181] Although there are multiple references to the existence of an official role for a προφήτης in the extant inscriptions from Didyma, there is minimal explanation of the actual function or purpose that the official served at the site.[182] The limited material that does remain, however, does not appear to provide any reason for moving away from the emphasis on proclamation established in the classical period. Rather, it seems reasonable to concur with Forbes that prophets at Didyma functioned 'as official [spokesmen] of the shrine, by publicly announcing the results of oracular consultations or by making other public statements on behalf of the shrine'.[183] A similar emphasis on the act of proclamation as the defining characteristic of the προφητ-terminology can be seen in later portions of the Greek tradition.[184] Thus, the distinction between the terms μάντις and προφήτης seen in the classical period appears to be the main point of emphasis within the Hellenistic material as well. Because of this distinction it is difficult to assert that the two terms were used interchangeably within any portion of the Hellenistic period prior to the rise of Christianity.[185] The practice in the LXX of rendering Hebrew

---

180. Contra Terrance Callan, 'Prophecy and Ecstasy in Greco-Roman Religion and in 1 Corinthians', *NovT* 27 (1985): 125-40 (128-29).

181. A portion of the oracular centre, located approximately 20 kilometers south of Miletus in Didim-Yenishar, is still extant. For a history of the site, see Joseph Fontenrose, *Didyma: Apollo's Oracle, Cult, and Companions* (Berkeley: University of California Press, 1988), 1-27.

182. For a comprehensive discussion of the epigraphic evidence from Didyma, see Forbes, *Prophecy*, 202-8; cf. Fontenrose, *Didyma*, passim.

183. Forbes, *Prophecy*, 206.

184. E.g. Dio Chrysostom, *Or.* 7.101; 36.42; Plutarch, *Mor.* 397B; 792F.

185. Contra M. Eugene Boring, *Sayings of the Risen Jesus: Christian Prophecy in the Synoptic Tradition* (SNTSMS 46; Cambridge: Cambridge University Press, 1982), 82-83. In particular, Boring's claim that 'Philo considers the authors of all Old Testament books to be prophets, who receive their revelations in Dionysian ecstasy' (83), is difficult to affirm in light of Philo's dependence on the Mosaic tradition for his own understanding of prophetic activity.

prophetic terms with προφητ-terminology, therefore, represents an apparently unique phenomenon within the Hellenistic era.

Although a seemingly unique practice within the Hellenistic period, the use of προφητ-terminology in the LXX may stem simply from a lexical necessity created by perceived conceptual differences between biblical and non-biblical figures. In spite of the fact that the semantic range of several Greek terms could reasonably describe certain portions of the Old Testament prophetic tradition (e.g. χρησμολόγος, ἐγγαστρίμυθος, and μάντις), the term προφήτης and its cognates may have proved the least problematic since they dealt primarily with the general activity of proclamation and not with particular forms of technical divination.[186] Conversely, Crone argues that προφήτης and its cognates were chosen due to a correlation in function between Greek prophetic figures and Israelite temple prophets, with both groups being understood under the rubric of cultic officials.[187] Although the precise reason for the use of προφητ-terminology in the LXX is not readily transparent, it seems that there is minimal overlap between its function in the biblical corpus and in the more representative Hellenistic literature apart from the general notion of proclamation. Lexically, therefore, there appears to be little correlation between the prophetic tradition of the Old Testament and Hellenistic prophetic traditions. This does not, however, preclude potential comparisons in terms of the existence of prophecy itself or even certain functions carried out by prophetic figures, irrespective of their particular title or religious position.[188]

In terms of the content and function of prophetic material in the Graeco-Roman period, Aune's extensive survey is indispensable. Aune notes that within the Graeco-Roman setting 'there were only three primary contexts or modes within which oracular activity was regarded as possible and appropriate'.[189] The third and final context for prophetic activity that Aune identifies is actually a mode of revelatory experience, namely oracular dreams. Dream oracles functioned both in a variety of

---

186. Forbes, *Prophecy*, 202. Reiling, 'ΨΕΥΔΟΠΡΟΦΗΤΗΣ', 154, notes that the term μάντις, for example, is always used pejoratively in the LXX (e.g. *4 Macc.* 7.5; 8.5; 10.13; Wis. 14.28).

187. Crone, *Early Christian Prophecy*, 14. Crone's argument, however, is based on the idea that the first prophetic passages to be translated into Greek were those dealing with temple prophets (e.g. Zech. 7.3). However, even if this historical reconstruction were accurate, the use of προφητ-terminology in texts dealing with temple prophets would not necessitate its use in texts dealing with other prophetic figures, especially if the προφητ-terminology was used because of its functional associations.

188. Cf. Forbes, *Prophecy*, 217.

189. Aune, *Prophecy*, 24.

settings and a multiplicity of ways in Graeco-Roman culture.[190] Their importance for Aune, however, is that all people could potentially receive dream oracles, thereby highlighting the universal reality of prophetic activity in the Graeco-Roman world.[191] The prior two contexts which Aune identifies provide more detail concerning the shape of 'professional' Hellenistic prophetic activity. The first category pertains to the activity that took place in established oracular shrines where official figures were present to provide messages from a particular deity. These types of religious venues were located throughout the Mediterranean world (e.g. Argos, Delphi, Didyma, Dodona, Olympia) and were associated with a number of famous deities, though most frequently with either Apollo or Zeus.[192] The wide geographical distribution of the oracular shrines was likely a catalyst for variations in the procedures used for the reception and distribution of oracles, as well as in the types of enquiries which were addressed to and by a particular oracular figure.[193] However, despite these individual variations, it seems that the existence of prophetic activity at the shrines in general was dependent both on the particular location of the site and on the specific ritual practices associated with it.[194] In broad terms, therefore, this form of prophetic activity was not necessarily validated by the presence of a particular individual, but through the programmatic fulfillment of a specific set of procedures in a designated location.

In light of the argument that the activity of ancient oracular shrines was validated by both its location and its ability to follow a particular set of procedures, there seems to be little evidence to suggest that the activities which took place at the oracular shrines could be described as primarily 'ecstatic' or 'frenzied'. Rather, it appears that a significant portion of the material which stems from the shrines represents activity that was both coherent and logical. This distinction is particularly transparent with regard to the behaviour of the Pythia at the Delphic oracle. Although several later witnesses attest to the incoherent and inarticulate character of the Pythia's statements,[195] this argument does not appear to

190. See Hanson, 'Dreams', 1395-427.
191. Aune, *Prophecy*, 24.
192. For the existence of oracular shrines in Syria and Phoenicia, see Youssef Hajjar, 'Divinités oraculaires et rites divinatoires en Syrie et en Phénicie à l'époque Gréco-Romaine', *ANRW* 18.4:2236-320.
193. J.R.C. Cousland, 'Prophets and Prophecy', *DNTB* 830-35.
194. Aune, *Prophecy*, 34.
195. E.g. Plato, *Phaed.* 244B-C; Plutarch, *Mor.* 405C; 407B; Strabo, *Geog.* 9.3.5. This view is also put forth in H.W. Parke and D.E.W. Wormell, *The Delphic Oracle I: The History* (Oxford: Blackwell, 1956), 36-40.

correlate with the material associated with proceedings at Delphi. The extant evidence points to the reality that the 'Pythia experienced enthusiasm, but not an uncontrolled and irrational frenzy'.[196] Additionally, the extant historical witnesses do not provide evidence for any figure apart from the Pythia mediating messages from Apollo. Thus, the argument that the Pythia would have been unable to offer responses to enquiries and needed additional mediators, such as official προφῆται, appears to be a misreading of the historical evidence.[197] Rather, like other oracular figures, the responses that the Pythia gave to her enquirers were understood as representative of the deity itself. Indeed, Maurizio argues that:

> [T]he Pythia at Delphi produced utterances that are a genuine expression of a cultural system which believed in and codified behaviours and speech that it understood as indicating the presence of the divine. To argue that spirit possession rendered the Pythia incapable of coherent prophetic speech or that the Pythia does not versify her words but waits patiently while someone else does so is to assume that the Pythia alone is an exception to the paradigm of spirit possession in early Greek culture.[198]

Apart from variations in practices at different locations, therefore, oracular shrines generally functioned as organized religious institutions that understood their own proceedings as resulting in the proclamation of inspired messages which stemmed from the divine world.

In spite of the fact that the existence of oracular shrines provides evidence that coherent communication with the divine world was an important aspect of Hellenistic culture, there are relatively few parallels between the activity that took place at the oracular shrines and the prophetic activity characteristic of the tradition developed in the Old Testament and continued, to some extent, in the Second Temple period. Specifically, the prophetic tradition developed in the Old Testament appears to be less concerned with establishing a particular set of procedures in a designated location as a means for legitimating the prophetic activity. There is, rather, a more direct emphasis on individual prophetic figures and their apparent connection with YHWH. Moreover, while the shrines may provide the most concrete evidence of divine inspiration within the Graeco-Roman setting, the influence of the shrines themselves

---

196. Joseph Fontenrose, *The Delphic Oracle: Its Responses and Operations* (Berkeley: University of California Press, 1978), 211; cf. Simon Price, 'Delphi and Divination', in *Greek Religion and Society* (ed. P.E. Easterling and J.V. Muir; Cambridge: Cambridge University Press, 1985), 128-54.

197. Fontenrose, *Delphic Oracle*, 217-24.

198. L. Maurizio, 'Anthropology and Spirit Possession: A Reconsideration of the Pythia's Role at Delphi', *JHS* 115 (1995): 69-86 (79).

likely decreased from the fourth to the first century B.C.E., due, at least in part, to fluctuations in the political situation of the Hellenistic world.[199] It is difficult, therefore, to determine how influential the shrines would have been in defining the scope of prophetic categories within the first century. For these reasons, it seems unlikely that this form of Hellenistic prophetic activity would have functioned as a primary paradigm either for Paul or for his Corinthian audience.

The second source of prophetic activity in the Graeco-Roman world that Aune identifies is the material associated with individual oracular figures with no particular association to religious venues or institutions. Aune categorizes these figures by separating them into four subdivisions based on the type of prophetic activity that they are normally associated with: (1) technical diviners, (2) inspired diviners, (3) collectors and interpreters of oracles, and (4) magical diviners.[200] Because of their lack of association with any particular religious location, Aune posits a close connection between these figures and the so-called free prophets who comprised a significant portion of the prophetic history developed in the Old Testament.[201] Of particular importance for this comparison are those oracular persons whom Aune categorizes as 'inspired diviners'. This category refers specifically to individual prophetic figures in the Graeco-Roman tradition who were dependent neither on technical practices of divination nor on revelatory magic, but on a form of direct revelation from a supernatural source. Thus, in terms of the apparent source of their statements, these figures may represent the closest parallel to Old Testament prophetic figures.

Potentially the most important type of prophetic figure within the category of inspired diviner, particularly in terms of subsequent impact on the literature, were the prophetesses known as Sibyls and the traditions associated with them. The sibylline tradition manifested itself within a number of social spheres and eventually gained a significant amount of influence within the Graeco-Roman world.[202] There are, however, relatively few extant examples of sibylline passages from Graeco-Roman sources.[203] In general, the sibylline oracles were individual statements that

    199.    Aune, *Prophecy*, 24; cf. Forbes, *Prophecy*, 300.
    200.    Aune, *Prophecy*, 35.
    201.    Aune, *Prophecy*, 35-48.
    202.    John J. Collins, *Seers, Sibyls and Sages in Hellenistic-Roman Judaism* (Leiden: Brill, 1997), 182-84.
    203.    This lack is due in part to the difficulty of locating copies of sibylline collections after a fire destroyed the Roman collection in 83 B.C.E. For an extensive discussion of the process of the re-collection of oracles, see H.W. Parke, *Sibyls and*

pertained to a variety of social issues, but regularly dealt with 'predictions of wars, political events or natural disasters'.[204] The oracles were subsequently gathered into collections and understood as representative of a single sibylline tradition. However, in contrast with the material attributed to the writing prophets of the Old Testament, the collections of sibylline oracles normally lacked a developed literary structure or context. For this reason the oracles rarely provided information outside of the individual events with which they were associated and, consequently, provided little insight into the larger stream of either Graeco-Roman or world history.[205] Structurally, therefore, the sibylline tradition does not provide a consistent parallel with the prophetic material in the biblical tradition.

However, apart from certain dissimilarities the sibylline tradition provides a unique point of comparison between Graeco-Roman and Jewish traditions due to the fact that certain segments of Second Temple Judaism appropriated the material associated with the Sibyls for use in their own contexts.[206] The use of the sibylline tradition within Jewish circles was likely an attempt to make the material attractive to non-Jewish audiences that would have been more familiar with the traditions associated with the Sibyls, as well as a warning to more overtly Hellenized Jews to avoid possible forms of idolatry.[207] Despite convergence between the two traditions in terms of the attribution to a sibylline figure and the use of particular forms (e.g. oracles of destruction) that were reminiscent of Graeco-Roman sibylline oracles, the Jewish sibylline tradition differs from that developed in the non-Jewish sources. The divergence between the two traditions can be seen most readily in the focus of the Jewish oracles on both universal history and ethical teaching, two foci that are nearly non-existent within Graeco-Roman sibylline literature.[208] Moreover, much of the ethical teaching presented in the Jewish sibylline tradition was likely meant to condemn practices associated with Hellenistic

*Sibylline Prophecy in Classical Antiquity* (ed. B.C. McGing; London: Routledge, 1988), 136-51. For an overview of the extant sibylline passages from Graeco-Roman sources, see Innocenzo Cervelli, 'Questioni Sibilline', *Studi Storici* 4 (1993): 895-934.

204. Collins, *Seers*, 184.
205. Arnaldo Momigliano, 'From the Pagan to the Christian Sibyl: Prophecy as History of Religion', in *Nono Contributo alla Storia Degli studi Classici e del Mondo Antico* (ed. Riccardo di Donato; Storia e Letteratura: Raccolta di Studi e Testi 180; Rome: Edizioni di Storia e Letteratura, 1992), 728-30.
206. Bauckham, 'Apocalypes', 185-87; John J. Collins, 'The Development of the Sibylline Tradition', *ANRW* 20.1:421-59.
207. Witherington, *Jesus the Seer*, 231.
208. Collins, *Seers*, 197.

religious traditions.[209] In other words, there appears to be little connection between Graeco-Roman and Jewish sibylline oracles in terms of their content or purpose. Thus, if the sibylline tradition provides the closest link between the inspired diviners of Hellenistic prophetic traditions and the prophetic figures associated with the Old Testament prophetic tradition, then there is relatively little to suggest that the two traditions were parallel in terms of their function within their individual social or religious settings.

There are general similarities between prophetic activity derived from the Graeco-Roman world and that associated with the Old Testament. In broad terms, both sources contain examples of revelatory material in which individual figures claim to receive information directly from a supernatural source. However, in spite of general connections derived from the existence of several parallel prophetic categories, the relationship between the prophetic material derived from Hellenistic sources and that developed in the Old Testament is subject to a number of complexities. Primarily, difficulty arises due to varying uses of prophetic terminology in the two traditions. Although both prophetic traditions use similar vocabulary, there is a significant amount of diversity in the meaning and function of the terminology in the sources. Secondly, while there are certain types or forms of prophetic activity that are parallel within the two traditions, there appears to have been a continued decline in the existence of inspired prophetic activity in the Graeco-Roman world from the fourth century B.C.E. to the first century C.E.[210] The two traditions, therefore, exhibit a divergence in terms of their favoured modes of prophetic activity, with the Hellenistic material being increasingly focused on forms of technical divination, practices that were frequently eschewed in the prophetic history of the Old Testament (e.g. Num. 22.1-7; Deut. 18.10-13; 2 Kgs 21.1-6; 2 Chron. 33.1-6; Isa. 44.24-26). Thirdly, it seems transparent that the development of Hellenistic prophetic traditions stemmed from social and religious presuppositions that were foreign both to the Yahwistic worldview presented in the Old Testament and the more contemporary worldviews displayed in the various segments of Second Temple Judaism (e.g. polytheism vs. Monotheism). In light of these differences it is likely inaccurate to affirm a direct correlation between the organic prophetic tradition that developed in the Old Testament and the material that represents prophetic activity in the larger Graeco-Roman setting. Nevertheless, it remains possible that early Christian understanding of prophetic categories was dependent

209. Bauckham, 'Apocalypses', 185-86.
210. See Forbes, *Prophecy*, 289-302.

on material from both the Old Testament prophetic tradition and Hellenistic prophetic traditions. It will be helpful, therefore, to analyse briefly the function of prophetic categories in the Gospel traditions, particularly the material associated with the prophetic activity of Jesus and his contemporaries.

## 5. The Prophetic Tradition in the Gospel Traditions

The form and function of prophetic activity within the earliest Christian communities were almost certainly shaped extensively by the Pauline tradition, particularly the material pertaining to prophecy and inspired speech in 1 Corinthians 12–14. Likely equal in terms of influence, however, is the prophetic material associated with Jesus and his contemporaries derived from the Gospel traditions, which, in terms of historical context, stands at the intersection of Old Testament, Second Temple, and Hellenistic backgrounds. The prophetic material derived from the Gospels, therefore, provides a unique window through which to view the ways that a particular prophetic tradition or multiple traditions were influential in the genesis and continuation of the Christian movement. In light of the potential importance of this material, the intention within this section will be to provide a brief survey of the prophetic traditions established within the Gospel material in order to determine their place in Israel's developing prophetic tradition and their significance for Paul's own presentation of prophetic history and material within 2 Corinthians.

In connection with particular prophetic figures and texts, the terminology associated with prophetic activity within the Gospels provides a helpful starting point for understanding the nature and function of prophets and prophecy in the view of Jesus and his contemporaries. As with the LXX, the Gospels (as well as the rest of the New Testament) most frequently use the προφητ-word group in order to refer to both prophetic figures and instances of prophetic activity. This correlation likely stems from the reality that a high proportion of the prophetic material in the Gospels either mentions Old Testament figures normally associated with Israel's prophetic history or references material from the canonical writing prophets.[211] These linguistic parallels may, however, attest to a broader connection between the New Testament and the LXX in terms of particular perceptions of the nature and function of prophetic activity. In other words, if the use of προφητ-terminology in the LXX represents a particular decision to avoid prophetic categories from the larger setting of the Graeco-Roman world, the Gospel writers may have been attempting to

---

211. Cf. Gerald F. Hawthorne, 'Prophets, Prophecy', *DJG* 637-39.

achieve the same type of categorical separation. At the very least, however, the terminological connection between the two sources highlights the likelihood of a connection between the prophetic traditions represented in each one.

However, within the Gospels there are a number of different uses for the terminology normally associated with prophetic activity. For example, the verb προφητεύω and the noun προφητεία are used primarily to refer to inspired speech, but the specific shape of the material in which the terms are used varies due to different contextual concerns, as well as the particular historical and theological emphases of each of the Gospel writers.[212] Moreover, it is necessary to note that the content associated with particular prophetic forms varied within the Gospel material.[213] Despite these variations, however, it does appear that a significant portion of the προφητ-terminology within the Gospels accords with the nature and function of the word group in the LXX. That is, both groups of texts appear to use the language primarily as a means to highlight the divine inspiration associated with a particular figure or a particular pronouncement.

In spite of the fact that a significant amount of the prophetic language within the Gospels pertains to Old Testament prophetic material, the Gospels are not devoid of references to contemporary prophetic activity. Luke's Gospel in particular highlights a number of persons who manifest certain prophetic characteristics. Although she is not labeled as a προφῆτις, Luke's description of Elizabeth as ἐπλήσθη πνεύματος ἁγίου in Lk. 1.41 highlights her prophetic character and leads Bock to conclude that '[s]he functions as a prophetess, declaring the divine significance of an action'.[214] Luke's connection between the Spirit and prophecy is made more explicit in Lk. 1.67, where the phrase ἐπλήσθη πνεύματος ἁγίου is repeated in conjunction with the verb ἐπροφήτευσεν in reference to Zechariah.[215] Zechariah's subsequent proclamation in Lk. 1.68-79, therefore, most likely functions as a type of prophetic announcement. The form and content of Zechariah's announcement are particularly important for the present discussion in light of the presence of a number of Old

---

212. Max Turner, *The Holy Spirit and Spiritual Gifts: Then and Now* (Carlisle: Paternoster, 1999), 193-96.

213. Turner, *Holy Spirit*, 200-201; cf. Aune, *Prophecy*, 231.

214. Darrell L. Bock, *Luke* (2 vols.; BECNT; Grand Rapids: Baker, 1994–96), 1:135.

215. For the importance of the connection between the Spirit and prophecy in Luke, see Robert P. Menzies, *The Development of Early Christian Pneumatology, with Special Reference to Luke–Acts* (JSNTSup 54; Sheffield: JSOT, 1991).

Testament and intertestamental parallels that point to a connection between the pronouncement and earlier prophetic material.[216] In addition to the prophetic activity seen within the birth narratives, Luke also places emphasis on prophetic activity in conjunction with Jesus' arrival in Jerusalem. While Simeon (Lk. 2.25-35), like Elizabeth, is never labeled with προφητ-terminology, his two statements (Lk. 2.29-32 and 2.34-35) are likely meant to be seen as prophetic in light of their seemingly divine source, evidenced by the participial phrase κεχρηματισμένον ὑπὸ τοῦ πνεύματος τοῦ ἁγίου in Lk. 2.26 and the prepositional phrase κατὰ τὸ ῥῆμά σου in Lk. 2.29. Likewise, the assertion in Lk. 2.25 that Simeon was προσδεχόμεονος παράκλησιν τοῦ Ἰσραήλ may serve as a connection with the prophetic emphasis on consolation seen especially in the Isaianic tradition (e.g. Isa. 40.1; 49.13; 51.3; 57.18; 61.2).[217] Simeon's pronouncements are coupled with that of Anna, who is explicitly identified as a προφῆτις in Lk. 2.36. The focus of Anna's pronouncement on the λύτρωσιν Ἰερουσαλήμ may also be rooted in the Old Testament prophetic tradition (e.g. Isa. 40.9; 52.9; 63.4).[218] These particular examples in Luke provide evidence for the existence of contemporary prophetic activity in the Gospels that can be connected with material in the Old Testament in terms of both function and content.

In addition to the prophetic figures that Luke identifies in the early portion of his Gospel, the most readily identifiable prophetic figure discussed by the Gospel writers apart from Jesus is John the Baptist. Although there is a certain amount of ambiguity surrounding particular portions of John's life, there is a general consensus concerning the basic features of his ministry.[219] In general terms, the Gospel writers provide evidence that John was a somewhat well-known figure in Judaea who announced oracles of judgment and gathered at least a small group of followers during the period prior to Jesus' public ministry (cf. Mk 1.4-8). In addition to the material pertaining to John in the New Testament, Josephus attests to the life and ministry of John in the midst of his

---

216. See, for example, the chart of parallel phrases and ideas in Raymond E. Brown, *The Birth of the Messiah: A Commentary on the Infancy Narratives in Matthew and Luke* (ABRL; New York: Doubleday, 1993), 386-89.

217. Bock, *Luke*, 1:238.

218. Bock, *Luke*, 1:253.

219. For an extensive discussion of John the Baptist within the context of the first century, see Robert L. Webb, *John the Baptizer and Prophet: A Socio-Historical Study* (JSNTSup 62; Sheffield: JSOT, 1991), and Webb, 'John the Baptist and His Relationship to Jesus', in *Studying the Historical Jesus: Evaluations of the State of Current Research* (ed. Bruce Chilton and Craig A. Evans; NTTS 19; Leiden: Brill, 1994), 179-229.

account of Herod Antipas (*Ant.* 18.116-19). Josephus' material consists of a brief overview of John's life and ministry in Judaea, in which he refers to John as an ἀγαθὸν ἄνδρα, details several aspects of his ministry, particularly his ethical message and emphasis on baptism, and connects his death with the political career of Herod.[220] The life and ministry of John are of particular importance in this context, however, in light of the unique position attributed to him within the Gospels as the forerunner to the prophetic ministry of Jesus (e.g. Mt. 3.1-6; Jn 5.33-36).

The importance of John's prophetic ministry is seen on a primary level in its consistent influence within the Gospel tradition. All four Gospels refer to some aspect of John's prophetic ministry, whether to describe his own particular actions, to differentiate between his ministry and other traditions, or to position him as a predecessor to Jesus' ministry (e.g. Mt. 11.9; 21.23-27; Mk 11.32; Lk. 3.2; 7.26; 20.6; Jn 1.19-28). In light of the public nature of John's ministry in Judaea and the surrounding area, as well as his influence over at least a small group of followers, he is, in the paradigm established by Webb, most readily understood as a 'leadership popular prophet'.[221] In essence, John's ethical and eschatological preaching resulted in the formation of a movement that was particularly focused on repentance (cf. Mk 1.4; Lk. 3.3). This emphasis on repentance and John's willingness to confront both religious (Mt. 3.7-10) and political (Mk 6.18) leaders parallel much of the material attributed to both the writing prophets and the so-called free prophets such as Elijah and Elisha.[222] Thus, although there is some scholarly contention concerning John's relationship to specific Old Testament prophets, particularly Elijah, it is relatively clear that a significant portion of John's ministry was reminiscent of certain traditions developed within the Old Testament prophetic material.[223] According to the testimony of the Gospel

---

220. Cf. Paul W. Hollenbach, 'John the Baptist', *ABD* 3:887-88; Webb, *John the Baptizer and Prophet*, 34-39. Josephus' portrait generally comports with that of the Gospels. The only significant difference is Josephus' claim that Herod executed John due to fear that John's preaching would lead to some type of στάσις (*Ant.* 18.118), while the Gospels understand his imprisonment and execution to be the result of John's condemnation of Herod's marriage to Herodias (e.g. Mk 6.17-29). Although the two scenarios have different emphases, they are not inherently incompatible. It is possible they focus on different aspects (e.g. political and personal) of the same event (so Ben Witherington III, 'John the Baptist', *DJG* 388-89).

221. See Webb, *John the Baptizer and Prophet*, 349-78.

222. Cf. Witherington, *Jesus the Seer*, 337.

223. Horsley and Hanson, *Bandits, Prophets, and Messiahs*, 175. John's relationship to Elijah is dependent, in part, on the existence of a tradition that understood Elijah as a forerunner to the Messiah. For the debate concerning the existence of

tradition, however, John perceived his own prophetic ministry as serving a penultimate function (cf. Mk 1.7-8). In spite of John's confusion with regard to certain portions of Jesus' ministry (e.g. Mt. 11.2-6; Lk. 7.18-23), the presentation of the Gospel writers normally conforms to the idea that John served 'both as the chronological and theological starting-point for [Jesus'] ministry'.[224] In reference to at least certain aspects, therefore, the prophetic tradition developed in the Old Testament appears to influence the shape of John's prophetic experience, which in turn provides foundational material for certain aspects of Jesus' own prophetic ministry and influence.

Although Jesus is not frequently associated with prophetic categories outside of the Gospel material (cf. Acts 3.22), it is possible to posit with Wright that a prophetic paradigm 'seems the most secure point at which to ground [a] study of Jesus' public career, and in particular of his characteristic praxis'.[225] This position stems from the realization that there are multiple instances within the Gospels in which Jesus' ministry is connected with portions of Israel's prophetic tradition (e.g. Lk. 4.16-21), as well as the possibility that Jesus presents himself as a prophetic figure at several points within the Synoptic tradition (e.g. Mt. 13.57; Mk 6.4; Lk. 13.31-33). Although these passages do not provide a significant amount of detail concerning Jesus' perception of the precise nature and function of his prophetic ministry, they do appear to represent a historically authentic window into the reality that his ministry was shaped by prophetic traditions.[226] Furthermore, apart from the possibility that Jesus understood himself as connected with certain prophetic paradigms, it is also helpful to note that a significant portion of the people who came into contact with Jesus perceived him to be some type of prophetic figure (e.g. Mt. 21.11, 46; Mk 6.14-16; 8.28; Lk. 7.16; 24.19; Jn 4.19; 7.52; 9.17). Thus, although the Gospel writers' presentation of Jesus' ministry undoubtedly moves beyond prophetic categories at certain points, there appears to be little room to argue against the reality that he was seen as a prophet by

---

such a tradition, see Dale C. Allison, 'Elijah Must Come First', *JBL* 103 (1984): 256-58; Morris M. Faierstein, 'Why Do the Scribes Say That Elijah Must Come First?', *JBL* 100 (1981): 75-86; Joseph A. Fitzmyer, 'More About Elijah Coming First', *JBL* 104 (1985): 295-96.

224. N.T. Wright, *Jesus and the Victory of God* (Christian Origins and the Question of God 2; London: SPCK, 1996), 161-62; cf. Hvidt, *Christian Prophecy*, 58-59; Webb, 'John the Baptist', 211-14, 229.

225. Wright, *Jesus*, 166.

226. Cf. Aune, *Prophecy*, 156-57.

diverse segments of his contemporaries.²²⁷ The existence of this perception, however, does not explicitly explain either the shape or function of Jesus' prophetic ministry.

Concerning the shape of Jesus' prophetic ministry there appears to be, at the very least, a conceptual connection with the ministry of John the Baptist, evinced particularly in Jesus' ongoing emphasis on the notions of repentance and the kingdom of God (e.g. Mk 1.14-15; 6.12; Lk. 10.13-15; 11.32; 13.3-5).²²⁸ Likewise, as with John the Baptist, comparing the shape and function of Jesus' ministry with a single prophetic figure (e.g. Elijah) would likely result in an oversimplification of the extant evidence. Rather, it seems that the material in the Gospels points more readily to the idea that the prophetic shape of Jesus' ministry is to be understood as part of the larger development of Israel's prophetic history.²²⁹ More specifically, different aspects of Jesus' ministry are parallel or reminiscent to those developed in the ministries of a number of earlier prophetic figures, such as Micaiah son of Imlach (Mt. 9.36; Mk 6.34), Ezekiel (e.g. Mt. 23.38; Lk. 13.35), Jeremiah (e.g. Mt. 21.12; Mk 11.15-19; Lk. 19.45-48), Jonah (Mt. 12.38-42; Lk. 11.29-32), Amos (Mt. 3.1-12; Mk 1.2-8; Lk. 3.1-20), and Elijah (e.g. Lk. 7.11-17).²³⁰ In addition to this multiplicity of associations the nature of Jesus' prophetic ministry took somewhat different forms depending on his presence in a particular geographical location, with different emphases being present in his activity in the north and the south. This geographical distinction may also reflect a connection with the different characteristics of the northern and southern prophets described in the Old Testament.²³¹ Due to these referential and geographical variations it seems that the shape of the prophetic portion of Jesus' ministry represents a diverse conglomeration of a variety of aspects connected with the development of Israel's own prophetic history. In essence, therefore, although the Gospel writers may present Jesus' prophetic ministry as conceptually and historically unique, its basis appears

---

227. Morna D. Hooker, *The Signs of a Prophet: The Prophetic Actions of Jesus* (Harrisburg, Pa.: Trinity Press International, 1997), 15; cf. Wright, *Jesus*, 196.

228. Witherington, *Jesus the Seer*, 249; contra John Dominic Crossan, *The Historical Jesus: The Life of a Mediterranean Jewish Peasant* (San Francisco: Harper, 1991), 237-38, who argues that Jesus' message eventually became completely distinct from John the Baptist's message. Webb, 'John the Baptist', 229, offers a seemingly more judicious analysis in showing both discontinuity (e.g. fasting, location) and continuity (e.g. forms of prophecy and leadership) between the ministries of John the Baptist and Jesus.

229. Wright, *Jesus*, 163.

230. Cf. Wright, *Jesus*, 166-67.

231. Witherington, *Jesus the Seer*, 251-53.

## 2. The Development of the Prophetic Tradition 67

to be predominantly confined to the prophetic history developed in the Old Testament and fostered throughout the Second Temple period.

The precise form and function of Jesus' prophetic ministry, however, is somewhat more difficult to define. Aune's study of certain proclamations attributed to Jesus leads to the conclusion that although Jesus does not use explicitly prophetic formulas to introduce his speech, his pronouncements may still be cautiously understood as prophetic in light of the larger prophetic matrix of his ministry, evidenced particularly by his symbolic actions.[232] Thus, although the material attributed to Jesus does not appear to contain any explicit prophetic formulas, there is some evidence for a connection between his speech-acts and those of Old Testament prophetic figures. Wright, for example, claims that the parabolic material in the Gospels can only be understood properly as an extension of earlier portions of Israel's prophetic history.[233] Furthermore, Wright argues extensively that a significant portion of Jesus' material on the kingdom reflects both prophetic teaching and practice.[234] A focus only on parabolic forms and kingdom material, however, may represent an oversimplification of the material attributed to Jesus. Because of the variegated nature of both the form of Jesus' teaching and his particular deeds Witherington contends that his prophetic teaching is more readily understood within the related tradition of the apocalyptic seer.[235] Specifically, Witherington understands the variegated historical material concerning Jesus' teachings in the Synoptic tradition as evidence for the notion that Jesus reflected the intersection of prophetic, apocalyptic, and sapiential traditions that took place primarily within the Second Temple period.[236] In general terms, therefore, there appears to be a wide spectrum

---

232. Aune, *Prophecy*, 171-88. Jesus' frequent use of the introductory phrase ἀμὴν [ἀμὴν] λέγω σοι/ὑμῖν (×31 times in Matthew; ×13 in Mark; ×6 in Luke; ×25 in John) is the most common example of a formula that may reflect Old Testament terminology. However, it seems that the phrase functions primarily as a means of indicating the respective social statuses of the speaker and the audience (cf. Aune, *Prophecy*, 164-65). With regard to Jesus, therefore, it seems that the phrase functions as a means of reflecting his authority, but not necessarily his *prophetic* authority (cf. D.A. Carson, *The Gospel According to John* [PNTC; Grand Rapids: Eerdmans, 1991], 162-63; John Nolland, *The Gospel of Matthew* [NIGTC; Grand Rapids: Eerdmans, 2005], 219).

233. Wright, *Jesus*, 177. Wright's emphasis on the connection between the parables and apocalyptic, however, seems to blur the presence of any formal literary distinctions between parabolic, prophetic, and apocalyptic literature.

234. Wright, *Jesus*, 198-368.
235. Witherington, *Jesus the Seer*, 277-90.
236. Witherington, *Jesus the Seer*, 290-91.

of associations between Jesus' teaching and prior prophetic material. For this reason it seems difficult to place Jesus within any singular prophetic category (e.g. eschatological, apocalyptic, or millenarian) due to the broad connections that the Gospel writers make with a number of prophetic emphases.

In spite of the formal variations in the prophetic aspects of Jesus' ministry, it seems reasonable to affirm that some of his statements and actions are parallel to the prophetic material established within Israel's prior history. Any eschatological or messianic dimensions that Jesus develops as a part of his prophetic ministry could then be seen to constitute a further extension of the singular, yet multi-faceted, prophetic tradition developed throughout the Old Testament. Although all of the Gospel writers provide insight into the prophetic character of Jesus' life and ministry, Luke's material is particularly illustrative of the connection between Jesus and Israel's preceding prophetic tradition. This is not meant to imply that Luke's presentation of Jesus is primarily or exclusively based on prophetic categories. On the contrary, Luke's use of prophetic categories is frequently paired with other themes used to explicate the importance of Jesus, such as kingship, servant-hood, and messianism. In other words, Luke's particular Christology revolves around a number of different axes, all of which intersect at certain points within his Gospel (e.g. Lk. 3.21-22, 30-35; 4.16-30; 9.19-20, 35).[237] Nevertheless, it seems that the prophetic theme is particularly important for the narrative movement of Luke's Gospel. More specifically, Jesus' relationship to particular prophetic figures and his personal fulfillment of prophetic texts provide a thematic background for a significant portion of the material from the infancy narrative to the Emmaus road discourse.[238]

Additionally, Luke's emphasis on Jesus' prophetic ministry may serve a broader purpose, functioning as a unifying theme in the description of salvation history throughout Luke–Acts.[239] Indeed, Luke's presentation of

---

237. See Bock, *Luke*, 1:30. This stands against J. Severino Croatto, 'Jesus, Prophet Like Elijah, and Prophet-Teacher Like Moses in Luke–Acts', *JBL* 124 (2005): 451-65, who argues that Luke presents Jesus as a prophet in his Gospel, but progresses away from Jesus as a prophet and toward Jesus as messiah in Acts, thereby placing a divide between the two categories. Likely more accurate, however, is the assertion of Jack Dean Kingsbury, 'Jesus as the "Prophetic Messiah" in Luke's Gospel', in *The Future of Christology* (Festschrift Leander E. Keck; ed. Abraham J. Malherbe and Wayne A. Meeks; Minneapolis: Fortress, 1993), 29-42, that Luke's use of both prophetic and messianic categories results in a picture of Jesus as 'the "prophetic Messiah"' (31).

238. Hooker, *The Signs of a Prophet*, 59-62.

239. Witherington, *Jesus the Seer*, 335-43

## 2. The Development of the Prophetic Tradition 69

the prophetic ministry of Jesus comports well with his later depiction of prophetic activity within the early Christian communities, since both appear to be rooted to some extent in Old Testament prophetic categories.[240] In this regard, the examples that Luke presents concerning Agabus are particularly important. In Acts 11.28 Agabus predicted (ἐσήμανεν διὰ τοῦ πνεύματος) that there would be a famine in the Roman world (i.e. τὴν οἰκουμένην), which Luke then claims (Acts 11.29) took place during the reign of Claudius (ca. 41–54 C.E.). Since the verb σημαίνω was common among Greek writers during the Hellenistic period, the use of the term here over against προφητεύω may suggest that Agabus' pronouncement reflects a common Graeco-Roman oracle paradigm.[241] The occurrences of the term within the rest of the New Testament (i.e. Jn 12.33; 18.32; 21.19; Acts 25.27; Rev. 1.1), however, do not appear to have any particular connection with Graeco-Roman prophetic practices and its use in this context may simply function as a stylistic variation.[242] Furthermore, the preceding comment that the prophets had come from Jerusalem to Antioch may strengthen the argument that their activity was unlikely to be associated with Hellenistic prophetic traditions. Further, in Acts 21.10-11 Agabus performs a sign act which demonstrates Paul's future arrest. The act is seemingly parallel in form with a variety of symbolic actions performed by prophetic figures within the Old Testament (cf. 1 Kgs 11.29-40; Isa. 8.1-4; Jer. 19.1-13; Ezek. 4–5). Although the details of Agabus' performance do not coincide entirely with Luke's later description of the predicted events, the act itself appears to function in the same way as the earlier Old Testament examples, providing a general picture of events that were to take place.[243] In general terms, therefore, Agabus provides a model of prophetic activity within the context of the Christian movement that is parallel to a certain degree with the prophetic

---

240. Witherington, *Jesus the Seer*, 341. The intent, however, of Witherington's further comment that Luke's presentation shows 'continuity…with the larger prophetic context of the Greco-Roman world' (341) is unclear since there appears to be little overlap between Luke's use of prophetic categories and those that were prevalent within the Graeco-Roman setting.
241. BDAG, s.v. σημαίνω; cf. Gottfried Schille, *Die Apostelgeschichte des Lukas* (THKNT 5; Berlin: Evangelische Verlagsanstalt, 1983), 266, who argues that the verb 'hat hier…den Sinn einer rätselhaften Orakelrede'.
242. C.K. Barrett, *A Critical and Exegetical Commentary on the Acts of the Apostles* (2 vols.; ICC 30; Edinburgh: T. & T. Clark, 1994–98), 1:562, argues that an occurrence of προφητεύεω would have followed 'clumsily upon the noun' προφῆται in Acts 11.27. For the use of σημαίνω in non-canonical Jewish literature see Josephus, *Ant.* 6.50; 8.409.
243. Barrett, *Acts*, 2:995-96; Witherington, *Jesus the Seer*, 341-42.

material of the Old Testament.²⁴⁴ Thus, if Luke's use of the prophetic material can, at a basic level, be seen as representative of the prophetic material in the larger Gospel tradition, then it seems reasonable to contend that references to prophecy and prophetic activity within the Gospels either stem from the Old Testament or represent contemporary prophetic material that is rooted primarily in the earlier prophetic tradition of the Old Testament.

It seems, therefore, that the predominant background for prophetic activity in the Gospel material was the prophetic tradition developed throughout the history of the Old Testament and which continued to influence prophetic material within the Second Temple period.²⁴⁵ This is not, however, an affirmation that prophetic categories within the Gospel tradition (or the rest of the New Testament) attest to a uniform understanding of either the form or function of prophetic activity within the Christian movement.²⁴⁶ Rather, the present argument is intended to highlight that the prophetic terminology and categories used to describe the words and actions of persons within the Gospel tradition place this portion of Christian material within the stream of Israel's own unique history. In other words, it seems that at least a portion of the early Christian material functioned with reference to the Old Testament prophetic material in much the same way as other Second Temple literature, specifically in its attempt to evaluate Israel's previous prophetic history in light of its contemporary situation and to create new prophetic material that related to the previous material in terms of both literary form and thematic concern. Thus, while the expansive course of prophetic history is characterized by a number of variegated emphases, the entire tradition appears to have provided the predominant background for the continued development of prophetic material and activity.

## 6. Conclusion

The prophetic history of the Old Testament can aptly be described as an organic entity that grows and develops with particular reference to the community to which it pertains. This organic development appears to

---

244. For the more specific discussion concerning the relationship between prophecy and authority with respect to Agabus, see Wayne Grudem, *The Gift of Prophecy in the New Testament and Today* (Wheaton: Crossway, 2000), 71-72, 77-83, and Witherington, *Jesus the Seer*, 441-42.

245. Cf. Aune, *Prophecy*, 198; Robin Lane Fox, *Pagans and Christians in the Mediterranean World from the Second Century AD to the Conversion of Constantine* (New York: Penguin, 1986), 376.

246. Cf. Aune, *Prophecy*, 231.

## 2. The Development of the Prophetic Tradition 71

be present throughout much of Israel's social, cultural, and political history, and can be seen within the Old Testament material itself, specifically with respect to the relationship between the prophetic material developed in the different literary corpora within the Old Testament. Additionally, the subsequent literature of the Second Temple period, as well as witnesses concerning the development of prophetic categories in the Gospel traditions, provide evidence for the continued development of the Old Testament prophetic tradition in their reliance on its form, function, content, and themes. Thus, in spite of the reality that much of the prophetic material in all three groups of literature represents a multiplicity of particular emphases, it seems reasonable to see continuity in the development of the material throughout Israel's history. Furthermore, the present argument sought to demonstrate the notion that the original prophetic material of the Old Testament provided the primary influence for the shape and function of both prophetic literature and activity throughout Israel's history from the time of Moses to the time of Jesus and his contemporaries. In other words, although Israel's developing prophetic tradition was not completely distinct from prophetic categories developed within other historical, social, and cultural settings, it remained unique in a variety of ways, allowing it to function as a separate entity from other prophetic traditions. The Old Testament prophetic material itself, therefore, seems to provide the most plausible background for Paul's own presentation of the prophetic tradition in 2 Corinthians, considering the relative dependence on the material by a significant portion of both his Christian and Jewish contemporaries. The purpose of the next chapter will be to examine portions of 1 Corinthians in order to investigate further the notion that Paul was particularly dependent on the Old Testament prophetic tradition and to provide a basis for his use of prophetic language and material in the latter portion of the Corinthian correspondence.

## Chapter 3

## THE PROPHETIC TRADITION IN 1 CORINTHIANS

### 1. *Introduction*

Although the occasional circumstances of 1 and 2 Corinthians differ widely, Paul's correspondence with the Corinthians provides a helpful textual lens through which to analyse the apostle's presentation of himself to a community with which he had more than a temporary relationship. Despite the disparity between the two epistles in terms of both content and structure, it seems reasonable to assert that the rhetorical material in 1 Corinthians provides a foundation, in some sense, for understanding Paul's presentation of himself and his relationship with the Corinthians manifest in 2 Corinthians. In light of this perceived importance of the social and rhetorical connection of the extant portions of the Corinthian correspondence, the purpose of the present chapter will be to provide a basis for the discussion of Paul's relationship to the prophetic tradition in 2 Corinthians through an analysis of aspects of that relationship that may be derived from 1 Corinthians. The aim at this point of the argument is not to provide an exhaustive treatment of all the material within 1 Corinthians pertaining to Paul's relationship to the prophetic tradition; rather, the intention is to examine portions of 1 Corinthians that offer insight into the prophetic aspects of Paul's self-presentation in order to explore more fully the historically subsequent and dependent material in 2 Corinthians. In some sense, therefore, the material in this section functions as a methodological precursor to the more detailed analysis of Paul's prophetic identity in 2 Corinthians. The primary focus of this chapter will be to delineate both Paul's personal relationship to the prophetic tradition and his use of the prophetic material as a basis for his rhetoric. The argument will begin with an analysis of 1 Cor. 9.15-18 as a piece of potential evidence for the notion that Paul presents his ministry as an extension of the preceding prophetic tradition and then move to an examination of 1 Cor. 14.20-25 as confirmation of the way in which Paul's rhetoric and understanding of prophecy are shaped by the prophetic tradition.

## 2. Prophetic Persona (1 Corinthians 9.15-18)

Paul's renunciation of his apostolic right to receive material support from the Corinthians in 1 Cor. 9.15-18 is part of the broader discussion pertaining to the question of meat offered to idols in 1 Cor. 8.1–11.1. Despite its textual location, the lack of transparent correlation between the argument of 1 Corinthians 9 and the surrounding material led an earlier generation of scholars to speculate that this portion of Paul's argument was either an editorial misplacement or a loosely related digression to the argument of 1 Corinthians 8 and 10.[1] More recently, however, an extensive consensus has emerged which understands 1 Corinthians 9 to be an integral part of the broader discussion of τὰ εἰδωλόθυτα in 1 Cor. 8.1–11.1.[2] The argument for the unity of the section is built upon a

---

1. See, e.g., Hans Conzelmann, *1 Corinthians* (Hermeneia; Philadelphia: Fortress, 1975), 151; Jean Héring, *The First Epistle of Saint Paul to the Corinthians* (trans. A.W. Heathcote and P.J. Allcock; London: Epworth, 1962), 75; Hans Lietzmann, *An die Korinther I, II* (rev. W.G. Kümmel; HNT 9; Tübingen: Mohr Siebeck, 1949), 43; Johannes Weiss, *Der erste Korintherbrief* (9th ed.; KEK 5; Göttingen: Vandenhoeck & Ruprecht, 1910), 231-49. For a more recent appraisal of 1 Cor. 9 as a 'digression' from the argument of 1 Cor. 8 and 10, see Joseph A. Fitzmyer, *First Corinthians* (AB 32; New Haven: Yale University Press, 2008), 353.

2. In addition to several of the more recent commentaries on 1 Corinthians, see, e.g., John C. Brunt, 'Love, Freedom, and Moral Responsibility: The Contribution of 1 Cor 8–10 to an Understanding of Paul's Ethical Thinking', in *SBL Seminar Papers, 1981* (ed. Kent Harold Richards; SBLSP 20; Chico, Calif.: Scholars Press, 1981), 19-33; Robinson Butarbutar, *Paul and Conflict Resolution: An Exegetical Study of Paul's Apostolic Paradigm in 1 Corinthians 9* (PBM; Milton Keynes: Paternoster, 2007), passim; Georg Galitis, 'Das Wesen der Freiheit: Eine Untersuchung zu 1 Ko 9 und seinem Kontext', in *Freedom and Love: The Guide for Christian Life (1 Co 8–10; Rm 14–15)* (ed. Lorenzo De Lorenzi; SMBen 6; Rome: St. Paul's Abbey, 1981), 127-47; Paul Douglas Gardner, *The Gifts of God and the Authentication of a Christian: An Exegetical Study of 1 Corinthians 8–11:1* (Lanham, Md.: University Press of America, 1994), 107-10; John Paul Heil, *The Rhetorical Role of Scripture in 1 Corinthians* (SBLSBL 15; Atlanta: Society of Biblical Literature, 2005), 12; David G. Horrell, *The Social Ethos of the Corinthian Correspondence: Interests and Ideology from 1 Corinthians to 1 Clement* (SNTW; Edinburgh: T. & T. Clark, 1996), 142-50; David G. Horrell, 'Theological Principle or Christological Praxis? Pauline Ethics in 1 Corinthians 8.1–11.1', *JSNT* 61 (1997): 83-114; Dale B. Martin, *Slavery as Salvation: The Metaphor of Slavery in Pauline Christianity* (New Haven: Yale University Press, 1990), 77-80; Helmut Merklein, 'Die Einheitlichkeit des ersten Korintherbriefes', *ZNW* 75 (1984): 153-83; Margaret M. Mitchell, *Paul and the Rhetoric of Reconciliation: An Exegetical Investigation of the Language and Composition of 1 Corinthians* (Louisville: Westminster John Knox, 1993), 130-38, 243-50; Richard Liong-Seng Phua, *Idolatry and Authority: A Study of 1 Corinthians 8.1–11.1 in the Light of*

number of interrelated points, including, for example, the rhetorical connection between 1 Cor. 8.13 and 1 Corinthians 9, the repetition of a number of significant terms throughout the section (e.g. ἐξουσία, ἐλευθερία, συνείδησις, ἀσθενής, and οἰκοδομεῖν), and the seemingly consistent link between this material and the notion of congregational factionalism present elsewhere in 1 Corinthians (e.g. 1 Cor. 1.10-17).[3]

In spite of this relatively extensive consensus concerning the unity of the broader context of 1 Cor. 8.1–11.1, there remains debate concerning the precise rhetorical function of 1 Corinthians 9 within Paul's argument. In light of the numerous rhetorical questions with which Paul begins the section and his overtly forensic statement in 1 Cor. 9.3 that this material represents his ἀπολογία τοῖς ἐμὲ ἀνακρίνουσιν, it has been argued that 1 Corinthians 9 functions primarily as Paul's defence of his apostolic behaviour, with specific regard either to his conduct surrounding the issue of idol-meat or to his renunciation of material support from the Corinthians.[4] The apparent change in the direction of the argument at 1 Cor. 9.15, however, has led a number of scholars to argue that 1 Corinthians 9 functions primarily as an example, with Paul establishing his own lifestyle as a paradigm by which the Corinthians might follow the sacrificial exhortation implicit in 1 Cor. 8.13.[5] In this analysis the successive rhetorical questions and forensic rhetoric form the basis upon which Paul establishes the stark nature of the divide between the rights to which he is entitled and his behaviour with respect to those rights. In order to bridge the gap between these two views it may be possible to argue that

*the Jewish Diaspora* (LNTS 299; London: T&T Clark International, 2005), 172-200; Wendell Willis, 'An Apostolic Apologia? The Form and Function of 1 Corinthians 9', *JSNT* 24 (1985): 33-48.

3. So Mitchell, *Paul and the Rhetoric of Reconciliation*, 237-40; cf. Anthony C. Thiselton, *The First Epistle to the Corinthians* (NIGTC; Grand Rapids: Eerdmans, 2000), 607-12.

4. E.g. Gerhard Dautzenberg, 'Der Verzicht auf das apostolische Unterhaltsrecht: Eine exegetische Untersuchung zu 1 Kor 9', *Bib* 50 (1969): 212-32; Gordon D. Fee, *The First Epistle to the Corinthians* (NICNT; Grand Rapids: Eerdmans, 1987), 392-94; John C. Hurd, *The Origin of 1 Corinthians* (London: SPCK, 1965), 126-31.

5. E.g. Mitchell, *Paul and the Rhetoric of Reconciliation*, 243; cf. Paul Bowers, 'Church and Mission in Paul', *JSNT* 44 (1991): 89-111; Joachim Jeremias, 'Chiasmus in den Paulusbriefen', *ZNW* 49 (1958): 145-56; F. Stanley Jones, *'Freiheit' in den Briefen des Apostels Paulus: Eine historische, exegetische und religionsgeschichtliche Studie* (GTA 34; Göttingen: Vandenhoeck & Ruprecht, 1987), 42; Joop Smit, 'The Rhetorical Disposition of First Corinthians 8:7–9:27', *CBQ* 59 (1997): 476-91; Willis, 'An Apostolic Apologia?', 40; Ben Witherington III, *Conflict and Community in Corinth: A Socio-Rhetorical Commentary on 1 and 2 Corinthians* (Grand Rapids: Eerdmans, 1995), 203.

1 Corinthians 9 contains elements of both defence and example.[6] This convergence of solutions, however, may not provide a seamless reading of Paul's argument. Both the position that regards 1 Corinthians 9 as a defence and that which understands there to be elements of both defence and example suffer from their inability to define precisely what charges were brought against Paul. In her extensive rhetorical analysis of this section Mitchell argues forcefully that attempts to explain 1 Corinthians 9 as a defence against real charges make little sense of Paul's broader argument.[7] The notion that Paul is here defending himself against real charges may also be weakened by the relative simplicity of the argumentation in 1 Cor. 9.1-14. Indeed, Willis goes so far as to argue that Paul's 'rhetorical arguments are numerous, not because their validity is problematic, but because it is obvious'.[8] Nevertheless, a more balanced analysis may see the forensic aspect of the argument as allowing Paul to overcome any negative implications that may have developed in light of his reluctance to use particular rights among the Corinthians as opposed to serving as evidence for the presence of a formal defensive speech.[9] It is this potentially less formal nature of Paul's defensive rhetoric that has led some proponents of the view which highlights both defensive and paradigmatic elements to affirm that it is the exemplary function of the passage which constitutes the crux of Paul's argument and that the call to imitation in 1 Cor. 11.1 finds its primary antecedent in the content of 1 Corinthians 9.[10]

Despite the complexity of the rhetorical movement of 1 Cor. 8.1–11.1 and the actual function of 1 Corinthians 9 in the epistle, the structure of the chapter is relatively clear. The first three verses of 1 Corinthians 9 provide a brief, though poignant, argument for the reality of Paul's apostolic status and provide a transition into the specific argument about apostolic rights in 1 Cor. 9.4-14. The argumentation of 1 Cor. 9.4-14 draws on evidence from daily human affairs, the Torah, temple practice, and the words of Jesus in order to support the notion that it is lawful for

---

6. E.g. Butarbutar, *Paul and Conflict Resolution*, 84-88; David L. Dungan, *The Sayings of Jesus in the Churches of Paul: The Use of the Synoptic Tradition in the Regulation of Early Church Life* (Philadelphia: Fortress, 1971), 5-6; Horrell, *Social Ethos*, 205; Martin, *Slavery as Salvation*, 77-80.

7. Mitchell, *Paul and the Rhetoric of Reconciliation*, 244-45 n. 330.

8. Willis, 'An Apostolic Apologia?', 35.

9. Thiselton, *First Corinthians*, 663; cf. John K. Chow, *Patronage and Power: A Study of Social Networks in Corinth* (JSNTSup 75; Sheffield: JSOT, 1992), 107-10.

10. E.g. Butarbutar, *Paul and Conflict Resolution*, 101; Horrell, 'Theological Principle', 92.

apostles to receive material support as recompense for their gospel ministry. Following this sustained argument for his right to receive material support Paul explains that he does not accept this right because of the nature of his specific relationship to the gospel (1 Cor. 9.15-18). This explanation of his renunciation then forms the basis for the rest of 1 Corinthians 9, which focuses primarily on the implications that Paul's renunciation has on his own ministry (1 Cor. 9.19-27).

In light of the likelihood that 1 Corinthians 9 functions as the apostle's personal example to the Corinthians, this section of the epistle appears to provide unique insight into Paul's presentation of his own apostolic ministry. The usefulness of this portion of 1 Corinthians for the present argument concerning Paul's relationship to the prophetic tradition, therefore, is derived primarily from Paul's description of his commission in 1 Cor. 9.15-18. For this reason, the primary aim of this section is not to develop an exegetical analysis of the whole of 1 Corinthians 9; rather, the intent at this point is to provide a detailed examination of 1 Cor. 9.15-18 in order to determine whether Paul's discussion of his apostolic commission provides insight into the nature of his connection with the prophetic tradition of the Old Testament.

a. *Renunciation of Rights (1 Corinthians 9.15)*
Paul's claim in 1 Cor. 9.15 that he has not used any of these 'rights' (οὐδενὶ τούτων) among the Corinthians harks back to the somewhat preemptive conclusion drawn in 1 Cor. 9.12 in which Paul asserted that he and Barnabas renounced their apostolic right in order to eliminate the possibility of creating barriers that could potentially prevent the progression of the gospel.[11] While 1 Cor. 9.12 and 9.15 generally revolve around the same concern, the transition away from the first person plural used in 1 Cor. 9.4-14 and the emphatic use of ἐγώ in 1 Cor. 9.15 introduce a particularly individual emphasis at this point of Paul's argument.[12] In

11. Wolfgang Schrage, *Der erste Brief an die Korinther* (4 vols.; EKKNT 7/1-4; Zurich: Benziger; Neukirchen–Vluyn: Neukirchener Verlag, 1991–2001), 2:319-20, argues convincingly that the parallels between 1 Cor. 9.12 and 9.15 point to the notion that τούτων refers to Paul's apostolic right(s). Contra Dungan, *Sayings of Jesus*, 21-22 n. 2, who argues that τούτων refers to the arguments enumerated in 1 Cor. 9.4-14 and is parallel to ταῦτα in the latter half of the verse. Dungan's primary concern that the plural τούτων cannot represent the singular ἐξουσία does not take account of the numerous, though related, rights which Paul discusses in the preceding section (cf. Fee, *First Corinthians*, 416 n. 12; David G. Horrell, '"The Lord Commanded... But I Have Not Used...": Exegetical and Hermeneutical Reflections on 1 Cor 9.14-15', *NTS* 43 [1997]: 587-603 [592-93 n. 33]).
12. Thiselton, *First Corinthians*, 693.

other words, this section appears to move from an abstract enumeration of proofs regarding the nature and validity of apostolic rights toward the particular relationship between Paul and the gospel, which will function as the primary exemplar for the way in which the Corinthians ought to approach their own 'rights'.[13] Paul's second assertion in 1 Cor. 9.15, that the preceding series of arguments were not meant as a plea for Corinthian financial support, likely serves as further evidence that the discussion of apostleship in the preceding portion of 1 Corinthians 9 functions as the basis of Paul's movement toward his emphasis on his example rather than as a formal defence against a specific Corinthian objection. That is, Paul's renunciation of his right to material support and his claim that the intent of the preceding arguments was not to gain that support illustrate that the emphasis at this point is not on the notion that Paul has apostolic rights, but on the way in which he uses those rights. It seems most likely, therefore, that Paul's stark contrast between his rights and his behaviour functions as the paradigm by which the Corinthians should approach their own rights and behaviour with regard to the internal contention surrounding the issue of τὰ εἰδωλόθυτα.[14]

The notion that this portion of the argument represents an expressly personal aspect of Paul's example is strengthened by the final (broken) assertion in 1 Cor. 9.15 (καλὸν γάρ μοι μᾶλλον ἀποθανεῖν ἤ—τὸ καύχημά μου οὐδεὶς κενώσει). This explanatory clause (cf. γάρ) emphasizes the importance of Paul's action with regard to his rights. The presence of aposiopesis and the resulting broken syntax of the claim seemingly emphasize the emotional character of Paul's argument, as well as highlight the significance of his refusal to accept material support (cf. Gal. 2.6).[15] It is not clear, however, whether this emotional outburst caused a disruption in Paul's logic. Despite some attempts to reconstruct the syntax of Paul's statement, Fee is likely correct that it is not possible to determine precisely how Paul would have completed the original

13. Thiselton, *First Corinthians*, 661-62; cf. Harry P. Nasuti, 'The Woes of the Prophets and the Rights of the Apostle: The Internal Dynamics of 1 Corinthians 9', *CBQ* 50 (1988): 246-64.

14. Mitchell, *Paul and the Rhetoric of Reconciliation*, 243-48; cf. Roy E. Ciampa and Brian S. Rosner, *The First Letter to the Corinthians* (PNTC; Grand Rapids: Eerdmans, 2010), 396-97.

15. Roger L. Omanson, 'Some Comments About Style and Meaning: 1 Corinthians 9:15 and 7:10', *BT* 34 (1983): 135-39; Christophe Senft, *La première épître de saint Paul aux Corinthiens* (CNT 7; Neuchâtel: Delachaux & Niestlé, 1979), 121. For a concise discussion of the textual tradition at this point, see Bruce M. Metzger, *A Textual Commentary on the Greek New Testament* (2d ed.; Stuttgart: Deutsche Bibelgesellschaft, 1994), 492.

sentence.¹⁶ It seems reasonable, however, to contend with Fee that the second portion of the statement in 1 Cor. 9.15 (i.e. τὸ καύχημά μου οὐδεὶς κενώσει) reflects the original direction of the logic, based on the importance of Paul's καύχημα in the argument that follows (i.e. 1 Cor. 9.16-18).¹⁷ In spite of the notion that the second half of the assertion constitutes the original direction of the argument, the import of Paul's first statement remains to be seen. In that regard, the infinitive ἀποθανεῖν likely serves to create a contrasting parallel with the infinitive ζῆν in the command of the Lord in 1 Cor. 9.14.¹⁸ Thus, one of the intentions of the incomplete comparison in 1 Cor. 9.15 may be to reaffirm the ministerial principle described in 1 Cor. 9.12, namely to avoid anything that may hinder the progress of the gospel, which in this instance would be Paul's acceptance of the Corinthians' patronage. Additionally, the reference to death at this point may foreshadow Paul's discussion of divine judgment in 1 Cor. 9.16 (i.e. οὐαὶ...μοί ἐστιν). In terms of that connection, Paul's statement appears to revolve around the notion that the acceptance of material support would negate his understanding of his divine commission to preach the gospel. This connection between death (1 Cor. 9.15) and divine judgment (1 Cor. 9.16) may be strengthened by Paul's introduction of his καύχημα, which defined by the present context is closely related to the apostle's proclamation of the gospel (cf. 1 Cor. 9.16-18).¹⁹ In broad terms, therefore, Paul is attempting to avoid a situation in which the nature of his commission to preach the gospel is undermined by the use of specific apostolic rights.

b. *Prophetic Constraint (1 Corinthians 9.16-17)*
Paul explains his renunciation of his right to remuneration through a brief analysis of the nature and form of his apostolic ministry in 1 Cor. 9.16-17. The explanation is developed predominantly in negative terms, with a description of what does not constitute the boast that Paul will not allow to be nullified by the Corinthians.²⁰ Paul's initial assertion in 1 Cor. 9.16 that his actual proclamation of the gospel is not his boast then serves as the catalyst for the subsequent discussion of the nature and form of his apostolic commission. With respect to the broader context of

16. Fee, *First Corinthians*, 417.
17. Fee, *First Corinthians*, 417.
18. David E. Garland, *1 Corinthians* (BECNT; Grand Rapids: Baker, 2003), 422; Nasuti, 'The Woes of the Prophets', 255.
19. Gardner, *Gifts of God*, 91; Garland, *1 Corinthians*, 422-23.
20. Fee, *First Corinthians*, 418; cf. Sandnes, *Paul—One of the Prophets?*, 122.

## 3. The Prophetic Tradition in 1 Corinthians

1 Cor. 8.1–11.1 Paul's argument establishes the basis for the potentially divisive renunciation of his apostolic rights and his potentially conflicting response with respect to the opinions of various segments of the Corinthian community. More specifically, the material in 1 Cor. 9.16-17 develops the idea that Paul's understanding of the nature of the gospel stands at the forefront of both his act of renunciation and his understanding of his commission.[21] It is in Paul's presentation of his relationship to the proclamation of the gospel that it becomes possible to see a connection between the apostle and the prophetic tradition of the Old Testament.

Paul affirms explicitly that his inability to boast in his proclamation of the gospel stems from the fact that ἀνάγκη…μοι ἐπίκειται (1 Cor. 9.16). Despite the concise nature of the statement, its meaning is not readily transparent. Ambiguity arises primarily in conjunction with the meaning of the noun ἀνάγκη in the present context. The semantic range of the term includes two distinct, though logically related, categories. The first refers to an abstract notion of compulsion or constraint, which may have either an external or internal source. The second category refers more concretely to particular instances of distress, calamity, or tribulation, which then result in some level of either emotional or physical constraint.[22] Both meanings are attested in the Pauline corpus, as well as in the Corinthian correspondence itself, with the former category functioning in Rom. 13.5; 1 Cor. 7.37; 2 Cor. 9.17; Phlm. 14, and the latter in 1 Cor. 7.26; 2 Cor. 6.4; 12.10; 1 Thess. 3.7. The meaning of the term in the present context, therefore, cannot be determined solely in terms of either lexical or statistical evidence. In contrast to the majority of interpretations, Nasuti posits that Paul's present use of ἀνάγκη is best understood through the lens of the second, more concrete semantic category and that it forms a specific parallel with the occurrences of ἐν ἀνάγκαις in the *Peristasenkataloge* of 2 Corinthians (i.e. 2 Cor. 6.4; 12.10).[23] Nasuti points particularly to the close connection between the terminology in 1 Cor. 9.12 (ἐγκοπὴν δῶμεν) and 2 Cor. 6.3 (διδόντες προσκοπήν), both of which elucidate Paul's desire to avoid hindering the progress of the gospel.[24] Nasuti's view may be strengthened by the predominance of this use of ἀνάγκη within the LXX (e.g. 1 Kgs 22.2; Job 5.19; 15.24; Pss. 24.17; 106.6,

---

21. Butarbutar, *Paul and Conflict Resolution*, 158-64.
22. BDAG, s.v. ἀνάγκη; cf. Heinz Schreckenberg, *Ananke: Untersuchungen zur Geschichte des Wortgebrauchs* (Zetemata 36; Munich: Beck, 1964).
23. Nasuti, 'The Woes of the Prophets', 256.
24. Nasuti, 'The Woes of the Prophets', 256.

13; Jer. 9.15).²⁵ These connections lead Nasuti to contend that Paul does not boast about his proclamation of the gospel because of the 'distress' which arises from it.²⁶

In spite of the possible contextual associations with both the LXX and 2 Corinthians, there appear to be several difficulties with rendering ἀνάγκη as 'distress' in 1 Cor. 9.16. First, if ἀνάγκη at this point is parallel to the sufferings and hardships that Paul encounters because of his apostolic ministry, then his assertion that his (distressed) ministry does not constitute his boast seems to contradict his subsequent claim in 2 Cor. 11.30 that he boasts particularly in those things that reflect his weakness (assuming that Paul did not change his view in the interlude between 1 and 2 Corinthians). Second, Nasuti's analysis does not appear to give enough weight to the concise nature of the present argument, highlighted by both the close syntactical connection of the section seen in Paul's successive use of the conjunction γάρ and the close logical connection between the discussion of ἀνάγκη and the subsequent assertions in 1 Cor. 9.16-17. More specifically, the actual terminology in the following clauses (e.g. οὐαί, ἑκών, ἄκων, and οἰκονομία) seems to establish logical categories that are more readily associated with a broader notion of constraint rather than those related to particular episodes of distress or hardship. For example, if the contrast between ἑκών and ἄκων in 1 Cor. 9.17 is primarily based on a divide between completing an action voluntarily or being forced to complete it against one's will (see below), then it seems likely that ἀνάγκη refers to a more abstract discussion of compulsion rather than specific physical or emotional hardships.²⁷ Furthermore, it may be possible to see a connection between Paul's affirmation that ἀνάγκη...μοι ἐπίκειται in 1 Cor. 9.16 and his claim in 1 Cor. 9.17 that he has been entrusted with an οἰκονομία. If ἀνάγκη and οἰκονομία are in some sense mutually interpretative (see below), then the strong notions of commission and forced labour frequently associated with οἰκονομία seemingly favour the notion that ἀνάγκη here denotes a form of (external) compulsion.²⁸ In light of the potential contextual

---

25. Cf. Walter Grundmann, 'ἀναγκάζω, κτλ.', *TDNT* 1:345; C. Maurer, 'Grund und Grenze apostolischer Freiheit', in *Antwort: Karl Barth zum siebzigsten Geburtstag am 10. Mai 1956* (ed. Ernst Wolf, Charlotte von Kirschbaum, and Rudolf Frey; Zollikon-Zurich: Evangelischer, 1956), 638.

26. Nasuti, 'The Woes of the Prophets', 256.

27. Hafemann, *Suffering and the Spirit*, 140-41; F. Hauck, 'ἑκών, κτλ.', *TDNT* 2:469-70; Sandnes, *Paul—One of the Prophets?*, 122-23.

28. John Reumann, 'Οἰκονομία-Terms in Paul in Comparison with Lucan *Heilsgeschichte*', *NTS* 13 (1967): 147-67 (158).

associations in 1 Cor. 9.16-17 it seems reasonable to argue at this point that ἀνάγκη here refers not to particular occurrences of distress or calamity but to broader notions of constraint, compulsion, or necessity. The actual character and function of this constraint, however, remain to be examined.

Although it is possible for ἀνάγκη to refer to a form of constraint that stems either from internal or external sources, it does not seem plausible that Paul's discussion focuses on internal notions of constraint. In his influential study of this portion of Paul's argument Käsemann argues concisely that the force behind ἀνάγκη at this point cannot stem from an internal ethical or psychological source, since both of these definitions stand in contrast to the passive voice of ἐπίκειται which points to the ostensible externality that characterizes the compulsion that affects Paul.[29] In contrast with the potentially impersonal notion of destiny or fate that may be associated with ἀνάγκη in Greek literature, the passive voice of ἐπίκειται is probably best understood as a divine passive, effectively making Paul's ἀνάγκη a divine constraint.[30] More specifically, Käsemann states that:

> *Ananke* describes here the power of the divine will which radically and successfully challenges man and makes its servant its instrument. This definition, then, makes it clear that, simply in his capacity as a Jew, Paul cannot be speaking, like the Greek with his *ananke* or the Roman with his *fatum*, of an impersonal force of blind ill-omen or chance. He may indeed be making use of the Greek concept, but only in order to delineate the character of the divine power as sovereign, inexorable and ineluctable.[31]

Thus, the external constraint which compels Paul arises from God's providential activity in the world (cf. Rom. 13.5).[32] In connection with this personal and active understanding of the divine constraint which affects Paul, the verb ἐπίκειται is probably best rendered as 'presses upon' rather than the more passive 'laid upon' as a means of emphasizing the overtly active character of both the act of compulsion and the constraint

---

29. Ernst Käsemann, 'A Pauline Version of the "Amor Fati"', in *New Testament Questions of Today* (London: SCM, 1969), 228-29.
30. Cf. Sandnes, *Paul—One of the Prophets?*, 122.
31. Käsemann, 'Pauline Version', 230. For a thorough discussion of the possible relationship between Paul's use of ἀνάγκη and Greek (especially Stoic) concepts of determinism, see Abraham J. Malherbe, 'Determinism and Free Will in Paul: The Argument of 1 Corinthians 8 and 9', in *Paul in His Hellenistic Context* (ed. Troels Engberg-Pedersen; Edinburgh: T. & T. Clark, 1994), 231-55.
32. Grundmann, *TDNT* 1:346; cf. Robert Morgenthaler, 'ἀνάγκη', *NIDNTT* 2:644.

itself.³³ Paul's proclamation of the gospel, therefore, does not allow for boasting because it is not an action derived from his own volition, but one that is forced upon him by means of divine constraint.

It is this notion of divine constraint which serves as the initial catalyst for identifying parallels between Paul and the prophetic material of the Old Testament. Certain strands of the prophetic tradition also bear witness to a form of divine constraint that compels the individual to complete a task or calling in spite of themselves (e.g. Exod. 3–4; Isa. 8.11; Jer. 20.7-10; Ezek. 3.14-19; 37.1; Amos 3.7-8; Jon. 1).³⁴ Sandnes' thorough analysis of the motif of prophetic constraint throughout the Old Testament and the rabbinic literature points to the reality that the prophets were understood both to be affected by divine constraint with regard to particular prophetic activities and, more broadly, to their entire self-conception as prophets.³⁵ In that regard it may be possible to argue broadly that Paul's own apostolic self-conception was rooted in the same type of divine constraint as that of the prophets. In more specific terms, the divine compulsion or constraint that affects Paul may provide a distinct parallel between the experience of the apostle and that of Jeremiah. Jeremiah was unable to overcome the word of the Lord and was forced to proclaim it in spite of persistent ridicule from his contemporaries (e.g. Jer. 20.7-10).³⁶ Paul's discussion of divine constraint may, therefore, be a deliberate reference to the prophetic commission of Jeremiah (cf. Gal. 1.15-16).³⁷ However, in light of the lack of any direct textual connection with Jeremiah at this point of Paul's argument, it seems more likely that his discussion of divine constraint belies a more general reference to the overall progression of the prophetic tradition. In other words, Paul appears to understand the origination of his commission as stemming from the same form of divine compulsion frequently reflected in the Old Testament prophetic material.

The connection with the prophetic tradition may be established further through Paul's following assertion that 'woe' will overtake him if he does not fulfill his commission to proclaim the gospel. The statement

33. Thiselton, *First Corinthians*, 696; cf. A.T. Robertson and Alfred Plummer, *A Critical and Exegetical Commentary on the First Epistle of St Paul to the Corinthians* (2d ed.; ICC 34; Edinburgh: T. & T. Clark, 1914), 189.

34. Ciampa and Rosner, *First Corinthians*, 416-47; Nicklas, 'Paulus—der Apostel als Prophet', 89; Schrage, *1 Korintherbrief*, 2:323-24.

35. See Sandnes, *Paul—One of the Prophets?*, 125-29.

36. Jack R. Lundbom, *Jeremiah* (3 vols.; AB 21; New York: Doubleday, 1999–2004), 1:858; John Arthur Thompson, *The Book of Jeremiah* (NICOT; Grand Rapids: Eerdmans, 1980), 460-61.

37. Cf. Conzelmann, *1 Corinthians*, 158 n. 26; Garland, *1 Corinthians*, 423-24.

οὐαὶ γάρ μοί ἐστιν reflects the prophetic woe-formulas that occur frequently throughout the Old Testament.[38] These prophetic woe-oracles vary somewhat in terms of vocabulary and syntax, but they generally function either as invectives against a particular person or group of people or as lamentation directed at the prophet himself.[39] The present woe-formula in 1 Cor. 9.16 undoubtedly reflects the self-directed form (cf. μοι), a fact that strengthens the connection between Paul and the prophetic tradition as this particular formula is often associated with the prophets' understanding of their prophetic commission (e.g. Isa. 6.5; Jer. 15.10; 45.3).[40] Jeremiah may again be the most useful paradigm for understanding Paul's relationship to the prophetic tradition as it pertains to his experience of the negative impact of divine constraint (cf. Jer. 15.10; 20.14-18). Indeed, Stuhlmacher contends that '[w]ie der Prophet Jeremia sieht sich Paulus auf Gedeih und Verderb mit der Verkündigung des Evangeliums betraut; würde er sie aufgeben, würde er dem Fluch Gottes verfallen'.[41] However, as with the connection between Paul and Jeremiah with respect to the notion of divine constraint, the parallels between their self-directed woes are not precise. The majority of self-directed woes in Jeremiah pertain primarily to the anguish and distress that arise in relation to his prophetic call (e.g. Jer. 4.13, 31; 6.4; 10.19; 15.10; 22.18; 34.5; 45.2).[42] Conversely, the focus of Paul's claim in 1 Cor. 9.16 appears to pertain less to notions of lamentation than it does to notions of eschatological judgment.[43] That is, Paul's focus at this point does not seem to be on the distress and suffering that arise in conjunction with his proclamation of the gospel, but on the possibility of

38. For a thorough analysis of the form and function of prophetic woe-oracles in the Old Testament, see Richard J. Clifford, 'The Use of Hôy in the Prophets', *CBQ* 28 (1966): 458-64; Erhard Gerstenberger, 'The Woe Oracles of the Prophets', *JBL* 81 (1962): 249-63; Waldemar Janzen, *Mourning Cry and Woe Oracle* (BZAW 125; Berlin: de Gruyter, 1972); Gunter Wanke, 'אוֹי und הוֹי', *ZAW* 78 (1966): 215-18; James G. Williams, 'The Alas-Oracles of the Eighth Century Prophets', *HUCA* 38 (1967): 75-91.
39. Nasuti, 'The Woes of the Prophets', 257.
40. Nasuti, 'The Woes of the Prophets', 257.
41. Peter Stuhlmacher, 'Das paulinische Evangelium', in *Das Evangelium und die Evangelien: Vorträge vom Tübinger Symposium 1982* (ed. Peter Stuhlmacher; WUNT 28; Tübingen: Mohr Siebeck, 1983), 160.
42. Nasuti's recognition of this distinction and his claim that 'Paul does not lament the distress which his preaching brings; he boasts of it' (Nasuti, 'Woes of the Prophets', 258) detracts further from his earlier hypothesis (256) that Paul's ἀνάγκη constitutes his apostolic distress(es) since Paul claims that his ἀνάγκη is precisely the reason he does not boast in his proclamation of the gospel (cf. γάρ in 1 Cor. 9.16).
43. Käsemann, 'Pauline Version', 229.

suffering divine judgment for avoiding his divinely constrained commission.[44] Despite the lack of similarity between the function of the woe-formulas here and in Jeremiah, the notion that Paul stands between divine constraint and divine judgment likely echoes the circumstances of Jer. 20.7-18 in which the prophet describes his own position with regard to his divine commission. The language and emphasis of 1 Cor. 9.16, therefore, seem to point to the notion that Paul understands his commission and its consequences as reflective of the prophetic material of the Old Testament.

The compact logic of Paul's rhetoric continues with an additional explanatory statement in 1 Cor. 9.17 that elucidates the material in the preceding verse. Paul here offers two contrasting conditional statements in order to describe further the nature and result of his commission to preach the gospel. The contrast revolves around two foci: the origin and form of Paul's commission. These two foci stem from the claims made in the respective protases and apodoses of Paul's two conditional statements. The aspect of Paul's argument developed in the protases pertains to the origin of his apostolic commission and centres on the distinction between that which is done ἑκών and that which is done ἄκων. In general terms, the difference between these two antonyms pertains to a simple distinction between the way in which one approaches an act, that is, either 'willingly' (ἑκών) or 'unwillingly' (ἄκων).[45] However, in light of the close syntactical association with the preceding verse (cf. γάρ) it seems likely that the distinction between the two terms is influenced by the discussion of ἀνάγκη in 1 Cor. 9.16. The divide then is not so much between one's own willingness and unwillingness as it is between one's willingness and God's compulsion. To combine the ideas of Gardner and Thiselton, the contrast at this point is between that done 'entirely by personal choice' and that done 'under God's compulsion'.[46] Thus, the focus of Paul's distinction is not upon the attitude with which he carries out his commission; rather, the focus is on the nature of the commission itself and, consequently, on Paul's apostolic status.[47] The notions behind ἄκων and ἀνάγκη stand in unison, therefore, against the semantic import

---

44. So Stuhlmacher, *Das paulinische Evangelium*, 87; cf. Eckhard J. Schnabel, *Der erste Brief des Paulus an die Korinther* (HTA; Wuppertal: Brockhaus, 2006), 497; Schrage, *1 Korintherbrief*, 2:324.

45. Cf. BDAG, s.v. ἄκων; ἑκών.

46. Gardner, *Gifts of God*, 92-93; Thiselton, *First Corinthians*, 696.

47. So Schnabel, *1 Korintherbrief*, 498, who argues, 'Paulus spricht also nicht von seinen Gefühlen im Blick auf seine Berufung zum Missionarsdienst, sondern von seinem Status'. Cf. Schrage, *1 Korintherbrief*, 2:325.

of ἑκών. In other words, the present contrast between ἑκών and ἄκων expresses the difference between an implied hypothetical state of freedom which Paul does not have and that of the necessity or constraint (i.e. ἀνάγκη) which actually defines his ministry.[48] Paul's commission originates not from his own volition but from divine constraint.

The second aspect of Paul's argument in 1 Cor. 9.17 pertains to the actual form of his apostolic commission. This aspect of the argument develops from the distinct references made in the apodoses of the conditional clauses with regard to the reception of payment (μισθὸν ἔχω) corresponding to work done through one's own decision (ἑκών) and the reception of a stewardship (οἰκονομίαν πεπίστευμαι) corresponding to work done on account of (divine) compulsion (ἄκων). In contrast with the distinct divide made between ἑκών and ἄκων in the protases of 1 Cor. 9.17, however, the apodoses do not form a strict contrast between a hypothetical right to remuneration and Paul's actual situation of having no such right. If Paul's assertion that he was entrusted with an οἰκονομία is meant to negate the idea that he has a right to receive material support, then both the preceding argument in 1 Cor. 9.4-14, in which the apostle argues stringently that he is entitled to payment, and his consequent refusal of that right in 1 Cor. 9.12, 15, 18, and 19 are rendered nonsensical.[49] The statements in the parallel apodoses in 1 Cor. 9.17 (μισθὸν ἔχω

---

48. The notion that the first conditional clause of 1 Cor. 9.17 (εἰ γὰρ ἑκὼν τοῦτο πράσσω, μισθὸν ἔχω) represents a real condition based solely on its grammatical form (e.g. Georges Didier, 'Le Salaire du Désintéressement [I Cor. ix,14-27]', *RSR* 43 [1955]: 228-51; Reumann, 'Οἰκονομία-Terms', 159; Weiss, *1 Korintherbrief*, 241) misunderstands both the nature of conditional clauses (the so-called first class condition is a *real* condition only in the sense that it assumes the argument [cf. BDF, 188-90; Daniel B. Wallace, *Greek Grammar Beyond the Basics: An Exegetical Syntax of the New Testament* (Grand Rapids: Zondervan, 1996), 690-94]) and the function of the second condition, which, according to this view, would also have to be reflective of Paul's situation. However, the notion that Paul preaches both ἑκών and ἄκων fails to account for both the grammatical distinction (i.e. δέ) in 1 Cor. 9.17 and the logical connection between ἄκων and ἀνάγκη in the progression of Paul's argument. Similarly, the assertion that Paul preaches ἑκών in spite of the fact that he faces divine constraint (e.g. Malherbe, 'Determinism and Free Will in Paul', 249-50; Vernon K. Robbins, *The Tapestry of Early Christian Discourse: Rhetoric, Society, and Ideology* [London: Routledge, 1996], 85-86) seems to misread the connection between the statements in 1 Cor. 9.16-17 (see the helpful critique of Malherbe's thesis in John K. Goodrich, 'Paul, the *Oikonomos* of God: Paul's Apostolic Metaphor in 1 Corinthians and its Graeco-Roman Context' [Ph.D. diss., Durham University, 2010], 197-202).

49. On this point, see especially Goodrich, 'Paul, the *Oikonomos* of God', 193-207. Goodrich's contention that there is not a strict contrast between μισθός and

and οἰκονομίαν πεπίστευμαι), therefore, do not represent a distinction in terms of reward, but in terms of the actual form of Paul's commission. In other words, the apodoses function as a further explanation of the contrast already made between working either ἑκών or ἄκων, denoting that the heart of Paul's contrast centres on notions of freedom and slavery. That the distinction here refers to the divide between freedom and slavery stems both from Paul's specific use of the term οἰκονομία in 1 Cor. 9.17 and the more general presence of terminology in 1 Cor. 9.16-17 dealing with the concepts of compulsion, volition, and payment, all of which are associated with the concept of slavery in the Graeco-Roman economy.[50] More specifically, Martin argues that Paul's language at this point 'clearly indicates to people of that society that [Paul] characterizes himself as Christ's slave agent'.[51] It seems, therefore, that Paul's particular self-description as a 'slave administrator' (οἰκονομίαν πεπίστευμαι) functions as the means by which he locates his labour within the context of 'God's program'.[52] For this reason, with respect to his apostolic commission it appears that the distinctive emphasis at this point is that Paul is a steward not of the Corinthians, but of God himself (cf. 1 Cor. 4.1).[53] Paul's presentation of his οἰκονομία may then relate specifically to the distinction made in 1 Cor. 9.17 between work done either ἑκών or ἄκων, with the divine commission inherent in οἰκονομία being closely associated

---

οἰκονομία in 1 Cor. 9.17 is based in large part on the actual historical situation of an οἰκονόμος with respect to status and remuneration (202-4). Thus, Paul's particular self-description as a 'slave administrator' (οἰκονομίαν πεπίστευμαι) functions both to confirm his status as a slave of God and his right to remuneration. The syntactical relationship between the conditional clauses in 1 Cor. 9.17 then parallels that between the statements in 2 Cor. 5.13, where Paul makes a primary distinction between his rhetorical ability (ἐξέστημεν or σωφρονοῦμεν) in order to illustrate that irrespective of either condition his ministry exists for the benefit of others (cf. Moyer V. Hubbard, 'Was Paul Out of His Mind? Re-Reading 2 Corinthians 5.13', *JSNT* 70 [1998]: 39-64). Paul's argument here, then, is that whether he preaches ἑκών or ἄκων, he is entitled to payment. That Paul is still entitled to payment explains the need for the apostle to define the actual nature of his μισθός in 1 Cor. 9.18.

50. Martin, *Slavery as Salvation*, 74-75; cf. Reumann, 'Οἰκονομία-Terms', 159.

51. Martin, *Slavery as Salvation*, 76.

52. John Reumann, 'Οἰκονομία = "Covenant"; Terms for *Heilsgeschichte* in Early Christian Usage', *NovT* 3 (1959): 282-92 (282).

53. That Paul is a steward of God at this point arises from the likelihood that πεπίστευμαι is a divine passive (cf. Sandnes, *Paul—One of the Prophets?*, 122). For an analysis of οἰκονόμους in 1 Cor. 4.1, see Andrew D. Clarke, *Secular and Christian Leadership in Corinth: A Socio-Historical and Exegetical Study of 1 Corinthians 1–6* (PBM; Milton Keynes: Paternoster, 2006), 121-22.

with the divine ἀνάγκη that conditions the reality of his apostolic labour. Because of this association it may be possible to argue that this compulsion and stewardship are mutually interpretative in the sense that they explain the interrelation of the source and form of Paul's commission to proclaim the gospel. This close rhetorical connection between the statements in 1 Cor. 9.16-17 may provide further evidence for the idea that Paul presents his commission as parallel to the Old Testament prophetic tradition inasmuch as the notion of constraint (e.g. Amos 3.7-8) and the language of slavery (e.g. Isa. 49.3, 5, 7) reflect concepts closely related to the prophetic persona. Paul's assertion that he was entrusted with an οἰκονομία, therefore, may serve as a recognition of his servant-status as a prophet of YHWH.

c. *Free Proclamation (1 Corinthians 9.18)*
Paul's introduction of the categories of freedom and slavery in 1 Cor. 9.17 via the distinction between the reception of payment (μισθὸν ἔχω) and the reception of a divine commission (οἰκονομίαν πεπίστευμαι) serves as the basis for the question that the apostle raises in 1 Cor. 9.18 concerning the actual nature of his remuneration (i.e. τίς οὖν μού ἐστιν ὁ μισθός;). Paul affirms that the reward of his οἰκονομία lies in preaching the gospel free of charge (ἀδάπανον θήσω τὸ εὐαγγέλιον), which is his practice. Somewhat ironically, therefore, Paul's payment is a lack of payment. In light of the closely connected rhetoric throughout the section, Paul's question and subsequent response may serve both as the logical conclusion to the labour dichotomy established in 1 Cor. 9.17 and as the positive contrast to his rhetorically negative statements concerning his boast in 1 Cor. 9.15-17. If this structural analysis is accurate then Paul's καύχημα and μισθός can be seen to refer to the same entity.[54] In more specific terms, his free proclamation of the gospel would constitute both his payment and his boast. A more nuanced understanding, however, may result from the idea that the two terms revolve around the same reality, with Paul boasting about his 'reward', which itself is the free proclamation of the gospel.[55] In spite of the concise nature of Paul's response to his own question, there is still some ambiguity with regard to the nature of the apostle's μισθός. Due to the fact that μισθός in 1 Cor. 9.17 refers ostensibly to immediate or present payment it seems reasonable to conclude that the use of the term in 1 Cor. 9.18 also refers to present payment. The basic thrust of 1 Cor. 9.18 would then be that Paul's

---

54. E.g. Fee, *First Corinthians*, 421; Sandnes, *Paul—One of the Prophets?*, 121.
55. So Fitzmyer, *First Corinthians*, 368.

remuneration is the fact that he preaches free of charge (ἀδάπανον).⁵⁶ Paul's concept of μισθός at this point, however, may move beyond the explicit statement of 1 Cor. 9.18 toward a broader, eschatological concept. Gardner, for example, provides four arguments that support the notion that μισθός here refers to an eschatological reward: (1) the meaning of οὐαί in 1 Cor. 9.17 is eschatological, (2) the earlier uses of μισθός in 1 Cor. 3.8 and 3.14 are eschatological, (3) the occurrences of μισθός in 1 Cor. 3.8 and 3.14 are the only other metaphorical uses of the term in the Pauline corpus, and (4) the immediate context of 1 Cor. 9.24-27 has an eschatological purview.⁵⁷ It may be helpful to recognize the existence of both associations since the present context contains material pertaining to notions of actual payment as well as to eschatological circumstance. Thus, Paul's immediate reward stems from the free proclamation of the gospel which itself clarifies his activity as an apostle (1 Cor. 9.19) and confirms his eschatological position (1 Cor. 9.27). Despite the debate concerning the precise meaning of μισθός at this point, however, it seems that Paul's response reaffirms the argument of 1 Cor. 9.17 that his μισθός is not defined by the Corinthians, but by God himself. In other words, Paul's assertion that he proclaims the gospel free of charge is a reaffirmation of his renunciation of material support in light of the nature and form of his apostolic commission (1 Cor. 9.15-17).

Paul preaches free of charge εἰς τὸ μὴ καταχρήσασθαι τῇ ἐξουσίᾳ μου ἐν τῷ εὐαγγελίῳ. The precise meaning of this phrase depends upon one's understanding of the infinitive καταχρήσασθαι. Some scholars have attempted to argue that Paul uses the intensive form of the infinitive χρῆσθαι at this point in order to distinguish between a proper (χρῆσθαι) and improper (καταχρήσασθαι) use of rights.⁵⁸ Thus, Paul is seen as foregoing this misuse of authority by not using those rights that would prevent the advancement of the gospel (cf. 1 Cor. 9.12, 15).⁵⁹ Although there may be a distinction between the two terms at this point, the argument that καταχρήσασθαι has a negative connotation is doubtful.⁶⁰ In light of the lack of textual evidence for the meaning 'misuse' in the first

---

56. E.g. Sandnes, *Paul—One of the Prophets?*, 121; Schrage, *1 Korintherbrief*, 2:326-27.

57. Gardner, *Gifts of God*, 94; cf. Hafemann, *Suffering and the Spirit*, 143-44; Nasuti, 'The Woes of the Prophets', 260.

58. E.g. Dungan, *Sayings of Jesus*, 24 n. 1; Darrell J. Doughty, 'The Presence and Future of Salvation in Corinth', *ZAW* 66 (1975): 61-90 (71 n. 47); Fee, *First Corinthians*, 421; Weiss, *1 Korintherbrief*, 200.

59. Fee, *First Corinthians*, 421.

60. Ciampa and Rosner, *First Corinthians*, 420; Schnabel, *1 Korintherbrief*, 499.

century it may be more likely that the difference here is one of degree (cf. 1 Cor. 7.31).[61] In this view, Paul's assertion is that he offers his proclamation free of charge as a means of not taking full advantage of the apostolic rights that he received from his gospel-oriented commission (ἐν τῷ εὐαγγελίῳ). This understanding seems to correlate well with the preceding argument in 1 Cor. 9.15-17 concerning the divinely constrained character of Paul's commission. Paul makes use only of those rights that are consistent with his status as a slave and with the prophetic constraint that defines his missionary activity. In terms of the argument of 1 Cor. 8.1–11.1, this divinely oriented commission functions as the basis upon which Paul is able to emphasize the gospel instead of particular rights. In broad terms, the notion that Paul's commission is divinely constrained in a manner similar to that seen in the Old Testament prophetic tradition forces him to function as a slave of Christ who proclaims the gospel irrespective of the societal constraints of patronage and remuneration.

d. *Conclusions*

Within 1 Cor. 9.15-18 Paul provides a portrait of his commission in order to explain his behaviour with regard to his renunciation of particular apostolic rights. The specific terminology and logic that Paul uses to paint this portrait reflect categories that are operative within the prophetic material of the Old Testament. It may be possible, therefore, to understand Paul's apostolic οἰκονομία as a prophetic commission. However, the lack of an explicit reference to the prophetic material at this point requires the potentially more nuanced conclusion that Paul's presentation of his commission is not derived from a specific portion of the Old Testament prophetic material, but from general conceptions associated with the prophetic tradition. In other words, although Paul's apostolic ministry and self-presentation may be built upon a variety of concepts and traditions, it seems reasonable to argue that the relationship between God and the prophets provided one framework within which the apostle was able to understand his own commission. To build on the terminology of Sandnes, Paul's position between divine ἀνάγκη and eschatological οὐαί places him within the locus of the Old Testament prophetic tradition.[62]

The notion that Paul presents his ministry as stemming, at least in part, from the prophetic tradition that developed within the Old Testament and persisted throughout the Second Temple period and among

---

61. So Thiselton, *First Corinthians*, 585, 697.
62. Sandnes, *Paul—One of the Prophets?*, 122.

the earliest Christian communities may be strengthened by the notion that the prophetic material itself functions to shape Paul's language and argumentation. That is, Paul's relationship to the prophetic tradition may stem not only from his connection with the prophetic persona developed in the Old Testament, but also from the correlation between his own rhetoric and that of the prophets. It will be helpful, therefore, to analyse 1 Cor. 14.20-25 as a means of highlighting the connection between Paul's rhetoric and that of the prophetic tradition.

### 3. *Prophetic Rhetoric (1 Corinthians 14.20-25)*

In relation to the discussion of spiritual gifts in 1 Corinthians 12–14, Paul's argument in 1 Cor. 14.20-25 has received a significant amount of attention. Scholarly interest at this point is due primarily to the relatively strict dichotomy that Paul establishes between the final effects of the use of unarticulated tongues and prophetic speech in the community.[63] In terms of the broader context of 1 Corinthians 12–14 there is a general consensus that 1 Cor. 14.20-25 serves as the final portion of Paul's argument regarding the need for intelligibility in the assembly (1 Cor. 14.1-19) as an extension of the way of love that is paradigmatic for activity within the community (1 Cor. 13).[64] More specifically, it is possible to argue that 1 Cor. 14.20-25 'is best understood as a corroboration and

---

63. For an extensive analysis of Christian glossolalia, see Forbes, *Prophecy*, 44-187. The phrase 'unarticulated tongues' is used throughout this section in order to illustrate that Paul's argument is not against the spiritual gift of γλῶσσαι in general, but against a misuse of the gift during public gatherings (cf. Wayne Grudem, '1 Corinthians 14.20-25: Prophecy and Tongues as Signs of God's Attitude', *WTJ* 41 [1979]: 381-96; contra Fitzmyer, *First Corinthians*, 521). The specific adjective 'unarticulated' stems from the proposal of Thiselton that γλῶσσαι are non-verbal, unconscious 'languages', which must be 'put into words' for intelligible use within the community (see Thiselton, *First Corinthians*, esp. 970-88, 1096-100, 1107-11; Anthony C. Thiselton, 'The "Interpretation" of Tongues: A New Suggestion in the Light of Greek Usage in Philo and Josephus', *JTS* 30 [1979]: 15-36). This particular understanding of γλῶσσαι is not, however, required for this portion of Paul's argument. The emphasis here is strictly on the unintelligible nature of tongues in contrast with the intelligible nature of prophetic speech.

64. E.g. Fee, *First Corinthians*, 652-53; Garland, *1 Corinthians*, 644; Schrage, *1 Korintherbrief*, 3:376-77; Thiselton, *First Corinthians*, 1074-77. For an alternative view, see Fitzmyer, *First Corinthians*, 508-9. For an analysis of the rhetorical unity of 1 Cor. 12–14, see Joop Smit, 'Argument and Genre of 1 Corinthians 12–14', in *Rhetoric and the New Testament: Essays from the 1992 Heidelberg Conference* (ed. Stanley E. Porter and Thomas H. Olbricht; JSNTSup 90; Sheffield: JSOT, 1993), 211-30.

reinforcement of the cumulative argument of [1 Cor. 14.]1-19'.[65] That is, Paul's preceding emphasis on the relationship between intelligible speech and communal edification in 1 Corinthians 14 forms the basis for the distinction between prophetic speech and unarticulated tongues at this point. In terms of its internal structure the argument of 1 Cor. 14.20-25 follows a fairly linear progression. The exhortation in 1 Cor. 14.20 frames the discussion of the usefulness of certain spiritual gifts within the public life of the assembly with the metaphor of childishness and maturity (cf. 1 Cor. 13.9-12). This exhortation is followed by a quotation of Isa. 28.11-12 in 1 Cor. 14.21 which is brought to bear on the Corinthian context through two brief assertions in 1 Cor. 14.22. The final three verses of the section, 1 Cor. 14.23-25, represent hypothetical illustrations of the consequences that stem from the preceding assertions.[66]

Despite the relative clarity of the general structure of the passage, there are a number of complex exegetical issues that obscure the relationship between the quotation (1 Cor. 14.21), the assertions (1 Cor. 14.22), and the illustrations (1 Cor. 14.23-25). These issues arise primarily from Paul's use of Isa. 28.11-12. In broad terms, the exegetical difficulties stem from the text-form of the quotation, the relationship between the quotation and the following assertions (cf. ὥστε in 1 Cor. 14.22), and the correlation, if any, between the Isaianic narrative and Paul's interaction with the Corinthians. Additionally, the relationship between the two assertions in 1 Cor. 14.22 and the two illustrations in 1 Cor. 14.23-25 is strained due to both the (potentially) elliptical syntax of the assertions and the meaning of the term σημεῖον. The complexity of the logic at this point has caused some interpreters either to abandon Paul's wording entirely or to express that the apostle may have followed his rhetoric beyond the point of his intended meaning.[67] In contrast, although these issues are multifaceted,

---

65. Thiselton, *First Corinthians*, 1118.

66. Fee, *First Corinthians*, 677; cf. Bruce C. Johanson, 'Tongues, A Sign for Unbelievers? A Structural and Exegetical Study of 1 Corinthians XIV.20-25', *NTS* 25 (1979): 180-203 (186-90). Contra Ralph P. Martin, *The Spirit and the Congregation: Studies in 1 Corinthians 12–15* (Grand Rapids: Eerdmans, 1984), 72, who argues that the section begins at 1 Cor. 14.21.

67. E.g. J.B. Phillips, *The New Testament in Modern English* (New York: Macmillan, 1960), 552 n. 5: '[First Corinthians 14.22] is the sole instance of the translator's departing from the accepted text. He felt bound to conclude from the sense of the next three verses [i.e. 1 Cor. 14.23-25] that we have here either a slip of the pen on the part of Paul, or, more probably, a copyists' error'. Likewise, Richard B. Hays, *First Corinthians* (IBC; Louisville: John Knox, 1997), 240, argues that 'Paul seems to have gotten carried away by the rhetorical antitheses of [1 Cor. 14.22] to say something that he does not strictly mean'. See also C.K. Barrett, *The First Epistle to*

it is possible to argue that they affirm, rather than detract from, the usefulness of this section for establishing certain boundaries with regard to Paul's presentation of the function of prophetic speech in Corinth. In other words, the specific exegetical issues concerning the relation of both γλῶσσαι and προφητεῖα to the Corinthian community, as well as their respective effects on the ἰδιῶται, ἄπιστοι, and πιστεύοντες, provide a helpful background for determining the purpose and implications of Paul's presentation of prophetic speech.[68] Furthermore, Paul's use of the Isaianic narrative may provide a more specific connection between his presentation of prophetic activity and the larger context of prophetic history developed in the Old Testament. The intention within this section, therefore, will be to provide a detailed analysis of 1 Cor. 14.20-25 in order to examine the nature of the influence of the prophetic tradition on Paul's argument concerning the shape and function of prophecy.

a. *Exhortation (1 Corinthians 14.20)*
Paul's exhortation in 1 Cor. 14.20 provides both a summation of the preceding argument and an introduction to the particular emphasis of the subsequent material. The reference to notions of childishness (παιδία) and maturity (τέλειοι) provides a contrast that harks back to the preceding argument of 1 Cor. 14.6-19 in which Paul succinctly argued that unintelligible discourse does not edify the community. There may also be correspondence at this point with the references to childishness in 1 Cor. 13.11.[69] Paul's intention, however, does not appear to be to disparage a particular gift, but to express to the Corinthians that their understanding of the gift and the behaviour resulting from its use created an inadequate, and potentially harmful, situation.

The verse itself is structured concentrically around the exhortation to avoid wickedness (τῇ κακίᾳ νηπιάζετε), with the first and third clauses providing the basic contrast between childishness and maturity in relation to the Corinthians' thought life (ταῖς φρεσίν). In light of the self-abasing paradigm established in 1 Corinthians 13 it seems likely that

---

the Corinthians (2d ed.; BNTC; London: Black, 1971), 324; Héring, *First Corinthians*, 152; Simon J. Kistemaker, *1 Corinthians* (Grand Rapids: Baker, 1993), 500; Jack W. MacGorman, *The Gifts of the Spirit: An Exposition of 1 Corinthians 12–14* (Nashville: Broadman & Holman, 1974), 96.

68. For an analysis of the terms ἰδιῶται and ἄπιστοι, see Stephen J. Chester, 'Divine Madness? Speaking in Tongues in 1 Corinthians 14.23', *JSNT* 27 (2005): 417-46 (418 n. 2). Within this section of Paul's argument the terms appear to function synonymously, referring primarily to those outside of the community.

69. Fitzmyer, *First Corinthians*, 519; Thiselton, *First Corinthians*, 1119.

Paul's use of the term κακός in the central portion of the exhortation refers more explicitly to a behavioural rather than a philosophical category, emphasizing the necessity to avoid activities that are unethical or result in the division of the community.[70] The emphasis of the admonition, therefore, likely refers back to 1 Cor. 14.13-17 where the Corinthians were encouraged to ensure that their use of tongues within the assembly resulted in the edification of the community and not simply themselves. In other words, there appears to be a focus on the value of the use of particular forms of speech for the benefit of others, and Paul is again exhorting the Corinthians to act sensibly with regard to the rest of the community.[71] Thus, as Fee aptly states: '[t]heir childishness consists of *thinking* improperly that tongues serves [sic] as evidence of their new transcendent spirituality…while in fact they evidence all kinds of ethical/ behavioural aberrations'.[72] Paul's initial exhortation, therefore, rephrases the preceding argument concerning the need to think and behave in a way that is cognizant of the entire community, or, in negative terms, in a way that does not seek only self-edification. The argument of the following verses continues to emphasize the effects of the Corinthians' actions in order to highlight that their level of maturity in using spiritual gifts will have both private and public consequences.

b. *Scriptural Quotation (1 Corinthians 14.21)*
Paul moves from the transitional exhortation in 1 Cor. 14.20 to a quotation of Isa. 28.11-12 in 1 Cor. 14.21.[73] The import of the quotation within the passage, however, is not immediately transparent. The opaque nature of Paul's argument at this point is the result of several exegetical difficulties stemming predominantly from the quotation itself. Initially, the narrative movement of the original context of the quotation is somewhat ambiguous due to several exegetical and literary complexities within Isaiah 28. These difficulties make the determination of the purpose of the quotation more complex, particularly with regard to the hermeneutical question of whether there is an immediate connection between the Isaianic and Corinthian situations. Furthermore, although it is relatively

---

70. Garland, *1 Corinthians*, 645.
71. Cf. Garland, *1 Corinthians*, 645; Thomas W. Gillespie, *The First Theologians: A Study in Early Christian Prophecy* (Grand Rapids: Eerdmans, 1994), 159; Schnabel, *1 Korintherbrief*, 815.
72. Fee, *First Corinthians*, 679. Original emphasis.
73. Paul's claim that the quotation is ἐν τῷ νόμῳ γέγραπται is likely a generic statement, with νόμος referring to the entire Old Testament, as in Rom. 3.19 and Jn 10.34; cf. Fitzmyer, *First Corinthians*, 519; Fee, *First Corinthians*, 679 n. 19.

transparent that Paul is in fact referencing at least a portion of Isaiah 28, identifying the apostle's *Vorlage* (or *Vorlagen*) at this point is nearly impossible.[74] The realization that Paul's text-form differs widely from earlier forms of Isaiah 28 raises further questions concerning Paul's presentation of the relationship between unarticulated tongues and prophetic speech at this point of the argument. Thus, although questions concerning the internal coherence of Paul's discourse, as well as broader hermeneutical questions concerning the relationship between the Isaianic narrative and the Corinthian situation, become more transparent in connection with the relationship between the two brief assertions (1 Cor. 14.22) and the following hypothetical illustrations (1 Cor. 14.23-25), the quotation itself functions as a catalyst for questions concerning both the form and rhetorical purpose of Paul's argument.

(1) *The Old Testament Context of Isaiah 28.11-12.* In order to examine the function of Paul's quotation in 1 Cor. 14.21 it will be helpful to provide a brief analysis of the context surrounding Isa. 28.11-12. Isaiah 28 stands as the first portion of the larger literary unit comprised of Isaiah 28–35. Despite numerous questions concerning the redaction history of this particular section of Isaiah, the unit likely pertains to the historical period between the fall of Samaria in 722 B.C.E. and the attack on Jerusalem by Sennacherib in 701 B.C.E., the so-called Assyrian crisis.[75] The literary structure of the larger unit is built primarily on a series of woe oracles.[76] In terms of the specific context of Paul's quotation, Isaiah 28 can be divided into four smaller units: Isa. 28.1-6, 7-13, 14-22, and 23-29. The first section, Isa. 28.1-6, represents the first of the representative woe oracles and functions as an introductory frame for the entire chapter. The section establishes the previous experience of the northern kingdom

---

74. See Christopher D. Stanley, *Paul and the Language of Scripture: Citation Technique in the Pauline Epistles and Contemporary Literature* (SNTSMS 74; Cambridge: Cambridge University Press, 1992), 197-205. Stanley surmises that '[d]etermining the precise relationship between the wording of 1 Cor. 14.21 and the text of the LXX is one of the greatest challenges in the entire corpus of Pauline citations' (198).

75. Isa. 28.1-6, however, may reflect a period before the fall of the northern kingdom. See, e.g., Brevard S. Childs, *Isaiah* (OTL; Louisville: Westminster John Knox, 2001), 199-200; cf. Childs, *Isaiah and the Assyrian Crisis* (SBT 2/3; London: SCM, 1967); Gerhard F. Hasel, *The Remnant: The History and Theology of the Remnant Idea from Genesis to Isaiah* (AUM 5; Berrien Springs, Mich.: Andrews University Press, 1982), 305.

76. Léo Laberge, 'The Woe-Oracles of Isaiah 28–33', *EgT* 13 (1982): 157-90; cf. Childs, *Isaiah*, 199.

as a means of warning concerning the impending judgment of Judah. The explicitly negative material within Isa. 28.1-4, however, is balanced by a somewhat different contextual emphasis in Isa. 28.5-6, marked grammatically by the introduction of the eschatological formula ביום ההוא.[77] The focus of Isa. 28.5-6 provides a positive contrast to the notion of judgment, describing the eschatological exaltation of the Lord and the corresponding restoration of a faithful remnant. Moreover, this succinct distinction between judgment and hope provides a framework for the following sections of Isaiah 28 and the larger section of Isaiah 28–35, expressing the particular contrast between the result of trusting either in foreign alliances or in 'God's wisdom and purpose'.[78]

The second unit of the passage, Isa. 28.7-13, returns to the initial emphasis on judgment through its negative portrayal of Judah's religious leaders.[79] The repetitive structure and terminology of Isa. 28.7-8 function literarily to emphasize the drunken and irresponsible state of the leaders, 'with these religious specialists staggering around, surrounded by vomit and excrement'.[80] The stark differences between the themes illustrated in Isa. 28.5-6 and those described in Isa. 28.7-8 bring forth an overtly negative picture of the leaders as those who have put themselves in a position in which they are completely incapable of fulfilling their political and religious duties. The result is a type of implicit *qal wahomer* (*a minore ad maius*) argument in which the reader is drawn to see the inevitability of the destructive result of such behaviour in light of the earlier situation faced by the northern kingdom (Isa. 28.1-4). Isaiah 28.9-10 provides more specific evidence of the failure of the religious leaders as they are placed in direct opposition with Isaiah himself. Although there is no specific grammatical evidence that these verses contain a change in speaker, it seems most likely, especially in view of the prophet's response in Isa. 28.13, that these two verses represent a quotation derived from the representatively negative approach of Isaiah's opponents.[81] In light of this

77. Childs, *Isaiah*, 205.
78. Childs, *Isaiah*, 206; cf. J. Cheryl Exum, '"Who Will He Teach Knowledge?": A Literary Approach to Isaiah 28', in *Art and Meaning: Rhetoric in Biblical Literature* (ed. David J.A. Clines, David M. Gunn, and Alan J. Hauser; JSOTSup 19; Sheffield: JSOT, 1982), 112-17.
79. Contra John N. Oswalt, *The Book of Isaiah* (2 vols.; NICOT; Grand Rapids: Eerdmans, 1986), 1:509, who argues that Isa. 28.7-13 represents a more specific accusation against the leaders of Ephraim.
80. Joseph Blenkinsopp, *Isaiah 1–39* (AB 19; New York: Doubleday, 2000), 389.
81. It is possible, however, that these verses represent an actual historical exchange between Isaiah and his opponents (Oswalt, *Isaiah*, 1:509). Several additional interpretations of these verses have arisen due to the lack of an explicit

understanding, Isa. 28.9-10 offers a negative reading of Isaiah's message as suitable merely for infants. This may provide support for the notion that the unintelligible Hebrew syllables in Isa. 28.10 (i.e. צו לצו צו לצו קו לקו קו לקו) represent a pattern of teaching the alphabet to small children.[82] The opponents' argument, therefore, would be that Isaiah's teaching is overtly simplistic and at a level beneath their educated position.[83] This succession of syllables, however, may merely represent a string of nonsensical mockery, in which the opponents claim that Isaiah's message sounds as if it is completely incomprehensible and consequently useless in light of their current situation.[84] Irrespective of the various historical backgrounds put forth for this string of syllables, their contextual purpose is made explicit within the judgmental context of Isa. 28.11-13. The religious leaders' irresponsible behaviour and rejection of the Lord's initial message (Isa. 28.12) become the catalyst for a word of judgment against the people through the use of לעגי שפה and לשון אחר. The word of judgment itself is brought forth in Isa. 28.13 through an exact repetition of the string of syllables in Isa. 28.10. The infantile or nonsensical words offered by Isaiah's opponents are turned against them as the word of God becomes completely unintelligible to them because of their rebellion.[85] The entirety of Isa. 28.7-13 seems to emphasize the notion that the 'stammering lips' and 'foreign speech' in Isa. 28.11 are a sign of judgment against the Israelites for their rejection of the divine message issued through Isaiah. The nonsensical speech given by the Lord in Isa. 28.13, therefore, points to the negative result of being obdurate with respect to the prophetic message.

The intersection between judgment and hope within this chapter continues in Isa. 28.14-22. The balance between these two themes is

---

definition of the speaker in Isa. 28.9-10. Apart from the present interpretation, the most common reading is that these verses represent a lament of either Isaiah or YHWH over the impoverished spiritual state of the southern kingdom (e.g. Exum, 'Whom Will He Teach', 120-21). For a list of additional interpretative possibilities, see Duke L. Kwon, 'Obfuscation and Restoration: Paul's Use of Isaiah in 1 Corinthians 14:20-25' (Th.M. thesis, Gordon-Conwell Theological Seminary, 2004), 24 n. 81; Oswalt, *Isaiah*, 1:512 n. 36.

82. The primary basis for this view is the study of William W. Hallo, 'Isaiah 28.9-13 and the Ugaritic Abecedaries', *JBL* 77 (1958): 324-38 (esp. 337 n. 34), where he builds on the work of R.H. Kennett, *Ancient Hebrew Social Life and Custom as Indicated in Law, Narrative and Metaphor* (Oxford: Oxford University Press, 1933).

83. Blenkinsopp, *Isaiah 1–39*, 389-90.

84. See Grudem, '1 Corinthians 14.20-25', 382-85, for the argument that these syllables were never meant to be understood as complete, intelligible words.

85. Childs, *Isaiah*, 207; Oswalt, *Isaiah*, 1:512.

upheld through a further description of the initial word of judgment pronounced in Isa. 28.13 and a more positive claim in Isa. 28.16-17 concerning God's promise to establish a new cornerstone that will not be subject to the same judgment. In spite of the impending judgment due to their willingness to create improper foreign alliances, hope of renewal is offered through the establishment of a cornerstone, which functions throughout Isaiah as a symbol for God's new work of restoration through the messianic rule.[86] Conversely, the stone metaphor also functions negatively within Isaiah, referring to a 'stumbling block' that causes the people to fall (cf. Isa. 8.14-15).[87] In light of this dual function, the stone imagery at this point of Isaiah 28 may conjoin the contextual notions of judgment and hope as it portrays the different effects of God's work in relation to different groups of people.

Connected with the theme of God's work, and potentially more important for Paul's use of Isaiah 28, is the characterization of God's work in Isa. 28.21 as both 'strange' (זר) and 'alien' (נכרי). As an analogy to the way in which God worked upon Mount Perazim (cf. 2 Sam. 5.17-25), God's plan is pictured as unintelligible. The word of judgment that was expressed in a language unknown to the people is now expressed in a divine action that is itself incomprehensible. Yet, as Childs argues, the final section of the chapter, Isa. 28.23-29, provides a theocentric analogy meant to establish that even though the work of the Lord may seem unintelligible to his people, it is still a part of his overarching wisdom (Isa. 28.29).[88] In light of this argument it seems reasonable to assert that Isaiah 28 provides evidence for the way in which divine work may have both positive and negative results depending upon the state of the people toward which the work is directed. With specific regard to the immediate context of Isa. 28.11-12, the foreign speech and strange tongues function as a sign of judgment upon those who have responded to the prophetic word with hard-hearted rebellion. The rhetorical progression of Isaiah 28–35, however, places this particular occurrence of judgment within the larger framework of the movement from exile to restoration. The judgment expressed in Isaiah 28 is reversed in Isa. 33.19 as the obscure speech (עמקי שפה) and stammering tongue (נלעג לשון) of the foreign invaders are removed from the people's presence. The close verbal parallels between these two passages seemingly move the narrative from the initial notion of judgment to the theme of eschatological restoration,

---

86. Childs, *Isaiah*, 209-10.
87. J. Alec Motyer, *The Prophecy of Isaiah* (Downers Grove, Ill.: InterVarsity, 1993), 95; cf. Childs, *Isaiah*, 210.
88. Childs, *Isaiah*, 210-11.

which frames a significant portion of the rest of Isaiah.[89] It may be helpful, therefore, to recognize that within the Isaianic narrative the unintelligible divine speech in Isa. 28.13 and its subsequent removal serve as a reference to the movement from exile to restoration.

(2) *Paul's Use of the Isaianic Material.* Paul's particular rendition of Isa. 28.11-12 comports neither with the MT nor with the LXX.[90] In terms of the logical flow of the passage, however, Paul's version appears to mirror more closely the narrative emphases within the MT. This assertion stems from the fact that the LXX departs from a strict translation of the Hebrew original at several points.[91] Nevertheless, Paul's version bears textual and logical discrepancies with both the Hebrew and Greek traditions. In contrast with the LXX, Paul's initial prepositional phrase, ἐν ἑτερογλώσσοις καὶ ἐν χείλεσιν ἑτέρων, replaces διὰ φαυλισμὸν χειλέων διὰ γλώσσης ἑτέρας. The two most significant variations within this substitution are the apparent reversal of γλῶσσα and χεῖλος and Paul's particular word choice.[92] It is difficult to determine the precise function of the first variation due to the fact that there is no extant textual evidence for the reversed order of γλῶσσα and χεῖλος found in Paul's version.[93] Although it is possible that either Paul or a previous translator simply rendered

---

89. Kwon, 'Obfuscation and Restoration', 49-50.

90. The extent of the differences depends primarily on the way in which the variations are classified. The number of presumably intentional changes ranges from four (e.g. Fee, *First Corinthians*, 680) to nine (e.g. Garland, *1 Corinthians*, 646-47; Kwon, 'Obfuscation and Restoration', 61-72).

91. For a comparative analysis of the MT and LXX versions, see Kwon, 'Obfuscation and Restoration', 57-60. For an analysis of the recent history of the text of Isaiah, see Armin Lange, *Die Handschriften biblischer Bücher von Qumran und den anderen Fundorten* (vol. 1 of *Handbuch der Textfunde vom Toten Meer*; Tübingen: Mohr Siebeck, 2009), 257-96.

92. The transition from διά to ἐν likely stems from the use of ב in the MT, but does not represent a significant variation from the LXX with regard to the second phrase, διὰ γλώσσης ἑτέρας. The use of διά plus the accusative in the first phrase of the LXX likely reflects the particle כִּי in the MT. The Lucianic LXX tradition, however, reads διὰ φαυλισμοῦ χειλέων, aligning the text more closely with the parallel structure of the MT.

93. Origen, *Philoc.* 9.2, however, claims, εὗρον γὰρ τὰ ἰσοδυναμοῦντα τῇ λέξει ταύτῃ ἐν τῇ τοῦ Ἀκύλου ἑρμενείᾳ κείμενα. Nevertheless, it may be inappropriate to understand τὰ ἰσοδυναμοῦντα as referring to a strict correspondence between the two versions since this type of divergence from the MT would not correlate well with Aquila's potentially more literal translation practice (so Emil Kautzsch, *De Veteris Testamenti locis a Paulo Apostolo allegatis* [Leipzig: Metzger & Wittig, 1869], 99; cf. Stanley, *Paul and the Language of Scripture*, 199).

בלעגי שפה and בלשון אחרת as ἐν ἑτερογλώσσοις and ἐν χείλεσιν ἑτέρων, respectively, it seems more likely that Paul reverses the order of the closely synonymous phrases in light of the contextual importance of the term γλῶσσα.[94] In addition, Paul's actual word choice diverges from the LXX tradition. Although the compound ἑτερόγλωσσος and the phrase χεῖλος ἑτέρων (cf. Acts 2.4) are found only here within the Pauline corpus, their meaning and function within the present verse are fairly clear. Both terms refer to the means (ἐν) by which the unintelligible divine discourse is spoken (λαλήσω). In other words, although there is variation with respect to both order and lexeme, there is likely no difference with respect to meaning between Paul and Isaiah at this point, with both focusing on the audience's inability to understand the message because of its unintelligible nature. If Paul does intend to offer a unique emphasis at this point of the quotation, then the best evidence for such a change may stem from his repeated use of the term ἕτερος. Kwon posits that the repeated use of the adjective reasserts Paul's emphasis on the potentially unintelligible character of unarticulated tongues (cf. 1 Cor. 14.11) and connects the present paragraph with the preceding argument concerning the edification of the entire community (cf. ὁ ἕτερος in 1 Cor. 14.17).[95] Thus, Paul does not appear to be appropriating the Isaiah passage because of a correlation between the types of languages being spoken in the two contexts; rather, the comparison at this point seems to revolve around the way in which the respective audiences perceive the speech forms.

Paul's potentially unique emphasis may also be evident in his use of the first person singular λαλήσω, which diverges both from the third person singular (ידבר) of the MT and the third person plural (λαλήσουσιν) of the LXX in Isa. 28.11. This variation represents the most substantial difference between the MT and the LXX. The LXX's use of the third person plural seemingly places the content of the following speech in the mouths of either the future invaders or the drunken leaders discussed in Isa. 28.1-7, in contrast to the third person singular of the MT in which the referent is either Isaiah or YHWH. In connection with this variation, the message of Isa. 28.12 is itself changed. Whereas the MT presents a *previous* (אמר) positive message from YHWH which was rejected, the LXX appears to present the speech as the message *expected* (λέγοντες in conjunction with λαλήσουσιν) to be given through the foreign enemies (διὰ

---

94. Fee, *First Corinthians*, 680; cf. Schnabel, *1 Korintherbrief*, 818. Contra Stanley, *Paul and the Language of Scripture*, 199.

95. Kwon, 'Obfuscation and Restoration', 62-64; cf. Conzelmann, *1 Corinthians*, 242 n. 19.

γλώσσης ἑτέρας).⁹⁶ Therefore, within the LXX the Israelites' disobedience (καὶ οὐκ ἠθέλησαν ἀκούειν) may actually be understood as a mark of 'valiant endurance' in which the people avoid capitulating to the Assyrians.⁹⁷ Within the LXX, however, the people are still eventually seen to be culpable due to their previous mocking of the prophetic message in conjunction with the disobedient leaders (Isa. 28.7-9), and they eventually suffer the same (exilic) fate described in the MT (Isa. 28.13). As with the MT, Paul's emphasis in 1 Cor. 14.21 appears to be on the divine origin of the speech, which in the Isaianic narrative eventually functions negatively as an 'anticipatory reference to the exile'.⁹⁸ Yet, it is precisely this strong notion of judgment against the Israelites (τῷ λαῷ τούτῳ) which is used as evidence that Paul either misunderstands or reinvents the meaning of Isaiah 28 within the context of 1 Corinthians.⁹⁹ It is likely going too far, however, to evaluate Paul's inclusion or exclusion of the judgmental nature of Isaiah 28 simply from the text-form of the quotation. In contrast, the theological import of the Isaiah passage more likely surfaces within Paul's application of the quotation in 1 Cor. 14.22-25. At this point, it seems plausible to argue that the beginning of Paul's quotation coheres with the rhetorical movement of the MT of Isaiah 28 and coordinates in at least some respects with his own preceding discussion about tongues and prophetic speech in 1 Corinthians 12–14.

The rest of Paul's quotation also diverges considerably from both the MT and the LXX. Primarily, Paul omits the content of the message given in Isa. 28.12. Although the content of the omitted material does not appear to factor largely into Paul's argument, the omission itself functions as a catalyst for the non-exact nature of the final portion of the

---

96. The correlation between God's speech and that of the foreign invaders may have been a catalyst for the LXX translator(s) to edit the text, in order to avoid any negative anthropomorphic connections between YHWH and the Assyrians. See, e.g., Charles T. Fritsch, 'The Concept of God in the Greek Translation of Isaiah', in *Biblical Studies in Memory of H.C. Alleman* (ed. Jacob M. Myers, O. Reimherr, and H.N. Bream; Locust Valley, N.Y.: Augustin, 1960), 155-69; cf. David A. Baer, *When We All Go Home: Translation and Theology in LXX Isaiah 56–66* (JSOTSup 318; Sheffield: Sheffield Academic, 2001); Marshall S. Hurwitz, 'The Septuagint of Isaiah 36–39 in Relation to That of 1–35, 40–66', *HUCA* 28 (1957): 75-83.

97. David E. Lanier, 'With Stammering Lips and Another Tongue: 1 Cor 14:20-22 and Isa 28:11-12', *CTR* 5 (1991): 259-86 (263).

98. Kwon, 'Obfuscation and Restoration', 65.

99. E.g. Karl Olav Sandnes, 'Prophecy—A Sign for Believers (1 Cor 14,20-25)', *Bib* 77 (1996): 1-15 (7); cf. Otto Michel, *Paulus und seine Bibel* (Darmstadt: Wissenschaftliche Buchgesellschaft, 1972), 167-68.

quotation. For example, Paul's use of the phrase οὐδ' οὕτως in place of οὐκ (or ולא) appears to serve 'a vital role in bridging the gap created by the elimination of Isa. 28.12a from the citation'.[100] Despite the fact that this substitution serves to connect the earlier and later portions of the quotation, the transition away from the simple adversative to the more concessive notion inherent in οὐδ' οὕτως seemingly results in a movement away from the idea in the MT that the unintelligible speech is caused by the unwillingness of the people to listen toward the notion that they will not listen (εἰσακούσονται) in spite of the unintelligible speech. Furthermore, the entire phrase, καὶ οὐδ' οὕτως εἰσακούσονταί μου, represents a departure from previous textual traditions of Isa. 28.12. The extensive differences between this part of the quotation and earlier textual traditions may point to the notion that Paul is no longer citing exclusively from Isaiah 28. Stanley posits that 1 Cor. 14.21 represents a conflated citation (cf. Rom. 9.27, 33; 10.6-8; 11.8), with the first portion of the material stemming from Isa. 28.11-12 and this final section referencing the frequently repeated prophetic indictment against the Israelites that οὐκ εἰσήκουσαν μου (e.g. Mic. 5.5; Jer. 7.24, 26; 13.11; 25.7; Zech. 1.4; cf. Zech. 7.13).[101] Kwon, however, argues that this terminology represents a consistent theme throughout the narrative of Isaiah concerning the continued spiritual obduracy of the people in spite of the exile (cf. Isa. 1.19, 20; 30.9, 15; 42.23, 24).[102] It is possible, however, that Paul's understanding at this point may simply reflect the conclusion of Isa. 28.13 in which the effect of the speech is also pictured in destructive terms.[103] The view that the phrase represents a broader connection to the larger prophetic corpus is strengthened by Paul's addition of λέγει κύριος at the close of the quotation. The phrase occurs in conjunction with forms of εἰσακούω in both Zech. 1.4 and 7.13, both of which relate to the rebellion against the earlier prophets and the consequential judgment associated with the exile. In light of this connection, it may be possible to argue with Kwon that 'Paul's specific phrasing serves as an echo/allusion to Zechariah's retrospective reflection upon Israel's history of obduracy according to the account of the former prophets'.[104] It seems likely, therefore, that Paul's final statement in 1 Cor. 14.21 (καὶ οὐδ' οὕτως εἰσακούσονταί μου, λέγει κύριος) echoes or alludes to broader themes within the prophetic

100. Stanley, *Paul and the Language of Scripture*, 203.
101. Stanley, *Paul and the Language of Scripture*, 203-5.
102. Kwon, 'Obfuscation and Restoration', 68-71.
103. Grudem, '1 Corinthians 14.20-25', 386 n. 19.
104. Kwon, 'Obfuscation and Restoration', 72.

literature which stem out of the context of Isaiah 28. Thus, Paul may locate his understanding of the judgment described in Isaiah 28 within the larger historical framework of the prophetic literature, potentially emphasizing the broader movement from exile to restoration pictured both within Isaiah 28–35 and the larger prophetic corpus.[105]

### c. *Inspired Speech in the Assembly (1 Corinthians 14.22-25)*

Although the quotation of Isaiah 28 in 1 Cor. 14.21 constitutes a starting point for understanding the intersection between the Isaianic and Corinthian situations, the material in 1 Cor. 14.22-25 appears to provide Paul's own understanding of the function of the quotation within the present context.[106] Rather than bringing immediate clarity to the use of the Isaiah passage, however, these verses add to the complexity of Paul's argument in this section of 1 Corinthians due to the apparent contradiction between the assertions in 1 Cor. 14.22 and their corresponding illustrations in 1 Cor. 14.23-25.[107] More specifically, it seems that what Paul affirms about the use of both unarticulated tongues and prophetic speech is reversed within the illustrations, particularly with regard to their effect on the hypothetical outsiders. In spite of the complexity of the argument at this point, however, these verses provide a helpful outline for a portion of Paul's understanding of the character and function of prophetic speech within the Corinthian community.

The assertions in 1 Cor. 14.22 likely represent Paul's rhetorical inference from the preceding quotation (cf. ὥστε), although the second assertion may function independently from the Isaiah quotation as an 'anticipated conclusion' derived from the final hypothetical illustration in 1 Cor. 14.24-25.[108] Apart from this grammatical connection between 1 Cor. 14.21 and 14.22, the actual rhetorical import of 1 Cor. 14.22 is constrained due to questions concerning both the structure of the verse and the meaning of the term σημεῖον.[109] It seems that the antithetic parallelism in both assertions provides evidence for reading the second half of the verse as an elliptical contrast of the first, with εἰς σημεῖόν εἰσιν

---

105. See, e.g., Mark J. Boda, 'From Fasts to Feasts: The Literary Function of Zechariah 7–8', *CBQ* 65 (2003): 390-407. Cf. VanGemeren, *Prophetic Word*, 194.
106. Contra Johanson, 'Tongues', 193-94.
107. Joop Smit, 'Tongues and Prophecy: Deciphering 1 Cor 14,22', *Bib* 75 (1994): 175-90, argues that 'the contradiction with the adjacent illustrations is insoluble' (175).
108. See Sandnes, 'Prophecy', 12-15, for the argument that 1 Cor. 14.22b does not stem primarily from the Isaiah quotation.
109. Cf. Fee, *First Corinthians*, 681.

functioning in both the assertion regarding unarticulated tongues and that pertaining to prophetic speech.[110] Furthermore, the prepositional phrase εἰς σημεῖον presumably functions in place of the predicate nominative expected with εἰσίν, rendering the initial portion of the two affirmations as 'tongues are a sign' and 'prophetic speech is a sign', respectively.[111] In terms of structure, therefore, the verse provides two separate assertions which relate unarticulated tongues and prophetic speech to the community (τοῖς πιστεύουσιν) and to outsiders (τοῖς ἀπίστοις).

More complex, however, is the determination of the way in which unarticulated tongues and prophetic speech relate to these two divergent groups. The ambiguous nature of the assertions arises primarily from Paul's use of the noun σημεῖον. The term occurs seven other times within Paul's epistles (i.e. Rom. 4.11; 15.19; 1 Cor. 1.22; 2 Cor. 12.12 [×2]; 2 Thess. 2.9; 3.17), but none of these occurrences provides a close parallel to the present argument.[112] In light of the rhetorical connection between the assertions and the quotation from Isaiah 28, the function of σημεῖον within the narrative of Isaiah may provide insight into the meaning of Paul's argument. Within the prophetic literature the term אוֹת (LXX: σημεῖον) frequently represents 'a special event, either ordinary or miraculous, that serves as a pledge by which to confirm the prophetic word'.[113] Based on this general definition, the term itself does not appear to be invested with either a strictly positive or negative meaning; rather, it seems to function more neutrally as that object or event which affirms the reality of the prophetic word. The semantic neutrality of the term lends credence to the notion that a prophetic sign can have a dual function within the same context, serving as a message of judgment against one group while simultaneously functioning as a means of blessing or restoration for another.[114] Because of this dual function the identity of the audience may play a prominent role in the determination of whether a

---

110. E.g. Fee, *First Corinthians*, 682; Garland, *1 Corinthians*, 648; Grudem, '1 Corinthians 14.20-25', 389-89; Sandnes, 'Prophecy', 10; Schrage, *1 Korintherbrief*, 3:408; contra O. Palmer Robertson, 'Tongues: Sign of Covenantal Curse and Blessing', *WTJ* 38 (1975): 43-53 (52); Krister Stendahl, *Paul Among Jews and Gentiles* (Philadelphia: Fortress, 1976), 116 n. 9.

111. BDAG, s.v. εἰς; BDF, 80-81; cf. Grudem, '1 Corinthians 14.20-25', 388 n. 23.

112. Garland, *1 Corinthians*, 649. For an extensive analysis of the term outside of the Pauline corpus, see Karl Heinrich Rengstorf, 'σημεῖον, κτλ.', *TDNT* 7:200-69.

113. Childs, *Isaiah*, 65; cf. Colin Brown and Otfried Hofius, 'σημεῖον', *NIDNTT* 2:626-33.

114. Paul A. Kruger, 'אוֹת', *NIDOTTE* 1:331-33.

sign is to be understood positively or negatively.¹¹⁵ The sign of Immanuel in Isaiah 7, for example, functions either as a word of judgment (Isa. 7.17) or as a word of salvation (Isa. 7.16) depending on the audience being addressed.¹¹⁶ This same type of dual function can be seen in the larger Old Testament corpus, with signs functioning either positively or negatively depending upon the identity of the addressees (e.g. the dual function of the 'signs' in the context of the exodus with respect to Pharaoh and the Israelites).¹¹⁷ In light of this overarching function it seems reasonable to argue that individual signs serve as the means by which God expresses his attitude concerning a particular situation, with either positive or negative consequences resulting depending on the particular audiences that are addressed.

If Paul's assertions in 1 Cor. 14.22 do in fact represent the inference being drawn from the Isaiah quotation, then the claim that unarticulated tongues serve as a sign for those who do not believe is arguably a negative assertion. That is, with Schnabel, it is possible to argue with regard to the way in which Paul is incorporating the Isaiah passage that 'Paulus greift diesen Gedanken auf: das Reden in anderen Sprachen in den Versammlungen der korinthischen Gemeinde wird nicht zur Bekehrung der Ungläubigen führen, sondern zu weiterer Entfremdung'.¹¹⁸ Just as the unintelligible speech functioned within the context of Isaiah 28 as a witness against the people of Israel because of their rejection of Isaiah's message, so too do unarticulated tongues represent a sign of judgment against those who do not believe.¹¹⁹ It is crucial to note, however, that the negative estimation of unarticulated tongues at this point represents Paul's own view. In other words, Paul understands a correlation between the

---

115. Cf. Kwon, 'Obfuscation and Restoration', 38; Sandnes, 'Prophecy', 10-12; Thiselton, *First Corinthians*, 1123.

116. Childs, *Isaiah*, 66-69.

117. Grudem, '1 Corinthians 14.20-25', 390. See, e.g., Exod. 10.1-2; 11.9-10; Deut. 4.34-35; 6.22; 7.19; Neh. 9.10. Cf. D.A. Carson, *Showing the Spirit: A Theological Exposition of 1 Corinthians 12–14* (Grand Rapids: Baker, 1987), 115.

118. Schnabel, *1 Korintherbrief*, 819.

119. The notion that σημεῖον is negative within this context has received wide support. See, e.g., Otto Betz, 'σημεῖον', *EDNT* 3:240; Carson, *Showing the Spirit*, 113-14; Fee, *First Corinthians*, 682; Garland, *1 Corinthians*, 650-51; Grudem, '1 Corinthians 14.20-25', 390; Gerald Hovenden, *Speaking in Tongues: The New Testament Evidence in Context* (Sheffield: Sheffield Academic, 2002), 145-48; Lanier, 'With Stammering Lips', 281; Rengstorf, *TDNT* 8:259; Schnabel, *1 Korintherbrief*, 819; Thiselton, *First Corinthians*, 1126; Weiss, *1 Korintherbrief*, 331-34; Antoinette Clark Wire, *The Corinthian Women Prophets: A Reconstruction Through Paul's Rhetoric* (Minneapolis: Fortress, 1990), 140.

foreign speech in Isaiah and the use of unarticulated tongues at Corinth because of their inability to bring about restoration. The improper use of tongues, therefore, does nothing to change the 'exilic' condition of the outsiders; they remain unconverted, as the contrast developed in 1 Cor. 14.24-25 illustrates (cf. δέ in 1 Cor. 14.24).

In contrast to his own view, Paul's presentation of the reaction to the activity in the assembly in 1 Cor. 14.23 (i.e. οὐκ ἐροῦσιν ὅτι μαίνεσθε;) may show that the outsiders' own perception of the Corinthians' unarticulated tongues was positive.[120] Debate at this point surrounds the contextual meaning of the verb μαίνομαι. Although Forbes has consistently shown that there is no *direct* correlation between any Graeco-Roman activity and the Christian phenomenon of glossolalia,[121] it seems plausible to argue that those outside of the Christian community in Corinth may have understood the use of unarticulated tongues as representative of the same types of activity normally associated with μαίνομαι and its cognates in the larger Hellenistic setting.[122] Witnessing unarticulated tongues within the Christian assembly may have alerted the outsiders to the fact that some form of divine activity was taking place within the Christian gathering.[123] With Forbes and Thiselton, however, it may be possible to read the outsiders' response negatively, as a simple affirmation of the insane nature of the congregation's activity. This would allow for Paul's presentation of the outsiders' claim to fit within the larger framework of μαίνομαι and its cognates in the LXX and the New Testament, where the terms uniformly have a negative connotation (e.g. *4 Macc.* 7.5; 8.5; 10.13; Wis. 14.28; Jn 10.20; Acts 26.24-25).[124]

Apart from the lexical debate surrounding μαίνομαι, it seems that Paul's contention becomes clear primarily in light of the quotation from Isaiah 28. Tongues are a spiritual gift (1 Cor. 12.10) and may be representative of divine activity to both those within the community and those outside it, but they do not result in the conversion of the outsider or, in terms of the larger Isaianic narrative, in the restoration of the community. Thus, in spite of the notion that μαίνομαι may in fact be positive with respect to the outsiders' perception (and possibly the Corinthians'),

120. Chester, 'Divine Madness', 417-46.
121. Forbes, *Prophecy*, 44-187.
122. Chester, 'Divine Madness', 428-29; cf. Dale B. Martin, 'Tongues of Angels and Other Status Indicators', *JAAR* 59 (1991): 547-89 (esp. 548 n. 4).
123. See the analysis of μαίνομαι in Chester, 'Divine Madness', 421-29. Forbes, *Prophecy*, 174, admits that unarticulated tongues may have been 'interpreted by [the outsiders] as evidence of some form of divine activity'.
124. Thiselton, *First Corinthians*, 1126; Forbes, *Prophecy*, 174; cf. Schrage, *1 Korintherbrief*, 3:409.

this does not require Paul's statement that 'tongues are a sign for unbelievers' to be positive.[125] Indeed, a positive association by the outsiders between the Corinthians' practice and other forms of Hellenistic religious activity would likely further Paul's negative estimation of the use of unarticulated tongues within the community, since it would reflect another instance of the Corinthians' view that their experience of the Spirit was (merely) a superior extension of their previous experience of Graeco-Roman religious activities (cf. 1 Cor. 12.2).[126] For this reason, it seems plausible to argue that Paul presents his own estimation of unarticulated tongues as representative of the judgmental context manifested in Isaiah 28 in contrast with that of the outsiders' perception in order to correct the Corinthians' inappropriate estimation and use of tongues.[127] Additionally, Paul's claim that unarticulated tongues are not a sign for the believing community may serve as secondary evidence that Paul's initial assertion in 1 Cor. 14.22 is negative. That is, those inside the community may be faced with a context in which judgment and obfuscation, represented by the use of unarticulated tongues, are prevailing over against the message of the gospel, resulting in the believing community feeling like outsiders within their own gathering, 'an inappropriate situation for the people of God'.[128] Despite the somewhat tentative nature of this secondary evidence, it seems reasonable to conclude, at least with respect to the relationship between unarticulated tongues and the unbelieving community, that the quotation in 1 Cor. 14.21 provided a means for Paul to reference the broad theme of judgment in Isaiah 28. The negative aspect of Paul's assertion, however, does not arise primarily from the specific use of the term σημεῖον, but from the larger contextual

---

125. Contra Chester, 'Divine Madness', 417-46. Chester is surely correct to emphasize the fact that the passage contains different estimations of unarticulated tongues (i.e. Paul's, the outsiders', and the Corinthians'), but he allows his understanding of the outsiders' response to determine his understanding of Paul's argument in 1 Cor. 14.22. Even if the outsiders understood the phenomenon as positive, Paul's contrast between unarticulated tongues and prophetic speech remains.

126. John M.G. Barclay, 'Thessalonica and Corinth: Social Contrasts in Pauline Christianity', *JSNT* 47 (1992): 49-74 (70).

127. For the argument that the Corinthians understood tongues as a status marker, see Martin, 'Tongues of Angels', 547-89.

128. Thiselton, *First Corinthians*, 1123. Against Thiselton at this point, see Chester, 'Divine Madness', 445 n. 105, and Garland, *1 Corinthians*, 650-51. Garland argues that the result of the use of unarticulated tongues *vis-à-vis* the believing community is simply a lack of edification, which he contends is 'a more neutral result' (651). In defence of Thiselton, it may be argued that edification is one of Paul's primary emphases in 1 Cor. 14 and, consequently, the problems associated with its absence may form the basis of Paul's argument.

association between the Isaianic narrative and the effect of using unarticulated tongues within the Corinthian assembly. As with its use in the broader prophetic corpus, the term σημεῖον at this point seems to function primarily as a neutral confirmation of the prophetic word relayed in 1 Cor. 14.21. The negative aspect of the statement stems from the observation that the use of unarticulated tongues is representative of divine activity, but not effective in terms of restoring a relationship between the Lord and τῷ λαῷ τούτῳ.

Even if the negative implications of the first assertion are rooted primarily in the contextual emphasis of the initial Isaiah quotation, the nature of the rest of Paul's argument is not immediately clear. If the second assertion in 1 Cor. 14.22 is also meant to reflect the negative implications of Isaiah 28, then the difficulty in correlating the assertion with the corresponding illustration in 1 Cor. 14.24-25 is compounded, since Paul does not describe any form of negative result. Additionally, to argue that prophetic speech is a negative sign would seem to contradict Paul's earlier association between prophetic speech and edification (e.g. 1 Cor. 14.1-5, 19).[129] In light of these difficulties it seems more likely that the second assertion is meant to reflect a positive contrast with the first, allowing δέ to have a distinctly adversative function.[130] Understanding the second assertion as reflecting a positive situation, however, does not instantly resolve the potential conflict between the assertion and the corresponding illustration in 1 Cor. 14.24-25. For example, Paul asserts that prophetic speech is not a sign for the outsiders, but then relates its positive effect upon them.[131] Likewise, Paul asserts that prophetic speech is a sign for believers, but seems to provide no explicit evidence for that part of the assertion. In spite of these persistent complexities, it is possible to argue that, as with the first assertion, the larger context of the Isaiah quotation contributes to the meaning of Paul's argument. In other words, Paul's argument may mirror the connection in Isaiah 28 between judgment and hope, while also relating to the overarching movement from exile to restoration developed within Isaiah 28–35. Thus, whereas the use of unarticulated tongues was representative of the negative dimension of the Isaiah passage, the use of prophetic speech may correspond

---

129. Barrett, *First Corinthians*, 324, however, contends that prophecy is here a judgment against the Corinthians for emphasizing unarticulated tongues over a form of prophetic speech that could potentially lead to salvation. See also Witherington, *Conflict and Community in Corinth*, 285, where he attempts to combine the concepts of judgment and exhortation.
130. Cf. Grudem, '1 Corinthians 14.20-25', 388-89.
131. Hays, *First Corinthians*, 240.

to the positive development of restoration described in the larger narrative of Isaiah.

The notion that Paul is referencing the movement of the Isaianic narrative from judgment to restoration in his description of the different effects of the use of unarticulated tongues and prophetic speech may be most readily illustrated in his description of a hypothetical outsider's response to prophetic speech in 1 Cor. 14.25. It is generally recognized that the outsider's assertion that ὄντως ὁ θεὸς ἐν ὑμῖν ἐστιν is reminiscent of material within the biblical tradition.[132] The precise identification of the text to which Paul is alluding at this point is somewhat more difficult, with several different contexts potentially serving as the background for the formulation (e.g. Deut. 4.7; 1 Kgs 18.39; Isa. 45.14; Dan. 2.46-47; Zech. 8.23).[133] In terms of verbal similarities, however, it seems that Isa. 45.14 (ὁ θεὸς ἐν σοι ἐστιν) and Zech. 8.23 (ὁ θεὸς μεθ' ὑμῶν ἐστιν) provide the most reasonable options. The possibility that the final portion of the earlier quotation in 1 Cor. 14.21 (καὶ οὐδ' οὕτως εἰσακούσονταί μου, λέγει κύριος) stems from material in Zechariah may provide support for the argument that Paul is here echoing the language of Zech. 8.23.[134] Two additional factors, however, point to the likelihood that Isa. 45.14 is the primary text in Paul's view at this point. First, Paul's use of προσκυνήσει seemingly reflects the use of προσκυνήσουσιν in Isa. 45.14. Secondly, the primary reference to Isaiah in 1 Cor. 14.21 supports for the continued influence of the Isaianic narrative on the shape of Paul's argument.[135]

Despite disagreement concerning the rhetorical unity of Isaiah 44–46, it seems clear that the material within Isaiah 45 pertains to the culmination of the exilic period and focuses primarily on 'the unexpected salvation wrought by God through Cyrus'.[136] More specifically, the Isaianic

132. Fee, *First Corinthians*, 687.
133. For the range of possibilities, see Raymond F. Collins, *First Corinthians* (SP 7; Collegeville, Minn.: Liturgical, 1999), 510; Richard B. Hays, 'The Conversion of the Imagination: Scripture and Eschatology in 1 Corinthians', *NTS* 45 (1999): 291-412 (391-93); Kwon, 'Obfuscation and Restoration', 77; Francois S. Malan, 'The Use of the Old Testament in 1 Corinthians', *Neot* 14 (1981): 134-70 (157); Wilk, *Die Bedeutung des Jesajabuches*, 331-33.
134. Kwon, 'Obfuscation and Restoration', 78-79, provides two further arguments for Paul's use of Zechariah at this point: (1) verbal similarities between Isa. 28.11-12 and Zech. 8.23 may link the passages within the prophetic corpus, and (2) the use of μετά in Zech. 8.23 may refer to Isaiah's Immanuel motif, which functions in the background of Isa. 28.
135. Cf. Hays, 'Conversion', 393.
136. Childs, *Isaiah*, 355. On the rhetorical structure of this section, see Yehoshua Gitay, *Prophecy and Persuasion: A Study of Isaiah 40–48* (Bonn: Linguistica Biblica, 1981), 191-205.

emphasis on the sovereignty of YHWH becomes the basis for the reversal of the exilic relationship between Israel and the foreign invaders, who come to recognize the unique presence of YHWH among the people (Isa. 45.14). The stark dichotomy between the notions of judgment and restoration is manifested even more clearly in Isa. 45.20-25 as the division between Israel and the nations gives way to the new, restorative work of the Lord.[137] In contrast to the use of foreign nations in Isaiah 28 as a means of judgment against the people, the nations are now provided an opportunity to become a part of YHWH's new work (Isa. 45.22-25).

In terms of Paul's argument in 1 Cor. 14.20-25, the allusion to Isa. 45.14 appears to function as a means of referencing the Isaianic themes of conversion and eschatological restoration. Paul's description in 1 Cor. 14.24 of the outsider's experience (ἐλέγχεται ὑπὸ πάντων, ἀνακρίνεται ὑπὸ πάντων) emphasizes notions of both conviction of sin (ἐλέγχω) and judicial examination (ἀνακρίνω).[138] The import of these dual notions seems to be that prophetic speech results in the outsider becoming 'sensitized to previously unrecognized sin'.[139] This view is made explicit in Paul's following statement in 1 Cor. 14.25 that τὰ κρυπτὰ τῆς καρδίας αὐτοῦ φανερὰ γίνεται. The apparent thrust of this statement is that prophetic speech affects the entire life of the person, drawing on information both known and unknown to the outsider.[140] In other words, the prophetic speech of the community has the effect of exposing the outsider to a new understanding of himself or herself. However, despite the clearly personal effect of the prophetic speech, Paul does not provide explicit information concerning either the form or content of the Corinthians' prophetic activity. In light of this ambiguity it seems that Chester provides a balanced conclusion concerning the Corinthians' prophetic speech:

> On the one hand, it need not necessarily be specifically addressed to the individual outsider; on the other, the content needs to be exact enough for an outsider to be able to recognize previously hidden truths about his or her own life. Something more precise than…general proclamation…is required, but not necessarily a detailed revelation of the particular sins of a named individual.[141]

137. Childs, *Isaiah*, 355-56.
138. Thiselton, *First Corinthians*, 1128.
139. Stephen J. Chester, *Conversion at Corinth: Perspectives on Conversion in Paul's Theology and the Corinthian Church* (SNTW; London: T&T Clark International, 2003), 120.
140. Thiselton, *First Corinthians*, 1129.
141. Chester, *Conversion*, 120-21. Contra Grudem, '1 Corinthians 14.20-25', 394-95, who maintains that the prophetic activity at this point *must* include a presentation of the outsider's particular sin(s).

The effect of the prophetic speech on the outsider, however, may provide more clarity concerning Paul's understanding of its function within the community.

Paul's description of the physical response of the outsider (πεσὼν ἐπὶ πρόσωπον προσκυνήσει τῷ θεῷ) alludes to broad biblical concepts of obeisance and worship,[142] while the apostle's formulation of the outsider's verbal claim (ὄντως ὁ θεὸς ἐν ὑμῖν ἐστιν) places the conversion scene within the more specific eschatological framework of Isaiah. In light of the context of Paul's formulation it seems plausible to argue that the hypothetical conversion experience that he outlines functions as a microcosm of the restoration and inclusion described within the Isaianic narrative. The close relationship between Paul's language and the material in Isaiah 45 strengthens the connection between Paul's argument in 1 Cor. 14.20-25 and the movement in Isaiah from judgment to restoration. Paul's description of the outsider's conversion, therefore, parallels the theme of restoration transparent in Isaiah 45 (and Zech. 8), with prophetic activity functioning as the means by which the outsider is made a part of the community. On this reading the two references to Isaiah in 1 Cor. 14.20-25 point to the idea that 'Paul expects Isaiah's script to be performed and his eschatological vision to be realized in the midst of the gathered community as it exercises its prophetic ministry'.[143] In contrast with the exilic character of unarticulated tongues brought forth in the preceding illustration, the Corinthians' prophetic activity functions as a type of restorative speech. Paul's emphasis on the function of prophetic speech in this context, therefore, appears to highlight the notion that the intelligible message of prophetic activity is representative of the Corinthians' present eschatological situation.

As with the negative emphasis of the first assertion, the positive emphasis of the second assertion does not stem primarily from the term σημεῖον itself; rather, the effect of the σημεῖον within the larger context of the Isaianic background becomes the focal point of the assertion. In contrast to the inability of unarticulated tongues to bring about understanding and edification, prophetic speech functions to reverse the effect of the judgmental context of the quotation from Isaiah 28 and to point to the post-exilic restoration of the people manifest in Isaiah 45. The allusion to Isa. 45.14, therefore, moves Paul's argument toward the notion

---

142. Fee, *First Corinthians*, 687; Thiselton, *First Corinthians*, 1129-30.

143. Roy E. Ciampa and Brian S. Rosner, '1 Corinthians', in *Commentary on the New Testament Use of the Old Testament* (ed. G.K. Beale and D.A. Carson; Grand Rapids: Baker, 2007), 742; cf. Ciampa and Rosner, *First Corinthians*, 707; Hays, 'Conversion', 393; Schnabel, *1 Korintherbrief*, 826.

that the use of prophetic speech within the community is a sign of God's presence as it functions as one of the means of the restoration and inclusion that form Isaiah's narrative.[144] The opposite side of the assertion, namely that prophetic speech is not a sign for unbelievers, may simply reflect the idea that prophetic speech is not evocative of the unbelievers' activity with regard to both the Isaianic and Corinthian settings.[145] In broad terms, therefore, Paul positions prophetic speech and unarticulated tongues against each other at this point in light of their association with the narrative movement from judgment to hope in Isaiah.

### d. Conclusions

The argument in 1 Cor. 14.20-25 provides insight into Paul's understanding of the shape and function of prophetic speech in the Corinthian community. The connection between Paul's presentation and that of the larger framework of Isaiah seems to locate the Corinthians' prophetic speech within the Isaianic movement from exile to eschatological restoration. That is, the hypothetical association between prophetic speech and conversion within the Corinthians' gathering supports the notion that Paul understands intelligible prophetic speech to be coordinate with Corinthians' eschatological situation. The dichotomy between the use of unarticulated tongues and prophetic speech, therefore, functions as a type of metonymy for the larger redemptive movement of Isaiah. In addition, the close correlation between Paul's language at this point and the earlier biblical tradition may highlight the divide between Paul's understanding of prophetic speech and that developed within the larger Hellenistic setting.[146] In other words, Paul's use of the Isaianic narrative at this point may demonstrate that the preceding prophetic tradition of the Old Testament served as the basis for both his own rhetoric and the development of prophetic speech within the Corinthian community.[147]

144. Cf. Ciampa and Rosner, *First Corinthians*, 703.
145. Thiselton, *First Corinthians*, 1123.
146. Fee, *First Corinthians*, 687 n. 65.
147. This is not an affirmation, however, that Paul saw no distinction between his own prophetic activity and that of the Corinthians. Paul's subsequent discussion concerning the need to differentiate (διακρίνω) between prophetic statements in 1 Cor. 14.29-33, for example, appears to signify a qualitative distinction in Paul's presentation between himself and the Corinthians in this regard. In terms of the outcome of prophetic activity with respect to the outsider in the present context, however, it may be possible to argue that the activity of both Paul and the Corinthians takes place on the same plane. For a discussion of the relationship between Paul's prophetic activity and that of the Corinthians, see Forbes, *Prophecy*, 251-78; Wayne A. Grudem, *The Gift of Prophecy in 1 Corinthians* (Lanham, Md.: University Press of America, 1982); Sandnes, *Paul—One of the Prophets?*, 244-46.

## 4. Conclusion

In light of the preceding analysis it seems reasonable to conclude that certain portions of 1 Corinthians support the notion that Paul's presentation of his apostolic ministry and the form of his argumentation were shaped by the prophetic tradition of the Old Testament. Although 1 Cor. 9.15-18 and 14.20-25 represent a relatively small sample of the epistolary material in 1 Corinthians, they serve as evidence that the prophetic tradition of the Old Testament functioned as at least one of the lenses through which Paul presents his apostolic ministry within this portion of the Corinthian correspondence. In other words, this material is meant neither to assert that the Old Testament prophetic tradition is the only framework with which Paul constructs his apostolic self-conception nor to elucidate every facet of the prophetic tradition that Paul may implicitly or explicitly coordinate with the origin and outworking of his apostleship. Rather, the continuity between aspects of the Old Testament prophetic tradition and the material in 1 Cor. 9.15-18 and 14.20-25 is meant to show that the Old Testament prophetic tradition was active in shaping Paul's presentation of himself with respect to the Christian community in Corinth. The intention within the following portions of the present argument will be to examine the ways in which Paul relates himself to the prophetic tradition in 2 Corinthians. The specific focus of the following chapter will be to highlight Paul's prophetic self-presentation in terms of his connection with particular persons associated with the prophetic tradition of the Old Testament (e.g. Moses, the Isaianic servant of the Lord, and Jeremiah). The subsequent chapter will then attempt to delineate the ways in which particular portions of Paul's rhetoric in 2 Corinthians are reflective of the prophetic tradition.

Chapter 4

## PAUL'S PROPHETIC SELF-PRESENTATION IN 2 CORINTHIANS

### 1. Introduction

It has long been argued that one of Paul's primary intentions in 2 Corinthians is to defend the nature, content, and purpose of his apostolic ministry. Indeed, at least one commentator claims that Paul's apostolic defence 'is a strand that runs through the letter from beginning to end'.[1] More specifically, past commentators have seen the apostle's defence as coming forth with particular clarity in the extended sections of 2 Cor. 2.14–7.4 and 2 Corinthians 10–13. Although there is a general consensus among scholars concerning the reality that Paul is, in some sense, discussing his own ministry within 2 Corinthians, there appear to be a number of remaining discrepancies concerning the nature and meaning of his defence. Of primary importance is the question of from where (or from what) Paul's defensive rhetoric originates. Numerous studies have concentrated on attempting to identify the opponents against whom Paul writes as a method for determining the nature and purpose of the defence.[2] Several more recent studies, however, have attempted to

---

1. Paul Barnett, *The Second Epistle to the Corinthians* (NICNT; Grand Rapids: Eerdmans, 1997), 42.
2. E.g. F.C. Baur, 'Die Christuspartei in der korinthischen Gemeinde, der Gegensatz des petrinischen und paulinischen Christentum in der ältesten Kirche, der Apostel Petrus in Rom', *TZT* 4 (1831): 61-206; Walter Schmithals, *Gnosticism in Corinth* (trans. John E. Steely; Nashville: Abingdon, 1971); Dieter Georgi, *The Opponents of Paul in Second Corinthians* (Edinburgh: T. & T. Clark, 1986); Ernst Käsemann, 'Die Legitimität des Apostels: Eine Untersuchung zu 2 Korinther 10–13', *ZNW* 41 (1942): 33-71. These works represent the seminal works in the discussion of the identity of the opponents in 2 Corinthians (i.e. Judaizers, Gnostics, divine men, or pneumatics). For a summary of the various methodologies and opinions concerning the identity of Paul's opponents in this epistle, see Jerry L. Sumney, *Identifying Paul's Opponents: The Question of Method in 2 Corinthians* (JSNTSup 40; Sheffield: JSOT, 1990).

develop Paul's defence as an extension of the apostle's own understanding of his place within the prophetic tradition. These works have primarily focused on the argument presented in 2 Corinthians 3-4 and the place of these two chapters within the larger framework of Paul's argument.[3] Thus, there has been a movement away from determining the nature of Paul's argument based on the situation he was facing toward an understanding that Paul himself was defining the terms and terminology of the discourse.

The purpose of the present chapter will be to discuss further the notion that Paul develops his defence based on his own understanding of his ministry and not, primarily, in response to his opponents. Although Paul's comments certainly address his opponents, as well as the faithful members of the Corinthian community, this chapter will attempt to show that Paul derives his argument from his own, apostolic self-understanding and not simply in response to the historical situation at Corinth. The argument will proceed by attempting to highlight the way in which Paul presents himself in relation to the prophetic tradition, particularly as it concerns Moses, the Isaianic servant, and Jeremiah, as well as highlighting the significance of Paul's assertion in 2 Cor. 3.6 that [θεός] ἱκάνωσεν ἡμᾶς διακόνους καινῆς διαθήκης.

## 2. The Relationship between Paul and Moses

Paul's use of the Mosaic tradition within 2 Corinthians, and his specific dialogue concerning the similarities and differences between his own ministry and Moses' ministry in 2 Cor. 3.7-18, have led to a continued debate concerning the relationship between Moses and the apostle. In relation to the extensive literature on 2 Cor. 3.7-18 and the relationship between the respective ministries of Paul and Moses,[4] there has been

---

3. E.g. Hafemann, *Paul, Moses, and the History of Israel*; Timothy B. Savage, *Power Through Weakness: Paul's Understanding of the Christian Ministry in 2 Corinthians* (SNTSMS 86; Cambridge: Cambridge University Press, 1996).

4. E.g. William R. Baker, 'Did the Glory of Moses' Face Fade? A Reexamination of καταργέω in 2 Corinthians 3:7-18', *BBR* 10 (2000): 1-15; Linda L. Belleville, *Reflections of Glory: Paul's Polemical Use of the Moses-Doxa Tradition in 2 Corinthians 3.1-18* (JSNTSup 52; Sheffield: JSOT, 1991); Belleville, 'Tradition or Creation? Paul's Use of the Exodus 34 Tradition in 2 Corinthians 3:7-18', in *Paul and the Scriptures of Israel* (ed. Craig A. Evans and James A. Sanders; JSNTSup 83; Sheffield: JSOT, 1993), 169-86; Nina L. Collins, 'Observations on the Jewish Background of 2 Corinthians 3:9, 3:7-8 and 3:11', in *Paul and the Corinthians: Studies on a Community in Conflict* (Festschrift Margaret Thrall; ed. Trevor J. Burke and J. Keith Elliot; NovTSup 109; Leiden: Brill, 2003), 75-92; Paul B. Duff, '"Glory in the Ministry

relatively little produced with regard to the relationship between the two leaders themselves.[5] This potential scholarly lacuna may stem from the perception that Moses, as a biblical figure, does not influence Paul's theological matrix to the same extent as others, such as Adam and Abraham.[6] With respect to the argument of 2 Corinthians, however, both Paul's explicit and implicit allusions to Moses and his ministry support the notion that the Mosaic tradition serves as one of the important

of Death": Gentile Condemnation and Letters of Recommendation in 2 Cor 3:6-18', *NovT* 46 (2004): 313-37; Duff, 'Transformed "from Glory to Glory": Paul's Appeal to the Experience of His Readers in 2 Corinthians 3:18', *JBL* 127 (2008): 759-80; William J. Dumbrell, 'The Newness of the New Covenant: The Logic of the Argument in 2 Corinthians 3', *RTR* 61 (2002): 61-84; Joseph A. Fitzmyer, 'Glory Reflected on the Face of Christ (2 Cor 3:7–4:6) and a Palestinian Jewish Motif', *TS* 42 (1981): 630-44; Randall C. Gleason, 'Paul's Covenantal Contrast in 2 Corinthians 3:1-11', *BSac* 154 (1997): 61-79; Sigurd Grindheim, 'The Law Kills but the Gospel Gives Life: The Letter-Spirit Dualism in 2 Corinthians 3:5-18', *JSNT* 84 (2001): 97-115; Hafemann, *Paul, Moses, and the History of Israel*, passim; Anthony T. Hanson, 'The Midrash in 2 Corinthians 3: A Reconsideration', *JSNT* 9 (1980): 2-28; Richard B. Hays, *Echoes of Scripture in the Letters of Paul* (New Haven: Yale University Press, 1989), 122-53; Sini Hulmi, *Paulus und Mose: Argumentation und Polemik in 2 Kor 3* (SFEG 77; Göttingen: Vandenhoeck & Ruprecht, 1999); Dietrich-Alex Koch, 'Abraham und Mose im Streit der Meinungen: Beobachtungen und Hypothesen zur Debatte zwischen Paulus und seinen Gegnern in 2 Kor 11,22-23 und 3,7-18', in *The Corinthian Correspondence* (ed. Reimund Bieringer; BETL 125; Leuven: Leuven University Press, 1996), 305-24; Thomas E. Provence, '"Who Is Sufficient for These Things?" An Exegesis of 2 Corinthians 2:15–3:18', *NovT* 24 (1982): 54-81; Siegfried Schulz, 'Die Decke des Moses: Untersuchungen zu einer vorpaulinischen Überlieferung in II Cor. 3.7-18', *ZNW* 49 (1958): 1-30; Carol Kern Stockhausen, *Moses' Veil and the Glory of the New Covenant: The Exegetical Substructure of II Cor. 3:1–4:6* (AnBib 116; Rome: Pontifical Biblical Institute, 1989); Margaret E. Thrall, 'Conversion to the Lord: The Interpretation of Exodus 34 in II Cor. 3:14b-18', in *Paolo, Ministro del Nuovo Testamento (2 Co 2,14–4,16)* (ed. Lorenzo De Lorenzi; SMBen 9; Rome: Benedictina, 1987), 197-232; Willem Cornelis van Unnik, '"With Unveiled Face": An Exegesis of 2 Corinthians iii 12-18', *NovT* 6 (1963): 153-69; Francis Watson, *Paul and the Hermeneutics of Faith* (London: T&T Clark International, 2004), 273-313; N.T. Wright, *The Climax of the Covenant: Christ and the Law in Pauline Theology* (Minneapolis: Fortress, 1992), 175-92.

    5. Both Hafemann, *Paul, Moses, and the History of Israel*, 29-35, 92-109, and Stockhausen, *Moses' Veil*, 82-85, devote time to a discussion of this relationship. Of primary importance, however, is the work of Jones. See Peter R. Jones, 'The Apostle Paul: A Second Moses According to II Corinthians 2:14–4:7' (Ph.D. diss., Princeton Theological Seminary, 1973), and Peter R. Jones, *La deuxième épître de Paul aux Corinthiens* (CEB 14; Edifac: Vaux-sur-Seine, 1992).

    6. Cf. Peter Oakes, 'Moses in Paul', in *La Construction de la figure de Moïse* (ed. Thomas Römer; Supplément à Transeuphratène 13; Paris: Gabalda, 2007), 249.

backdrops for the apostle's presentation of his relationship with the Corinthian community. It will be helpful, therefore, to analyse the way in which Paul sees his own connection with Moses in terms of his ministerial call, the nature of his ministry, and his overarching role as a minister of the new covenant.

a. *The Ministerial Call of Paul*
The first point of similarity between Moses and the apostle may be seen in their respective divine callings. Connections have previously been drawn between the contextual argument of 2 Cor. 3.1-6 and the narrative of Exodus 3–4.[7] Although the connection between the two texts does not derive simply from linguistic similarities, the language of 'sufficiency' plays an important role in the determination of the nature of the relationship between the calls of Paul and Moses. Thus, although the term ἱκανός exhibits a number of meanings within both Graeco-Roman literature and the LXX itself, there is little evidence to dissuade from the observation that it functions to form a linguistic connection between Exodus and 2 Corinthians at this point. In addition, the eventual source of the sufficiency (God himself) and the reason for the sufficiency (the execution of a ministry) outlined in both Exodus 3–4 and 2 Cor. 3.1-6 seemingly constitute broad thematic associations between the two texts, offering further support for the notion that the Exodus narrative constitutes one of the intertexts that establish Paul's rhetorical framework at this point of the epistle.[8] In light of these connections it may be reasonable to argue that Paul's presentation of his ministerial call in 2 Cor. 3.1-6 is defined by the same structure and purpose reflected in the Lord's commission of Moses, namely, to show that even though the work of God is exhibited in the lives of these two men, it is not derived from within either of them.[9] Paul's particular emphasis on the divine source of his ministerial sufficiency, therefore, may represent a unique association with the Mosaic tradition.

In terms of a structural analysis, the call of Moses stands within a broad paradigm for the way in which the Lord commissions prophets to minister in and among the people. While the work of Zimmerli was foundational in determining the existence of a consistent form (or forms)

---

7. Hafemann, *Suffering and the Spirit*, 90-98.
8. Stockhausen, *Moses' Veil*, 84; cf. Edith M. Humphrey, 'Ambivalent Apocalypse: Apocalyptic Rhetoric and Intertextuality in 2 Corinthians', in *The Intertexture of Apocalyptic Discourse in the New Testament* (ed. Duane F. Watson; SBLSymS 14; Leiden: Brill, 2002), 117-18.
9. John I. Durham, *Exodus* (WBC 3; Nashville: Thomas Nelson, 1987), 49.

of prophetic call narratives in the Old Testament, there is little consensus concerning either the exact structure of the form or the precise quantity of elements of which it is comprised.[10] Apart from the continued fluctuation of ideas concerning the number of elements in the precise form, however, there are four elements that can consistently be identified in the majority of the prophetic call narratives. These elements follow a basic movement from an initial theophany, to the presentation of a divine commission, to the recognition by the prophet of his own insufficiency, to a divine work of grace that overcomes the prophet's deficiency.[11] This basic structure can be seen not only in the narrative of Exodus 3–4, but also in the calls of Gideon (Judg. 6.11-24), Isaiah (Isa. 6.1-3), Jeremiah (Jer. 1.4-10), and Ezekiel (Ezek. 1.1–3.11).[12] Thus, in spite of the structural complexity exhibited in the prophetic call narratives, the relatively consistent presence of these particular structural dimensions seems to support the assertion that there is a general scheme or overarching structure that is characteristic of prophetic call narratives.

It may also be feasible to argue that Paul's own ministerial call fits within this structure. Hafemann's extensive work on 2 Cor. 2.14–3.18 posits a close association between the call of Moses developed in Exodus 3–4 and Paul's apostolic call within the narrative structure of Acts, as well as Paul's own particular discussion of his sufficiency and call in 2 Corinthians.[13] In other words, Paul's own divine call is seen to take place within the boundaries of the same narrative movement (i.e. an initial theophany, to the presentation of a divine commission, to the recognition by the prophet of his own insufficiency, to a divine work of grace that overcomes the prophet's deficiency) exhibited in the prophetic call narratives of the Old Testament prophets. While Luke's triad

10. Walther Zimmerli, *Ezekiel 1* (Hermeneia; Philadelphia: Fortress, 1979), 97-100. For a summary of the debates that have arisen from Zimmerli's initial work, see Rudolf Kilian, *Studien zu alttestamentlichen Texten und Situationen* (ed. W. Werner and J. Werlitz; SBAB 28; Stuttgart: Katholisches Bibelwerk, 1999), 53-76, and Dieter Vieweger, *Die Spezifik der Berufungsberichte Jeremias und Ezechiels im Umfeld ähnlicher Einheiten des Alten Testaments* (BEATAJ 6; Frankfurt: Peter Lang, 1986), 11-24. For a helpful recent analysis of the dissimilarities between the prophetic call narratives, see Kathleen Rochester, 'Prophetic Ministry in Jeremiah and Ezekiel' (Ph.D. diss., Durham University, 2009), 13-70.

11. The existence of these particular elements stems from the suggestion of Hafemann, *Paul, Moses, and the History of Israel*, 49. This basic narrative structure eliminates Zimmerli's distinction between the presence of the word of YHWH or a vision of YHWH and focuses on the common parallels between the prophetic calls.

12. For a more thorough outline of the call structure in these particular prophets, see Hafemann, *Paul, Moses, and the History of Israel*, 50-59.

13. See Hafemann, *Paul, Moses, and the History of Israel*, 100-106.

of narratives concerning Paul's call detail his encounter with the Lord (Acts 9.1-19; 22.2-16; 26.9-18), the apostle's own rhetorical question in 2 Cor. 2.16 and his admission of a lack of self-sufficiency in 2 Cor. 3.5 stand as evidence of God's message to him, his own realization of his insufficiency, and the Lord's act of grace in providing the necessary level of apostolic competence. Thus, part of Paul's apostolic defence hinges on the connection between himself and the prophetic tradition. His argument depends on understanding that in spite of his insufficiency, his ministry among the Corinthians, and the rest of the Pauline communities, was both divinely appointed and genuine.

With regard to 2 Corinthians in particular, the starting point for understanding Paul's connection with the call of Moses and the prophets is the stark rhetorical question put forth in the final clause of 2 Cor. 2.16: καὶ πρὸς ταῦτα τίς ἱκανός; Though it is possible that this question alludes to the discussion of the day of the Lord in Joel 2.11, the positive nuance of Paul's argument in the subsequent verses seems to negate the possibility that the apostle's question is to be answered in the same negative fashion as Joel's.[14] Rather, there may be a more direct connection between Paul's question and Moses' own admission of insufficiency before the Lord (οὐχ ἱκανός εἰμι [Exod. 4.10 LXX]). As with the Exodus narrative, Paul's argument appears to turn on the notion of sufficiency. Like Moses, Paul is sufficient *because* of his insufficiency.[15] In this way, the answer to Paul's question in 2 Cor. 2.16 may reflect a more positive nuance. This more positive notion of sufficiency may be supported by the subsequent explanatory clause in 2 Cor. 2.17 (cf. γάρ) in which Paul contrasts those who are insufficient for the apostolic ministry (οἱ πολλοὶ καπηλεύοντες τὸν λόγον τοῦ θεοῦ) and those whom God sent (ὡς ἐκ θεοῦ). In other words, Paul is not here claiming that the apostolic ministry is an impossible task for which no one is sufficient; rather, he is stating that God made him sufficient for the ministry to which he was called (cf. 2 Cor. 3.6).

14. Barnett, *Second Corinthians*, 155.
15. Hafemann, *Paul, Moses, and the History of Israel*, 50, does well to note the relationship between sufficiency and insufficiency, but seems to err in thinking that the prophetic call exhibits a theme of '*sufficiency in spite of insufficiency*' (50; original emphasis). In contrast, Paul seems to be making the point throughout 2 Corinthians that his insufficiency is the conduit for the Lord's powerful work (cf. Savage, *Power Through Weakness*, 189-90). Likewise, Ulrich Heckel, *Kraft in Schwachheit: Untersuchungen zu 2. Kor 10–13* (WUNT 2/56; Tübingen: Mohr Siebeck, 1993), 119, argues that the related category of weakness developed in 2 Cor. 10–13 can be understood in similar terms: 'Der Gegensatz von Kraft und Schwachheit ist für die Gegner ein kontradiktorischer, für Paulus ein polarer.'

Similarly, Paul's assertion in 2 Cor. 3.5, οὐχ ὅτι ἀφ' ἑαυτῶν ἱκανοί ἐσμεν λογίσασθαί τι ὡς ἐξ ἑαυτῶν, highlights his understanding of his own self-deficiency. The basic structure of the verse (οὐχ...ἀλλά) points to the reality that Paul 'rejects even the capacity to discern that anything could emanate from him'.[16] His sufficiency derives not from himself (ἐξ ἑαυτῶν) but from God (ἐκ τοῦ θεοῦ). Indeed, as Schmeller notes '[d]ie Antwort von [2 Kor. 3.5] auf die in [2 Kor. 3.1a] gestellte Frage ist also: Ich empfehle mich nicht selbst, weil schon meine Fähigkeit zur Selbstbeurteilung von Gott stammt'.[17] The import of the argument at this point is similar to Paul's discussion of his sufficiency (οὐκ εἰμί ἱκανὸς καλεῖσθαι ἀπόστολος) in 1 Cor. 15.9-10, where he roots his apostolic ministry in the grace of God.[18] Moreover, this particular dichotomy with regard to the potential sources of Paul's sufficiency supports the notion that the apostle's previous assertion of confidence in 2 Cor. 3.4 (πεποίθησιν... τοιαύτην ἔχομεν) was not meant to be a statement of self-recommendation. In contrast, just as his confidence came διὰ τοῦ Χριστοῦ πρὸς τὸν θεόν (2 Cor. 3.4), so too does his sufficiency come only ἐκ τοῦ θεοῦ (2 Cor. 3.5). The key to both the question in 2 Cor. 2.16 and the assertion in 2 Cor. 3.6 is that Paul's confidence and sufficiency as an apostle are not derived from him, even though they exist within his own self-understanding.[19] The apostle can be simultaneously aware of his ministerial sufficiency and of the source of its derivation.

Like Moses, Paul's authority derives from God's external call and his internal work of grace in giving him the necessary sufficiency for his new covenant ministry. Paul's claim stands in line with much of the historical literature, including the Apocrypha, Pseudepigrapha, and rabbinic traditions, which note that the ability to connect one's ministry with Moses serves as a way in which to express the viability of one's own ministry.[20] The basic structure of Moses' call to ministry, therefore, becomes paradigmatic not only for Paul, but for the rest of the prophetic community. In this way, Moses is seen as a 'fountainhead' for the entire prophetic tradition not only in terms of the content of his message, but also with

16. Barnett, *Second Corinthians*, 173.
17. Thomas Schmeller, *Der Zweite Brief an die Korinther (2Kor 1,1–7,4)* (EKKNT 8/1; Neukirchen–Vluyn: Neukirchener Verlag; Ostfildern: Patmos-Verlag, 2010), 183.
18. Murray J. Harris, *The Second Epistle to the Corinthians* (NIGTC; Grand Rapids: Eerdmans, 2005), 268-69.
19. Hafemann, *Paul, Moses, and the History of Israel*, 98.
20. E.g. *T. Mos.* 1.14; 11.16; 12.6-7; Pseudo-Philo, *LAB* 9.7-8; *Targum Neofiti*; *Targum Pseudo-Jonathan*; Hafemann, *Paul, Moses, and the History of Israel*, 74-81, also highlights the place of Moses' call within the works of Philo and Josephus.

regard to the method and manner that he was brought forward as a servant of the Lord.[21] At this stage of Paul's argument, the importance of his relationship with Moses is not in the functions the two of them perform, but in the way that they were called to fulfill those functions. That is, while it can be argued that Paul's call is structurally related to that of Moses, it remains to be examined whether the structural parallels of their calls necessitate parallels between the nature and function of their respective ministries.

b. *The Nature of Paul's Ministry*
Having established that Paul's presentation of his call exhibits the normal structure of biblical calls to prophetic ministry, it may then be asked whether or not this parallel comes forth through the purpose or intent of Paul's ministry. Does the notion that Paul's call exhibits structural similarities with previous call narratives signify the nature of Paul's presentation of his apostolic ministry within the Corinthian community? More precisely, it is important to determine whether Paul's apostolic self-presentation consists of the notion that his ministry is representative of the nature and function of the Mosaic ministry. Furthermore, it will be helpful to work through the idea that Paul represents a second Moses, in order to attempt to determine whether Paul's presentation of his ministry is simply similar to that of Moses or whether the apostle sees himself as the fulfillment of the Lord's promise to establish a new prophet like Moses (cf. Deut. 18.15-18).

Initially, it is possible to note that Paul's own allusion to Moses' prophetic call establishes that the apostle understands Moses as a point of reference for his own ministry in some sense. In light of the discussion of divine sufficiency coming only through the Lord, it seems reasonable to argue that Paul views Moses as someone who was sufficient only because of the Lord's work.[22] What is relatively remarkable, however, is not that Paul connects himself with Moses and the prophetic tradition, but that he is so readily able to compare and contrast his ministry with that of Moses based on this similarity (cf. 2 Cor. 3.7-18). As Humphrey notes, 'the proto-seer Moses becomes for Paul…a model and also an *inverse* model of perception and of ministry'.[23] Paul not only places himself on

---

21. VanGemeren, *Prophetic Word*, 45; cf. Christopher R. Seitz, 'The Prophet Moses and the Canonical Shape of Jeremiah', *ZAW* 101 (1989): 3-27, especially the comment that 'Moses is the first prophet, the type against which others are measured' (5).

22. John Lierman, *The New Testament Moses* (WUNT 2/173; Tübingen: Mohr Siebeck, 2004), 170.

23. Humphrey, 'Ambivalent Apocalypse', 117. Original emphasis.

the same level as Moses in 2 Cor. 3.7-18, he also uses Moses as a foundation upon which to build an argument for the reality of his own apostolic ministry. In this way, Paul shows that, like Moses, he too is the mediator or messenger of a divine ministry.[24]

This understanding of Paul's use of Moses, however, is based on a particular reading of 2 Cor. 3.7-11, which understands Paul not to be defaming the ministry of the old covenant, but to be supporting the glory of his own new covenant ministry by favourably comparing it with the glory that was part of the old covenant. In broad terms, the material in 2 Cor. 3.7-11 introduces Paul's commentary on the narrative of Exodus 32–34 in which he illustrates the relationship between the two covenants in terms of their differing functions with respect to the people of God. In more specific terms, the argument in 2 Cor. 3.7-11 centres primarily on a comparison between the δόξα inherent in the ministries of both Moses and Paul built upon a series of *qal wahomer* (*a minore ad maius*) arguments that demonstrate the surpassing greatness of the ministry of the new covenant in light of the negative function of the old.[25] The predominant emphasis on glory at this point of the argument stems primarily from Paul's multiple uses of the noun δόξα (2 Cor. 3.7 [×2], 8, 9 [×2], 10, 11 [×2]) and the verb δοξάζω (2 Cor. 3.10 [×2]). The frequent occurrence of the δόξα language at this point suggests that the argument functions in large part as an explication of the relationship between the two covenants with respect to their corresponding manifestations of God's glory. In other words, the import of Paul's δόξα language is that there is a crucial point of similarity between the two covenants. The particular points of dissimilarity between the two covenants that Paul highlights in 2 Cor. 3.7-11, therefore, are based on the logical affirmation that both covenants are representative of God's glory.[26] Moreover, Paul's particular focus on the concept of glory at this point of the argument looks forward to the apostle's dramatic discussion of the Lord's glory in the climatic conclusion of the passage in 2 Cor. 3.18.[27] In terms of the specific argument in 2 Cor. 3.7-11, however, it seems that Paul here establishes the way in which the glory manifested in the old covenant functions as an affirmation of the glorious nature of his own new covenant ministry. In other words, although the glory inherent in Moses' ministry was indeed representative

---

24. Lierman, *New Testament Moses*, 168.
25. Barnett, *Second Corinthians*, 180.
26. Hafemann, *Paul, Moses, and the History of Israel*, 269-71; Jason C. Meyer, *The End of the Law: Mosaic Covenant in Pauline Theology* (NACSBT 6; Nashville: Broadman & Holman, 2009), 87.
27. Dumbrell, 'New Covenant', 70.

of God's glory in Paul's view, the differences between them reflect the notion that the inauguration of the new covenant results in the creation of a ministry that is even more glorious. Paul's description of the surpassing glory (τῆς δικαιοσύνης δόξῃ) of his ministry in 2 Cor. 3.10, therefore, becomes the evidence for an eschatological distinction between his own ministry and that of Moses.[28] The essential feature of Paul's argument with respect to the present work, however, is that the apostle's comparison with Moses centres not only on the previous parallels with respect to their prophetic calls, but also on the notion that their respective ministries stem from the same basis, namely the glory of God.

In spite of Paul's ostensible dependence on the narrative of Exodus 32–34 in 2 Corinthians 3, it remains to be explored whether or not the Corinthians would have understood the allusions either to Moses' call or to the nature of his old covenant ministry. That is, although it is clear from Jewish tradition that Moses was seen as the supreme prophet, it remains to be examined whether an abrupt discussion of Moses' ministry would have surpassed the knowledge of a predominantly Gentile audience.[29] Although certain authors in the ancient world detracted from the ministry of Moses,[30] it is clear that 'Moses was not only by far the most widely known Jewish figure in Graeco-Roman antiquity, he was also the most respected'.[31] This claim finds its basis not only among the intellectual elite,[32] but also within the common magical papyri that were prevalent in antiquity.[33] Moreover, the affirmation in Acts that Paul reasoned with both Jews and Gentiles in the Corinthian synagogue stands as evidence of the fact that at least some of the Corinthian Gentiles would have been familiar with the teaching of the Old Testament and the ministry of Moses (cf. Acts 18.1-4).[34]

This fascination with Moses, which likely stems from his reception of the Torah (Exod. 19–31), his knowledge of the divine name (Exod. 3.14), and his personal encounters with the Lord (Exod. 32–34), affirms the dramatic nature of Paul's argument in 2 Corinthians 3. Paul places his apostleship next to the ministry of Moses in order to use the differences

28. Meyer, *The End of the Law*, 87, 93.
29. For Moses' place within the Jewish tradition, see *As. Mos.* 11.6; *Sir.* 45.2; Josephus, *Ant.* 3.180.
30. E.g. Quintilian, *Inst.* 3.7.21; Tacitus, *Hist.* 5.4-5.
31. Savage, *Power Through Weakness*, 106; cf. Steve Moyise, *Paul and Scripture* (London: SPCK, 2010), 48.
32. E.g. Strabo, *Geogr.* 16.2.39; Justin, *Epit.* 36.2.11-6; Longinus, *Subl.* 9.9.
33. K. Preisendanz and A. Vogliano, 'Laminetta Magica Siciliana', *Acme* 1 (1948): 73-85 (77).
34. Barrett, *Acts*, 2:864.

between their respective functions to present his own apostolic ministry as the greater of the two. Indeed, the stark contrast between the notions established by the distinct semantic ranges of καταργέω and μένω in 2 Cor. 3.11 'epitomizes [Paul's] view of religious history in the light of the cross of Christ'.[35] It is this salvation-historical divide that allows Paul to emphasize the distinction between the new and the old in the present context, and to present his own apostolic ministry as an extension of the reality brought about by this new order. The unique aspect of Paul's ministry is its representation of the *newness* that defines the present covenantal reality. As Watson helpfully notes:

> It is the order established by the life-giving Spirit of the living God, who writes in fleshly hearts a letter of recommendation for the apostle that is also Christ's message to the world—Christ addressing the world by way of the Spirit-filled community. This new order endures for ever; it is final and definitive, and will not be superseded by any still newer order. In it, the 'righteousness' and 'life' which constitute true human fulfilment are finally established. Its surpassing glory is its own and does not fade; and this is the transforming glory of the risen Christ. It is *this* glory that eclipses the temporary, borrowed glory that shone at Sinai.[36]

In other words, the nature of Paul's apostolic ministry stems directly from the nature of the new covenant, which in Paul's view represents God's complete and final word to humanity.

It seems reasonable to argue at this point that Paul illustrates the validity of his own call by establishing the eschatological position of his ministry over against that of the inoperative ministry of Moses (cf. 2 Cor. 3.7, 11).[37] Thus, the present paragraph, 2 Cor. 3.7-11, is seemingly linked with the larger theme of Paul's apostolic defence expressed in the argument of 2 Cor. 2.14–4.6. In broad terms, Paul appears to be arguing that his apostolic ministry in Corinth is evidence of his assertion in 2 Cor. 3.6 that τὸ...πνεῦμα ζωοποιεῖ. The surpassing glory of the new covenant

---

35. Harris, *Second Corinthians*, 291; cf. Fee, *God's Empowering Presence*, 298.

36. Watson, *Paul and the Hermeneutics of Faith*, 312. Original emphasis. Cf. Jan Lambrecht, *Second Corinthians* (SP 8; Collegeville, Minn.: Liturgical, 1999), 42-43.

37. The use of the term 'inoperative' in relation to the Mosaic ministry is an intentional reference to the semantic domain of καταργέω and its cognates. Within the Pauline corpus this term functions as a key word for Paul in his description of the effect of God's new work in Christ on the world. To use the term with reference to the Mosaic ministry, therefore, is to highlight the end of the negative effects of that ministry because of the new work of the Spirit. For a complete discussion of this word group, its use within the Pauline corpus, and its particular function within 2 Corinthians see Hafemann, *Paul, Moses, and the History of Israel*, 301-13. For an alternative analysis, see Meyer, *The End of the Law*, 90-93.

ministry solidifies its function within the community and stands against those who would argue for the Sinaitic covenant as the source of life within the community.[38] This ministry is characterized by a surpassing glory because it brings neither condemnation nor death, but results in the justification of the believer in light of the powerful work of the Spirit. The essential deficiency of the old covenant was not in its representation of God's glory; rather, its deficiency lay in the fact that it was ineffectual and, consequently, representative of God's judgment.[39] In contrast, the authority and significance of Paul's apostolic ministry does not lie in letters of commendation or the condemnation brought about by the old covenant, but in the power of the new covenant, which is effectual because of the life and ministry of the Spirit in the καρδίαι σαρκίναι of the Corinthians.

Paul's continued argument in 2 Cor. 3.12-18 provides the exegetical conclusion to the entirety of the preceding argument in 2 Cor. 3.1-11. In other words, both of Paul's particular sets of arguments concerning his apostolic ministry in the new covenant in 2 Cor. 3.1-6 and 3.7-11 provide the theological basis from which the apostle can make his dramatic conclusions in 2 Cor. 3.12-18.[40] The glory that is representative of the new covenant, therefore, becomes the basis upon which Paul is able to make the claims concerning the significance of his own ministry and the state of believers within the new covenant. His conclusions in 2 Cor. 3.12-18 are made in light of the fact that the new covenant contains the glory of God and produces righteousness through the life-giving work of the Spirit.[41] It is only divine power that founds and sustains the new covenant and allows for the bold nature of Paul's ministry.

In addition, the contextual focus on the customary activity of Moses in veiling himself (2 Cor. 3.13), the current state of the Israelites in relation to the Law (2 Cor. 3.14-15), and the freedom of Christian believers (2 Cor. 3.16-18) are evidence of the functional difference between the two covenants. In other words, it seems that one of Paul's purposes is to show the distinct work of the Spirit within the ministry of the new covenant in contrast to the old covenant ministry, which remains devoid of the Spirit's life-giving power (cf. 2 Cor. 3.6). While Paul sees several similarities between himself and Moses, there is also a clear distinction

---

38. A. Andrew Das, *Paul, the Law, and the Covenant* (Peabody, Mass.: Hendrickson, 2001), 93.
39. Witherington, *Conflict and Community in Corinth*, 379; cf. Meyer, *The End of the Law*, 63.
40. Dumbrell, 'New Covenant', 76.
41. Hafemann, *Paul, Moses, and the History of Israel*, 266.

between them in light of the differing audiences they address, and the consequent outcomes of their respective ministries.[42] In more general terms, there are key *differences* between the character and ministry of Moses and the character and ministry of the apostle. It is seemingly important, therefore, to distinguish between Paul as one who is in line with much of the prophetic tradition, with Moses at its forefront, and Paul as a fulfillment of the Lord's promise to establish another prophet like Moses among his people (Deut. 18.15-18). Paul does not appear to establish himself and Moses as pillars of the two covenants; rather, it seems that the parallels between the two figures establish a more general connection between the ministry of Paul and the preceding prophetic tradition of the Old Testament. In light of this more general association, the paradigmatic nature of Moses' call and ministry, although thoroughly important to Paul's self-presentation in 2 Cor. 2.14–4.6, does not seem to support Jones' overarching thesis that Paul consciously or unconsciously fits into the mould of a second Moses.[43]

The primary difficulty in identifying Paul as the specific embodiment of the second Moses tradition is the relative uncertainty that exists concerning the presence of a consistent or crystallized notion of a second Moses figure prior to the time of Christ.[44] Although there is discussion of a return of Moses within the rabbinic tradition at *Sifre* Deut. 33.21, the tradition behind this text stems, at the earliest, from the middle of the second century (ca. 120–140 C.E.).[45] In conjunction with this tradition it has been argued that both 1 Macc. 4.46 and 14.41 allude to a prophet who functions within the same scheme as Moses.[46] The difficulty with this view, however, is the opaque nature of the Maccabaean texts themselves. Both texts contain only the accusative anartharous noun προφήτην as part of an ambiguous temporal clause with no specific referent (cf. the particles μέχρι and ἕως). Thus, as Banks has already noted, it is by no means certain that Deut. 18.15-18 stands behind these passages, or that the coming prophet will have 'any detailed similarity with the actual role

42. Cf. Wright, *Climax of the Covenant*, 180, 183.
43. E.g. Jones, 'Apostle Paul', 375.
44. Robert Banks, 'The Eschatological Role of Law in Pre- and Post-Christian Jewish Thought', in *Reconciliation and Hope: New Testament Essays on Atonement and Eschatology* (Festschrift L.L. Morris; ed. Robert Banks; Grand Rapids: Eerdmans, 1974), 182.
45. Banks, 'Eschatological Role', 179.
46. This view was first put forward in William D. Davies, *Torah in the Messianic Age and or Age to Come* (JBLMS 7; Philadelphia: Society of Biblical Literature, 1952), 44. Jones, 'Apostle Paul', 184-85, provides further support for the notion that the 'prophet' in 1 Maccabees can be associated with Moses.

of Moses'.[47] Moreover, it is difficult to support Jones' use of specific New Testament texts, particularly in John, to support a reading of a second Moses figure back into the texts in 1 Maccabees.[48]

Of more increasing interest, however, is the possible connection between the Teacher of Righteousness within the Qumran community and the expectation of a prophet like Moses. Three documents are of particular significance in this discussion: the *Damascus Document*, the *Testimonia*, and the *Hodayot*.[49] Within the *Damascus Document* there are several clear connections between titles given to Moses and those given to the interpreter of the Law, who is possibly the same figure as the Teacher of Righteousness (cf. CD 6.3). Although it is difficult to state that the interpreter of the Law and the Teacher of Righteousness are one and the same, there does seem to be room to argue that the Teacher took part in some of the same functions that were characteristic of the Mosaic ministry.[50] For example, CD 1.10-12 establishes the notion that the function of the Teacher of Righteousness 'is that of setting out instructions for the life of the community rather than making alterations in the Mosaic Law or giving utterance to new Torah'.[51] Apart from these similarities, it does not appear that the *Damascus Document* understands the Teacher of Righteousness to be the singular fulfillment of the second Moses tradition. More appropriately, it seems that the function and work of the Teacher of Righteousness are simply being described in terms that refer back to the ministry of Moses. The claim is not one of equality, but of progression.

Similarly, both the *Testimonia* and the *Hodayot* correlate the Teacher of Righteousness with certain aspects of Moses' ministry, but neither makes an explicit assertion that the Teacher is indeed a fulfillment of Deut. 18.15-18. The particular difficulty with the *Testimonia* is its fragmentary nature and the resulting ambiguity concerning to whom the document refers. While it does appear likely that the document pertains to the Teacher of Righteousness, it is unclear to what stage of his life and ministry the quotations refer (e.g. past or future).[52] The *Hodayot* scroll

---

47. Banks, 'Eschatological Role', 180.
48. Contra Jones, 'Apostle Paul', 184-85. However, Jones does assert that 'any attempt [including his own] to solve the problem of origin must be somewhat hypothetical' (185).
49. For a full synopsis of those who affirm the connection between the Teacher of Righteousness and a second Moses, see Jones, 'Apostle Paul', 186 n. 1.
50. Jones, 'Apostle Paul', 201-2.
51. Banks, 'Eschatological Role', 180.
52. Cf. Jones, 'Apostle Paul', 204.

provides several close verbal connections between the self-perception of the Teacher of Righteousness and a figure that resembles the characteristics of Moses' prophetic ministry.[53] The hymns do not, however, directly link the Teacher of Righteousness with a concrete notion of a second Moses or a fulfillment of this part of the prophetic tradition. Indeed, the portrait in the *Hodayot* of the Teacher as having greater insight into God's plan than that of the prophets seemingly suggests that his connection with the Mosaic tradition is based primarily on his mediation of the law and not on prophetic categories.[54] It seems that the relatively consistent thought that runs through the Qumran community is not that the Teacher of Righteousness was a fulfillment of Deut. 18.15-18, but that the community and the Teacher himself attempted to describe his ministry in terms of the ministry of Moses.

Apart from the rabbinic tradition and the Qumran material, the New Testament may also shed light on the possible crystallization of the second Moses tradition. Despite the fact that there are several possible allusions to Deut. 18.15-18 in the New Testament (e.g. Mt. 11.9, 14; 17.5, 12; Mk 6.15; 8.28; 9.7; Lk. 24.27; Jn 1.21, 25, 45; 5.46; 6.14; 7.40), there are only two texts, both in Acts (3.22; 7.37), which make direct reference to the passage. Both of these references, however, are clearly focused upon the life and ministry of Jesus as the fulfillment of the second Moses tradition.[55] Although the presence of these quotations and allusions seems to reflect the notion that the New Testament contains an expectation of the fulfillment of Deut. 18.15-18, there are still two problematic points with Jones' thesis. First, there is still a significant amount of ambiguity in these texts, particularly the allusions, concerning the background for the prophetic tradition (e.g. Mt. 11.9; Jn 7.40).[56] Second, as with the quotations, most of the allusions have their main referent in the person of Jesus. Thus, Hafemann is likely correct in his assertion that if a singular expectation for a second Moses 'did exist as a crystallized belief, [it] is focused in the New Testament on Jesus alone'.[57] Indeed, Jones' own review of

---

53. Jones, 'Apostle Paul', 209-11, points to six particular similarities based on the *Hodayot* scroll: (1) they teach only true Torah based on divine revelation, (2) they both posses divine secrets, (3) they both struggle with internal opposition, (4) they both spend time in 'exile', (5) they both found communities, and (6) they struggle with external opposition.

54. See Leonhardt-Balzer, 'Minor Prophets', 9-13.

55. F.F. Bruce, *Commentary on the Book of the Acts* (NICNT; Grand Rapids: Eerdmans, 1984), 92-93, 152-53.

56. Banks, 'Eschatological Role', 181.

57. Hafemann, *Paul, Moses, and the History of Israel*, 103.

Hafemann's work provides a more satisfactory notion when he posits a '*deutero*-mosaic prophecy of the *New* Covenant for the *eschatological* people of God'.[58]

Furthermore, Paul's own argumentation within 2 Corinthians supports the idea that he did not see himself as the second Moses, but as one who stood in line with the message of the prophets and served as a mediator between God and his people. The discussion of the similarities between the call of Moses and Paul is crucial, therefore, in showing how Paul adapts the structural form of the prophets to highlight the fact that he too is called in the same way. Paul's use of the Mosaic tradition is evidence that he fulfills the expectation for a second Moses only in the same terms that all prophets fulfill this expectation, namely in the structure of their divine call and their function as a mediator between God and his people.[59] This may also explain Paul's relatively infrequent reference to Moses throughout his epistles.[60] The correlation between them is one of ministerial type, not ontological identity. In other words, Paul and Moses are both mediators, but they do not function in precisely the same ways. The key distinctions outlined in 2 Cor. 3.7-11, for example, highlight that Paul does not mediate the covenant, but the Spirit. That is, Paul was called to be a minister of the new covenant in order that he might be a mediator of the Spirit (and not a new law) that transforms the new covenant community.[61]

Although it may reasonably be argued that Paul does not present himself as a fulfillment of the promise of a prophet like Moses, there are several important notions to be drawn from Paul's comparison of his own ministry and the ministry of Moses. First, even though Paul does not see himself as the embodiment of Deut. 18.15-18, it is possible to show that Paul conceives of his ministry in terms of the overarching purpose of the prophetic tradition.[62] However, this notion of fulfillment places Paul on a slightly different plane than Moses and the rest of the prophets. Instead of standing in entirely the same position, Paul's view of his ministry is comparatively different in terms of its perspective upon the Lord's work in the gospel.[63] In other words, the 'eschatological prophets

---

58. Peter R. Jones, review of Scott J. Hafemann, *Suffering and the Spirit: An Exegetical Study of II Cor. 2:14–3:3 within the Context of the Corinthian Correspondence*, *EvQ* 59 (1987): 374. Original emphasis.
59. Hafemann, *Paul, Moses, and the History of Israel*, 103.
60. Cf. Oakes, 'Moses in Paul', 249, 260.
61. Hafemann, *Paul, Moses, and the History of Israel*, 102 n. 32.
62. So Sandnes, *Paul—One of the Prophets?*, passim.
63. Sandnes, *Paul—One of the Prophets?*, 243-44.

proclaiming the final comfort in the Last Days are the apostles of Jesus Christ proclaiming the gospel'.[64] In this way, Paul's comparisons between his ministry and the ministry of Moses in 2 Cor. 3.7-11 serve to show not a deficiency in the ministry of Moses, but a transition in God's dealings with his own people and a difference in the nature of the ministry of his servants.

Likewise, Paul's discussion of the difference between his own ministry and that of Moses in 2 Cor. 3.13 again highlights not a deficiency in Moses, his ministry, or the glory he received from the Lord, but a transition because of the Father's work through the Spirit.[65] In contrast to the judgment brought forth through the ministry of Moses, Paul's own apostolic ministry, understood through the material in Ezekiel 36 and Jeremiah 31 that provides the foundational background for the argument in 2 Cor. 3.1-6, serves as evidence for the notion that God is bringing his new covenant promise to achieve a proper and personal relationship between himself and his people to fruition within the Corinthian community.[66] Paul's intention in 2 Cor. 3.12-13, therefore, is not to contrast his open and truthful behavior with an act of deception by Moses; rather, he is seemingly expressing the idea that his ministry is characteristic of a glory that has its τέλος in the life-giving work of the Spirit.[67]

Third, as with Paul's allusion to the call of Moses (cf. 2 Cor. 2.16; 3.4), his discussion of the similarities and differences between their ministries serves as a historical argument for the authoritative nature of his ministry. Hafemann's work in outlining the place of the call of Moses in historical interpretation leads to the conclusion that this comparison 'could effectively silence the criticism of his opponents that his prior persecution of the Church and present ongoing weakness rendered him insufficient for the apostolic ministry'.[68] Paul's discussion of the call and ministry of Moses are not necessarily pre-conditioned by the rhetoric and actions of his opponents in Corinth. Although his allusions to Moses do not undermine any claim against his apostleship, Paul uses the Mosaic tradition in order to explain the effects and characteristics of his ministry.

---

64. Sandnes, *Paul—One of the Prophets?*, 244.
65. David E. Garland, *2 Corinthians* (NAC 29; Nashville: Broadman & Holman, 1999), 190.
66. Hafemann, *Paul, Moses, and the History of Israel*, 361. See also C.F.D. Moule, 'Fulfilment-Words in the New Testament', *NTS* 14 (1968): 293-320.
67. Margaret E. Thrall, *A Critical and Exegetical Commentary on the Second Epistle to the Corinthians* (2 vols.; ICC 34; Edinburgh: T. & T. Clark, 1994–2000), 1:256.
68. Hafemann, *Paul, Moses, and the History of Israel*, 105.

The opponents were questioning what they could see of Paul's ministry and this led to Paul's composition of his own formulation for the foundation and outworking of his place as a minister of the new covenant.

### c. *The Function of Paul's Ministry*

If it can be argued that Paul presents the call and nature of his ministry as parallel to that of Moses, it may then be helpful to determine how this association with the Mosaic tradition impacts the actual function of Paul's ministry. More specifically, if Paul is defining his apostolic ministry as a corollary to the prophetic tradition, how is this connection worked out pragmatically in the course of his ministry? It may be possible to define at least two specific ways in which the Mosaic tradition affects the outworking of Paul's apostolic ministry. The first is in Paul's use of the term διάκονος, which serves a key role in 2 Corinthians in defining the functional nature of Paul's ministry. The second is Paul's emphasis in the epistle on the reality of his physical suffering, which may create an implicit connection with both the Mosaic tradition and the entire prophetic tradition.

Within the New Testament, the διακον-terminology is used primarily, though not exclusively, in the Pauline corpus. Difficulty arises, however, when one accounts for the overwhelming number of contexts within which Paul can use the terminology.[69] In his monograph on the word group, Collins attempts to show that Paul's use of the word διάκονος is consistent with that of non-Christian writers and that it comes to have a specific and technical meaning. In more specific terms, Collins asserts that Paul's use of the noun connotes the idea of 'messengers on assignment from God'.[70] Collins, therefore, attempts to show that the word group, in and of itself, does not bring forth any idea of inferiority or inadequacy. In contrast, he argues that the word group, and particularly the noun διάκονος, establishes the notion of a 'go-between' or representative. This act of mediation or representation, however, does not refer specifically to the social status associated with the work. The service can reflect either a notion of humility or dignity.[71] However, as Clarke shows, Collins' analysis does not provide an adequate reading of the entire word

---

69. See Andrew D. Clarke, *A Pauline Theology of Church Leadership* (LNTS 362; London: T&T Clark International, 2008), 60-61.

70. John N. Collins, *Diakonia: Re-interpreting the Ancient Sources* (Oxford: Oxford University Press, 1990), 195. A similar notion of emissary can be found in Georgi, *Opponents*, 29-31.

71. Collins, *Diakonia*, 194.

group, especially in light of its use within the Synoptic tradition.[72] Clarke helpfully notes that Paul's use of the word group, particularly within 2 Corinthians, is often coupled with the overarching theme of suffering.[73] It appears, therefore, that Paul's use of the word group neither refers only to his authoritative position as a divine spokesman nor only to his position as a lowly servant. Instead, it seems that one of the main ideas behind Paul's usage is that of his activity as both an apostle and a servant of Christ.

As a result, Paul's use of the διακον-terminology seems to be more general in nature. His specific use of διάκονος in 2 Cor. 3.6 does not refer particularly to his apostolic status but to the functional nature of his apostleship. In other words, Paul's use of this particular word group is not the means by which he expresses the reality of his apostolic authority to the Corinthians; rather, it functions as an additional argument, in conjunction with the testimony offered in the actual existence of the Christian community in Corinth (2 Cor. 3.2), that Paul's ministry is sufficient and God-ordained.[74] It seems likely, therefore, that Paul's designation of himself as a διάκονος καινῆς διαθήκης is meant to highlight the fact that he has been called to function as a mediator of the Spirit among the new covenant community in spite of any lack of status or suffering that may accompany that activity.

The thrust of Paul's use of the διακον-terminology, including the specific uses of διάκονος and διάκονοι in 2 Cor. 3.6, 6.4, and 11.23, points to the notion that the apostle is a minister whose authority is not derived from his status, but by his work of ministering the gospel even amidst his continual sufferings and hardships. Although Collins does well to emphasize the notion of mediation that is part of the term, a sense of menial servant-hood can also be seen to fall into the semantic range of the terminology. Paul is able, therefore, to use the term of numerous people and in a variety of contexts because it does not refer to a precise title, but brings forth a notion of mediated service, which often deals with the ministry of the gospel. In connection to the ministry of Moses, Paul can be seen again to be an insufficient individual who is called to difficult service by God.[75]

---

72. Clarke, *Pauline Theology*, 65-66.
73. Clarke, *Pauline Theology*, 67.
74. Cf. Hafemann's critique of Collins in *Paul, Moses, and the History of Israel*, 113 n. 73.
75. It should be noted again that the διακον-terminology itself does not establish this notion. Moreover, all the occurrences of the word group need not express this meaning in its entirety. The argument here is that Paul's use of the word group

As noted in the discussion of the διακον-terminology, there is a strong connection between the function of Paul's ministry and the reality of the suffering that accompanies it. Again, Moses serves as a helpful parallel for Paul. Of particular importance in this parallel is Moses' intercession with the Lord in Exod. 32.31-32. Within these verses Moses is seen to be willing to suffer on behalf of sinful Israel.[76] This passage is important for two reasons. First, the narrative of Exodus 32–34 serves as the primary background to Paul's extended discussion in 2 Cor. 3.7-18. In light of this contextual association it seems likely that Paul was aware of Moses' willingness to suffer for his people and that it helped shape his own self-presentation to some degree. This can be seen, for example, in Paul's own use of Mosaic terminology when he speaks of his willingness to suffer for Israel in Rom. 9.3.[77] If Paul sees both his call and the nature of his ministry as parallel with that of Moses, it is possible to posit that he perceives parallels with regard to their functions as well. Secondly, as Hafemann's precise exegetical study of 2 Cor. 2.14-16 illustrates, Paul understands suffering to be a distinctive part of his ministry.[78] Paul seems not only to be aware of the logical implications of the connections between the two ministries (2 Cor. 3.7-18), but also of the pragmatic connections between himself and Moses. Just as Moses, an insufficient human, was called to minister among and suffer for his people, so too is Paul called to be a minister who suffers for his people and one who ministers through those sufferings (cf. 2 Cor. 12.10; 13.4).

d. *Conclusions*
Paul's close relationship with Moses can be seen in the similar structures of their ministerial calls, the parallel natures of their ministries, and the related characteristics of their ministerial functions. The structure of

---

within 2 Corinthians supports the idea that he is an authoritative minister of the gospel because of the sufficiency he received from the Lord (cf. 2 Cor. 3.1-6).

76. It is important to note, however, that Moses would not be able to atone for the sins of Israel. This point is seen transparently in the Lord's response to Moses in Exod. 32.33-34; cf. Durham, *Exodus*, 432. Albert Gelin, 'Moses im Alten Testament', in *Moses in Schrift und Überlieferung* (ed. Albert Gelin; Düsseldorf: Patmos, 1963), 31-37, makes a similar argument concerning Moses' willingness to suffer for Israel in light of Num. 11.12.

77. Douglas J. Moo, *The Epistle to the Romans* (NICNT; Grand Rapids: Eerdmans, 1996), 558-59; Johannes Munck, *Christ and Israel: An Interpretation of Romans 9–11* (trans. Ingeborg Nixon; Philadelphia: Fortress, 1967), 29; Gordon P. Wiles, *Paul's Intercessory Prayers: The Significance of the Intercessory Prayer Passages in the Letters of Paul* (SNTSMS 24; Cambridge: Cambridge University Press, 1974), 256.

78. Hafemann, *Suffering and the Spirit*, 41-87.

Paul's call points to the reality that the sufficiency of his ministry is derived solely from the gracious work of the Lord and not from himself. The similarities and differences between the ministries of the two men likewise highlight the nature of the Lord's work among his people. Paul's argument in 2 Cor. 3.7-18 serves not to disparage Moses and his ministry, but to highlight the Lord's new work through Paul in the present age. In addition, Paul's use of the διακον-terminology and his focus upon his suffering (e.g. 2 Cor. 2.14-16) exhibit a correlation between himself and Moses. Both serve the Lord in and through their insufficiency and suffering. It is important to note, however, that these parallels do not establish Paul as the second Moses. More accurately, these distinct parallels support the thesis that Paul conceives of at least a general connection between his own ministry and that manifest in the preceding prophetic tradition of the Old Testament, even if his place within salvation history was distinct from it.

The assertion that Paul should not be seen as a fulfillment of the second Moses tradition can also be seen in the fact that other prophetic figures play a significant role within Paul's self-presentation and rhetoric. That is, Paul's self-presentation stems not only from his relationship with Moses, but also from other portions of the prophetic tradition. Therefore, it will be helpful to analyse further the way in which Paul models his ministry in light of the lives and writings of other members of the prophetic tradition, particularly the Isaianic servant and Jeremiah.

## 3. *The Relationship between Paul and the Isaianic Servant*

As with Paul's use of various aspects of the Mosaic tradition to formulate his apostolic self-presentation within 2 Corinthians, the Isaianic tradition arguably plays a prominent role in Paul's presentation of his self-conception, and likely provides a basis for his discourse with the Corinthian community.[79] Complexity arises, however, when one attempts

---

79. It is beyond the scope of this work to discuss exhaustively the various partition theories that pertain to the book of Isaiah. Although it is possible to delineate two, or possibly three, different portions within Isaiah, it is relatively clear that Paul does not make this authorial distinction, using the formula Ἡσαίας γὰρ λέγει to refer to all of the major sections of the book (cf. Rom. 10.16, 20; 15.12). Thus, even though much of Paul's use of Isaiah in 2 Corinthians represents material from so-called Deutero-Isaiah, the separation does not appear to affect Paul's own understanding of the theological import of Isaiah. For a full discussion of the partition theories for the book of Isaiah, see Oswalt, *Isaiah*, 1:17-28; Christopher R. Seitz, 'On the Question of Divisions Internal to the Book of Isaiah', in *SBL Seminar Papers, 1993* (ed. Eugene H. Lovering, Jr.; SBLSP 32; Atlanta: Scholars Press, 1993), 260-66.

to determine the specific way in which the Isaianic material influences Paul. The apostle's close reading of the Exodus narrative in the early portion of the epistle focused on the relationship between the respective ministries of Moses and himself, as well as the particular relationship between the two figures. Similarly, Paul's use of the narrative of Isaiah and its accompanying theological message seemingly provide much of the background for Paul's discourse both in 2 Corinthians as a whole and in the specific argument of 2 Cor. 5.11–6.10.[80] However, Paul's use of Isaiah appears to move in at least one distinct direction. This distinction revolves around Paul's incorporation of specific aspects of the Isaianic material in the presentation of his own apostolic ministry. This point is seen most clearly in the relationship between the Isaianic servant of the Lord and the apostle.[81] Paul's relationship with Isaiah, therefore, does not

---

80. It can be argued that the text of Isaiah plays a critical role throughout the entire Pauline corpus. C.J.A. Hickling, 'Paul's Reading of Isaiah', in *Papers on Paul and Other New Testament Authors* (vol. 3 of *Studia Biblica 1978: Sixth International Congress on Biblical Studies, Oxford 3–7 April 1978*; ed. Elizabeth A. Livingstone; JSNTSup 3; Sheffield: JSOT, 1980), 215-23, posits that 26 percent of Paul's Old Testament quotations are derived from Isaiah. Savage, *Power Through Weakness*, 113 n. 50, places the number at 28 percent. Although staggering, neither one of these figures is able to account for the potential myriad of allusions or echoes of Isaiah within the Pauline corpus.

81. The idea that Paul is in some way related to the Isaianic servant of the Lord is, in and of itself, not a novel idea. Some semblance of a relationship has been noticed over the last several decades of New Testament scholarship. See, for example, G.K. Beale, 'The Old Testament Background of Reconciliation in 2 Corinthians 5–7 and Its Bearing on the Literary Problem of 2 Corinthians 6.14–7.1', *NTS* 35 (1989): 550-81; William S. Campbell, 'Israel', *DPL* 445; Lucien Cerfaux, 'Saint Paul et le 'serviteur de Dieu' d'Isaïe', in *Recueil Lucien Cerfaux* (3 vols.; BETL 6-7; Gembloux: Duculot, 1954), 2:439-54; Craig A. Evans, 'Prophet, Paul as', *DPL* 762-65; Paul E. Dinter, 'Paul and the Prophet Isaiah', *BTB* 13 (1983): 48-52; Anthony T. Hanson, *The Living Utterances of God: The New Testament Exegesis of the Old* (London: Darton, Longman & Todd, 1983), 39; Tom Holland, *Contours of Pauline Theology: A Radical New Survey of the Influences on Paul's Biblical Writings* (Fearn: Christian Focus, 2004), 69-82; Seyoon Kim, *The Origin of Paul's Gospel* (WUNT 2/4; Tübingen: Mohr Siebeck, 1981), 91-99; Kar Yong Lim, *'The Sufferings of Christ Are Abundant in Us' (2 Corinthians 1.5): A Narrative Dynamics Investigation of Paul's Sufferings in 2 Corinthians* (LNTS 399; London: T&T Clark International, 2009), 128-39; Ralph P. Martin, *Reconciliation: A Study of Paul's Theology* (Atlanta: John Knox, 1981), 90-110; Munck, *Paul*, 26; Walter Radl, 'Alle Mühe umsonst? Paulus und der Gottesknecht', in *L'Apôtre Paul: Personnalité, style et conception du ministère* (ed. Albert Vanhoye; BETL 73; Leuven: Leuven University Press, 1986), 144-49; Thomas R. Schreiner, *Paul, Apostle of God's Glory in Christ: A Pauline Theology* (Downers Grove, Ill.: InterVarsity, 2001), 47-49; David M. Stanley, 'The Theme of the Servant

appear to parallel the prophet himself, but the content of his prophetic message.[82] In light of this particular function of the Isaianic material, the intention within this section is to analyse Paul's relationship with the Isaianic servant of the Lord in order to determine its significance for the apostle's presentation of his ministry in 2 Corinthians.

a. *Paul and the Servant Outside of 2 Corinthians*
Prior to discussing the significance of the ministry of the servant of the Lord within 2 Corinthians it will be helpful to survey Paul's use of the tradition outside of the Corinthian correspondence. In addition, it will be useful to address the way in which the Lukan material describes the relationship between Paul and the servant. This brief survey will provide some insight into the surrounding tradition concerning the connection between Paul's ministry and that of the servant. It should be noted, however, that there is likely a certain amount of inter-dependence between these traditions. The purpose of this survey is not to establish either the historical significance or the theological implications of the relationship between Paul and the servant tradition; rather, it is meant to highlight the fact that this relationship is not merely contingent upon the Corinthian community and, consequently, not upon the particular adversity which Paul is facing in 2 Corinthians.

The Lukan tradition contains several essential texts in this regard. Of preeminent importance is Acts 13.47. When Paul and Barnabas are confronted negatively by Jews in Pisidian-Antioch because of the content of their preaching, they respond by quoting the mission given to the servant of the Lord in Isa. 49.6: τέθικά σε εἰς φῶς ἐθνῶν τοῦ εἶναί σε εἰς σωτηρίαν ἕως ἐσχάτου τῆς γῆς. These words, which stem from the second of the so-called servant songs, seem to highlight the notion that the apostolic ministry is a continuation of the mission given to the servant of the Lord. Interestingly, however, similar thematic connections are made between the ministry of Jesus and the ministry of the servant in Lk. 2.32. Thus, within the Lukan tradition both Christ and his followers are connected to

---

of Yahweh in Primitive Christian Soteriology, and Its Transposition by St. Paul', *CBQ* 16 (1954): 385-425; William J. Webb, *Returning Home: New Covenant and Second Exodus as the Context for 2 Corinthians 6.14–7.1* (JSNTSup 85; Sheffield: JSOT, 1993), 128-31, 145, 150.

82. It is of course possible that the servant of the Lord tradition in Isaiah has its historical referent in Isaiah (or Deutero-Isaiah) himself. However, it appears, that one of the important aspects of the four so-called servant songs is the overarching anonymity of the servant; see Childs, *Isaiah*, 414; cf. Claus Westermann, *Isaiah 40–66* (OTL; London: SCM, 1969), 93.

the commission of the servant.[83] However, as Barrett points out, Luke's imagery, whether it is intentional or not, does not give Christ and the apostles equal status. More accurately, Paul and Barnabas achieve their mission of bringing light to the Gentiles by preaching Christ, but Christ is a light to the Gentiles because he is the object of their proclamation.[84]

Similar themes can be seen in the narration of Paul's call in his dialogue with Agrippa in Acts 26. The notion in Acts 26.17-18 that part of Paul's mission was to open the eyes of the Gentiles is also rooted in the surrounding context of the servant's commission in the first servant song (Isa. 42.7).[85] Bruce is even willing to assert that 'the commission of Paul and of all Christian witnesses is the perpetuation of the Servant's commission'.[86] Although it is important to see the connection between Paul and the Isaianic servant, it is likely progressing too far at this point to claim a precise perpetuation between the two, particularly because Luke himself also sees a connection between the servant and Jesus (cf. Lk. 2.32). It will be beneficial, therefore, to examine the way in which Paul conceives of his relationship with the servant. At this point, however, it is helpful simply to note that there is some basis for seeing a connection between Paul and the servant, whether intentional or unintentional, outside of the Pauline corpus.

Within the Pauline corpus there are several references to the servant tradition in Deutero-Isaiah.[87] Of first importance is Paul's autobiographical statement in Gal. 1.15 that God set him apart ἐκ κοιλίας μητρός μου. Even though it is possible that Paul is here alluding to the call narrative found in Jer. 1.5 (πρὸ τοῦ με πλάσαι σε ἐν κοιλίᾳ ἐπίσταμαί σε καὶ πρὸ τοῦ σε ἐξελθεῖν ἐκ μήτρας ἡγίακά σε), it is also likely that the words echo the

83. I. Howard Marshall, 'Acts', in Beale and Carson (eds.), *Commentary*, 588.
84. Barrett, *Acts*, 1:658.
85. Although there is some debate concerning the precise content of the songs within Isaiah, this work will delineate the four songs as follows: (1) 42.1-4, (2) 49.1-6, (3) 50.4-9, (4) 52.13–53.12. This programmatic delineation, however, is not an affirmation that the songs themselves are either a later interpolation or irrelevant to the overall message of Isa. 40–66; contra the seminal argument of Bernhard Duhm, *Das Buch Jesaia* (HKAT; Göttingen: Vandenhoeck & Ruprecht, 1892). Attempts to read the songs within their literary context have recently become more prevalent; e.g. W.A.M. Beuken, 'Mispat: The First Servant Song in Its Context', *VT* 22 (1972): 1-30; Childs, *Isaiah*, 323.
86. Bruce, *Acts*, 492.
87. For the sake of clarity this work will refer to all of Isa. 40–66 as 'Deutero-Isaiah'. This identification is not, however, a judgment on the level of connection between these chapters and Isa. 1–39. For the relationship between Isa. 1–39 and 40–66, see Christopher R. Seitz, 'How Is the Prophet Isaiah Present in the Latter Half of the Book? The Logic of Chapters 40–66', *JBL* 115 (1996): 219-40.

servant's claim in Isa. 49.1 that ἐκ κοιλίας μητρός μου ἐκάλεσεν τὸ ὄνομά μου.[88] Apart from the discrepancy concerning the primary referent of Paul's allusion, this autobiographical statement has been used as one of the foundations upon which to build the argument that Paul is to be uniquely identified with the servant of the Lord.[89] However, in light of the fact that both Jeremiah and the servant describe their divine calling as taking place prior to their birth, it may be more feasible to affirm that the relationship between Paul and the servant is not ontological, but historical.[90] That is, Paul's assertion that God called him prior to his birth seemingly supports the notion that his apostolic ministry is an extension of the preceding prophetic tradition.[91] In this way, the allusion to the servant material is not one of precise identification, but of historical correspondence. Paul, as with his allusion to the call of Moses, here places his own ministry within the stream of the prophetic tradition.

This ministerial connection is also seen in Paul's use of the servant tradition in his letter to the Romans. In Rom. 10.15-16 Paul quotes two texts from the fourth servant song, Isa. 52.7 and 53.1, in reference to the proclamation of the gospel. Paul's likely logical thrust in the passage is to affirm that the proclamation of the gospel completes the necessary conditions for the message of salvation to go forth (cf. Rom. 10.14).[92] In other words, Paul here quotes from Deutero-Isaiah in order to show that the apostolic proclamation is itself a fulfillment of the message of this

88. Although commentators vary on their understanding of the primary text in Paul's mind, there is little disagreement that the language of the text compares both to the Isaianic servant and to Jeremiah; see, e.g., F.F. Bruce, *The Epistle to the Galatians* (NIGTC; Grand Rapids: Eerdmans, 1982), 92; Ronald Y.K. Fung, *The Epistle to the Galatians* (NICNT; Grand Rapids: Eerdmans, 1988), 63; Richard N. Longenecker, *Galatians* (WBC 41; Nashville: Thomas Nelson, 1990), 30; Ben Witherington III, *Grace in Galatia: A Commentary on St Paul's Letter to the Galatians* (Grand Rapids: Eerdmans, 1998), 105.

89. E.g. Campbell, 'Israel', 445; Roy E. Ciampa, *The Presence and Function of Scripture in Galatians 1 and 2* (WUNT 2/102; Tübingen: Mohr Siebeck, 1998), 111-18; Stanley, 'The Theme of the Servant', 420. For a concise analysis of the Isaianic elements of Gal. 1.15-16, see Seyoon Kim, *Paul and the New Perspective: Second Thoughts on the Origin of Paul's Gospel* (WUNT 140; Tübingen: Mohr Siebeck, 2002), 101-27.

90. Peter T. O'Brien, *Gospel and Mission in the Writings of Paul: An Exegetical and Theological Analysis* (Grand Rapids: Baker, 1995), 7, 12; cf. Ferdinand Hahn, 'Der Apostolat im Urchristentum: seine Eigenart und seine Voraussetzungen', *KD* 20 (1974): 54-77 (68).

91. See, e.g., J. Louis Martyn, *Galatians* (AB 33A; New York: Doubleday, 1997), 157; Nicklas, 'Paulus—der Apostel als Prophet', 84; Schnelle, *Apostle Paul*, 89-90.

92. Moo, *Romans*, 664.

portion of the Isaianic tradition. However, it does not appear that Paul is asserting a direct connection between himself and the servant at this point. The argument here is not primarily a defence of his apostolic ministry; rather, these quotations help form the basis for the larger argument in this section of the epistle that the message of salvation for both Israel and the nations that was proclaimed in Isaiah has now become available.[93] Additionally, Paul references the fourth servant song (i.e. Isa. 52.15) in Rom. 15.21 with reference to his call to preach to the Gentiles. The key distinction at this point, as in Acts, is that Paul serves by proclaiming about the servant (περὶ αὐτοῦ). It seems, therefore, that Paul is not asserting that he is the servant of the Lord, but that he serves as a herald of the message *about* the servant of the Lord.[94] Moreover, although these references provide a basis for seeing that Paul, at least in some way, understood the servant tradition Christologically, the present emphasis is more readily understood in either missiological or ministerial categories.[95] More specifically, Paul affirms that the servant tradition provides a basis for understanding the content of his ministry with regard specifically to his work of proclamation.

Three additional texts within the Pauline corpus (i.e. Gal. 2.2; 1 Thess. 3.5; Phil. 2.16) represent potential allusions to the servant of the Lord material. As with the discussion of Gal. 1.15, the argument surrounding the connection of these texts with the servant songs is lexically based, with particular reference to the noun κενός and its cognates. It is argued that the presence of the prepositional phrase εἰς κενόν, which occurs in each of the three New Testament passages, echoes the cry of the servant in Isa. 49.4: κενῶς ἐκοπίασα. Just as the servant momentarily feared that his labour would come to nought, so too is Paul periodically fearful that the difficult labour of his ministry would not come to fruition. Thus, not only does the content of Paul's ministry have some connection with the servant, his own character and ministerial concerns are formed, at least in part, from the servant tradition. To some extent, therefore, it seems reasonable to confirm that the Isaianic servant tradition serves as a template for the nature and function of his own apostolic ministry.[96]

---

93. Thomas R. Schreiner, *Romans* (BECNT; Grand Rapids: Baker, 1998), 569.
94. J. Ross Wagner, 'The Heralds of Isaiah and the Mission of Paul: An Investigation of Paul's Use of Isaiah 51–55 in Romans', in *Jesus and the Suffering Servant: Isaiah 53 and Christian Origins* (ed. William H. Bellinger Jr. and William R. Farmer; Harrisburg: Trinity Press International, 1998), 221-22.
95. Wagner, 'Heralds of Isaiah', 222.
96. Cf. Lim, *'The Sufferings of Christ'*, 131-32.

It is again helpful to notice, however, that these allusions, though strong, do not create an explicit link between the identity of the servant and the apostolic persona of Paul. What can be said at this point is that Paul's ministry is in some way parallel to that of the servant, as well as to the rest of the prophetic tradition. As was seen in Paul's relationship with Moses, Paul's call and ministerial function reflect the call and function of the servant tradition. To help clarify Paul's particular relationship with the servant, as a way to determine one of the ways in which Paul uses the Isaianic tradition, the analysis will now turn to the function and place of the relationship between Paul and the servant within 2 Corinthians.

b. *Paul and the Servant Within 2 Corinthians*
Paul's use of the servant tradition in 2 Corinthians is particularly apparent in 2 Cor. 6.2, which contains a direct quotation from Isa. 49.8, a verse found within the immediate context of the second servant song. While the quotation occurs in the midst of Paul's apostolic defence, the importance of the quotation is not derived solely from this structural reality. More helpful is the realization that the quotation plays an important role in Paul's specific argument in 2 Cor. 5.11–6.10.[97] This particular portion of Paul's argument is based significantly on the narrative movement of Isaiah 40–66.[98] The quotation, therefore, appears to serve as a more transparent manifestation of the elusive notion that Paul's argument here centres on the theological import of the whole of Isaiah 40–66. Furthermore, the quotation and its surrounding context within 2 Corinthians provide an important window through which to view Paul's conception of Jesus' position with respect to the Isaianic servant tradition. It will be beneficial, therefore, to analyse briefly both the context of the passage quoted and the material preceding the quotation. This will allow for a consistent understanding of this portion of Paul's argument and help to elucidate the way in which the apostle's ministry may parallel that of the servant.

---

97. The thesis of Gignilliat, *Paul and Isaiah's Servants*, that Paul's apostolic self-conception lies in an identification with the servants of Isaiah, as found in Isa. 56–66, is discussed below.

98. The influence of Isa. 40–66 on this portion of 2 Corinthians is well documented. See, e.g., Beale, 'Old Testament Background'; Webb, *Returning Home*; Gignilliat, *Paul and Isaiah's Servants*. Although these three works differ in their particular conclusions about the function of the passage in Paul's argument, they are in agreement that Paul is reading the Isaianic narrative in light of its own context.

(1) *The Old Testament Context of Isaiah 49.8.* Prior to discussing the intent and function of Paul's quotation of Isa. 49.8, it will be helpful to discuss both the overarching message of Isaiah 40–66 and the logical progression in the four servant songs themselves. Apart from continued discussion of matters of authorship, discussion of this portion of Isaiah's prophecy has centred on determining the nature of the historical background of the text. Most frequently the historical referent of this section of Isaiah is located within the context of the Babylonian exile.[99] For this reason, the overarching message of the text is seen to be a call for the people to return to the land from their captivity in Babylon. It can be questioned, however, whether this historical circumstance provides enough of a foundation to support all of the material in Isaiah 40–66, or even the material spanning Isaiah 40–55. The realization that Deutero-Isaiah itself contains very few historical references may lead to the conclusion that this exilic background, though potentially present, is not the most helpful lens through which to analyse the text or its message. Indeed, it has even been argued that an understanding of this material as being formulated from this background is 'unnecessary and less plausible, both on literary and on historical grounds'.[100] More useful, arguably, is the idea that the content of these chapters is focused on the more expansive notion of God's eschatological work in the world to bring about a new reality for both Israel and the nations. It is likely that references to the Babylonian exile (e.g. Isa. 45.1; 52.10-12) are part of a more extensive discussion of God's work in bringing about a new exodus or new creation.[101]

This eschatological message can be delineated in several ways throughout Deutero-Isaiah.[102] Most clearly, there is a continued focus on the dichotomy between the old, former things and those that are new (e.g.

---

99. E.g. Westermann, *Isaiah 40–66*; Arvid S. Kapelrud, 'The Main Concern of Second Isaiah', *VT* 32 (1982): 50-58. See, however, Lena-Sofia Tiemeyer, *For the Comfort of Zion: The Geographical and Theological Location of Isaiah 40–55* (VTSup 139; Leiden: Brill, 2010), who argues extensively that the material in Isa. 40–55 reflects a Judahite setting.

100. Christopher R. Seitz, 'Isaiah 40–66', *NIB* 6:316; cf. Tiemeyer, *For the Comfort of Zion*, passim.

101. The presence of this eschatological message likely serves as one of the factors for Paul's incorporation of the Isaianic tradition in 2 Corinthians; cf. Lim, 'The Sufferings of Christ', 135.

102. Much of the following discussion of the eschatological theme is dependent on Childs, *Isaiah*, 446. Significantly, Childs uses these characteristics to show the literary and theological unity between Isa. 40–55 and 56–66, which have commonly been thought to represent two distinct historical and literary traditions.

## 4. Paul's Prophetic Self-Presentation in 2 Corinthians 141

Isa. 43.18-19; 65.16-17). The passing away of the old things and the creation of the new are the primary characteristics of God's work in bringing about a new age. This new age involves an exilic return and freedom for both Israel and the nations (cf. Isa. 43.1-9). Of additional importance is the role of the Spirit as one of the primary agents of this new work (Isa. 42.1; cf. 2 Cor. 3). The work of the Spirit is also connected with the work of the servant, which is itself a continuing theme throughout Isaiah 40–66.

As with the overarching message and historical continuity of the material in Deutero-Isaiah, discussion of the creation, form, and function of the so-called servant songs has had a sustained history in biblical scholarship.[103] Questions have particularly centred on the relation of the songs to their surrounding context and the identity, both historical and narrative, of the servant. The intent of the following discussion is not to deal with all of the exegetical (or theological) questions tied up with the songs, but to highlight the internal progression of the songs within the context of Isaiah 40–66. Consideration will also be given to the identity of the servant, as this relates particularly to Paul's own presentation of his relationship with the servant.

Within the eschatological theme of Isaiah 40–66, the term משפט comes to the forefront and could be regarded as a technical term for the content of God's new work. Childs defines the term as 'the restoration of God's order in the world' and discusses the connection of Israel's complaint in Isa. 40.27 with the mission of the servant as it is expressed in Isa. 42.1-4.[104] While this first song is relatively clear concerning the mission of the servant and his connection with God's new eschatological work, the issue of his identity is more complex. The actual terminology of עבד only serves to cloud the picture. Throughout the Old Testament the term is used for a variety of offices and persons, including the patriarchs (Gen. 24.14), the Levites (Ps. 113.1), prophets (Isa. 20.3), kings (2 Sam. 3.18), and Israel (Jer. 30.10).[105] That final reference (i.e. Israel) becomes even more problematic when one realizes that עבד does not occur initially in Isaiah within the first servant song, but in relation to Israel (Isa. 41.8). Aside from possible ambiguity within the other three songs, it is difficult to assert at this point that the servant is not in some way associated with the nation of Israel.[106] Although the context seems to demand the

---

103. Works pertaining to the songs, whether collectively or individually, are myriad and it would be impossible to survey the entire historical progression here. For an introductory survey of the literature, see Oswalt, *Isaiah*, 2:113-15.
104. Childs, *Isaiah*, 324-25.
105. Childs, *Isaiah*, 324.
106. Childs, *Isaiah*, 325.

recognition that Israel and the servant are related, the actual nature of the relationship is fairly opaque. In other words, even though there is a connection between their identities, there is a differentiation between their present character and role.[107] At this point, therefore, the servant's mission is related to God's work of eschatological restoration and his identity is, in some way, tied up with the nation of Israel.

The situation becomes more complex with the added content of the second song (i.e. Isa. 49.1-6). Of primary significance for this discussion is the nature of the identity of the servant within these verses. Although the first servant song linked the servant's identity with the nation, that identification becomes less clear within the parameters of this song. At first glance it appears that the servant is again designated *as* Israel in Isa. 49.3, only to receive a mission with reference *to* Israel in Isa. 49.5-6. The difficulty stems from the somewhat ambiguous statement in Isa. 49.3 that עבדי־אתה ישראל. Syntactically, it is possible to render the noun 'Israel' as a vocative, an appositive, or a predicative.[108] Several scholars contend that the noun here stands in the predicate position and, consequently, that Isa. 49.3 functions as an affirmation of the notion that the servant is representative of corporate Israel.[109] This argument also makes sense within the larger context of Deutero-Isaiah. Although the nation had originally been identified as the Lord's servant, the rebuke found in Isa. 42.18-19 and 48.8 highlights the idea that the nation had not completed the task assigned to the servant. It appears possible, therefore, that a progression from corporate to individual takes place within the songs themselves. An individual servant is now beginning to take on 'the role originally designated for Israel'.[110]

Although the third song (Isa. 50.4-9) contains its own linguistic and exegetical difficulties, Westermann claims that it is the easiest to comprehend out of the four.[111] Within these verses it appears that the servant

107. Peter Wilcox and David Paton-Williams, 'The Servant Songs in Deutero-Isaiah', *JSOT* 42 (1988): 79-102 (88).

108. Namely, 'You are my servant, O Israel', 'You are my servant, who is Israel', or 'You are my servant, you are Israel'. Cf. Childs, *Isaiah*, 383-84. The syntactical ambiguity persists in the LXX, which translates the verse 'literally' with the words Δοῦλός μου εἶ σύ, Ἰσραηλ. For a comprehensive study on the servant songs in the LXX, see Eugene Robert Ekblad Jr., *Isaiah's Servant Poems According to the Septuagint: An Exegetical and Theological Study* (CBET 23; Leuven: Peeters, 1999).

109. Childs, *Isaiah*, 384; Gignilliat, *Paul and Isaiah's Servants*, 73; Seitz, 'Isaiah 40–66', 429; Wilcox and Paton-Williams, 'The Servant Songs', 90.

110. Gignilliat, *Paul and Isaiah's Servants*, 73; cf. Christopher R. Seitz, '"You Are My Servant, You Are the Israel in Whom I Will Be Glorified": The Servant Songs and the Effect of Literary Context in Isaiah', *CTJ* 39 (2004): 117-34 (128).

111. Westermann, *Isaiah 40–66*, 226.

is again the speaker and that he is most readily identified as an individual. Significantly, this individual now suffers oppression (Isa. 50.6). The significance at this point is not necessarily in the oppression itself, but in the servant's obedience to the Lord and recognition of the Lord's faithfulness in spite of his physical suffering. The nation had failed to be obedient to their calling, but the servant now embodies faithful service. Here again the narrative of Deutero-Isaiah itself appears to point to a movement from a corporate understanding of the servant to an individual identification.[112] The particular identity of this individual, however, is still not explicit within the text.

If the third servant song can be described as the least complex of the four, then the fourth (i.e. Isa. 52.13–53.12) would likely have to be deemed the most complex. Difficulty with this text emerges not only from its place and function within the Isaianic corpus, but also from the long history of its interpretation within the Christian tradition.[113] Apart from textual, literary, and linguistic questions, the song plays a crucial role within the narrative movement of Deutero-Isaiah. Significantly, this passage serves to highlight the convergence between God's eschatological work in bringing about the new creation and the servant's role within that work. Of particular importance here is the notion that the servant will be raised, lifted up, and highly exalted (Isa. 52.13). Within the Isaianic corpus these descriptions 'are virtually technical terms, applied almost exclusively to Yahweh'.[114] Thus, even in the early stages of the song there appears to be a close connection developed between the identity of YHWH and the identity of the servant. Crucial here is the work of Bauckham, who argues based on the linguistic connections between Isa. 6.1, 52.13, and 57.15 that Isa. 52.13 is meant to express the narrative identification between God and the servant, who 'belongs to the identity of the unique God'.[115]

This convergence of identities becomes even more important as one attempts to understand the overall theological import of the passage. Although much can be said about the value of Isaiah 53 in a discussion of the systematic category of atonement, it is difficult to avoid the implication of the text that the servant plays a crucial role in God's new work

112. Childs, *Isaiah*, 395; Gignilliat, *Paul and Isaiah's Servants*, 76.
113. For a survey of the use of this song in the interpretative history of the Christian tradition, see John Sawyer, *The Fifth Gospel: Isaiah in the History of Christianity* (Cambridge: Cambridge University Press, 1996).
114. Wilcox and Paton-Williams, 'The Servant Songs', 95.
115. Richard Bauckham, *Jesus and the God of Israel: God Crucified and Other Studies on the New Testament's Christology of Divine Identity* (Grand Rapids: Eerdmans, 2009), 36-37.

among Israel and the nations. In this way, it appears that the intercession of the servant goes beyond that of Moses (cf. Exod. 32.31-34), and is in some way more effectual.[116] Apart from this distinction, however, it may also be important to recognize a positive connection between Moses and the servant.[117] Deutero-Isaiah's description of God's eschatological work is reminiscent of the description of God's divine action in bringing his people out of Egypt. These potential references (e.g. Isa. 40.3-5; 41.17-20; 42.14-16; 43.1-3, 14-21; 49.8-12; 51.9-10; 52.11-12; 55.12-13) seem to support the notion that the exodus serves as one of the controlling themes of this portion of the Isaianic narrative. Furthermore, the plurality of these allusions may suggest a particular connection between the Isaianic servant and Moses himself.[118] Indeed, Hugenberger lists no fewer than twelve possible connections between the servant and Moses, including the ideas that Moses provides a helpful background for understanding the connection between the corporate and individual notions of the servant's identity and the connection between the call of the servant in Isa. 49.1-6 and the call of Moses in Exodus 3–4.[119] Although it can be argued that Deutero-Isaiah is formulated from a thematic understanding of a second exodus, it is probably moving too far beyond the context of Isaiah 40–66 to argue that the servant is the sole fulfillment of the Mosaic expectation expressed in Deut. 18.15-18. As with the earlier discussion of the relationship between Paul and Moses, it is seemingly more contextually feasible to argue that the servant's persona and ministry correspond to the preceding prophetic tradition in more general terms. In spite of this connection, it does appear that one of the implications of Isa. 52.13–53.12 is that the servant moves beyond the bounds of the prophetic

---

116. Gignilliat, *Paul and Isaiah's Servants*, 86. The way in which the servant's work is effectual is a matter of continual debate. The purpose of the statement here is not to argue for a specific understanding of the servant's work, but to affirm that within this song the servant has an important role in God's work of redemption and reconciliation.

117. As with Paul's connection to the servant, a connection between the servant and Moses is not a novel formulation in itself; cf. Ronald E. Clements, 'Isaiah 53 and the Restoration of Israel', in Bellinger and Farmer (eds.), *Jesus and the Suffering Servant*, 461-62; Gignilliat, *Paul and Isaiah's Servants*, 79-80; Gordon P. Hugenberger, 'The Servant of the Lord in the "Servant-Songs" of Isaiah: A Second Moses Figure', in *The Lord's Anointed: Interpretation of Old Testament Messianic Texts* (ed. Philip E. Satterthwaite, Richard S. Hess, and Gordon J. Wenham; Grand Rapids: Baker, 1995), 119-40.

118. Gerhard von Rad, *Old Testament Theology* (trans. D.M.G. Stalker; 2 vols.; San Francisco: Harper & Row, 1965), 2:261.

119. Hugenberger, 'The Servant of the Lord', 130-33.

tradition in some sense and becomes uniquely connected with the identity of YHWH himself. It is, however, the somewhat broader notion that the narrative foundation of Isaiah 40–55 is built, at least in part, on the thematic development of a second exodus motif and God's new, eschatological work that forms the essential point of correspondence with Paul's specific rhetorical developments in 2 Cor. 5.14-21 and 6.1-2.

(2) *The Argument of 2 Corinthians 5.14-21.* The content of 2 Corinthians 5–7 has been the subject of numerous debates with regard to its structure. Though important, the focus of the present analysis is not to determine the merits of the various redactional theories pertaining to this portion of the letter. Rather, the material in 2 Cor. 5.11–6.10 will be seen to form a cohesive unit and an attempt will be made to see how the rhetorical developments that Paul makes in both 2 Cor. 5.14-21 and 6.1-2 function within the defence of his apostolic ministry that forms the basis for the larger argument in 2 Cor. 2.14–7.4.[120] Following the basic structure of this unit proposed by Lambrecht, 2 Cor. 5.11-13 functions as an introduction to a new portion of Paul's defence, namely the discussion of the ministry of reconciliation.[121] The following material in 2 Cor. 5.14-21 then highlights the actual content and essence of this ministry in terms of its Christological and eschatological implications. The analysis will proceed with both an exegetical and a thematic discussion.

Paul's argument in 2 Cor. 5.14-15 functions as a bridge between the introductory comments concerning commendation (cf. 2 Cor. 3.1-3) and the subsequent discussion of the apostle's ministry of reconciliation. The initial phrase, ἡ γάρ ἀγάπη τοῦ Χριστοῦ συνέχει ἡμᾶς, provides the basis for the following material. Though συνέχω can have either a positive or negative meaning (e.g. compels vs. restrains), the idea here is more likely representative of the negative sphere. Christ's love (subjective genitive) is 'a dominating power that effectively eradicates choice in that it leaves [Paul] no option but to live for God'.[122] That this love represents a uniquely forceful entity stems from Paul's prior conviction ὅτι εἷς ὑπέρ πάντων ἀπέθανεν. This somewhat enigmatic statement is elucidated by the following clause and Paul's further discussion in 2 Cor. 5.15. This one died ὑπέρ πάντων so that those who live would be turned from

---

120. For an example of the view that this section does not cohere with the larger framework of 2 Corinthians, see Hendrikus Boers, '2 Corinthians 5:14–6:2: A Fragment of Pauline Christology', *CBQ* 64 (2002): 527-47.

121. Jan Lambrecht, '"Reconcile Yourselves ...": A Reading of 2 Corinthians 5,11-21', in Bieringer and Lambrecht (eds.), *Studies on 2 Corinthians*, 364-65.

122. Harris, *Second Corinthians*, 419; cf. Schmeller, *2 Korintherbrief*, 1:321-22.

self-sufficiency to a focus on the one who died and was raised ὑπέρ αὐτῶν. The complex nature of Paul's argument at this point arises primarily from the difficulty involved in determining the way in which one is to render the recurring preposition ὑπέρ, which could function to develop notions of either representation or substitution.[123] Paul's immediately subsequent affirmation in 2 Cor. 5.14, ἄρα οἱ πάντες ἀπέθανον, may suggest that the representative dimension of Christ's work is primary at this point, since the notion of substitution would seemingly require that others do not die.[124] Conversely, the particular emphasis on Christ's unique work in 2 Cor. 5.21 may indicate that Paul's terminology contains a nuanced balance of both the representative and substitutionary dimensions of Christ's work.[125] In more specific terms, the basic assertion of 2 Cor. 5.14-15 may contain reference to both notions, so that Christ is seen to have died both on behalf and in place of the all.[126]

It is this assertion that begins to establish parallels with the context of Deutero-Isaiah and the servant tradition. The potential impasse between the notion of representation and the notion of substitution also plagues discussions about the servant of the Lord in Deutero-Isaiah.[127] Placing the earlier discussion of the songs, particularly the fourth, and Paul's argument here in 2 Corinthians next to each other, it may be possible to see a connection between Paul's presentation of Christ and the presentation of the servant in Deutero-Isaiah. Both are seen to suffer on behalf of, and for, others. However, although the passages are somewhat parallel, there is at this point neither a precise connection between the servant and Jesus nor an explicit association between the ministry of Paul and the ministry of the servant.

The following verses, 2 Cor. 5.16-17, further clarify Paul's argument. If the death and resurrection of Christ (cf. 2 Cor. 5.15) function as a preliminary basis upon which the apostle can present his ministry of reconciliation, then 2 Cor. 5.16-17 can be seen as its consequence. There are again several difficult exegetical issues within these two verses. Of

123. This is, however, not the only issue. Ambiguity also surrounds the identification of the referent(s) for both πάντες and οἱ ζῶντες. With Harris, *Second Corinthians*, 420-21, it seems likely that the former deals with humanity as a whole and the latter refers only to those who are 'in Christ'. Cf. Moyer V. Hubbard, *New Creation in Paul's Letters and Thought* (SNTSMS 119; Cambridge: Cambridge University Press, 2002), 173; Lambrecht, *Second Corinthians*, 95.

124. So Hubbard, *New Creation*, 172.

125. Ralph P. Martin, *2 Corinthians* (WBC 40; Nashville: Thomas Nelson, 1986), 130-31.

126. So Harris, *Second Corinthians*, 421.

127. Gignilliat, *Paul and Isaiah's Servants*, 94.

primary importance for determining the message of 2 Cor. 5.16 is an analysis of the complexity surrounding the repeated prepositional phrase κατὰ σάρκα. Two specific questions arise. First, is the phrase adjectival or adverbial? Several considerations point to an adverbial understanding. As Harris notes, when the phrase κατὰ σάρκα is used to modify a noun it always follows the noun (or nominal participle).[128] Also, since the verb οἴδαμεν separates the noun from the prepositional phrase in the first part of the verse, it seems unlikely that the phrase can modify the noun οὐδένα in that instance. Because of this, it appears that at least the first occurrence is adverbial. This evidence, however, likely suggests that the parallel occurrence of the phrase in the latter section of the verse is also adverbial, being rendered appropriately with ἐγνώκαμεν and not Χριστόν. The second question concerns the actual meaning of κατὰ σάρκα in the present context. Three distinct possibilities emerge among the commentaries: (1) humanly, (2) worldly, or (3) externally.[129] Although all of these options may hold weight within the context, it seems that Paul's thrust is that his transformed conception about Christ (2 Cor. 5.14-15) ultimately shapes the way he views all people and all things. This becomes particularly transparent in light of Paul's following assertion in 2 Cor. 5.17.

Though brief, Paul's initial statement in 2 Cor. 5.17 is profound: ὥστε εἴ τις ἐν Χριστῷ, καινὴ κτίσις. The explicit introduction of the new creation theme makes it clear that Paul is focusing primarily on the new spiritual reality of those who are in Christ. Moreover, the discussion of the transition between old and new harks back to the overall context of Isaiah 40–55.[130] It appears, therefore, that Paul is alluding in some sense to the eschatological context of the Isaianic narrative. Although this will become more transparent in 2 Cor. 5.18-21, it is already possible to see at this point that the narrative movement in Deutero-Isaiah with respect to God's eschatological work through the servant parallels Paul's argument concerning the nature and function of Christ's death and resurrection in the present age. That is, although it is likely going too far to eliminate anthropological notions from the text, there is here an eschatological or cosmological focus on the new situation that has come about because of Christ's coming into the world.[131] To regard neither humans nor Christ κατὰ σάρκα, therefore, is to understand that God's work in Christ

---

128. E.g. Rom. 1.3; 4.1; 9.3, 5; 1 Cor. 1.26; 10.18; Harris, *Second Corinthians*, 428.
129. See Harris, *Second Corinthians*, 427, for a summary of the positions.
130. Beale, 'Old Testament Background', 553.
131. T. Ryan Jackson, *New Creation in Paul's Letters* (WUNT 2/272; Tübingen: Mohr Siebeck, 2010), 119-23; Martin, *2 Corinthians*, 152. For the notion that Paul's argument is entirely anthropological, see Hubbard, *New Creation*, 177-83.

affected the present era in such a way that the new creation and new eschatological age have become a present reality (cf. 2 Cor. 6.2).

The following verses, 2 Cor. 5.18-21, deal primarily with the topic of reconciliation, both in terms of its divine initiation and its function within the apostolic proclamation. Prior to discussing the function of καταλλάσσω and its cognates, however, it may be helpful to emphasize the identity of the primary actor within this portion of Paul's argument. Even a surface reading of the passage reveals that the primary work of reconciliation stems from God himself. This particular emphasis on divine initiative and action is also present within the Isaianic narrative, manifest primarily in the intersection between God's work and the mission of the servant.[132] For example, it is God who calls the servant (Isa. 49.1-6) and the servant's mission in the fourth servant song is earlier described as the arm of the Lord (Isa. 52.10). Paul's unique focus on God's activity with respect to the language of reconciliation, therefore, may suggest that the apostle is reliant at this point on the concept of restoration developed broadly in the Isaianic narrative and, more specifically, in God's work through the servant's sacrificial activity in Isa. 52.13–53.12.[133]

With regard to a more specific discussion of Paul's actual terminology in the present argument, it is helpful to note that the apostle's language of reconciliation has previously been analysed both categorically and lexically.[134] It is not the intent of this discussion to rehearse all of what can be said about the term, but to highlight its function within this portion of Paul's argument. In this vein, the discussion of Furnish is particularly lucid: 'In and of itself the tradition [of reconciliation] emphasizes three things: (a) that *God...was reconciling the world to himself*; (b) that *Christ* was the agent of this reconciliation; and (c) that reconciliation means *not charging* trespassers with *their trespasses*'.[135] In other

---

132. Cf. Gignilliat, *Paul and Isaiah's Servants*, 100.
133. Cf. Otfried Hofius, 'Erwägungen zur Gestalt und Herkunft des paulinischen Versöhnungsgedankens', in *Paulusstudien* (2d ed.; WUNT 51; Tübingen: Mohr Siebeck, 1994), 1-14.
134. Categorically, the most comprehensive study is Martin, *Reconciliation*. For lexical analyses, see Cilliers Breytenbach, *Versöhnung: Eine Studie zur paulinischen Soteriologie* (WMANT 80; Neukirchen–Vluyn: Neukirchener Verlag, 1989); I. Howard Marshall, 'The Meaning of "Reconciliation"', in *Unity and Diversity in New Testament Theology* (Festschrift George E. Ladd; ed. Robert A. Guelich; Grand Rapids: Eerdmans, 1978), 117-32; Stanley E. Porter, *Καταλλάσσω in Ancient Greek Literature, with Reference to the Pauline Writings* (Cordoba: El Almendro, 1994).
135. Victor Paul Furnish, *II Corinthians* (AB 32A; New York: Doubleday, 1984), 334. Original emphasis.

### 4. Paul's Prophetic Self-Presentation in 2 Corinthians                149

words, the initial focus of Paul's use of the καταλλάσσω word group is the fact that God is the one working to bring about the reconciliation. The problem being overcome is a divide between God and the world. Secondly, this divide is overcome through Christ. This notion of Christological agency nearly presupposes a notion of substitution, lending more credence to the earlier use of the preposition ὑπέρ.[136] Related is the idea that this agency involves Christ taking on the trespasses or sin of others (cf. ἁμαρτίαν ἐποίησεν in 2 Cor. 5.21). Thus, although Paul may know of a variety of backgrounds for καταλλάσσω and its cognates, his unique use of the term in these verses focuses on the divine initiative in removing the divide between God and humanity through the death of Christ.

Of greater significance for the present discussion, however, are the association of this work of reconciliation with Isaianic restoration and the association of Christ with the servant tradition. The focus of the Isaianic restoration was not solely on a return to the land, but on a restoration of Israel (and the nations) from sin and disobedience. Likewise, the work of the servant is not primarily centred on bringing people back to the land but in proclaiming salvation through his atoning work (Isa. 42.18-25; 43.24; 53.5-6, 10, 12).[137] The overarching context of Isaiah 40–66 appears to be in Paul's mind in 2 Cor. 5.14-21. It is here worth quoting Beale's judicious statements at length:

> In the light of the thematic overview of Isaiah 40–66 it is plausible to suggest that 'reconciliation' in Christ is Paul's way of explaining that Isaiah's promises of 'restoration' from the alienation of exile have begun to be fulfilled by the atonement and forgiveness of sins in Christ. The believer's separation and alienation from God because of sin have been overcome through the divine grace expressed in Christ, who has restored the believer into a reconciled relationship of peace with God.[138]

Here, therefore, Christ himself becomes the conclusion of the Isaianic narrative and the fulfillment of the servant tradition in terms both of the servant's mission and the manner in which the mission is carried out.

(3) *Exegetical Analysis of 2 Corinthians 6.1-2.* In terms of both grammar and context it can be argued that the first two verses of 2 Corinthians 6 belong together, with the particle γάρ functioning as a causal link

---

136. Furnish, *II Corinthians*, 335.
137. Gignilliat, *Paul and Isaiah's Servants*, 102.
138. Beale, 'Old Testament Background', 556; cf. Hofius, 'Erwägungen', 14, who argues that '[d]er paulinishce Versöhnungsgedanke ist…entscheidend durch die Botschaft Deuterojesajas geprägt… Er hat damit zugleich aus dem Alten Testament die Sprache empfangen, in der er des Heilshandeln Gottes in Jesus Christus auszusagen vermochte'.

between them. Together, these verses serve as a pragmatic conclusion to the complex theological argument that preceded them in 2 Cor. 5.14-21.[139] The initial thrust of the exhortation is clear. Paul, as a fellow worker, does not want the Corinthians (ὑμᾶς) to receive the grace of God εἰς κενόν. After this initial observation, however, several questions present themselves. First, with whom is Paul working? And, second, how does this appeal relate to the preceding section? With regard to the initial question, the close verbal parallels between 2 Cor. 5.20 and 6.1 make it likely that God is in view in the present verse.[140] That is, as Paul's work as an ambassador stems from God's exhortation through him (2 Cor. 5.20), so too is Paul's own exhortation based on his connection with God's work (2 Cor. 6.1). Paul's exhortation to the Corinthians, therefore, is seen to be an extension of God's own plea.

The content of the present exhortation deals with the reception of τὴν χάριν τοῦ θεοῦ. Although χάρις will take on a slightly different nuance in 2 Corinthians 8–9, it appears that Paul's use of the term at this point in the discourse is meant to be a reference to the entire expanse of blessings that stem from the gospel.[141] It is particularly likely that Paul has in mind at this point the benefits of God's work in bringing about a new eschatological reality. This assertion stems from the idea that Paul's argument in the previous section (2 Cor. 5.14-21) hinged on this divine act of reconciliation, as well as the continued eschatological focus in the following verse (2 Cor. 6.2). Furthermore, the Corinthians are urged not to receive this grace εἰς κενόν. It seems that the general meaning of Paul's exhortation is that he does not want the Corinthians to fail to profit from the gracious work described in 2 Cor. 5.14-21. Paul is not explicit at this point, however, with regard to the way in which the Corinthian community is to avoid this form of negative reception. Nevertheless, it is possible to argue implicitly that Paul has the same concern here for the Corinthians that he expressed in relation to his own ministry (cf. εἰς κενόν in

---

139. Harris, *Second Corinthians*, 456.

140. Other options include Christ (cf. 2 Cor. 5.20) or other of Paul's human co-workers, such as Timothy. It is difficult to argue, however, that human co-workers provide a sufficient basis for the present appeal (cf. Thrall, *Second Corinthians*, 1:451). Although the fact that τοῦ θεοῦ is the subject of παρακαλοῦντος in 2 Cor. 5.20 stands as likely evidence that God is in view here, this does not diminish the Christocentric nature of Paul's ministry. Whether God or Christ is viewed as the implied subject in 2 Cor. 6.1, the implication is that Paul's exhortation has a divine source (cf. Harris, *Second Corinthians*, 457). For a consistent reading of the passage with Christ as the referent, see Lim, 'The Sufferings of Christ', 123-57.

141. Thrall, *Second Corinthians*, 1:451.

Gal. 2.2; 1 Thess. 3.5; Phil. 2.16). Paul does not want the Corinthians to neglect the ministry of reconciliation that God has established.

Paul then grounds his appeal with a quotation from Isa. 49.8 in 2 Cor. 6.2. This verse and its use of the Isaianic tradition have received varying amounts of attention. Although the verse and its content should likely not be seen as merely a parenthetical statement that gives little additional insight into the course of Paul's argument, it is likely moving too far to affirm with Barnett that the verse is the key for understanding Paul's apostolic defence and the whole of 2 Corinthians.[142] Primarily, the verse serves as a foundation for Paul's appeal in 2 Cor. 6.1. The purpose of the quotation, as expressed in Paul's repetition of its salient points in the latter half of the verse, is to highlight the fact that the present era (νῦν) is to be equated with the eschatological era of God's new work.[143] The primary focus of the verse, therefore, is to show the Corinthians why they ought not to receive the grace of God in vain. God's grace is not to be received in vain because the present era is that in which God is completing his eschatological work of reconciliation in Christ. It seems that the conclusion of Gignilliat that 2 Cor. 6.2 summarizes 'Paul's deep reflection on the redemptive drama of Isaiah 40–66' provides a more helpful way in which to view the function of the verse itself.[144]

Secondarily, however, it is helpful to determine whether or not this verse and the quotation it contains serve to magnify an understanding of Paul's presentation of his own ministry. In other words, does Paul's use of the Isaianic tradition here in 2 Cor. 6.2 establish any form of a relationship between himself and the prophetic material in Deutero-Isaiah? Of particular importance for this question is determining the referent for the pronouns σου and σοι. Even though there is near unanimity that the pronouns refer to the servant of the Lord in Deutero-Isaiah, there is a fair amount of ambiguity concerning their referent in 2 Corinthians. It is possible to link the pronouns with the preceding ὑμᾶς.[145] That is, although the pronouns differ in number, it is possible to assert that they all refer to the Corinthian community to whom Paul writes. However, it is also feasible to argue that the two singular pronouns in 2 Cor. 6.2

---

142. Barnett, *Second Corinthians*, 318; cf. Lim, 'The Sufferings of Christ', 131.

143. It may also be possible that Paul's use of εὐπρόσδεκτος in place of δεκτῷ strengthens the force of his argument. In this context, however, the words are likely functional synonyms. The force of the eschatological reality is more readily seen in Paul's repetition of ἰδοὺ νῦν.

144. Gignilliat, *Paul and Isaiah's Servants*, 60.

145. So Barnett, *Second Corinthians*, 318; Lambrecht, *Second Corinthians*, 108-9; Thrall, *Second Corinthians*, 1:453.

refer to Paul himself.¹⁴⁶ The fact that the preceding verse is addressed to the Corinthians highlights the notion that Paul's focus in 2 Cor. 6.2 is to express to the Corinthians that they need to recognize the reality that their present situation is part of the new eschatological age. This overarching recognition, however, also includes a more specific recognition of the apostle himself and his authority among the Corinthians. God has given him authority (cf. συνεργοῦντες in 2 Cor. 6.1) and Paul's use of Isa. 49.8 is a way in which to claim that God is reaffirming the apostle's work among the Corinthians.¹⁴⁷ Although this conclusion is controversial, it is supported by the fact that the subsequent section (i.e. 2 Cor. 6.3-10) pertains to Paul's ministry and its specific characteristics. These two verses, therefore, serve to connect the discussion of God's work of reconciliation with Paul's description of his own ministry. It remains to be examined, however, how Paul's presentation and defence of his ministry in this section relates to the servant tradition in Deutero-Isaiah.

(4) *Paul's Relationship with the Servant of the Lord.* From the outset of this discussion it is important to note that Paul's use of the servant tradition in 2 Cor. 6.2 does not constitute an explicit claim that the apostle is the embodiment of *the* servant of the Lord. As will be discussed, this precise identification seems to neglect Paul's own presentation of the servant tradition in 2 Cor. 5.14-21 and does not appear to coordinate with his earlier use of the Mosaic tradition as part of his apostolic defence. It is possible, however, to see some correlation between Paul and the servant within 2 Corinthians. This correlation has two primary foci: authority and mission. In terms of authority, this entire section, 2 Cor. 5.14–6.10, is part of the defensive rhetoric that began in 2 Cor. 2.14. Paul's quotation of the servant tradition in 2 Cor. 6.2 is, therefore, a part of this defence. By discussing his own authority in relation to the authority of the servant, Paul provides a further foundation upon which his ministry may be constructed.¹⁴⁸ In fact, it is possible to argue that one

---

146. So Beale, 'Old Testament Background', 561-62; contra Christopher D. Stanley, *Arguing with Scripture: The Rhetoric of Quotations in the Letters of Paul* (London: T&T Clark International, 2004), 103, who argues that understanding Paul as the referent renders the meaning of the verse 'obscure'.

147. Beale, 'Old Testament Background', 563; cf. Lim, 'The Sufferings of Christ', 133-34; Florian Wilk, 'Isaiah in 1 and 2 Corinthians', in *Isaiah in the New Testament* (ed. Steve Moyise and Maarten J.J. Menken; London: T&T Clark International, 2005), 151-52.

148. Peter Balla, '2 Corinthians', in Beale and Carson (eds.), *Commentary*, 768.

of the primary functions of Paul's preceding discussion of reconciliation was to encourage the Corinthians to accept him as an apostle because of his status as a co-worker with God and as an ambassador for Christ.[149] Thus, in the same way that Paul used the Mosaic tradition to underscore the authority of his own ministry, so too does he use the Isaianic tradition to confirm his apostolic authority.

Secondly, a correlation exists between the mission of the servant and Paul's presentation of his mission in 2 Corinthians. Paul presents his ministry as an extension of the mission given to the servant.[150] A similar connection was seen in the earlier discussion of the relationship between Paul and the servant outside of 2 Corinthians. It is possible, therefore, to see a connection between the Lukan and Pauline traditions at this point. That is, the commission that Paul received from Christ could serve as the basis for the apostle's use of the Isaianic tradition in 2 Corinthians and for his identification with the servant tradition.[151] Furthermore, the aspect of suffering within the servant's mission can be seen in the shape of Paul's own mission (cf. 2 Cor. 6.3-10).[152] The suffering of the servant may, therefore, prefigure Paul's own apostolic suffering.[153]

In spite of the presence of these two foci within the present context of 2 Corinthians it is still difficult to make the explicit assertion that Paul personally embodies the Isaianic servant tradition. The most significant difficulty with an explicit identification between Paul and the servant is the apostle's own presentation of Christ as the primary fulfillment of the servant material. Within the earlier discussion of Paul's argument in 2 Cor. 5.14-21 it was possible to see that Paul viewed God's work in Christ as an event that corresponded with God's work through the servant. This close association between Christ and the servant tradition in 2 Cor. 5.14-21 makes it difficult to argue that Paul would present

---

149. Beale, 'Old Testament Background', 552.
150. Cerfaux, 'Saint Paul', 2:452. Interestingly, Cerfaux also claims with regard to Paul that: 'Il n'est pas sans vraisemblance qu'il ait appris clairement, dans la vision du chemin de Damas, que le Christ lui assignait un rôle en relation avec les prophéties d'Isaïe'. Kim, *Paul's Gospel*, 93, also asserts that Paul saw the Damascus event as relating to both the second servant song and Isa. 6.
151. Beale, 'Old Testament Background', 580.
152. For a helpful introduction to Paul's *Peristasenkataloge* in the Corinthian correspondence, see John T. Fitzgerald, *Cracks in an Earthen Vessel: An Examination of the Catalogues of Hardships in the Corinthian Correspondence* (SBLDS 99; Atlanta: Scholars Press, 1988).
153. Colin G. Kruse, 'Servant, Service', *DPL* 870; Lim, *'The Sufferings of Christ'*, 136-37.

himself as the servant within the same context (i.e. 2 Cor. 6.2).[154] Nevertheless, Paul's application of the Isaianic material to his own ministry signifies a close connection between his own apostolic mission and that reflected in the servant tradition.[155] This connection, however, appears to revolve around Christ's own relationship with the work of the servant. In other words, it seems that Paul's use of the servant tradition in this context is not an explicit identification of himself with the Isaianic servant, but a presentation of his ministry as an extension of God's new eschatological work in Christ, which itself corresponds to God's work through the servant in the context of Deutero-Isaiah.

Ambiguity remains, however, concerning the way in which Paul's ministry relates to the servant tradition and the larger context of Deutero-Isaiah. A recent proposal seeks to show that Paul implicitly identifies himself with the servants of the servant, the main narrative figures in Isaiah 56–66.[156] In this view, Paul's *Peristasenkatalog* in 2 Cor. 6.3-10 (cf. 2 Cor. 4.7-15; 11.23-29; 12.9-10) is the means by which he presents his ministry as an extension of the work of Christ and, consequently, the servant tradition. In light of this connection the main thrust of both 2 Cor. 4.8-10 and 6.3-10 is to show that Paul's own sufferings are rooted in God's overarching work of reconciliation in Christ. Paul's sufferings are not vicarious in their own right, but are consequential because of their particular connection with the sufferings of Christ.[157] Likewise, the servants of the servant are uniquely connected to

---

154. Jan Lambrecht, 'The Favorable Time: A Study of 2 Corinthians 6,2a in Its Context', in Bieringer and Lambrecht (eds.), *Studies on 2 Corinthians*, 524; cf. Gignilliat, *Paul and Isaiah's Servants*, 108.

155. See especially Lim, 'The Sufferings of Christ', 134-39. Although Lim attempts to identify Paul as the Isaianic servant, his argument is necessarily dependent on Paul's historical position with respect to Christ (135). Paul's presentation of his relationship with the servant, therefore, is seemingly constructed only in light of the fact that Christ himself is the servant of the Lord.

156. This is the main thesis of Gignilliat, *Paul and Isaiah's Servants*. The thesis is, in large measure, based on the notion that Paul's argument in 2 Cor. 5.14–6.10 represents a figural reading of Deutero-Isaiah. In Gignilliat's view, 2 Cor. 6.2 is the 'hermeneutical key' for this section as it serves both to highlight the fact that Paul is dependent upon the Isaianic tradition and to draw the reader into the narrative of Deutero-Isaiah itself (108). Gigniliat's thesis is also transparent in two earlier articles: Mark Gignilliat, 'A Servant Follower of the Servant: Paul's Eschatological Reading of Isaiah 40–66 in 2 Corinthians 5:14–6:10', *HBT* 26 (2004): 98-124, and Gignilliat, '2 Corinthians 6:2: Paul's Eschatological "Now" and Hermeneutical Invitation', *WTJ* 67 (2005): 147-61. Cf. Jackson, *New Creation*, 127.

157. Gignilliat, *Paul and Isaiah's Servants*, 110.

the mission and suffering of the servant himself within Isaiah 56–66.[158] As with the narrative movement from the servant to the servants in Isaiah 40–66, Gignilliat sees a movement from Christ (*the* servant) to Paul (*a* servant of *the* servant) in 2 Cor. 5.14–6.10. The connection between Paul and the servants is seen in the apostle's use of διακον-terminology, his function as a herald (cf. Isa. 52.7; 53.1; 61.1-4), his suffering (cf. Isa. 57.2), his righteousness or faithfulness (cf. Isa. 57.1), and his role in the current eschatological tension (cf. Isa. 59).[159] In these ways, Paul is connected typologically with the servant's offspring (cf. Isa. 53.10) and not with the servant himself, since Paul presents Christ as the typological fulfillment of the servant tradition (cf. 2 Cor. 5.14-21).

Despite the fact that this connection is helpful in analysing the nature and function of Paul's presentation of his own ministry, it is likely moving too far to assert that Paul is the typological fulfillment of the servant's offspring in Isaiah 56–66. The notion that Paul is to be connected with the servants of the servant is subject to the same criticism as the statement that Paul is to be identified with the servant himself, namely that Paul does not explicitly claim a connection with the tradition of the servants.[160] This is not meant to diminish the necessity of seeing the dramatic influence of the Isaianic narrative on Paul's thought at this juncture of 2 Corinthians; rather, the significance of this insight needs to be incorporated into the whole of Paul's apostolic defence. If Paul is implicitly related to the servant tradition through the fact that the presentation of his ministry parallels that of the servant's offspring, how does this relationship correlate with Paul's earlier presentation of his ministry as parallel with the Mosaic tradition? Stating that Paul's presentation of his ministry is based solely on the identity and role of the servants of the servant seems to neglect one of the purposes of Paul's earlier argument.

---

158. Gignilliat, *Paul and Isaiah's Servants*, 112-31, provides a helpful overview of the function and characteristics of the servants within the Isaianic narrative. Of particular importance are his conclusions about the narrative identity of the servants: 'the servants' work and mission are intricately connected to that of the Servant, but in a subordinate role, a role that finds its distinctiveness in its continuation of the work of the Servant' (131). In other words, the servants in Isa. 56–66 are connected with the servant in Isa. 40–55 not in terms of status or precise identity, but in the similar nature of their respective functions within God's act of restoration.

159. Gignilliat, *Paul and Isaiah's Servants*, 132-42.

160. It could be argued that the quotation of Isa. 49.8 in 2 Cor. 6.2 is an explicit connection between Paul and the servant, but that connection does not take into account the overarching argument of 2 Cor. 5.14–6.10 and the particular connection that Paul makes between Christ and the servant tradition in 2 Cor. 5.14-21.

Interestingly, however, it is possible to see a connection between the Mosaic tradition and the Isaianic servant tradition. The context of the servant songs appears to draw a connection between the servant and the new-Moses tradition. In addition to the similarities surrounding the call of Moses and the servant, God sustains both figures (cf. Exod. 4.10-12; Isa. 49.2; 50.4) and both figures are seen to exercise prophetic, kingly, and priestly roles within their ministries.[161] Paul's use of Isaiah 49 in 2 Corinthians 6, therefore, may in fact highlight the convergence of these two traditions. In other words, Paul's quotation of Isa. 49.8 is not meant to identify his ministry as the precise fulfillment of the servant tradition; rather, it seems that one of the functions of the quotation is to show that Paul's ministry is parallel to the ministry of the servant (Christ) and stems from it. In a similar fashion to the way in which Paul connected his ministry to Moses, he here presents his ministry as being shaped by the characteristics of the servant tradition. Thus, it is possible that since Paul sees both the Mosaic tradition and the servant tradition as coming to fruition ultimately in Christ, his presentation of his own ministry is shaped by the trajectory manifested in the characteristics and functions of those two traditions.[162] Arguably, both the ministry of Moses and the ministry of the servant provide a functional outline for Paul's presentation of his ministry to the Corinthians.

Similar to the discussion of Paul's use of the Mosaic tradition, it seems that the main emphasis of Paul's use of the Isaianic servant tradition is to present himself as a member of the prophetic tradition. Thus, the earlier thesis of Sandnes again seems to hold true: Paul conceives of his apostolic ministry through the lens of the prophetic tradition.[163] This conception, however, may also be subject to the same criticism as that of the earlier identifications of Paul's ministry with that of the servant or the servant's offspring. That is, Paul never explicitly claims that he is a prophet. This particular omission may suggest that Paul understands his ministry to be part of 'a stage of the *Heilsgeschichte* fundamentally different from that of the Old Testament prophets'.[164] Paul's lack of an explicit identification

---

161. Jones, 'Apostle Paul', 124-25.

162. Cf. William L. Lane, 'Covenant: The Key to Paul's Conflict with Corinth', *TynBul* 33 (1982): 3-29 (9); contra Webb, *Returning Home*, 145 n. 1. Webb argues that Paul functions as a new Moses only secondarily, but that his function as the 'new' servant is forthright and primary in his self-understanding.

163. Sandnes, *Paul—One of the Prophets?*, 242.

164. Kim, *Paul's Gospel*, 93 n. 2; cf. Jürgen Roloff, *Apostolat-Verkündigung-Kirche: Ursprung, Inhalt und Funktion des kirchlichen Apostelamtes nach Paulus, Lukas und den Pastoralbriefen* (Gütersloh: Gütersloher, 1965), 42-45. Sandnes,

of himself as a prophet, however, does not immediately detract from the relatively striking similarities between Paul and the prophetic tradition evinced by both the apostle's call and ministry as a messenger or herald.[165] Thus, a parallel between Paul and the prophetic tradition may provide a more general conception for the way in which he presents his ministry. It seems reasonable to suggest, therefore, that Paul uses both the Mosaic tradition and the Isaianic servant tradition to illustrate his authority to the Corinthians and to highlight the notion that his ministry parallels the trajectory of the prophetic tradition.

c. *Conclusions*

Paul's discourse in 2 Cor. 5.14–6.10 provides significant insight into the way in which he presents his ministry to the Corinthian community. Paul's use of Deutero-Isaiah within this section points to a close connection between the apostle and the Isaianic servant tradition. The relationship between the two figures can be seen predominantly in the similarities between their respective authority and mission. Through these two foci the servant tradition is seen to be representative of Paul's overarching mission and serves as a means for the apostle to express his authority as a divine co-worker (2 Cor. 6.1). However, the close association created by Paul between Christ and the servant tradition in 2 Cor. 5.14-21 highlights the notion that Paul is not here presenting himself as the typological embodiment of the servant. Rather, the similarities and differences between Paul's presentation and that of the servant tradition appear to point to a more general correlation between Paul's own apostolic ministry and that of the prophetic tradition. Thus, Paul's use of both the Mosaic tradition and the Isaianic servant tradition provides a means for his presentation of his prophetic self-understanding.

Although it can be argued that his position within salvation history is categorically distinct from the prophets, Paul presents himself as one who is involved with the new eschatological work of God as his representative co-worker among the Corinthians. As part of this representation Paul proclaims the notion that the present age is equal with the eschatological age described within Deutero-Isaiah (cf. 2 Cor. 6.1-2) and seeks to encourage the Corinthians to recognize the authority of his ministry among them (cf. 2 Cor. 6.11-13). The distinct parallels between Paul and

*Paul—One of the Prophets?*, 243-44, offers two additional explanations for the lack of an explicit declaration by Paul that he was a prophet: his ministry was thoroughly, and distinctly, Christological, and it was directed externally toward the nations.

165. Kim, *Paul's Gospel*, 93 n. 2.

both the Mosaic and Isaianic traditions seem to highlight a correlation between Paul's presentation of his ministry and the prophetic tradition. In order to elucidate further the argument that Paul's presentation of his ministry is rooted in an overarching understanding of his ministry as parallel to that of the prophetic tradition, it will be helpful to analyse the relationship between Paul and Jeremiah.

## 4. The Relationship between Paul and Jeremiah

As with the discussion of Paul's relationship with Moses and the Isaianic servant, there are several points of comparison between the apostle's presentation of his ministry and the prophetic persona of Jeremiah. Within 2 Corinthians Paul references Jeremiah in order to elucidate the nature of his ministry (i.e. 2 Cor. 3.4-6) and to substantiate his authority among the Corinthians (i.e. 2 Cor. 10.8, 17; 13.10).[166] On the surface, therefore, it appears that both the person and message of Jeremiah play a crucial role in Paul's presentation of his ministry.[167] Thus, as with the apostle's relation to Moses and the Isaianic servant, it may be possible to assert that Paul, in some sense, views himself as a second Jeremiah. However, it may be more reasonable to state that Paul's multiple references to the Jeremianic tradition in 2 Corinthians further illustrate the connection between the apostle and the overarching prophetic tradition (cf. 1 Cor. 1.31). The aim of this section is to examine the way in which

---

166. There is a small minority, however, which claims that the prophetic tradition of Jeremiah had no impact on Paul, particularly with reference to Jer. 31 and the institution of the new covenant (e.g. Dietrich-Alex Koch, *Die Schrift als Zeuge des Evangeliums: Untersuchungen zur Verwendung und zum Verständnis der Schrift bei Paulus* [BHT 69; Tübingen: Mohr Siebeck, 1986]; Christian Wolff, *Jeremia im Frühjudentum und Urchristentum* [TUGAL 118; Berlin: Akademie-Verlag, 1976]). Following Koch, Helmut Utzschneider, 'Flourishing Bones: The Minor Prophets in the New Testament', in *Septuagint Research: Issues and Challenges in the Study of the Greek Jewish Scriptures* (ed. Wolfgang Kraus and R. Glenn Wooden; SBLSCS 53; Atlanta: Society of Biblical Literature, 2006), 280 n. 12, claims that '[i]t is remarkable, but not entirely surprising, that there are no citations at all from Jeremiah in Paul's writings'. This statement, however, appears to overlook the likely citation of Jer. 9.22-23 (LXX) in both 1 Cor. 1.31 and 2 Cor. 10.17.

167. The authorship and content of the book of Jeremiah, however, are highly disputed. For an introduction to the literary problems surrounding the book, see William L. Holladay, *Jeremiah* (2 vols.; Hermeneia; Philadelphia: Fortress, 1986), 2:10-70. For the sake of clarity this work will refer to all portions of Jeremiah as the product of the prophet himself. There does not appear to be any evidence in the Pauline corpus to suggest that the apostle saw any fragmentation within Jeremiah.

## 4. Paul's Prophetic Self-Presentation in 2 Corinthians

Paul's presentation of his ministry relates to Jeremiah in terms of the prophet's call, new covenant prophecy, prophetic mission, and prophetic action in order to determine the significance of Paul's use of Jeremiah in 2 Corinthians.

### a. *The Call of Paul in Relation to Jeremiah*

Prior to discussing the specific correlation between Paul and Jeremiah established in 2 Corinthians, it will be helpful to see that Paul's discussion of his call in Galatians 1 provides additional insight into the apostle's understanding of his relationship with Jeremiah and the rest of the prophetic tradition. As noted in the discussion of Paul's relationship with the Isaianic servant of the Lord, Paul's statement in Gal. 1.15 that God set him apart ἐκ κοιλίας μητρός μου could be attributed either to the call of Jeremiah (cf. Jer. 1.5) or to that of the Isaianic servant (cf. Isa. 49.1). While the precise vocabulary of Galatians is more closely associated with that of Isaiah, it is not entirely possible to eliminate the Jeremianic tradition as a background for Paul's statement.[168] However, as with the discussion of the Isaianic servant, Paul's use of this passage may derive its significance not from its reference to a particular prophetic figure, but from its potential allusion to broader realities within Israel's prophetic tradition. The veracity of this understanding is made more explicit through an analysis of the structural similarities between the calls of Jeremiah and Paul.

In the prior discussion of the relationship between Paul and Moses it was argued that the apostle's presentation of his call within 2 Corinthians parallels that of Moses with regard to form and purpose. Additionally, the basic elements of the calls of both Moses and Paul (i.e. the movement from an initial theophany, to the presentation of a divine commission, to the recognition by the prophet of his own insufficiency, to a divine

---

168. Sandnes, *Paul—One of the Prophets?*, 63-64, offers three reasons for seeing an allusion to Jeremiah in Galatians: (1) the discussion of legitimacy in Galatians parallels the situation of Jeremiah (cf. Jer. 20.11; 23.18-22; 26.15; 28.5-17), (2) there is a close conceptual association between ἀφορίζω and ἁγιάζω, and (3) the phrase ἐκ κοιλίας μητρός may simply be a standard way of referring to the beginning of life in the LXX (e.g. Judg. 16.17; Job 1.21; Ps. 21.10) and, therefore, Paul's statement could be parallel to the concept in Jeremiah. See also J. Christiaan Beker, *Paul the Apostle: The Triumph of God in Life and Thought* (Edinburgh: T. & T. Clark, 1980), 10, 116; Kathy Ehrensperger, *Paul and the Dynamics of Power: Communication and Interaction in the Early Christ-Movement* (LNTS 325; London: T&T Clark International, 2007), 83-85; L.J. Lietaert Peerbolte, *Paul the Missionary* (CBET 23; Leuven: Peeters, 2003), 167-68.

work of grace that overcomes the prophet's deficiency) are also found in the call narratives of several other Old Testament prophetic figures. The paradigmatic nature of Moses' call, however, may be seen to function most prominently within the call of Jeremiah due to parallels not only with regard to form, but also in terms of content.[169] That is, in addition to the presence of the characteristic call formula, Jeremiah's call parallels Exodus 4 in terms of the particular problem that Jeremiah recognizes (i.e. the inability to speak expressed in Jer. 1.6) and in terms of God's provision to Jeremiah (i.e. the Lord's promise to put his words in the mouth of the prophet in Jer. 1.9).[170] Furthermore, there is a close connection between the call of Jeremiah and the expectation of a prophet like Moses in Deut. 18.15-18. Both passages contain the instruction that the prophet is to speak what the Lord commands (Deut. 18.18; Jer. 1.7), as well as the promise that the Lord will put his words in the mouth of the prophet (Deut. 18.18; Jer. 1.9). In light of these connections it may be possible to assert that Jeremiah himself is the fulfillment of the second Moses tradition. More likely, however, is the notion that Jeremiah's prophetic ministry was shaped through the same lens used to formulate the prophetic dimensions of Moses' ministry.[171] In this way, the call and ministry of Jeremiah stand as further evidence of the notion that the prophetic tradition stemmed primarily from the figure of Moses. Thus, Paul's primary reference to the call of Moses in 2 Cor. 2.16 by means of the discussion of sufficiency may also represent a secondary reference to the call of Jeremiah since the ministry of Jeremiah is also shaped by the essential characteristics of the prophetic call tradition.

---

169. Hafemann, *Paul, Moses, and the History of Israel*, 55.

170. Hafemann, *Paul, Moses, and the History of Israel*, 55. However, while both Moses and Jeremiah see a problem with their speech, the deficiency stems from a different source in each man: Moses' from a lack of eloquence and potential speech impediment (Exod. 4.10) and Jeremiah's from his youth (Jer. 1.6).

171. Norman Habel, 'The Form and Significance of the Call Narratives', *ZAW* 77 (1965): 297-323 (306-7). The precise nature of the relationship between Moses and Jeremiah, however, is disputed. Holladay argues that Jeremiah was cognizant of the relationship and fulfilled his prophetic ministry in light of the Mosaic tradition (see William L. Holladay, 'The Background of Jeremiah's Self-Understanding: Moses, Samuel, and Psalm 22', *JBL* 83 [1964]: 153-64; Holladay, 'Jeremiah and Moses: Further Observations', *JBL* 85 [1966]: 17-27). Seitz, 'The Prophet Moses', 3-27, however, argues that it was the later editors of Jeremiah who made the connection between the prophet and the Mosaic tradition in Deuteronomy. The relationship may also stem simply from the fact that a standard form for a prophetic call is used in both Exodus and Jeremiah, cf. Hafemann, *Paul, Moses, and the History of Israel*, 56.

This point is further established in light of the conceptual connection between Paul's autobiographical statement in Galatians 1 and the prophet's call narrative in Jeremiah 1. Paul's allusion to the Jeremianic tradition and the Isaianic tradition in Gal. 1.15 may serve as a way for Paul to establish himself within the same tradition as those two figures. In other words, Paul's formulation of his call in the same manner as the prophetic tradition seemingly points to the idea that Paul views his own ministry as related to that of the prophets in terms of both its form and mission.[172] However, the text of Galatians also exhibits two key distinctions between the call of the prophets and that of Paul. First, God's revelation to Paul dealt primarily with the revelation of his Son (Gal. 1.16). That is, there is a Christological dimension in Paul's call that is not explicitly present in any of the Old Testament prophetic call narratives. Related to this, the second distinction is seen in the fact that the revelation given to Paul stands as the actual content of the message that he is called to proclaim (ἵνα εὐαγγελίζωμαι αὐτὸν ἐν τοῖς ἔθνεσιν).[173] In light of these two distinctions, there appears to be a progression between the Old Testament prophets and the apostle. The basis for this progression, however, may already be present within the Old Testament prophetic tradition itself. The specific ministerial distinctions between the prophetic personas of Jeremiah and Ezekiel, for example, appear to stem in large part from the unique realities of their respective contextual settings.[174] The distinct aspects of Paul's own call, therefore, would represent the unique dimensions of his ministerial context. The significance of this progression for Paul's presentation of his apostolic ministry may be seen more clearly in his understanding of Jeremiah in 2 Corinthians and his specific designation of himself as a minister of the new covenant in 2 Cor. 3.6.

### b. *Paul as a Minister of the New Covenant*

Paul's claim in 2 Cor. 3.6 that he is a minister of the new covenant is primarily an extension of the preceding argument in 2 Cor. 3.1-5. The first portion of Paul's argument (2 Cor. 3.1-3) appears to point to a historical situation in which uncertainty had developed in Corinth concerning the validity of Paul's ministry due in part to the fact that

---

172. Fung, *Galatians*, 63; cf. Lietaert Peerbolte, *Paul the Missionary*, 167-68; Munck, *Paul*, 26.
173. Sandnes, *Paul—One of the Prophets?*, 60. The antecedent of αὐτόν is τὸν υἱόν.
174. This is the primary thesis of Rochester, 'Prophetic Ministry in Jeremiah and Ezekiel'.

the apostle never presented a written letter of recommendation to the Corinthians. The import of the two rhetorical questions in 2 Cor. 3.1 is not to condemn the practice of writing letters of recommendation; rather, Paul's intent appears to be to condemn the notion that he needs any external evidence for the character and sufficiency of his ministry as expressed in 2 Cor. 2.16-17.[175] In order to affirm that his ministry is characterized by divine sufficiency, Paul composes a 'brilliant metaphor' that establishes that it is the Christian Corinthians themselves who are Paul's ἐπιστολή (2 Cor. 3.2).[176] Thus, the existence of the Corinthian church becomes the deeply internal (ἐγγεγραμμένη ἐν ταῖς καρδίαις ἡμῶν) and overtly public (γινωσκομένη καὶ ἀναγινωσκομένη ὑπὸ πάντων ἀνθρώπων) evidence of Paul's ministry in Corinth.

Paul's continued description of the Corinthians as his letter of recommendation in 2 Cor. 3.3 places primary emphasis on the divine agency of Christ and appears to point to the notion that Paul views his own proclamation of the gospel as the means by which Christ establishes the Corinthians as Paul's letter of recommendation.[177] The following two comparisons that Paul makes in 2 Cor. 3.3 serve to explicate further the nature of Paul's ministry among the Corinthians. Read as succeeding affirmations, the two comparisons serve to highlight initially that the Spirit is responsible for the Christian community in Corinth and, subsequently, that the Spirit has accomplished this work in the specific locality

---

175. Scott J. Hafemann, *Suffering and Ministry in the Spirit: Paul's Defense of His Ministry in II Corinthians 2:14–3:3* (Grand Rapids: Eerdmans, 1990), 185. If Paul were condemning the practice of writing letters of recommendation he would be discrediting his own practice (cf. Rom. 16.1-2; 2 Cor. 8.16-24; Phil. 2.19-23; Col. 4.7-9; Philemon). For a full discussion of the place and purpose of commendation letters in the Graeco-Roman world, see Peter Marshall, *Enmity in Corinth: Social Conventions in Paul's Relations with the Corinthians* (WUNT 2/23; Tübingen: Mohr Siebeck, 1987), 259-77.

176. Morna D. Hooker, 'Beyond the Things That Are Written? St. Paul's Use of Scripture', *NTS* 27 (1981): 295-309 (296); cf. Erich Grässer, 'Paulus, der Apostel des neuen Bundes (2 Kor 2,14–4,6)', in De Lorenzi (ed.), *Paolo, Ministro del Nuovo Testamento*, 15. That Jer. 38 (LXX) is in view in 2 Cor. 3.2 is supported by Hays, *Echoes of Scripture*, 128, and Earl Richard, 'Polemics, Old Testament, and Theology: A Study of II Cor. III,1-IV,6', *RB* 88 (1981): 340-67. However, this argument is primarily based on the later allusion to Jeremiah in 2 Cor. 3.6 and not on direct parallels between Jer. 38 (LXX) and 2 Cor. 3.2.

177. Hays, *Echoes of Scripture*, 127; cf. Robert Sloan, '2 Corinthians 2:14–4:6 and "New Covenant Hermeneutics"—A Response to Richard Hays', *BBR* 5 (1995): 129-54 (136). More specifically, the emphasis on Christ's agency is derived from understanding the genitive Χριστοῦ as subjective (i.e. 'the letter Christ wrote'), while the phrase διακονηθεῖσα ὑφ' ἡμῶν highlights Paul's mediatory function.

of the Corinthians' hearts.[178] At this point of the argument, therefore, Paul appears to be defending the validity of his ministry based on the Corinthians' own experience. The apostle then moves to a more specific discussion concerning the nature of his new covenant ministry in 2 Cor. 3.4-6.

As noted in the discussion of the relationship between Paul and Moses the emphasis on sufficiency in 2 Cor. 3.4-6 highlights that God works in spite of, and through, Paul's weakness. It is this divine sufficiency that enables Paul to become a minister of the new covenant (2 Cor. 3.6). The import of the διακον-terminology, therefore, is crucial in this comparison as well. Paul's self-designation as a διάκονος καινῆς διαθήκης is illustrative of the notion that he has been called to mediate the Spirit among the Corinthians, since he defines this covenant as pertaining not to the letter (γράμματος) but to the Spirit (πνεύματος). Of primary importance for the present argument, however, is Paul's explicit allusion to Jer. 38.31 (LXX) in 2 Cor. 3.6. While Paul earlier presented his ministry as connected with the prophetic tradition, a notion evidenced in this context by his association with the call and ministry of Moses, he now appears to connect himself particularly with the prophetic ministry of Jeremiah by stating that the ministry for which he was made sufficient is shaped by a καινὴ διαθήκη.[179]

---

178. Hafemann, *Suffering and the Spirit*, 200-203. Paul's allusion to writing on stone tablets likely stems from Exod. 24.12; 31.18; 32.15-16; 34.1, while the reference to καρδίαις σαρκίναις is most likely derived from Ezek. 11.19 and 36.26 (cf. John W. Yates, *The Spirit and Creation in Paul* [WUNT 2/251; Tübingen: Mohr Siebeck 2008], 108-9). Therefore, it is unlikely that Jer. 38 (LXX) forms part of the immediate background of 2 Cor. 3.3 (contra Yates, *Spirit and Creation*, 108 n. 8). However, the precise identity of the texts in Paul's mind at this point is a matter of continual debate. Potential backgrounds include material from Exodus, Deuteronomy, Proverbs, Jeremiah, and Ezekiel. For a survey of the various positions and a sustained argument for the position taken here, see Hafemann, *Suffering and the Spirit*, 204-7. For an alternative analysis, see Stockhausen, *Moses' Veil*, 54-71.

179. Paul's use of the phrase καινὴ διαθήκη likely stems from the last supper tradition maintained by the Synoptic Gospels (i.e. Mt. 26.28; Mk 14.24; Lk. 22.20), as evidenced by the apostle's use of the same terminology in the Eucharistic setting of 1 Cor. 11.25. However, contra Koch, *Die Schrift als Zeuge des Evangeliums*, 45-46, this connection does not preclude Jer. 38 (LXX) as part of the background to Paul's argument (cf. Lambrecht, *Second Corinthians*, 43). The contextual discussion of the relationship between the two covenants in 2 Cor. 3.7-18 further supports Paul's dependence on the message of Jeremiah. For this reason, the position of Heikki Räisänen, *Paul and the Law* (WUNT 29; Tübingen: Mohr Siebeck, 1983), 240-45, that Paul could not be referring to Jeremiah in this instance since he is condemning the Law, appears to misunderstand Paul's following discussion of the relationship between the two covenants (so Hafemann, *Paul, Moses, and the History of Israel*,

This connection, however, is often overlooked in light of the complexity of Paul's assertion in the latter section of 2 Cor. 3.6 that τὸ... γράμμα ἀποκτέννει, τὸ δὲ πνεῦμα ζωοποιεῖ.[180] Exegetically, this contrast has been seen either as an affirmation of a true dichotomy between the two covenants, with the old being abrogated in light of the place of the new, or as evidence of a salvation-historical movement, with the work of the Spirit enabling believers to follow after the stipulations of the old covenant.[181] This divide stems primarily from discrepancy concerning the meaning of the term γράμμα in the present context, which has taken on a variety of meanings in the history of New Testament interpretation.[182] In light of the reference to Jeremiah in 2 Cor. 3.6, however, it is difficult to assert that Paul is here denigrating the Law, in and of itself, since the message of Jeremiah argues that it is the Law that would be written on the hearts of the people (Jer. 38.33 LXX). That is, in Jeremiah, the need for a new covenant does not stem initially from a problem with the Law itself, but from the inability of the Israelites to obey the Law.[183] It appears, therefore, that Paul's statement concerning the letter and the Spirit in 2 Cor. 3.6 is not pointing to a divide between the character of the Law and the Spirit, but to a separation between their respective functions.[184]

---

127). Furthermore, the possibility that Paul's opponents were the catalyst for the covenant language at this point (e.g. Annie Jaubert, *La notion d'alliance dans le judaïsme aux abords de l'ère chrétienne* [Patristica Sorboniensia 6; Paris: Seuil, 1963], 447-48; Jerome Murphy-O'Connor, 'A Ministry Beyond the Letter [2 Cor 3:1-6]', in De Lorenzi [ed.], *Paolo, Ministro del Nuovo Testamento*, 116-17; Mathias Rissi, *Studien zum zweiten Korintherbrief: Der alte Bund–Der Prediger–Der Tod* [ATANT 56; Zurich: Zwingli, 1969], 23-24) does not necessarily imply that Paul's argument represents 'a shift in perspective' between 1 and 2 Corinthians (contra Thomas R. Blanton IV, 'Spirit and Covenant Renewal: A Theologoumenon of Paul's Opponents in 2 Corinthians', *JBL* 129 [2010]: 129-51).

180. For a survey of the historical interpretation of the divide between the letter and the Spirit, see Gleason, 'Paul's Covenantal Contrast', 61-79.

181. For an overview of the exegetical divide, see Grindheim, 'The Law Kills', 97-115. Grindheim does not discuss issues of continuity between the covenants, but attempts to show that 2 Cor. 3.6 should be understood in terms of a 'dualism between law and gospel' (97).

182. See Thrall, *Second Corinthians*, 1:234-35, for a summary of the options and their proponents.

183. Robert P. Carroll, *Jeremiah* (OTL; Philadelphia: Westminster, 1986), 610-14; Thompson, *Jeremiah*, 580-81; Hans Walter Wolff, *Confrontations with Prophets: Discovering the Old Testament's New and Contemporary Significance* (Philadelphia: Fortress, 1983), 49-62.

184. Meyer's contention that the difference between the covenants stems from an *ontological* distinction between the covenants themselves (e.g. Meyer, *The End of*

## 4. Paul's Prophetic Self-Presentation in 2 Corinthians

This conclusion explains the following discussion in 2 Cor. 3.7-11, where Paul is able to affirm the glory of both his own ministry and that of Moses, while also recognizing the opposite outcomes which each brought about. If this position is tenable, then Paul's thesis statement in 2 Cor. 3.6 that τὸ...γράμμα ἀποκτέννει, τὸ δὲ πνεῦμα ζῳοποιεῖ functions as both an explicit explanation of the function of the new covenant and an implicit description of the character and function of his apostolic ministry.[185] As Meyer helpfully notes, 'Paul's ministry and God's new covenant become identified to such a degree that Paul can speak of his ministry as a ministry of the Spirit ([2 Cor.] 3:8)'.[186] In this way, the effective work of the Spirit among the Corinthians becomes additional evidence for the validity of Paul's ministry in Corinth. Thus, Paul's personal defence at this point rests primarily on his prior understanding that God made him sufficient to be a minister of the new covenant.

Moreover, the notion that Paul presents himself as a minister of the new covenant highlights his potential association with Jeremiah. In contrast with the ministry of Moses as described in 2 Cor. 3.7-18, Paul's ministry deals primarily with the mediation of the Spirit, as opposed to the Law.[187] Paul's ministry, therefore, is partially a fulfillment of the promise made explicit in Jeremiah 38 (LXX), where God begins a new work, through the Spirit (cf. Ezek. 36.26), in which he inscribes the Law on the hearts of his people. Thus, while the allusion to Jeremiah 38 (LXX) in 2 Cor. 3.6 is brief, it is possible to argue that by this comparison Paul is presenting his ministry as the eschatological counterpart of Jeremiah's.[188] For this reason, however, it appears that instead of creating an explicit parallel between his own ministry and that of Jeremiah, Paul is claiming that his ministry reflects the redemptive historical movement of the prophetic tradition. In other words, Paul is here defending his ministry by presenting it through the framework of God's work in bringing about

---

*the Law*, 64, 84) appears not to account for his own insightful argument that Christ's writing on the Corinthians' πλαξὶν καρδίαις σαρκίναις (2 Cor. 3.3) evinces the prior divine action that changed the spiritual condition of the covenant recipients (74). The salvation-historical divide between the letter and the Spirit, therefore, seems not to stem from a distinction between the extrinsic and intrinsic presence of the Spirit, but from the prior replacement of τὴν καρδίαν τὴν λιθίνην with a καρδίαν σαρκίνην (Ezek. 36.26-27).

185. Meyer, *The End of the Law*, 77 n. 54; cf. Schmeller, *2 Korintherbrief*, 1:154-61.

186. Meyer, *The End of the Law*, 77 n. 54.

187. Hafemann, *Paul, Moses, and the History of Israel*, 173.

188. Lane, 'Covenant', 9-10; cf. Hafemann, *Paul, Moses, and the History of Israel*, 136.

the new covenant as prophesied by Jeremiah. The idea that Paul sees his ministry as connected to Jeremiah is further supported through the apostle's discussion of his apostolic authority in 2 Corinthians 10-13.

### c. *Jeremiah's Mission and Paul's Authority*
Paul further describes the shape of his new covenant ministry in the latter section of the epistle, 2 Corinthians 10-13. While Paul's self-designation as a minister of the new covenant may stem merely from the language of Jeremiah, there is additional support for the connection between the apostle and the prophet in this section of the Corinthian correspondence. On two occasions in 2 Corinthians 10-13 Paul refers explicitly to the authority that was given to him εἰς οἰκοδομὴν καὶ οὐκ εἰς καθαίρεσιν (2 Cor. 10.8; 13.10). Although Paul uses architectural language at several points throughout his epistles, the close comparison between the notions of construction and destruction seems to point to Jeremiah as the source of these two statements. The notions of 'building up' and 'tearing down' are repeated throughout the book of Jeremiah as a way in which to view the mission of the prophet (e.g. Jer. 1.10) and a lens through which to understand the Lord's work among both Israel and the nations (e.g. Jer. 12.14-17; 18.7-11; 24.6; 31.27-28; 42.10; 45.4).[189] It is difficult, however, to determine whether Paul has any precise section of Jeremiah in view at either 2 Cor. 10.8 or 13.10 since neither verse exhibits a precise verbal overlap with the passages in Jeremiah that contain parallel vocabulary.[190] Conceptually, Paul's language closely resembles Jer. 24.6 and 42.10, where there is also a contrast between the notions of 'building up' and 'tearing down', even though the vocabulary does not coordinate precisely.[191] Yet, if the previous discussion of the relationship between the calls of Jeremiah and Paul is seen to be valid, then the presence of similar language in Jer. 1.10 may also provide the background for Paul's presentation here in 2 Corinthians.[192] The lack of precise verbal correspondence, however, may serve as evidence that Paul does not have a particular

---

189. Cf. Lane, 'Covenant', 9.

190. The themes of restoration ('building up') and judgment ('tearing down') are found in numerous contexts in Jeremiah (e.g. Jer. 1.10; 12.14-17; 18.7-11; 24.6; 29.5, 28; 31.4-5, 27-28; 35.7; 42.10; 45.4).

191. All the words in Jeremiah are verbal forms as opposed to the nouns in 2 Cor. 10.8 and 13.10, which here have verbal connotations. Moreover, Jer. 24.6 utilizes ἀνοικοδομέω while Jer. 42.10 (49.10 LXX) has a parallel form of οἰκοδομέω. Both passages in Jeremiah have verbal forms of καθαιρέω, from which Paul's term, καθαίρεσις, stems.

192. Cf. Harris, *Second Corinthians*, 695; Lambrecht, *Second Corinthians*, 156-57; Thrall, *Second Corinthians*, 1:476.

passage of Jeremiah in mind, but is referring, more generally, to the overarching theme of restoration and judgment that moves throughout the course of Jeremiah's prosaic and poetic language.

The claim that Paul's vocabulary stems from a Jeremianic theme and not from a particular passage within Jeremiah may be substantiated within the text of Jeremiah itself. The numerous occurrences of the dual themes of restoration and judgment throughout the book of Jeremiah highlight their conceptual importance for the prophet. The MT of Jeremiah utilizes four verbs to describe the negative aspect of Jeremiah's mission, while the LXX translates these words with eight terms.[193] Though important, the fluidity of these terms does not prove definitive in the argument that Jeremiah was primarily concerned with the idea of judgment and not with the specific terms themselves. This concept is derived more concretely from the conflation of the terms within the various parts of Jeremiah and their ability to function as synonyms within the passages dealing with restoration and judgment (e.g. Jer. 1.10; 12.14-17; 18.7-11; 24.6; 31.27-28; 42.10; 45.4). This notion of fluidity can be seen most clearly in the relation of the poetic and prosaic material within Jeremiah, as well as the various ways in which the terms appear within the passages, including their specific sequence.[194] Thus, although the specific verbs concerning judgment are not always interchangeable, they do normally refer to the negative dimension of Jeremiah's call.[195] For this reason, it seems that Jeremiah's language of judgment is more relevant in terms of its conceptual significance than its lexical form.

In contrast with the terminology used to describe the negative aspect of Jeremiah's call and subsequent mission, the vocabulary associated with

---

193. The Hebrew terms are אבד (1.10; 12.17; 18.7; 31.28), הרס (1.10; 24.6; 31.28; 42.10; 45.4), נתץ (1.10; 18.7; 31.28), and נתש (1.10; 12.14 [×2], 15, 17; 18.7; 24.6; 29.5; 31.28; 42.10; 45.4). The LXX uses ἀπόλλυμι (1.10; 18.7), ἀποσπάω (12.14), ἐκβάλλω (12.14, 15), ἐκριζόω (1.10), ἐκτίλλω (24.6; 49.10; 51.35), ἐξαίρω (12.17; 18.7), καθαιρέω (24.6; 38.28; 49.10; 51.35), and κατασκάπτω (1.10).

194. For an extensive discussion of the relationship between the poetry and prose sections in Jeremiah, see William L. Holladay, 'Prototype and Copies: A New Approach to the Poetry-Prose Problem in the Book of Jeremiah', *JBL* 79 (1960): 351-67. For his discussion of the particular verbs in question, see 363-64. It may also be possible to posit that the LXX itself condenses these negative terms into one concept of destruction in Jer. 38.28 where the infinitive καθαιρεῖν may replace the four Hebrew verbs that are used in the MT (אבד, הרס, נתץ, נתש); see Bob Becking, 'Jeremiah's Book of Consolation: A Textual Comparison. Notes on the Masoretic Text and the Old Greek Version of Jeremiah xxx–xxxi', *VT* 44 (1994): 145-69. Lundbom, *Jeremiah*, 2:460, however, argues that the LXX contains only one word due to two instances of haplography.

195. Thompson, *Jeremiah*, 508.

the positive notion of restoration is more consistent. The prophet normally uses the terms בנה and נטע to describe the restorative action of the Lord. These terms are rendered most frequently in the LXX with forms of (ἀν)οικοδομέω ('to build up') and (κατα)φυτεύω ('to plant').[196] In addition to the contrast in the actual amount of terms used to describe the negative and positive aspects of Jeremiah's ministry, the positive terms do not undergo the same amount of fluctuation with respect to their sequence. When the two concepts appear together, the notion of building always precedes that of planting. This observation was one of the factors that led Bach to conclude that the terms were not given to Jeremiah (or the rest of the prophets) as individual terms, but as a 'Begriffspaar' or 'Wortpaar'.[197] Together, therefore, the two terms form a sort of hendiadys in the Old Testament that refers primarily to God's restorative action.

While it is probable that Paul's language in these two passages is related to the dual theme of restoration and judgment in Jeremiah, it remains to be seen how Jeremiah's language affects Paul's own presentation of his apostolic ministry. Is the connection merely verbal, or is there a contextual link at this point between the ministry of Jeremiah and the ministry of Paul? While it can be argued that there is a distinct movement within the ministry of Jeremiah from judgment to hope, it may be more accurate to see these two themes as running concurrently throughout the prophet's ministry. The call and mission of Jeremiah, which are an extension of God's own activity, are never entirely devoid of either judgment or restoration. The two themes often occur simultaneously within Jeremiah (e.g. Jer. 1.13-19; 21.8-10).[198] The themes of restoration and judgment, therefore, do not move in a simple progression from the beginning of Jeremiah to the end; rather, they function to create a framework for understanding the overall mission of the prophet and the outworking of that mission with respect to both Israel and the nations.[199]

It is within this framework, namely the outworking of the prophet's call and mission, that Paul's use of the Jeremianic tradition in 2 Corinthians appears to take shape. Paul's first mention of his authority εἰς

196. There appears to be little distinction in Jeremiah with regard to the semantic domains of either ἀνοικοδομέω and οἰκοδομέω or καταφυτεύω and φυτεύω.

197. Robert Bach, 'Bauen and Pflanzen', in *Studien zur Theologie der alttestamentlichen Überlieferungen* (Festschrift Gerhard von Rad; ed. Rolf Rendtorff and Klaus Koch; Neukirchen–Vluyn: Neukirchener Verlag, 1962), 11, 17. Bach also discusses the theme of building and planting as it occurs outside of Jeremiah (cf. Deut. 6.10-11; 20.5-6; Ezek. 36.36; Amos 9.14; Zeph. 1.13).

198. Lundbom, *Jeremiah*, 1:149.

199. Lundbom, *Jeremiah*, 1:235.

οἰκοδομὴν καὶ οὐκ εἰς καθαίρεσιν in 2 Cor. 10.8 occurs within the rhetorically charged section of 2 Corinthians 10 and, more specifically, as part of Paul's response to the negative assessment of his character in 2 Cor. 10.1-11. It seems that Paul's thrust in this passage is to explain to the Corinthians that he has a divinely appointed authority (2 Cor. 10.7-8) that can be worked out potently in *both* written discourse and personal speech (2 Cor. 10.6, 11).[200] The metaphorical language, drawn from the realms of warfare (2 Cor. 10.3-5), the legal system (2 Cor. 10.6), and architecture (2 Cor. 10.8), therefore, serves as a foundation for Paul's description of his own character and the outworking of his authority.[201] Paul is urging the Corinthians to recognize the divine authority that he has received. The context of the second occurrence of the phrase in 2 Cor. 13.10 is similar to that of the first.[202] Paul again addresses the criticism of the apparent differences between his character as expressed in his letters and in his personal appearances (2 Cor. 13.1-4), and presents his ministry as stemming from divine power (2 Cor. 13.4, 10). In addition, Paul here urges the Corinthians to examine themselves (2 Cor. 13.5) so that the apostle's subsequent visit to the city will be marked by the positive nature of his ministry among the Corinthians and will not result in their harsh destruction (2 Cor. 13.10).[203] The two occurrences of the phrase εἰς οἰκοδομὴν καὶ οὐκ εἰς καθαίρεσιν, therefore, create a type of *inclusio* for this section of 2 Corinthians.

In addition to these two occurrences, Paul utilizes similar architectural metaphors throughout his epistles, and the idea of 'building up' frequently functions as a metaphor for his description of the way in which the church is to be constructed and maintained (e.g. Rom. 14.19; 15.2; 1 Cor. 3.9-10, 12, 14; 8.1, 10; 10.23; 14.3, 12, 26; Eph. 2.21; 4.12-13, 16, 29; 1 Thess. 5.11). Several studies have attempted to analyse the origin and function of this word group in the Pauline corpus in order to determine

---

200. Harris, *Second Corinthians*, 664; Thrall, *Second Corinthians*, 2:597.
201. Harris, *Second Corinthians*, 664. That Paul is discussing his own authority seems transparent from his use of two first person verbs in 2 Cor. 10.8 (i.e. καυχήσωμαι and αἰσχυνθήσομαι), as well as the addition of the personal pronoun μοι in 2 Cor. 13.10. The plural pronoun ἡμῶν in 2 Cor. 10.8, therefore, should likely be regarded as an epistolary plural which refers particularly to Paul. For Paul's use of epistolary plurals in other portions of 2 Corinthians, see Hafemann, *Suffering and the Spirit*, 12-18.
202. For an analysis of the material correspondence between 2 Cor. 10 and 13 see Jan Lambrecht, 'The Fool's Speech and Its Context: Paul's Particular Way of Arguing in 2 Cor 10–13', *Bib* 83 (2001): 305-24 (esp. 314-16).
203. Cf. Thrall, *Second Corinthians*, 2:871.

the specific meaning of οἰκοδομή and its cognates.²⁰⁴ Vielhauer's analysis presents four possible backgrounds for Paul's use of the terminology: biographical, sociological, mythological, and biblical.²⁰⁵ With relation to Paul's use of the term in 2 Cor. 10.8 and 13.10, Vielhauer argues that the metaphor refers to the 'Gründung, Erhaltung und Förderung der Gemeinde'.²⁰⁶ This notion of communal edification can also be seen to be part of Paul's use of the word group within his other epistles. Paul's use of the term in Rom. 14.19 and 15.2 highlights that edification or 'building up' is one of the exhortations that the community should seek to fulfill.²⁰⁷ This act of οἰκοδομή in Romans is given further definition through the presence of the imperative κατάλυε in Rom. 14.20. The second verb, καταλύω, is used throughout the New Testament to refer to both literal and figurative destruction (e.g. Mt. 5.17; 24.2; 26.61; Mk 13.2; 14.58; 15.29; Lk. 9.12; 19.7; 21.6; 23.2; Acts 5.38, 39; 6.14; 2 Cor. 5.1; Gal. 2.18). The communal edification, therefore, is not defined simply in terms of productivity but in the positive construction of communal life. Without the process of edification the community itself would be subject to destruction.²⁰⁸ Similar themes can be found in the letter to the church at Ephesus where leaders are said to receive gifts in order to 'build' up the church (Eph. 4.12) and the church is seen to 'build' itself up in love (Eph. 4.16).²⁰⁹ Primarily in these cases the metaphor of building parallels the

---

204. The standard analysis is Philipp Vielhauer, 'Oikodome: Das Bild vom Bau in der christlichen Literatur vom Neuen Testament bis Clemens Alexandrinus', in *Oikodome: Aufsätze zum Neuen Testament* (ed. Günter von Klein; TBü 65; Munich: Kaiser, 1979), 1-168. See also Pierre Bonnard, *Jésus-Christ édifiant son Eglise: Le concept d'édification dans le Nouveau Testament* (CahT 21; Neuchâtel: Delachaux & Niestlé, 1948); Mark W. DeNeui, 'The Body, the Building and the Field: Paul's Metaphors for the Church in 1 Corinthians in Light of Their Usage in Greco-Roman Literature' (Ph.D. diss., University of Aberdeen, 2008), 136-85; Ingrid Kitzberger, *Bau der Gemeinde: Das paulinische Wortfeld οἰκοδομή/(ἐπ)οικοδομεῖν* (FzB 53; Würzburg: Echter, 1986); Otto Michel, 'οἶκος, κτλ.', *TDNT* 5:119-59; Josef Pfammatter, *Die Kirche als Bau: Eine exegetisch-theologische Studie zur Ekklesiologie der Paulusbriefe* (Analecta Gregoriana 110; Rome: Gregorian University Press, 1960).
205. Vielhauer, 'Oikodome', 110-15. Vielhauer argues that the Old Testament provides the normal background for Paul's use of the terms (114).
206. Vielhauer, 'Oikodome', 73; cf. David Peterson, *Engaging with God: A Biblical Theology of Worship* (Leicester: Apollos, 1992), 206.
207. Moo, *Romans*, 859, 867.
208. Schreiner, *Romans*, 735; cf. James D.G. Dunn, *Romans* (2 vols.; WBC 38; Dallas: Word, 1988), 2:825.
209. Cf. Peter T. O'Brien, *The Letter to the Ephesians* (PNTC; Grand Rapids: Eerdmans, 1999), 304-5, 316.

actual construction of a building. The metaphor is meant to show that the church must be constructed in a way that is architecturally sound so that the building will not crumble or be torn down.

Apart from this material, however, the Corinthian correspondence itself provides a unique window through which to understand Paul's use of this terminology. The word group appears on several occasions in 1 Corinthians (e.g. 1 Cor. 3.9-10, 12, 14; 8.1, 10; 10.23; 14.3, 12, 26) and may function thematically to unite the message of the entire epistle. In other words, the metaphorical language of 1 Cor. 3.9-10 serves as a foundation for Paul's later distinction between the effects of love and knowledge in 1 Cor. 8.1, as well as for the function and order of the community described in 1 Corinthians 12–14.[210] That is, it appears that one of the functions of the architectural language in 1 Corinthians is to show the clear contrast between building the church in love and inflating it with knowledge that is devoid of love.[211] In line with this view Mitchell sees Paul's use of the word group as a consistent metaphor 'to refer to the stable construction, peaceful maintenance and improvement of the Corinthian community'.[212] Mitchell, however, argues that Paul adapts this terminology from its use as a political *topos* in order to deal with the pervasive factionalism that was threatening the existence of the Corinthian church.[213] More broadly, DeNeui argues that Paul's use of the building metaphor parallels its use in a variety of Graeco-Roman sources in terms of both its form and function.[214] Although Mitchell and DeNeui rightly observe a connection between Paul's use of the οἰκοδομή word group and his attempt to unite the Corinthian Christians, neither explicitly discusses Paul's use of the term in 2 Corinthians nor the possible Jeremianic background from which the references in 2 Cor. 10.8 and 13.10 are likely derived. Thus, while both Mitchell and DeNeui highlight important backgrounds for understanding the function of the metaphor

---

210. Paul also employs an agricultural metaphor in 1 Cor. 3, which may be an additional reference to the context of Jeremiah, which uses both agricultural and architectural metaphors; cf. J. Goetzmann, 'οἰκοδομέω', *NIDNTT* 2:252.

211. This is the central distinction made in Kitzberger, *Bau der Gemeinde*, 73-78. Kitzberger's study focuses primarily on the distinction between the οἰκοδομή word group and its oppositional referents (e.g. φυσίοω).

212. Mitchell, *Paul and the Rhetoric of Reconciliation*, 101; cf. Karl Maly, *Mündige Gemeinde* (Stuttgart: Katholisches Bibelwerk, 1967).

213. Mitchell, *Paul and the Rhetoric of Reconciliation*, 101-11, esp. 101 n. 219. For the οἰκοδομή word group in contexts referring to concord and discord see Xenophon *Mem.* 4.4.16-17; Dio Chrysostom *Or.* 48.14.

214. DeNeui, 'The Body, The Building, and the Field', 156-69.

within the Corinthian correspondence, it seems reasonable to affirm that Paul's various uses of the architectural metaphor may incorporate information from a variety of backgrounds.[215] Additionally, the building metaphor may function as a means for Paul to disparage the self-exaltation of the Corinthians by serving as an image of manual labour, which was often associated with low social status in the purview of Graeco-Roman society.[216] Within 1 Corinthians, however, it appears that Paul's use of οἰκοδομέω and its cognates is meant to refer primarily to the positive and cohesive activity needed for the formation of the community.[217]

In the first instance this understanding of the οἰκοδομέω word group appears to be part of Paul's presentation in 2 Corinthians as well. The specific dichotomy that Paul presents between construction and destruction in both 2 Cor. 10.8 and 13.10 probably affirms the idea that the apostle is presenting his ministry primarily in terms of its positive function. Paul's claim that his authority from the Lord is εἰς οἰκοδομήν likely refers to his power 'both to create a new community of believers and also to promote, guide and nurture the development of their spiritual life'.[218] Difficulty arises, however, when one attempts to determine the significance of Paul's additional statement that his authority is οὐκ εἰς καθαίρεσιν. While the dual themes of judgment and restoration are likely drawn from the Jeremianic background, it is not initially transparent why

---

215. This reasoning seems to be in accord with DeNeui, 'The Body, The Building, and The Field', 136-37, who argues that one should not dismiss Graeco-Roman backgrounds for the metaphor simply because of a *heilgeschichtlich* approach. In addition to the initial four backgrounds proposed by Vielhauer (i.e. biographical, sociological, mythological, and biblical) and the language of political concord discussed in Mitchell, it is also possible that Paul's language (at least in 1 Cor. 3.9-15) mirrors epigraphic sources which contain architectural terminology; see Jay Shanor, 'Paul as Master Builder: Construction Terms in First Corinthians', *NTS* 34 (1988): 461-71. For additional backgrounds, see DeNeui, 'The Body, The Building, and the Field', 140-56.

216. Clarke, *Secular and Christian Leadership*, 120; cf. Ronald F. Hock, 'Paul's Tentmaking and the Problem of His Social Class', *JBL* 97 (1978): 555-64; Ronald F. Hock, *The Social Context of Paul's Ministry: Tentmaking and Apostleship* (Philadelphia: Fortress, 1980). However, the notion that Paul views his own manual labour negatively (i.e. Hock, *Social Context*, 66-67) has been contested by Todd D. Still, 'Did Paul Loathe Manual Labor? Revisiting the Work of Ronald F. Hock on the Apostle's Tentmaking and Social Class', *JBL* 125 (2006): 781-95.

217. Cf. Thiselton, *First Corinthians*, 1088; Bruce W. Winter, *Seek the Welfare of the City: Christians as Benefactors and Citizens* (vol. 1 of *First-Century Christians in the Graeco-Roman World*; ed. Andrew D. Clarke; Grand Rapids: Eerdmans, 1994), 175.

218. Cf. Thrall, *Second Corinthians*, 2:625.

Paul states that his ministry is *not* for tearing down. This lack of clarity stems from an apparent contradiction between Paul's statement that his ministry is not destructive and several prior assertions concerning his ministry in 2 Cor. 10.3-6. In 2 Cor. 10.3-5 Paul affirms that he uses weapons to destroy (καθαίρεσιν) strongholds and to destroy (καθαιροῦντες) arguments that stand against the knowledge of God. Additionally, Paul expresses in 2 Cor. 10.5 that part of his mission is to take captive (αἰχμαλωτίζοντες) every thought, and he also states in 2 Cor. 10.6 that is he willing to punish (ἐκδικῆσαι) acts of disobedience. In light of this particularly forceful language, it seems necessary to assert that Paul's ministry is indeed destructive at one level. Paul asserts that the intent of this destructive activity (cf. εἰς in 2 Cor. 10.5), however, is to draw all things into obedience to Christ, which due to the surrounding military language likely involves all things being forced to render allegiance to Christ.[219] Since the apostle presents the destructive aspects of his ministry within this Christological framework, it may be possible that Paul understands the negative function of his ministry as serving a beneficial purpose within the community.[220]

Conversely, the destructive nature of Paul's ministry may be reserved only for those he perceives to be opponents of his ministry in Corinth. In other words, the negative dimension of Paul's ministry may reflect the same destructive notion evidenced in the ministry of Jeremiah, who called for the Lord to destroy his opponents at several points (e.g. Jer. 11.20; 12.1-3; 15.15; 17.18; 18.21-23).[221] This may explain Paul's exhortation concerning the restoration of the Corinthians in 2 Cor. 13.5-10. While he was capable of destructive actions, the intent of his exhortation in the latter section of the epistle was to provide the Corinthians a way in which to avoid the potentially harsh nature of his authority (i.e. ἵνα παρὼν μὴ ἀποτόμως χρήσωμαι in 2 Cor. 13.10).[222] With reference to the Corinthians, therefore, it seems that Paul was reticent, though willing if necessary, to assert a negative dimension of his authority that was primarily reserved for his opponents (2 Cor. 13.2-4). In this way, Paul's apostolic mission parallels the message of Jeremiah, which affirmed both God's willingness to act destructively in response to the disobedience of his people (e.g. Jer. 25.4-11) and the notion that God's eventual purpose

---

219. Harris, *Second Corinthians*, 684; cf. Jan Lambrecht, 'Paul's Appeal and the Obedience to Christ: The Line of Thought in 2 Corinthians 10,1-6', *Bib* 77 (1996): 398-416 (410).
220. Carl Schneider, 'καθαιρέω, καθαίρεσις', *TDNT* 3:413.
221. Cf. Thompson, *Jeremiah*, 90-91.
222. Thrall, *Second Corinthians*, 2:900.

was to draw the people into a proper relationship with him (e.g. Jer. 30.3-22).[223] The conflation of positive and negative themes can also be seen in the prophet's description of the Lord's action with respect to Israel and the nations (cf. Jer. 24.6; 42.10). Moreover, the idea of building up *after* judgment or destruction provides a key distinction within the prophecy of the new covenant in Jeremiah 31. The combination of judgment and restoration also surfaces earlier in the call narrative of Jer. 1.4-10, where the prophet receives both a negative and positive mission. However, the preponderance of negative terms in Jer. 1.10 may signify that the prophet's mission was more acutely focused on notions of judgment rather than restoration.[224] Although it is difficult to delineate a strict progression from judgment to hope in the ministry of Jeremiah, part of Jeremiah's description of the Lord's work in establishing a new covenant does exhibit a movement away from destruction and toward restoration (e.g. Jer. 31.27-40). Paul's claim that his ministry is εἰς οἰκοδομὴν καὶ οὐκ εἰς καθαίρεσιν likely establishes that the apostle understood his ministry as an extension of the transition from judgment to restoration exhibited in God's work in Jeremiah 31. Thus, because of their distinct positions with regard to the old and new covenants, the ministries of Jeremiah and Paul are characterized by different primary functions, with Jeremiah's pertaining primarily to destruction and judgment (cf. Jer. 1.10), and Paul's to edification and construction.[225] The apparent contradiction in Paul's statement in 2 Cor. 10.8 and 13.10 that his ministry is not οὐκ εἰς καθαίρεσιν dissipates, therefore, when the function of the destructive language in 2 Corinthians 10–13 is seen as part of a movement from destruction to edification.

Furthermore, because of the conceptual similarities between the language of Paul and Jeremiah, some have argued that Paul's use of this language in this portion of 2 Corinthians is evidence of the idea that this particular vocabulary, or the dual conception to which it refers, is germane to Paul's own apostolic authority.[226] In other words, Paul's thematic

---

223. Harris, *Second Corinthians*, 694.
224. Lundbom, *Jeremiah*, 1:235.
225. Cf. Scott J. Hafemann, 'Paul's "Jeremiah" Ministry in Reverse and the Reality of the New Covenant', in *Remapping Mission Discourse* (Festschrift Rev. George Kuruvila Chavanikamannil; ed. Simon Samuel and P.V. Jospeh; Dehradum: NTC; Delhi: ISPCK, 2008), 80-81. A similar assertion is made by Hafemann in his commentary on 2 Corinthians; see Scott J. Hafemann, *2 Corinthians* (NIVAC; Grand Rapids: Zondervan, 2000), 398.
226. E.g. Gillespie, *First Theologians*, 142-44; Hafemann, 'Paul's "Jeremiah" Ministry', 78-79; E.A. Judge, 'Cultural Conformity and Innovation in Paul: Some Clues from Contemporary Documents', *TynBul* 35 (1983): 3-24 (23-24); Lane,

reference to the content of Jeremiah's ministry is evidence of the notion that 'Paul understood his task as the eschatological ministry of establishing the New Covenant, an act of God prophesied through Jeremiah and achieved through Paul as the servant of the new covenant'.[227] Paul, in this view, is presenting his ministry as an authoritative extension of God's own work among the Corinthians (cf. 2 Cor. 6.1). Just as Jeremiah was called to express God's work of restoration and judgment through his prophetic ministry, so too does Paul understand his ministry as an authoritative extension of God's own activity.[228] In some sense, therefore, Paul categorizes himself as a second Jeremiah. However, it appears more reasonable not to assert that Paul sees himself as the embodiment of Jeremiah, but that the apostle perceives his ministry to be an extension of the prophetic tradition. In other words, the dual mission of Jeremiah 'to build up' and 'to tear down' (cf. Jer. 1.10) becomes part of the framework through which Paul presents his own covenantal ministry.[229] That Paul positions his ministry within a Jeremianic framework may also be seen in the apostle's conception of appropriate boasting.

### d. *Paul's Act of Boasting in the Lord*

After an initial response to the critical assessment of his character in 2 Cor. 10.1-11, Paul offers further validation for the authority given to him by the Lord (2 Cor. 10.8) through an act of self-commendation or boasting in 2 Cor. 10.12-18. In the conclusion to his argument in this section Paul attempts to establish the validity of this particular rhetorical action through a reference to Jer. 9.22-23 (LXX; cf. 1 Cor. 1.31).[230] In

---

'Covenant', 9-10; John Howard Schütz, *Paul and the Anatomy of Apostolic Authority* (SNTSMS 26; Cambridge: Cambridge University Press, 1975), 224-25.

 227. Lane, 'Covenant', 10.
 228. Schütz, *Paul*, 224-25; cf. Michel, *TDNT* 5:140.
 229. Lane, 'Covenant', 9.
 230. Paul's quotation differs from the LXX in several ways: (1) the initial ἀλλ' ἤ is removed, (2) the subject, ὁ καυχώμενος, has been moved to the first position, and (3) the prepositional phrase ἐν κυρίῳ has replaced ἐν τούτῳ. It is also possible that the citation derives from 1 Kgdms 2.10, which contains a nearly identical text to that of Jer. 9.22-23 (LXX). Contextually, it appears that the theme of Jeremiah more closely parallels Paul's statement in both the present passage and 1 Cor. 1. For an extended argument which favours Jer. 9.22-23 (LXX) as the background of this portion of Paul's argument, see Ulrich Heckel, 'Jer 9,22f. als Schlüssel für 2 Kor 10–13: Ein Beispiel für die methodischen Probleme in der gegenwärtigen Diskussion über den Schriftgebrauch bei Paulus', in *Schriftauslegung im antiken Judentum und im Urchristentum* (ed. Martin Hengel and Hermut Löhr; WUNT 73; Tübingen: Mohr Siebeck, 1994), 206-25; Josef Schreiner, 'Jeremia 9,22.23 als Hintergrund des paulinischen "Sich-Rühmens"', in *Neues Testament und Kirche* (Festschrift Rudolf

broad terms, therefore, Paul's use of self-commendation as a logical device is rooted, at least in part, in the context of Jeremiah.[231] In more specific terms, it may be possible to argue that the prophet's recitation of the Lord's command concerning the boasting of human beings functions as one of the foundational supports for Paul's use of self-commendation as a legitimate way in which to assert his apostolic authority within the Corinthian community. Further analysis of this portion of 2 Corinthians is needed, however, to determine in more precise terms how the reference to Jeremiah in the present context is significant for Paul's presentation of his ministry.

It appears that Paul's primary purpose in 2 Cor. 10.12-18 is to defend the legitimacy of his apostleship to those Corinthians who have questioned the potentially inconsistent nature of both his character and his boasting. In other words, while Paul's intent in the previous part of 2 Corinthians 10 was seemingly to describe the reality of his apostolic ministry, the present section of the argument appears to constitute an attempt to show that his ministry is rightly practised in the context of the Corinthian church.[232] The apostle's discussion of his boasting in 2 Cor. 10.12-18, therefore, may function as an extension of his claim in 2 Cor. 10.7-11 that he would not be ashamed of boasting simply because there was a significant amount of dissonance within the community concerning the nature of his ministry.[233] This lack of shame in his act of

---

Schnackenburg; ed. Joachim Gnilka; Freiburg: Herder, 1974), 530-42. For the possibility that the passage stems from LXX 1 Kgdms 2.10, see Kasper Ho-yee Wong, *Boasting and Foolishness: A Study of 2 Cor 10,12-18 and 11,1a* (JDDS 5; Hong Kong: Alliance Bible Seminary, 1998), 173-76. Wong, however, ultimately concludes that Jeremiah provides the most reasonable background for Paul's quotation (176).

231. For a discussion of self-commendation as an important form of logical argumentation for Paul, as well as the crucial role it plays in the whole of 2 Corinthians, see Scott J. Hafemann, '"Self-Commendation" and Apostolic Legitimacy in 2 Corinthians: A Pauline Dialectic?', *NTS* 36 (1990): 66-88. On the Graeco-Roman nature of Paul's boasting, see Christopher Forbes, 'Comparison, Self-Praise and Irony: Paul's Boasting and the Conventions of Hellenistic Rhetoric', *NTS* 32 (1986): 1-30; Duane F. Watson, 'Paul and Boasting', in *Paul in the Greco-Roman World: A Handbook* (ed. J. Paul Sampley; Harrisburg, Pa.: Trinity Press International, 2003), 77-100; 'Paul's Boasting in 2 Corinthians 10–13 as Defense of His Honor: A Socio-Rhetorical Analysis', in *Rhetorical Argumentation in Biblical Texts: Essays from the Lund 2000 Conference* (ed. Anders Eriksson, Thomas H. Olbricht, and Walter Übelacker; ESEC 8; Harrisburg, Pa.: Trinity Press International, 2002), 260-75.

232. Harris, *Second Corinthians*, 704.

233. Hafemann, 'Self-Commendation', 74. While the connection between 2 Cor. 10.8 and 10.12-18 is primarily thematic (e.g. the association between authority and boasting), it is also possible to assert that the γάρ in 2 Cor. 10.12 is a link to 10.8 (so

boasting likely stems from Paul's belief that his ministry is reflective of a divine prerogative, as evidenced by his original proclamation of the gospel in Corinth.

The first portion of 2 Cor. 10.12 involves an ironical and negative comparison between Paul and his opponents in Corinth. In terms of irony, Paul, who was thought by some in Corinth to be ταπεινός (2 Cor. 10.1), now affirms that he lacks the boldness (τολμῶμεν) to classify or compare himself with those who commend themselves.[234] Conversely, those who are claiming that Paul is 'bold' (cf. 2 Cor. 10.1, 10-11) are now faced with the apostle's own contrary admission. The nature of the irony is that Paul's timidity in this regard becomes one of the foundations for his self-commendation.[235] Paul's ironic admission of timidity in this case may represent a further connection between his ministry and that of Jeremiah. Jeremiah's so-called confessions (e.g. Jer. 11.18–12.6; 15.10-21; 17.12-18; 18.18-23; 20.7-18) often express the prophet's own timidity with regard to his mission because of the opposition that he faced as a response to the negative dimension of his call.[236] Furthermore, the 'confessions', which function in part to validate the prophetic ministry of Jeremiah over against the 'false prophets', may serve as a background for Paul's subsequent rhetoric against his opponents.[237] In terms of the negative assertion, Paul avoids the form of comparison used by his opponents since he believes it to be evidence of their errant method of commendation. It is a method that shows that they are without understanding (οὐ συνιᾶσιν).[238] This negative assertion likely concerns the

---

Jan Lambrecht, 'Dangerous Boasting: Paul's Self-Commendation in 2 Corinthians 10–13', in Bieringer [ed.], *The Corinthian Correspondence*, 332). The γάρ, however, should likely be seen as either a transitional or affirmative particle in this instance (so Harris, *Second Corinthians*, 706).

234. Wong, *Boasting and Foolishness*, 79-83, 112.

235. Forbes, 'Comparison', 16; cf. Hafemann, 'Self-Commendation', 76.

236. Holladay, *Jeremiah*, 1:359-60. The form, content, and purpose of Jeremiah's 'confessions', however, are subject to continual debate. See, e.g., John Maclennan Berridge, *Prophet, People, and the Word of Yahweh: An Examination of Form and Content in the Proclamation of the Prophet Jeremiah* (BST 4; Zurich: EVZ-Verlag, 1970); A.R. Diamond, *The Confessions of Jeremiah in Context: Scenes of Prophetic Drama* (JSOTSup 45; Sheffield: JSOT, 1987); Kathleen M. O'Connor, *The Confessions of Jeremiah: Their Interpretation and Role in Chapters 1–25* (SBLDS 94; Atlanta: Scholars Press, 1984); Timothy Polk, *The Prophetic Persona: Jeremiah and the Language of the Self* (JSOTSup 32; Sheffield: JSOT, 1984).

237. Cf. O'Connor, *Confessions*, 26, 51.

238. George Brown Davis, 'True and False Boasting in 2 Cor 10–13' (Ph.D. diss., University of Cambridge, 1999), 182, argues that the language of understanding echoes the Jeremianic narrative.

improper standards or measures that the opponents were using to evaluate both their own ministry and that of Paul.[239] In the first instance, therefore, Paul does not appear to be condemning the opponents because of their act of self-commendation; rather, the condemnation seems to be rooted in the apparent illegitimacy of the criteria that the opponents put forth to support themselves.[240] The notion that Paul here focuses primarily on the opponents' particular criteria is supported by the rest of the apostle's argument in 2 Cor. 10.13-18.

The frequency of language pertaining to measurement in 2 Cor. 10.13 (i.e. εἰς τὰ ἄμετρα ἐμέρισεν, τὸ μέτρον τοῦ κανόνος, and μέτρου) highlights Paul's specific emphasis at this point on the criteria that both he and his opponents offer in order to support their claims to authority over the Corinthians.[241] Although this emphasis is relatively clear, the argument itself is difficult to understand due to the somewhat ambiguous meaning of several of Paul's terms (i.e. μέτρον and κανών) and the complex nature of the syntactical relationships between the subordinate clauses in 2 Cor. 10.13. With respect to the meaning of μέτρον, Paul normally uses the term as a figurative reference to the measured part or section that results from the process of measuring (cf. Rom. 12.3; Eph. 4.7, 13, 16).[242] This figurative sense allows Paul to use the term as a reference to a type of limit or boundary derived from the act of measuring. This affirmation points to the notion that the preceding portion of the contrast, οὐκ εἰς τὰ ἄμετρα καυχησόμεθα, refers, in this instance, to boasting *beyond* the boundary created by the process of measuring. That is, Paul does not seem to be stating that he will not partake in immeasurable boasting; rather, his emphasis appears to be on his lack of willingness to boast outside of the proper boundaries of his own work (cf. 2 Cor. 10.15). The basic distinction in 2 Cor. 10.13, therefore, is not between proper and improper boasting, but between boasting based on proper and improper measures. How these measures are to be understood in the present context, however, is dependent on the relationship between τὸ μέτρον and τοῦ κανόνος, the function of the repeated occurrence of μέτρον within the relative clause (οὗ ἐμέρισεν ἡμῖν ὁ θεὸς μέτρου), and the relationship between the final infinitive clause (ἐφικέσθαι ἄχρι καὶ ὑμῶν) and the rest of the verse.

---

239. Thrall, *Second Corinthians*, 2:642-43; cf. C.K. Barrett, *A Commentary on the Second Epistle to the Corinthians* (BNTC; London: Black, 1973), 263; Forbes, 'Comparison', 16.

240. Cf. Hafemann, 'Self-Commendation', 76-77.

241. Cf. Barnett, *Second Corinthians*, 484 n. 22.

242. K. Deissner, 'μέτρον, κτλ.', *TDNT* 4:632; H.W. Beyer, 'κανών', *TDNT* 3:599 n. 12.

The complex nature of the prepositional phrase κατὰ τὸ μέτρον τοῦ κανόνος arises both from the meaning of the term κανών and the contextual function of the genitive case. Concerning the meaning of κανών, the term may be associated with a variety of conceptual categories, including carpentry, construction, athletics, geography, and administration.[243] Although there is certainly an emphasis on the geographical sphere of Paul's ministry in the subsequent material, it seems unlikely that this notion stems only from Paul's use of κανών.[244] In contrast, the term likely connotes the more general idea of 'rule' or 'standard', allowing it to function usefully in a variety of contexts, including those invested primarily with geographical concerns. In light of this more general definition it seems likely that the genitive κανόνος should here be regarded as subjective. On this reading Paul would be asserting that he is willing to boast according to the limit, or within the boundary, defined by this standard.[245] Paul then clarifies the definition of this standard in the following relative clause (οὗ ἐμέρισεν ἡμῖν ὁ θεὸς μέτρου). The standard is that which God apportioned to Paul as a limit or boundary, with μέτρου standing in apposition to the relative pronoun.[246] The boundary by which Paul constrains his boasting is determined by the standard that God apportioned.

243. See Harris, *Second Corinthians*, 711-12, for a survey of the categories and the particular renderings of the term that stem from them.

244. Beyer, *TDNT* 3:599 n. 20. Beyer's assertion has been challenged by James F. Strange, '2 Corinthians 10:13-16 Illuminated by a Recently Published Inscription', *BA* 46 (1983): 167-68 (cf. Furnish, *II Corinthians*, 471), primarily on the basis of a bilingual document from the first century that pertains to the responsibility of local communities to provide certain services to Roman officials with regard to transportation (see *NewDocs* 1.36-45). However, Judge's comments on the document highlight that the term itself is not invested with geographical notions but is simply embedded within a context that deals primarily with geographical concerns (Judge, *NewDocs* 1.45). For *1 Clem.* 41.1 as another example of the term having geographical connotations, see Hafemann, 'Self-Commendation', 78 n. 41.

245. That this is a subjective genitive is well represented in the literature, e.g. Beyer, *TDNT* 3:599 n. 12; Hafemann, 'Self-Commendation', 79; Adolf Schlatter, *Paulus, Der Bote Jesu, Eine Deutung seiner Briefe an die Korinther* (Stuttgart: Calwer, 1969), 624. Thrall, *Second Corinthians*, 2:645, however, believes that this rendering may result in varied understandings of the precise content of the κανών. This problem is removed, however, when the content of the κανών is seen to be expressed in the following infinitive clause. Harris, *Second Corinthians*, 713-14, argues that the genitive is here functioning epexegetically and that Paul is simply equating the two concepts. This, however, appears to create an unhelpful tautology within Paul's argument.

246. The standard (i.e. τοῦ κανόνος), therefore, is the antecedent of the relative pronoun, not the limit (i.e. τὸ μέτρον), contra Hafemann, 'Self-Commendation', 79. See Harris, *Second Corinthians*, 714.

The following infinitive phrase, ἐφικέσθαι ἄχρι καὶ ὑμῶν, may be related either to the preceding aorist verb (ἐμέρισεν) or to the antecedent of the relative pronoun (τοῦ κανόνος). Although it is possible to argue that there is a connection between the two aorist forms (ἐφικέσθαι and ἐμέρισεν), it seems that Paul's primary intent at this point is to clarify the nature of the κανών in question. It may be more helpful, therefore, to understand the infinitive phrase as an epexegetical definition of τοῦ κανόνος.[247] In this way, the actual content of the standard is Paul's divinely appointed mission to reach even to Corinth with the message of the gospel.[248] Paul's distinction between himself and his opponents at this point revolves around the respective value of the criteria with which they attempt to establish their boast. Paul contends that the opponents establish their claim for authority by pointing merely to themselves, while arguing that his own authority is the result of a divinely appointed mission to bring the gospel to Corinth.[249] This emphasis on Paul's missionary work as the basis for his boasting becomes more transparent in 2 Cor. 10.14-16.

In 2 Cor. 10.14 Paul reestablishes that his boast is appropriate and does not reach beyond its appropriate boundaries (οὐ...ὑπερεκτείνομεν). The implied contrast between Paul and the opponents in 2 Cor. 10.13 (εἰς τὰ ἄμετρα vs. κατὰ τὸ μέτρον τοῦ κανόνος) is made again in 2 Cor. 10.14. Interestingly, the proof (cf. γάρ) that Paul offers for his assertion that he has not overreached his limit is that he was the first to bring the gospel to Corinth (cf. ἐφθάσαμεν).[250] The legitimacy of Paul's boast is again seen to stem from his mission to preach the gospel among the Corinthians. Moreover, Paul explicitly defines going εἰς τὰ ἄμετρα as καυχώμενοι ἐν ἀλλοτρίοις κόποις in 2 Cor. 10.15. The implied contrast is that his opponents are boasting in a work that they neither initiated nor brought to fruition. Paul, however, claims that he boasts only in light of the standard

---

247. If the infinitive is connected with the finite verb it could be rendered either as an infinitive of purpose ('in order that we might reach as far as you') or as an infinitive of result ('with the result that we reached as far as you'); cf. Harris, *Second Corinthians*, 715.

248. Hafemann, 'Self-Commendation', 79.

249. Thrall, *Second Corinthians*, 2:647.

250. Although φθάνω normally means simply 'to arrive' in the New Testament (e.g. Mt. 12.28; Rom. 9.31; Phil. 3.16; 1 Thess. 2.16), its emphasis on priority is well attested in classical Greek, cf. LSJ, s.v. φθάνω. The classical definition appears to fit more readily the following discussion about foundational ministry and the negative statements about working in someone else's territory (2 Cor. 10.16-17); cf. Harris, *Second Corinthians*, 718; Wong, *Boasting and Foolishness*, 146.

which God gave him, namely to reach the Corinthians with the gospel.[251] Thus, the very existence of the Corinthian church becomes the standard which defines the limit of Paul's boast (cf. 2 Cor. 3.2-3).[252] Furthermore, Paul hopes that his missionary work will be expanded among and through the Corinthians so that the gospel can continue to go forth and that he can continue to boast only in the work apportioned to him by God.

Paul's repeated contrast in 2 Cor. 10.12-16 revolves primarily around the distinction he perceives between his own legitimate standard and that of his opponents. It is within this framework that Paul quotes from Jer. 9.22-23 (LXX). Because of its place within the present context it appears that the quotation serves to establish the proper criterion or standard for boasting in Paul's view.[253] Within the context of Jeremiah 9 (LXX) the admonition to boast in the Lord is placed in direct contrast with a form of boasting that is reliant primarily on the human standards of σοφία, ἰσχύς, and πλοῦτος. This specific contrast points to the notion that the apparent thrust of Jeremiah's argument at this point is to portray a stark divide between anthropocentric and theocentric boasting.[254] The contrast itself suggests that boasting is legitimate only when it is based on a boast about knowing the Lord, which, for Jeremiah, entails knowing the Lord's character and way (Jer. 5.4-5).[255] In other words, the act of boasting in the Lord is both a doxological and ethical activity, in which one recognizes who God is and then responds to that knowledge by participating within the divine economy.[256] The admonition in Jeremiah, therefore, is not that one should refrain from boasting, but that one's boast should centre on, and consequently represent, the legitimate work of the Lord. This same emphasis can be seen in the intertextual associations that Paul develops with his reference to Jeremiah 9 (LXX) in 1 Corinthians.[257] As with Jeremiah's audience, the Corinthians were apparently boasting about certain symbols of their cultural status, such as σοφός, δυνατός, and εὐγενής (1 Cor. 1.26). Paul concludes, however, that these particular marks of high status are devoid of legitimacy in light of the Lord's work among the Corinthians (1 Cor. 1.27-30). That is, it seems that one of the

---

251. Hafemann, 'Self-Commendation', 80.
252. Lambrecht, 'Dangerous Boasting', 334.
253. Lim, 'The Sufferings of Christ', 169-70; Wong, Boasting and Foolishness, 171.
254. So Lim, 'The Sufferings of Christ', 165.
255. Lundbom, Jeremiah, 1:572.
256. So Davis, 'True and False Boasting', 77-80.
257. See especially Gail R. O'Day, 'Jeremiah 9:22-23 and 1 Corinthians 1:26-31: A Study in Intertextuality', *JBL* 109 (1990): 259-67; cf. Hays, 'Conversion', 404-6.

main emphases of Paul's argument in 1 Cor. 1.26-31 is to express to the Corinthians that they could boast legitimately only about what the Lord had accomplished among them in spite of their high social status.[258] The specific argument in 1 Corinthians, therefore, reasserts the contrast between anthropocentric and theocentric boasting developed in the context of Jeremiah 9 (LXX).[259] Likewise, in the context of 2 Cor. 10.12-18, Paul implicitly presents his opponents as endeavouring to commend themselves on illegitimate grounds. Paul asserts that he had been given divine authority to preach the gospel in Corinth (cf. 2 Cor. 10.8) as evidenced by the existence of the new covenant community in Corinth, while the opponents had received no such commission. For this reason, Paul believes that the opponents' boast is unfounded and, consequently, that it could not be characterized as boasting in the way or knowledge of the Lord.

This distinction between Paul and the opponents is further established by the generic dichotomy between those who commend themselves and those whom the Lord commends in 2 Cor. 10.18. Indeed, this verse is viewed by Hafemann 'as the *crux interpretum* for understanding how Paul himself judged his own apologetic, as well as that of his opponents'.[260] Primarily, this verse functions as the grounds (cf. γάρ) for Paul's use of Jeremiah 9 (LXX). One ought to boast only in the Lord because of the implications it has for one's approval before the Lord. Thus, both the explicit positive assertion concerning boasting in the Lord and the implicit negative assertion about not boasting in objects other than the Lord are restated in 2 Cor. 10.18 in order to highlight the emphasis on the apparent illegitimacy of the opponents' claim. This last segment of Paul's argument, therefore, reformulates the contrast already made in 2 Cor. 10.14-16 and 10.17. The boast of Paul and the boast of his opponents differ primarily in terms of the objective criteria that provide the basis for their commendatory action.

In this view, Paul boasts unashamedly in the authority given to him by God to proclaim the gospel even as far as Corinth (cf. 2 Cor. 10.8), emphasizing, in the first instance, his own missionary activity. However, Paul presents this activity as rooted solely in his divine commission (2 Cor. 10.13) so that he is able to present his missionary work in Corinth as an extension of God's own work among the Corinthians. Consequently, Paul's conception of appropriate boasting may reflect the dual notions of doxology and ethics inherent in the Jeremianic narrative, with

258. Garland, *1 Corinthians*, 80; cf. Clarke, *Secular and Christian Leadership*, 96.
259. Lim, 'The Sufferings of Christ', 168.
260. Hafemann, 'Self-Commendation', 74.

Paul's apostolic mission evincing both his knowledge of the Lord and his activity as the Lord's human co-worker (cf. 2 Cor. 6.1).[261] It may be possible, therefore, to equate Paul's boast in the present context with Jeremiah's admonition to boast only in the Lord. In both contexts boasting in the Lord most plausibly refers to boasting in what the Lord has accomplished through the person in spite of himself or herself.[262] In Jer. 9.22-23 (LXX), it is God alone who brings about ἔλεος, κρίμα, and δικαιοσύνη. In 2 Corinthians, it is God who defines Paul's apostolic mission to the Corinthians. In other words, it seems that Paul considers his boast to be appropriate in light of the Lord's work through him, a reality attested to by the very existence of the Christian community in Corinth (cf. 2 Cor. 3.2-3). For this reason, it appears that Paul uses the Jeremiah passage to substantiate both the character and criteria of his boast. Paul's boast is legitimate in character because it can be confirmed by the objective reality of his missionary work in Corinth. The general principle in the Jeremianic narrative becomes the framework through which Paul presents the legitimacy of his ministry to the Corinthians. Although this connection with the text of Jeremiah may not, in and of itself, provide a concrete connection between the prophet and the apostle, it does seem reasonable to assert that this textual correlation provides additional support for the idea that Paul presents his ministry in 2 Corinthians as connected with the prophetic tradition.

### e. Conclusions

The relationship between Paul and Jeremiah can be seen in the similarities between their respective calls (cf. Gal. 1.15-16), Paul's role as a minister of the new covenant (2 Cor. 3.6), Paul's expression of his apostolic authority for edification and not for destruction (2 Cor. 10.8; 13.10), and Paul's presentation of the proper criteria for evaluating one's boast (2 Cor. 10.17). These particular connections appear to affirm the more general point that Paul is presenting his own ministry as an extension of the new covenant framework established in Jeremiah 38 (LXX). Thus, while Paul particularly references Jeremiah at several distinct points in 2 Corinthians, it seems probable that these references highlight Paul's connection with the prophetic tradition. This is primarily apparent in Paul's discussion of himself as a minister of the new covenant and in

---

261. Lim, 'The Sufferings of Christ', 170.
262. Hafemann, 'Self-Commendation', 81; cf. Glenn Holland, 'Speaking Like a Fool: Irony in 2 Corinthians 10–13', in Porter and Olbricht (eds.), *Rhetoric and the New Testament*, 253-54; Schreiner, 'Jeremia 9,22.23', 532. This also appears to be the thrust of Paul's use of the quotation in the context of 1 Corinthians.

his description of his authority for building up and not for tearing down, both of which highlight Paul's connection to Jeremiah, as well as the distinctive aspects of the apostle's ministry. In conjunction with the similarities noted between Moses and the servant of the Lord, Paul's relationship with Jeremiah in 2 Corinthians points toward the notion that the apostle understood his ministry as an extension of the prophetic tradition.

## 5. Conclusion

The assertion that Paul understands his ministry as an extension of the prophetic tradition stems from the connections that the apostle draws in 2 Corinthians between his own ministry and that of Moses, the Isaianic servant of the Lord, and Jeremiah. Although it is possible to argue at one level that Paul is either the expected prophet like Moses, the fulfillment of the servant tradition in Isaiah, or a type of second Jeremiah, the combination of all of these parallels within 2 Corinthians seems to favour the understanding that Paul's emphasis is not on his connection with each prophet individually, but with the prophetic tradition corporately. Thus, while particular insights can be gleaned from Paul's relationship with each of these prophetic figures, the overarching import of the connections in 2 Corinthians seems to be that Paul is presenting his ministry as a further extension of God's work through the prophets.[263] Moreover, the particular sections of 2 Corinthians discussed in this chapter highlight the notion that Paul's response to his opponents and to the faithful Corinthians was derived initially from this prophetic self-understanding. That is, the defensive rhetoric in which Paul engages in this epistle appears to be derived primarily from his understanding that God commissioned him to be part of the prophetic tradition. However, while the reason and content of Paul's rhetoric may be linked to this prophetic commission, the influence of this commission on the shape or form of Paul's rhetoric remains to be explored. The focus of the next chapter, therefore, will be to consider particular sections of 2 Corinthians in order to discern the influence of Paul's prophetic self-presentation on the conceptual framework of his rhetoric.

---

263. Sandnes, *Paul—One of the Prophets?*, 65; Frances Young and David F. Ford, *Meaning and Truth in 2 Corinthians* (BFT; London: SPCK, 1987), 78.

Chapter 5

PAUL'S PROPHETIC RHETORIC IN 2 CORINTHIANS

1. *Introduction*

The potentially prophetic nature of Paul's presentation of his apostolic ministry outlined in the preceding chapter may suggest that the way in which the apostle shapes the message of 2 Corinthians is also dependent on a prophetic framework. In other words, it may be possible to argue that if Paul conceives of his ministry as an extension of the Old Testament prophetic tradition, then his rhetorical activity may also be conditioned by a distinctly prophetic hermeneutic.[1] Paul's specific use of prophetic texts and concepts would then provide an important dimension of the formation of particular portions of his argument in 2 Corinthians.[2] That is, instances which reflect the intersection between the Old Testament prophetic material and the content of Paul's argument may provide a unique window through which to view the way in which the apostle constructs his rhetorical agenda in 2 Corinthians.[3] In light of this potential connection the purpose of the present chapter will be to examine a variety of texts from 2 Corinthians in order to discern the influence of Paul's prophetic self-presentation on the actual shape and course of his rhetoric in the epistle. Although the apostle's rhetoric may be defined by a number of conceptual and cultural backgrounds, the present chapter

---

1. Cf. Beker, *Paul the Apostle*, 116; Ehrensperger, *Paul and the Dynamics of Power*, 93.
2. Contra D. Moody Smith, 'The Pauline Literature', in *It Is Written: Scripture Citing Scripture* (Festschrift Barnabas Lindars; ed. D.A. Carson and H.G.M. Williamson; Cambridge: Cambridge University Press, 1998), 175, and Stanley, *Arguing with Scripture*, 97-98. For a concise overview of the biblical framework of Paul's thought in 2 Corinthians, see Scott J. Hafemann, 'Paul's Use of the Old Testament in 2 Corinthians', *Int* 52 (1998): 246-57; Hubbard, *New Creation*, 150-61.
3. The term rhetoric and its derivates are used throughout this chapter as broad references to Paul's development of his argument with respect to the Corinthians.

will attempt to analyse the ways in which Paul's argument is particularly defined by the Old Testament prophetic tradition. The intention within the chapter is not merely to discuss points at which Paul explicitly interacts with prophetic texts through means of a direct quotation, but to delineate the ways in which the apostle's rhetorical framework is itself an extension of Paul's presentation of his prophetic persona. The argument will proceed, therefore, through an analysis of four sections of Paul's argument (2 Cor. 2.14-16; 4.1-6; 6.14–7.1; 12.1-10) in order to observe the ways in which the prophetic tradition of the Old Testament shapes the course and content of Paul's rhetoric in 2 Corinthians.

## 2. Prophetic Triumph in 2 Corinthians 2.14-16

The material in 2 Cor. 2.14-16 functions in broad terms as an introduction to the defence of Paul's apostleship that extends from 2 Cor. 2.14–7.4, and, more specifically, as the initial stage of the closely constructed argument regarding the nature and function of his ministry in 2 Cor. 2.14–4.6. In light of this general structural outline, the argument within 2 Cor. 2.14-16 likely serves as an entryway into the subsequent discourse and may, consequently, provide insight into the theoretical outline within which the apostle formulates his rhetoric in 2 Corinthians. The meaning of the argument at this point, however, is mired in ambiguity due to uncertainty concerning the origin of the metaphorical language Paul uses to describe God's action and his apostolic ministry in 2 Cor. 2.14-15, as well as the complexity involved in defining the conceptual relationship between the metaphors themselves. These two related issues have generated a substantial divide with regard to the function of the thanksgiving formula in relation to Paul's subsequent argument on the nature of his apostolic ministry in Corinth, with the metaphors becoming a near *crux interpretum* for the shape of this portion of 2 Corinthians. Of particular importance for the present work is Paul's potential reliance on the prophetic tradition in the construction of his metaphorical framework. The intention within this section, therefore, is to provide a brief analysis of 2 Cor. 2.14-16 in order to examine the level of influence that the Old Testament prophetic tradition may have on this section of Paul's argument.

### a. *Paul's Apostleship as Defeated Sacrifice*
Despite the relative consensus concerning the broadly introductory function of 2 Cor. 2.14-16, the internal structure of the passage itself is contested at several points. The first issue pertains to the syntactical relationship between the two participial clauses that follow the initial

thanksgiving formula (τῷ δὲ θεῷ χάρις) in 2 Cor. 2.14. In specific terms, it may be possible to consider the fragrance metaphor in the second clause (τὴν ὀσμὴν τῆς γνώσεως αὐτοῦ φανεροῦντι δι' ἡμῶν ἐν παντὶ τόπῳ) as logically subordinate to the preceding triumph metaphor (τῷ πάντοτε θριαμβεύοντι ἡμᾶς ἐν τῷ Χριστῷ), with the result that the conceptual background inherent in the triumph metaphor controls the progression of Paul's argument.[4] However, the grammatical parallels between the two clauses suggest that the metaphors function as equal marks of identification for the action of God.[5] If the two participial phrases form a single unit of parallel thoughts, then the subsequent clause in 2 Cor. 2.15, ὅτι Χριστοῦ εὐωδία ἐσμὲν τῷ θεῷ, likely serves as the logical basis of the entire thanksgiving formula and not simply as an extended explanation of the particular nuances of the directly preceding reference to τὴν ὀσμὴν τῆς γνώσεως αὐτοῦ.[6] Paul's status as the 'aroma of Christ' is defined by both aspects of God's action described in 2 Cor. 2.14. A limited amount of ambiguity also persists with regard to the syntactical relationship between the prepositional phrases in 2 Cor. 2.15 and the related relative clauses in 2 Cor. 2.16. Carrez's hypothesis that the four phrases are direct parallels, so that those who are being saved (ἐν τοῖς σῳζομένοις) are the ones among whom the fragrance leads to death (οἷς…ὀσμὴ ἐκ θανάτου εἰς θάνατον) and those who are perishing (ἐν τοῖς ἀπολλυμένοις) are the ones among whom the fragrance leads to life (οἷς…ὀσμὴ ἐκ ζωῆς εἰς ζωήν), however, has received little support in light of the potentially more reasonable view that the phrases form a concise structural chiasm.[7] If the phrases are read within a chiastic structure, then the import of 2 Cor. 2.15-16 is seemingly to stress the divisive implications involved in either accepting or rejecting Paul's apostolic message, a distinction that governs a large portion of Paul's rhetoric in 2 Corinthians. In general terms, therefore, the present argument allows Paul to establish a broad outline for both the nature of his apostolic ministry (2 Cor. 2.14) and its potential result with respect to the Corinthians (2 Cor. 2.15-16).

Paul's initial participial phrase, τῷ πάντοτε θριαμβεύοντι ἡμᾶς ἐν τῷ Χριστῷ, functions as the first of two explanatory statements that elucidate the nature and scope of God's action in 2 Cor. 2.14. Paul's unique use of

---

4. E.g. Hafemann, *Suffering and the Spirit*, 43; Martin, *2 Corinthians*, 46.
5. See especially Lim, 'The Sufferings of Christ', 64-65.
6. Contra Harris, *Second Corinthians*, 248; cf. Lim, 'The Sufferings of Christ', 65.
7. See, e.g., Maurice Carrez, 'Odeur de mort, odeur de vie (à propos de 2 Cor 2:16)', *RHPR* 64 (1984): 135-42. The chiastic structure of the material is generally assumed (e.g. Furnish, *II Corinthians*, 177; Harris, *Second Corinthians*, 250-51; Thrall, *Second Corinthians*, 1:202-3).

the participle θριαμβεύοντι, however, introduces a number of barriers to an immediate understanding of the argument at this point. The verb θριαμβεύω, which corresponds to the Latin verb *triumphare*, pertains specifically to the elaborate triumphal processions that were common in Graeco-Roman antiquity.[8] Throughout the extant literature the term predominately occurs with the intransitive sense of 'to celebrate a (prior) victory by means of a triumphal procession'. With regard to the transitive sense of the verb, Breytenbach's extensive lexical analysis demonstrates that when the verb takes a personal direct object (e.g. θριαμβεύω τινά) the object always denotes the conquered enemy over whom the triumph is celebrated.[9] Paul's own position with respect to the triumphal procession in 2 Cor. 2.14, therefore, is as God's previously conquered enemy.[10] The apostle's presentation of his actual position *within* the metaphorical triumphal procession, however, is disputed. Hafemann asserts that the transitive use of θριαμβεύω '*always* refers to the one having been conquered and subsequently led in the procession'.[11] In contrast, Breytenbach contends that the use of the verb with a direct object does not, in and of itself, contain this sense. Rather, he argues that θριαμβεύω τινά functions only as a reference to the celebration of the triumph over the conquered enemy rather than as a specific reference to the enemy's

---

8. So Cilliers Breytenbach, 'Paul's Proclamation and God's "Thriambos" (Notes on 2 Corinthians 2.14-16b)', *Neot* 24 (1990): 257-71; cf. Breytenbach, 'Christologie, Nachfolge/Apostolat', *BTZ* 8 (1991): 183-98. Contra Rory B. Egan, 'Lexical Evidence on Two Pauline Passages', *NovT* 19 (1997): 34-62. For descriptions of the Roman triumphal procession, see Appian, *Bell. civ.* 2.15.101-102; *Hist. rom.* 8.9.66; Josephus, *J.W.* 7.132-57; Plutarch, *Aem.* 32.1-36.6 (cf. Dio Cassius, *Hist.* 6.23). The standard treatment in the secondary literature is H.S. Versnel, *Triumphus: An Inquiry into the Origin, Development and Meaning of the Roman Triumph* (Leiden: Brill, 1970); cf. Mary Beard, *The Roman Triumph* (Cambridge: Belknap, 2007).
9. Breytenbach, 'Paul's Proclamation', 261-68.
10. The earlier argument that the occurrence of θριαμβεύω in 2 Cor. 2.14 reflects either a causative sense, Paul as victorious conqueror (e.g. John Calvin, *The Second Epistle of Paul the Apostle to the Corinthians and the Epistles to Timothy, Titus and Philemon* [trans. T.A. Smail; CNTC 10; Grand Rapids: Eerdmans, 1964], 33), or the derivative nuance of co-victory, Paul as one of God's victorious generals (e.g. Barrett, *Second Corinthians*, 98), remains linguistically impossible in light of the extant textual evidence. For a helpful survey of the various interpretations of θριαμβεύω in 2 Cor. 2.14, see Jan Lambrecht, 'The Defeated Paul, Aroma of Christ: An Exegetical Study of 2 Corinthians 2:14-16b', *LS* 20 (1995): 170-86; Schmeller, *2 Korintherbrief*, 1:154-61.
11. Hafemann, *Suffering and the Spirit*, 33. Original emphasis. Cf. Lamar Williamson, 'Led in Triumph: Paul's Use of *Thriambeuō*', *Int* 22 (1968): 317-32 (esp. 319).

physical participation or position in the procession.[12] However, none of the transitive uses of θριαμβεύω that Breytenbach presents detracts from the possibility that the phrase may be rendered as 'lead someone as a captive in a triumphal procession'.[13] Consequently, the significance of this portion of 2 Cor. 2.14 appears to be that God continually leads Paul as a captive in his triumphal procession.[14] Hafemann's particular contention that Paul uses the metaphor in order to express that God is leading him to his death, however, may stretch the metaphor beyond its logical boundaries, since captives led in triumphal processions were not always executed.[15] This minor qualification, however, does not detract from the dramatic nature of the metaphor, which is manifest in the realization that Paul offers thanksgiving to God for always leading him around as a defeated captive.

Although Paul's defeated position within the triumphal procession is a demonstrable aspect of the metaphor, it is also important to note that the primary intention of a triumphal procession was not to exploit the captives, but to offer thanks to the deity who granted the preceding

12. Breytenbach, 'Paul's Proclamation', 261-62; cf. Lambrecht, 'Defeated Paul, Aroma of Christ', 183-86. One of Breytenbach's primary examples is Herodian, *Hist.* 1.6.6 (θριαμβεύοντί τε καὶ δεσμίους ἀπάγοντι καὶ αἰχμαλώτους βασιλεῖς τε καὶ σατράπας βαρβάρους), which he uses to separate the notion of leading from the semantic range of θριαμβεύω in light of the subsequent occurrence of ἀπάγω. In the context, however, θριαμβεύω is intransitive. Breytenbach's assertion would be valid only if the participle was transitive (e.g. θριαμβεύοντι αὐτούς).

13. E.g. Appian, *Hist. rom.* 12.11.77; Plutarch, *Arat.* 54.3; *Comp. Thes. Rom.* 4.2; Strabo, *Geogr.* 12.3.35 (Breytenbach, 'Paul's Proclamation', 262). In particular, the example from Appian, *Hist. rom.* 12.11.77 (οὐ γὰρ ἐδόκει Ῥωμαῖον ἄνδρα βουλευτὴν θριαμβεύειν. Ἀλέξανδρος δὲ ἐς τὴν πομπὴν ἐφυλάσσετο) appears to prove the opposite of Breytenbach's position, as Lucullus presumably orders Varius' execution so that he would not be led in the triumphal procession, as the contrast with the fate of Alexander makes clear. Furthermore, Breytenbach's examples from Plutarch (*Mor.* 201E; 318B) and Eutropius (*Brev.* 1.11) contain forms of θριαμβεύω with impersonal objects (i.e. τὸ δεύτερον, νίκην ἄδακρυν, τὴν νίκην) and do not, consequently, fit the pattern present in 2 Cor. 2.14 in which the verb takes a personal direct object (cf. Col. 2.15). The meaning of the verb, therefore, is seemingly dependent upon both its sense (intransitive or transitive) and, if appropriate, the nature of its direct object (impersonal or personal).

14. On the parallel, though somewhat distinct, imagery in 1 Cor. 4.9 see V. Henry T. Nguyen, 'God's Execution of His Condemned Apostles: Paul's Imagery of the Roman Arena in 1 Cor 4,9', *ZNW* 99 (2008): 33-48; Nguyen, 'The Identification of Paul's Spectacle of Death Metaphor in 1 Corinthians 4.9', *NTS* 53 (2007): 489-501.

15. So Beard, *Roman Triumph*, 107-42; Frederick W. Danker, *II Corinthians* (ACNT; Minneapolis: Augsburg, 1989), 50; Harris, *Second Corinthians*, 245-46; Lim, 'The Sufferings of Christ', 70.

victory and to honour the military general who oversaw it.[16] In addition to Paul's status as a defeated captive, therefore, it seems necessary to emphasize God's role within the metaphor as the one who leads the procession.[17] This particular emphasis on the divine aspect of Paul's metaphor may already be transparent in the somewhat distinctive word order of the initial thanksgiving formula, in which τῷ θεῷ is placed in the primary position (cf. 1 Cor. 15.57) instead of χάρις (cf. Rom. 6.17; 7.25; 2 Cor. 8.16; 9.15).[18] In light of both the historical purpose of the triumph and the grammatical emphasis on God as the subject of 2 Cor. 2.14, it seems reasonable to argue that Paul's metaphorical language moves beyond his own defeated position to the more comprehensive picture of God as the triumphant warrior leading Paul as a captive in the triumphal procession in Christ.

The second participial clause, τὴν ὀσμὴν τῆς γνώσεως αὐτοῦ φανεροῦντι δι' ἡμῶν ἐν παντὶ τόπῳ, denotes an additional dimension of the divine action for which Paul offers his thanksgiving. In contrast to the initial phrase the basic import of the second statement seems to be relatively transparent: Paul's apostolic ministry is the vehicle through which (δι' ἡμῶν) God manifests the knowledge of Christ (τῆς γνώσεως αὐτοῦ) in the world (ἐν παντὶ τόπῳ).[19] The metaphorical language introduced in τὴν ὀσμὴν τῆς γνώσεως αὐτοῦ, however, clouds the relationship between the present statement and the preceding material. Debate at this point primarily revolves around whether Paul's specific use of the term ὀσμή constitutes an extension of the triumphal procession metaphor or a transition to the cultic language of Old Testament sacrifice that likely governs the meaning of 2 Cor. 2.15.[20] The structural relationship between

---

16. So Hafemann, *Suffering and the Spirit*, 31.

17. For the emphasis on God as the subject of θριαμβεύω, see Lim, 'The Sufferings of Christ', 74-75; James M. Scott, 'The Triumph of God in 2 Cor 2:14: Additional Evidence of Merkabah Mysticism in Paul', *NTS* 42 (1996): 260-81 (263-65).

18. Cf. Harris, *Second Corinthians*, 243; Lim, 'The Sufferings of Christ', 74.

19. There is some debate whether the antecedent of αὐτοῦ is θεός or Χριστός. Although Paul refers unambiguously to the knowledge of God at several points (e.g. Rom. 11.33; Gal. 4.9; 2 Cor. 4.6; 10.5), the immediately preceding reference to Christ in 2 Cor. 2.14 (ἐν τῷ Χριστῷ) and the subsequent assertion in 2 Cor. 2.15 (Χριστοῦ εὐωδία ἐσμέν) suggest that Christ is in view at this point (cf. Harris, *Second Corinthians*, 247).

20. For a summary of the various positions, see Thrall, *Second Corinthians*, 196-99; cf. Harold W. Attridge, 'Making Scents of Paul: The Background and Sense of 2 Cor 2:14-17', in *Early Christianity and Classical Culture: Comparative Studies in Honor of Abraham J. Malherbe* (ed. John T. Fitzgerald, Thomas H. Olbricht, and L. Michael White; NovTSup 110; Leiden: Brill, 2003), 72-79.

the two participial clauses in 2 Cor. 2.14 may suggest that the triumphal procession influences the contextual meaning of the fragrance metaphor.[21] The background of the Roman institution seemingly provides an adequate framework within which to explain Paul's introduction of the olfactory language at this point, since the dissemination of certain scents and types of incense was a relatively common part of the Roman processional tradition.[22] In contrast, Hafemann argues extensively in his analysis of ὀσμή and εὐωδία (cf. 2 Cor. 2.15) that when the terms are used in the same context they denote the conceptual framework inherent in the phrase ὀσμὴ εὐωδίας, which operates as a near *terminus technicus* for sacrifice in the LXX (e.g. Gen. 8.21; Exod. 29.18; Lev. 1.9; Ezek. 20.41).[23] Thus, the combination of the assertion in 2 Cor. 2.15 that Χριστοῦ εὐωδία ἐσμὲν τῷ θεῷ with the occurrences of ὀσμή in both 2 Cor. 2.14 and 2.16 suggests that Paul's metaphor takes on a sacrificial dimension at this point. On this reading it is Paul's position as a defeated captive in God's triumphal procession that allows him to manifest the fragrance of the knowledge of Christ, which in light of the sacrificial nature of the language seemingly constitutes an implicit reference to Christ's suffering and death on the cross.[24] This association with the narrative of Christ is supported by the lexical and thematic parallels between the present argument and that of 2 Cor. 4.7-12, where Paul presents the suffering and death of Jesus as one of the paradigms which shapes his apostolic existence.[25] Paul's subsequent assertion in 2 Cor. 2.15 that Χριστοῦ εὐωδία ἐσμέν confirms the Christological dimension of the apostle's ministry inasmuch as it highlights the notion that his own defeated existence reflects the pleasant sacrificial aroma associated with the death of Christ.[26] The apostle's defeated position in God's continuous (πάντοτε)

21. So Harris, *Second Corinthians*, 246.
22. E.g. Suetonius, *Nero* 25.2; Appian, *Hist. rom.* 8.9.66; cf. Attridge, 'Making Scents of Paul', 79-83; Breytenbach, 'Paul's Proclamation', 267-69; Harris, *Second Corinthians*, 246.
23. Hafemann, *Suffering and the Spirit*, 43-49. The import of Hafemann's linguistic argument is that the reference to the sacrificial language becomes a key transition away from the Roman metaphor, where sacrifice may also have been present, toward the conceptual background of the LXX (cf. Lim, 'The Sufferings of Christ', 71-73).
24. Cf. David A. Renwick, *Paul, the Temple and the Presence of God* (BJS 224; Atlanta: Scholars Press, 1991), 80.
25. Lim, 'The Sufferings of Christ', 88.
26. Lim, 'The Sufferings of Christ', 88-91; cf. Steven J. Kraftchick, 'Death in Us, Life in You: The Apostolic Medium', in *1 and 2 Corinthians* (ed. David M. Hay; vol. 2 of *Pauline Theology*; ed. Jouette M. Bassler, David M. Hay, and E. Elizabeth Johnson; Minneapolis: Fortress, 1993), 169-77.

and universal (ἐν παντὶ τόπῳ) triumphal procession, therefore, becomes the very definition of his apostolic existence.[27] That is, the dual metaphors in 2 Cor. 2.14 create the window through which Paul views both the character (defeated captive) of his apostleship and its function within the Corinthian community (representation of Christ's sacrificial activity). It remains to be examined, however, why Paul constructs this particular metaphorical framework for the description of his apostolic ministry.

b. *Paul's Prophetic Framework*
Although nearly all discussions of 2 Cor. 2.14-16 are dependent in some way on the Roman institution of the triumphal procession, several more recent interpretations have sought to analyse the potential influence of other processional traditions on Paul's thought at this point.[28] In general terms, these analyses attempt to demonstrate that while the initial point of reference for the metaphor ostensibly lies within the Roman tradition in light of Paul's unique use of θριαμβεύω, the combination of multiple metaphors in the present context may suggest that Paul's rhetorical structure extends beyond the Roman background inherent in the context. Webb, in particular, argues that Paul's specific focus on the action of God and Christ, combined with the subsequent sacrificial imagery in 2 Cor. 2.14-15, is evidence that the apostle here intentionally imports theological categories into the cultural metaphor.[29] Webb's specific argument is that Paul's reference to the Roman institution is the means by which the apostle introduces processional motifs derived from the Old Testament prophetic tradition into the present context (e.g. Isa. 40.1-10; 57.14; Mal. 3.1). He contends that the Old Testament background offers a better explanation for both the sacrificial imagery developed in the fragrance metaphor in 2 Cor. 2.14-15 and the subsequent prominence of covenantal themes in 2 Corinthians 3. Furthermore, Webb argues that Paul's specific language parallels the actual shape of the Old Testament processional tradition in terms of its dual agency (God and Christ are representative of YHWH and the Isaianic servant), universal scope (πάντοτε and ἐν παντὶ τόπῳ), and emphasis on exalted suffering (thanksgiving as a defeated

---

27. Cf. Peter Marshall, 'A Metaphor of Social Shame: ΘΡΙΑΜΒΕΥΕΙΝ in 2 Cor 2:14', *NovT* 25 (1983): 302-17 (316).

28. E.g. Paul Brooks Duff, 'Metaphor, Motif, and Meaning: The Rhetorical Strategy Behind the Image "Led in Triumph" in 2 Corinthians 2:14', *CBQ* 53 (1991): 79-92; Lim, '*The Sufferings of Christ*', 64-96; Scott, 'Triumph of God', 260-81; Webb, *Returning Home*, 75-84.

29. Webb, *Returning Home*, 84.

captive).³⁰ In sum, Paul's language 'redresses' the Roman triumphal procession with theological concepts derived from the Old Testament prophetic tradition.

Lim closely follows Webb in positing that Paul here explicitly invests the Roman triumphal metaphor with a distinctly Old Testament background, focusing specifically on the processional material present in the Isaianic narrative.³¹ Lim's thesis primarily revolves around the Isaianic description of God as the divine warrior who inaugurates a new eschatological era (e.g. Isa. 26.16–27.6; 42.13; 51.4-11; 59.15-20; 63.1-6). That is, for Lim, Paul's emphasis on God as the subject of the triumphal procession in 2 Cor. 2.14 serves as the means by which the apostle is able to introduce the theological motifs of new creation and eschatological restoration developed in the Isaianic narrative into the rhetorical matrix of 2 Corinthians (cf. 2 Cor. 4.6; 5.17; 6.2, 17).³² Moreover, Lim argues that the connection in Isaiah between the divine warrior motif and the concept of a triumphal procession (e.g. Isa. 40.1-10; 51.9-10) enables Paul to define his ministry as an extension of the Isaianic emphasis on God's formation of a new eschatological community. In this way, Paul's position as a defeated captive in God's triumphal procession becomes a metaphorical testimony to God's universal sovereignty, with the apostle himself serving as 'an instrument that witnesses the ingathering of the gentiles to Zion'.³³ Paul's apostolic ministry, therefore, forms a necessary aspect of the eschatological renewal pictured in the narrative of Isaiah.

In addition, Lim helpfully points out the necessity of defining the Christological dimension (ἐν τῷ Χριστῷ) of Paul's statement in 2 Cor. 2.14 in the development of an accurate understanding of the contextual background of the triumph metaphor. He argues concisely that the prepositional phrase ἐν τῷ Χριστῷ should be rendered instrumentally so that the entire metaphor refers specifically to '*God's messianic triumphal procession*'.³⁴ In other words, Paul intends the triumph metaphor to represent a dynamic picture of the way in which God leads him as a defeated captive because of Christ's death and resurrection. This reading appears to support Webb's earlier contention that Paul's rhetoric parallels the dual agency present in the processional tradition of the

---

30. Webb, *Returning Home*, 79-83.
31. Lim, 'The Sufferings of Christ', 79-86.
32. Lim, 'The Sufferings of Christ', 79-83.
33. Lim, 'The Sufferings of Christ', 82.
34. Lim, '*The Sufferings of Christ*', 78. Original emphasis. Cf. Thrall, *Second Corinthians*, 1:196.

Isaianic material in which both YHWH and his servant play key roles in the narrative. The metaphor emphasizes that God is the one responsible for the prior victory over Paul and that Christ, like the Isaianic servant, is the instrument through which the victory was brought about. In light of this potential association between Paul's metaphorical language and the narrative movement of the Isaianic material, it may be possible to argue that the potentially negative aspect of defeated suffering that characterizes Paul's ministry in 2 Cor. 2.14 becomes the positive evidence for the apostle's unique position with respect to the in-breaking eschatological reality that Paul believes defines the present situation in Corinth (2 Cor. 6.1-2).

In view of the conceptual similarities between Paul's metaphorical language in 2 Cor. 2.14-15 and the processional material developed in the Old Testament prophetic literature, it seems reasonable to assert that Paul's rhetorical framework at this point of 2 Corinthians is defined in some sense by the preceding prophetic tradition. In other words, the theological shape of the metaphorical language in 2 Cor. 2.14-15 supports the notion that the apostle's conceptual background is rooted in the processional narratives that form a part of the Old Testament prophetic tradition. That the triumph metaphor is here invested with concepts derived from the prophetic tradition provides an adequate explanation for Paul's immediate transition to the cultic language of the Old Testament, since the prophetic picture of God's universal triumph was commonly supplemented with the language of cultic celebration and sacrifice (e.g. Isa. 56.7; 60.4-7; Ezek. 20.41). Furthermore, this particularly prophetic dimension of Paul's rhetoric likely provides insight into the language that the apostle uses in 2 Cor. 2.15-16 to define the distinct results which his ministry brings about. Paul's particular reference to those who are being saved (τοῖς σῳζομένοις) and those who are perishing (τοῖς ἀπολλυμένοις) coordinates with the eschatological picture developed in the prophets' presentation of God's universal triumphal procession.[35] The distinct divide that Paul presents between life and death, therefore, seemingly functions as a summary of the dichotomy between eschatological restoration and eschatological judgment manifest in the victory that brought about God's triumphal procession.[36] Thus, while the Corinthians' geographical position as citizens of Roman Corinth and Paul's particular use of θριαμβεύω may suggest that the initial point of reference for the processional language in 2 Cor. 2.14 was the Roman processional

---

35. Martin, *2 Corinthians*, 48-49.
36. Lim, 'The Sufferings of Christ', 92-93.

5. *Paul's Prophetic Rhetoric in 2 Corinthians* 195

tradition, the expansive nature of Paul's metaphorical portrait appears to parallel the prophetic processional material, illustrating that God leads him as a defeated captive in order to manifest the universal implications of the Christ event through his apostolic existence and ministry.

c. *Conclusions*

Paul's thanksgiving to God in 2 Cor. 2.14-16 serves as an introduction to the discussion of his apostolic nature and function that defines the argument in 2 Cor. 2.14–4.6. In broad terms, Paul here portrays himself as a captive whose defeated position is the conduit through which God manifests the fragrant sacrificial aroma of Christ's suffering and death. This broad picture may be particularly rooted in the prophetic narrative of the Old Testament, in which God's triumphal procession in celebration of his messianic victory is connected with the creation of a new, eschatological community. Paul's defensive rhetoric, therefore, derives in part from the theoretical framework developed in the Old Testament prophetic tradition. However, the notion that Paul's rhetoric in 2 Corinthians is shaped in part by the Old Testament prophetic tradition cannot be sustained by a single, complex allusion at this point of the epistle. The following material, therefore, will attempt to examine several other portions of 2 Corinthians (4.1-6; 6.14–7.1; 12.1-10) in order to determine the level of influence of the prophetic material on the shape and content of Paul's rhetoric.

### 3. *Prophetic Proclamation in 2 Corinthians 4.1-6*

Paul's argument in 2 Cor. 4.1-6 serves in large part as the essential conclusion to the material in 2 Cor. 2.14–3.18 concerning the reality and viability of his apostolic ministry in Corinth.[37] In structural terms, the argument developed in the larger section of 2 Cor. 2.14–4.6 can likely be separated into three distinct units that form a concentric relationship (i.e. 2 Cor. 2.14–3.6; 3.7-18; 4.1-6).[38] That the larger section is structured concentrically, however, does not necessarily detract from the unity of its overarching argument. The close structural and verbal similarities between the material in 2 Cor. 2.14-17 and 4.1-6 likely confirm that the

---

37. That the argument of 2 Cor. 4.1-6 pertains primarily to Paul's ministry is dependent in large part on one's understanding of the apostle's use of first person plurals throughout 2 Corinthians. For a defence of the position taken here, see Hafemann, *Suffering and the Spirit*, 12-18.

38. E.g. Jan Lambrecht, 'Structure and Line of Thought in 2 Cor 2,14–4,6', in Bieringer and Lambrecht (eds.), *Studies on 2 Corinthians*, 260-61.

present section continues the primarily apologetic force of Paul's argument at this point.³⁹ Similarly, concepts present in both 2 Cor. 3.7-18 and 4.1-6 (e.g. διακονία, δόξα, and νοήματα) seemingly connect the entirety of Paul's rhetoric in this section of the epistle.⁴⁰ The internal argument of 2 Cor. 4.1-6 may also be defined in terms of a concentric structure, with the material in 2 Cor. 4.1-2 and 4.5-6 pertaining specifically to the nature of Paul's apostolic ministry and 2 Cor. 4.3-4 to its perceived effect among the Corinthians.⁴¹ The relatively close syntactical progression of the material, however, likely points to the unified nature of Paul's argument at this point. All of the material in 2 Cor. 4.1-6, therefore, appears to represent an extension of the apostle's discourse on the origin and nature of his new covenant ministry. Nevertheless, Paul's present argument introduces several original insights with regard to the nature and function of his apostolic ministry. Of primary importance for the present argument is the potential impact of the biblical allusion in 2 Cor. 4.6 on the overall shape of Paul's rhetoric at this point. The intention within this section, therefore, will be to provide a detailed analysis of 2 Cor. 4.1-6 in order to examine the significance of the prophetic tradition on the rhetorical form and content of Paul's apostolic ministry.

a. *Paul's Apostolic Character (2 Corinthians 4.1-2)*
The first portion of Paul's argument centres primarily on a description of the basic character of his apostolic ministry. The introductory formula διὰ τοῦτο refers back to the extensive argument developed in 2 Corinthians 2–3, which is succinctly summarized in the following participial phrase (ἔχοντες τὴν διακονίαν ταύτην καθὼς ἠλεήθημεν). That Paul is here giving a synopsis of the preceding argument arises from his particular reference to τὴν διακονίαν ταύτην, a phrase that likely relates back to the entire discourse in 2 Cor. 2.14–3.18 concerning the sufficiency, validity, and character of his new covenant ministry.⁴² Thus, in contrast with the more universal discussion of Christian experience in 2 Cor. 3.18, the present material seemingly constitutes a return to Paul's presentation of his apostolic ministry. This transition is further reflected in the comparative phrase καθὼς ἠλεήθημεν, which functions as a direct parallel to the notion that Paul's call as a minister of the new covenant stemmed

---

39. Harris, *Second Corinthians*, 320.
40. Gerhard Dautzenberg, 'Überlegungen zur Exegese und Theologie von 2 Kor 4,16', *Bib* 82 (2001): 325-26; Harris, *Second Corinthians*, 320-21; Lambrecht, 'Structure', 260-63.
41. E.g. Lambrecht, 'Structure', 275-76.
42. Cf. Schmeller, *2 Korintherbrief*, 1:237.

only from the divine sufficiency granted to him and was not the result of either his own action or human commendation (cf. 2 Cor. 2.16; 3.4-6). The relationship between the notions of received mercy (2 Cor. 4.1) and divine sufficiency (2 Cor. 3.4-6) may also signify that the apostle is referring specifically to his theophanic experience on the Damascus road (cf. ἠλεήθην in 1 Tim. 1.13).[43] Although it is likely going too far to posit a connection between Paul's call narratives in Acts and the present context based solely on the aorist tense form of ἠλεήθημεν,[44] the likelihood that Paul is referring to the inauguration of his apostolic ministry at this point is solidified by both the close contextual association with the preceding argument and the thematic importance of the notions of call and divine illumination in the subsequent material. Apart from the specific nuances of these possible connections, their general function appears to be to allow Paul to reassert the divine authority that stands behind his ministry.[45] In other words, as he begins to conclude this portion of his apostolic defence, Paul returns to the origination of his commission in order to establish the framework for the following discussion concerning the form and function of his new covenant ministry.

Paul then uses this brief summary of the preceding argument as the rhetorical basis for the contrast that he develops in 2 Cor. 4.1-2 concerning the character of his apostolic commission. The initial negative statement in the contrast, οὐκ ἐγκακοῦμεν, likely refers to Paul's refusal to allow his ministry to be characterized by a notion of remissness or reluctance. That is, while it is possible to understand ἐγκακέω as referring to notions of weariness or physical dependency (e.g. 'lose heart'; 'grow weary'), it may be more helpful to understand Paul's present use of the term as pertaining specifically to negative behavioural action, the notion to which the term more commonly refers in extra-biblical material.[46] Paul's emphasis at this point would then revolve around a desire to avoid the perception (potentially already present in Corinth) that he was negligent with respect to his apostolic ministry.

---

43. Harris, *Second Corinthians*, 323; Thrall, *Second Corinthians*, 1:298.
44. Contra Kim, *Paul's Gospel*, 11.
45. Cf. Susan R. Garrett, 'The God of this World and the Affliction of Paul: 2 Cor 4:1-12', in *Greeks, Romans, and Christians: Essays in Honor of Abraham J. Malherbe* (ed. David L. Balch, Everett Ferguson, and Wayne A. Meeks; Minneapolis: Fortress, 1990), 101.
46. E.g. Polybius, *Histories* 4.19.10: τὸ ... πέμπειν ... ἐνεκάκησαν; cf. LSJ, s.v. ἐγκακέω. See also the extensive discussion in Norbert Baumert, *Täglich Sterben und Auferstehen: Der Literalsinn von 2 Kor 4,12–5,10* (SANT 34; Munich: Kösel, 1973), 318-46.

That the statement οὐκ ἐγκακοῦμεν is a claim against improper ministerial action by Paul is solidified in light of the following comparison. The apostle asserts that he does not partake in actions that would reflect an improper level of reluctance; rather, he actively seeks to repudiate τὰ κρυπτὰ τῆς αἰσχύνης. Despite its brevity, this phrase can be understood in a variety of ways.[47] In light of the contextual emphasis on the notion of sight (cf. 2 Cor. 3.7, 13, 18; 4.4, 18), it seems most likely that τὰ κρυπτά concerns concealed or secretive acts. The genitive τῆς αἰσχύνης would then provide the necessary contrast with the previous assertion by representing notions parallel to those inherent in ἐγκακέω. The entire phrase, therefore, would pertain to secret or concealed actions that are defined by their overt level of disgracefulness. The actual shape of τὰ κρυπτὰ τῆς αἰσχύνης, however, is defined by the two following participial clauses, both of which describe specific activities that Paul repudiates and consequently seeks to avoid in the same way as the characteristic of reluctance. More specifically, Paul claims that his ministry involves neither deception (πανουργίᾳ) nor distortion of the word of God (δολοῦντες τὸν λόγον τοῦ θεοῦ). Both phrases refer to particular behaviours that would have marked Paul as a fraudulent minister of the gospel.[48] The specificity of these assertions may be evidence that Paul's Corinthian opponents had accused the apostle of these particular activities. However, due to the close connection with his preceding explanation of the shape of his new covenant ministry, it may be more accurate to understand these phrases as Paul's own method of legitimizing his ministry in Corinth.[49]

That Paul is here defining the boundaries of the discussion becomes more transparent in the final contrast developed in 2 Cor. 4.2, in which the apostle positively asserts that his ministry is an open presentation of the truth (τῇ φανερώσει τῆς ἀληθείας). Paul's claim that this open aspect of his ministry is the means by which he seeks self-commendation from πᾶσαν συνείδησιν ἀνθρώπων ἐνώπιον τοῦ θεοῦ places this portion of the epistle within the broader theme of commendation developed throughout 2 Corinthians and likely highlights that the present argument stems from the apostle's larger rhetorical purpose in the epistle.[50] There may also be a connection at this point with the preceding argument in

47. See Harris, *Second Corinthians*, 324, for an exhaustive list of the exegetical possibilities.
48. Furnish, *II Corinthians*, 218.
49. Cf. Thrall, *Second Corinthians*, 1:301.
50. On the importance of the theme of commendation in 2 Corinthians, see Linda L. Belleville, 'A Letter of Apologetic Self-Commendation: 2 Cor. 1:18–7:16', *NovT* 31 (1989): 142-63; Hafemann, 'Self-Commendation', 66-88.

2 Corinthians 3, specifically Paul's claim in 2 Cor. 3.2 that the Corinthians were the evidence of Paul's apostolic ministry, known and read ὑπὸ πάντων ἀνθρώπων. That is, Paul remains confident that the character of his apostolic ministry and its spiritual effect, represented in the existence of the Corinthian Christians themselves, affirm the reality of his apostolic ministry in Corinth. Thus, Paul appears to be arguing that the mode of his ministry is intended to result in his human audience coming to the same (positive) conclusion as God concerning the authority and validity of his new covenant ministry.[51]

b. *Christocentric Proclamation (2 Corinthians 4.3-4)*
In contrast to the assertion that his ministry constitutes an open presentation of the truth, Paul concedes in 2 Cor. 4.3 that his gospel may in fact be veiled to some in Corinth (ἔστιν κεκαλυμμένον).[52] The apostle's veil language undoubtedly arises from the previous analogy with the ministry of Moses in 2 Corinthians 3. In the specific argument of 2 Cor. 3.14-16 Paul uses the veil metaphor derived from the narrative of Exodus 32–34 as a metonymy for the hard-hearted condition that prevented his contemporaries from beholding the glory of the Lord (cf. 2 Cor. 3.18).[53] The veil metaphor seemingly functions in a similar way in the present context. A certain group of people (τοῖς ἀπολλυμένοις) were unaffected by Paul's new covenant ministry because of the presence of a veil over their minds (cf. 2 Cor. 3.14; 4.4). Paul's specific identification of this group as 'the ones who are perishing' (τοῖς ἀπολλυμένοις) confirms that the metaphor pertains primarily to a distinction based on the spiritual condition of his audience. In 2 Cor. 2.15-16 he describes his ministry as an ὀσμὴ ἐκ θάνατον εἰς θάνατον with respect to τοῖς ἀπολλυμένοις, a direct contrast to the way in which it was perceived by τοῖς σῳζομένοις (i.e. as an ὀσμὴ ἐκ

---

51. Margaret E. Thrall, 'The Pauline Use of ΣΥΝΕΙΔΗΣΙΣ', *NTS* 14 (1967–1968): 118-25 (125); cf. Erich Grässer, *Der zweite Brief an die Korinther* (2 vols.; ÖTK 8; Gütersloh: Gütersloher Verlagshaus; Würzburg: Echter, 2002), 1:151.

52. The degree to which Paul concedes this point, however, depends upon the introductory formula εἰ δὲ καί. It may represent either an acknowledged fact (e.g. 'even if'; 'although') or a more subjective possibility, where δέ points to a contrast with τῇ φανερώσει and καί emphasizes the entire protasis (i.e. 'if our gospel is *actually* veiled'). In light of the repetition of ἔστιν κεκαλυμμένον it may be more accurate to affirm that Paul is positing, not confirming, the veiled status of his proclamation (cf. Margaret E. Thrall, *Greek Particles in the New Testament: Linguistic and Exegetical Studies* [NTTS 3; Leiden: Brill, 1962], 81; Thrall, *Second Corinthians*, 1:303 n. 792).

53. See the nuanced discussion in Hafemann, *Paul, Moses, and the History of Israel*, 363-86.

ζωῆς εἰς ζωήν). In light of the strict contrast between τοῖς σῳζομένοις and τοῖς ἀπολλυμένοις in 2 Cor. 2.15-16 and the correlation between τοῖς ἀπολλυμένοις and ἄπιστοι in 2 Cor. 4.4 (see below), it seems reasonable to assert that Paul is referring at this point specifically to unbelievers, and potentially to the more limited group comprised of his opponents in Corinth.[54] Although Paul concedes that not everyone in Corinth perceives his ministry as an open presentation of the truth, he does not view this rejection as a reflection upon the effective nature of his ministry in Corinth, but upon the spiritual condition of his audience.

The spiritual aspect of Paul's argument comes forth more plainly in 2 Cor. 4.4, where the association between the veil metaphor and those who are perishing is drawn together through the description of the negative activity of ὁ θεὸς τοῦ αἰῶνος τούτου. In spite of the uniqueness of this construction in the Pauline corpus, the negative connotations associated with τοῦ αἰῶνος τούτου (cf. Rom. 12.2; 1 Cor. 1.20; 2.6, 8; 3.18; Gal. 1.4; Eph. 1.21) and the dichotomy established with ὁ θεὸς ὁ εἰπών in 2 Cor. 4.6 (see below) leave little doubt that the referent in Paul's mind at this point is Satan.[55] The inability of those who are perishing to understand the true nature of Paul's gospel, therefore, is attributed to demonic activity, with Satan functioning as the catalyst for their lack of perception (ἐτύφλωσεν τὰ τῶν ἀπίστων εἰς τὸ μὴ αὐγάσαι).[56] This distinction in perception is again considered primarily in terms of the spiritual condition of Paul's audience, with the former designation τοῖς ἀπολλυμένοις here equated with τῶν ἀπίστων,[57] a term frequently used by Paul to refer

---

54. Cf. Garrett, 'God of this World', 101 n. 12; Harris, *Second Corinthians*, 327; Thrall, *Second Corinthians*, 1:305. The suggestion that τοῖς ἀπολλυμένοις is neuter and refers to the perishing aspects of the old covenant (so John A. Bain, '2 Cor iv.3-4', *ExpTim* 18 [1906–1907]: 380; S. Davies, 'Remarks on the Second Epistle to the Corinthians 4:3,4', *BSac* 25 [1868]: 23-30 [27]; cf. Martin, *2 Corinthians*, 78) correlates neither with Paul's use of the term in 2 Cor. 2.16 nor with the syntax of 2 Cor. 4.3-4.

55. Cf. Garland, *2 Corinthians*, 210-11; Harris, *Second Corinthians*, 328; Schmeller, *2 Korintherbrief*, 1:242; Thrall, *Second Corinthians*, 1:306-8. Contra Young and Ford, *Meaning and Truth*, 115-17. Young and Ford's primary objection that Paul never uses the term θεός to refer to an entity other than a member of the Godhead cannot be sustained (cf. ὁ θεὸς ἡ κοιλία in Phil. 3.19).

56. This conception of Satan's activity generally correlates with the way in which he is presented throughout the Pauline corpus. See Garrett, 'God of this World', 104-9; cf. Mohan Uddin, 'Paul, the Devil and "Unbelief" in Israel (with Particular Reference to 2 Corinthians 3–4 and Romans 9–11)', *TynBul* 50 (1999): 265-80 (273-79).

57. In light of the grammatical ambiguity that results from the introductory ἐν οἷς, the precise relationship between τοῖς ἀπολλυμένοις and τῶν ἀπίστων may be

to unbelievers (e.g. 1 Cor. 6.6; 7.12-15; 10.27; 14.22-24; 2 Cor. 6.14-15; 1 Tim. 5.8; Tit. 1.15). That it is specifically unbelievers who are in view at this point suggests that what is being prevented is a form of 'spiritual illumination'. In other words, the metaphorical activity of blinding pertains to the unbelievers' inability to comprehend the proclamation of the gospel in a way agreeable to Paul.

The specific purpose of Satan's blinding activity is to prevent the unbelievers from seeing τὸν φωτισμὸν τοῦ εὐαγγελίου τῆς δόξης τοῦ Χριστοῦ, ὅς ἐστιν εἰκὼν τοῦ θεοῦ. In contrast with the predominantly pneumatological emphasis of the preceding argument in 2 Corinthians 3, Paul formulates the discussion of his apostolic ministry in primarily Christological terms at this point. The specific discussion of Christ's glory ostensibly relates to the repeated emphasis on the theme of δόξα in 2 Cor. 3.7-11. The glory which Moses reflects (2 Cor. 3.7, 13) and through which believers are transformed (2 Cor. 3.18) is now explicitly described as manifest in Christ himself, who is the essential object of Paul's proclamation (2 Cor. 4.5; cf. 1 Cor. 1.23). Christ is not here presented as an entity which reflects the glory of God, but is in fact presented as the glory of God himself.[58] The reality of this equation is further established by means of the structural relationship between 2 Cor. 4.4 and 4.6, with the present phrase functioning as a parallel to τῆς δόξης τοῦ θεοῦ in the latter verse. In basic terms, therefore, Paul presents his apostolic proclamation as an explanation of the way in which Christ embodies the glory of God.

The assertion that Christ is the εἰκὼν τοῦ θεοῦ strengthens the close connection between Christ and the Father that Paul appears to be emphasizing at this point (cf. Phil. 2.6; Col. 1.15-19).[59] However, an understanding of the precise function of Paul's argument depends in large part on the conceptual background of the apostle's εἰκών language.[60] The

---

either epexegetic (i.e. 'unbelievers' as sub-group of 'those who are perishing') or resumptive (i.e. 'unbelievers' as equal to 'those who are perishing'). In light of the contrast between τοῖς ἀπολλυμένοις and τοῖς σῳζομένοις in 2 Cor. 2.15-16, it seems most likely that τοῖς ἀπολλυμένοις and τῶν ἀπίστων are synonyms in the present context.

58. Hafemann, *Paul, Moses, and the History of Israel*, 416.
59. Cf. Harris, *Second Corinthians*, 330-31.
60. For a comprehensive analysis of Paul's εἰκών language, see Stefanie Lorenzen, *Das paulinische Eikon-Konzept: Semantische Analysen zur Sapientia Salomonis, zu Philo und den Paulusbriefen* (WUNT 2/250; Tübingen: Mohr Siebeck, 2008), and Georg H. van Kooten, *Paul's Anthropology in Context: The Image of God, Assimilation to God, and Tripartite Man in Ancient Judaism, Ancient Philosophy and Early Christianity* (WUNT 232; Tübingen: Mohr Siebeck, 2008).

present notion of 'image' may reflect a specific allusion to Jewish wisdom traditions. Both the Wisdom of Solomon and Philo develop their understanding of wisdom through the use of iconographic language. In Wis. 7.24-26 σοφία is described as the image of God's goodness (εἰκὼν τῆς ἀγαθότητος αὐτοῦ, Wis. 7.26) and Philo refers to wisdom as both an image and vision of God (εἰκόνα καὶ ὅρασιν θεοῦ).[61] The general impact of these texts on Paul's argument would be to see Christ as the essential embodiment of wisdom. However, Paul's language may derive generally from the creation narrative in Genesis 1–2 and specifically from the declaration in Gen. 1.27 that humanity was made according to the image of God (κατ' εἰκόνα θεοῦ). If the Genesis narrative is the primary text in view at this point, then Paul's εἰκών language likely points to a significant theological connection between Adam and Christ, particularly in terms of their respective expressions of humanity. In other words, while the notion of Christ as the embodiment of wisdom may play some role in Paul's thought at this point, the primary emphasis appears to be on the notion of Christ as the quintessential human.[62] Apart from these significant theological considerations, however, the rhetorical force of Paul's Christological argument at this point likely stems from its impact upon the standing of his own apostolic ministry. More specifically, if the content of Paul's proclamation (although veiled to some) is the presentation of Christ as the embodied glory of God, then this may be offered as further evidence of the glorious nature of the apostle's own new covenant ministry.[63]

### c. Prophetic Light (2 Corinthians 4.5-6)

Paul's assertion that οὐ...ἑαυτοὺς κηρύσσομεν ἀλλὰ Ἰησοῦν Χριστὸν κύριον in 2 Cor. 4.5 returns the argument to a more explicit discussion of his apostolic ministry. The brief description of the content of his proclamation as Ἰησοῦν Χριστὸν κύριον (cf. Rom. 10.9; 1 Cor. 12.3; Phil. 2.11), however, continues the emphasis from the preceding verse on the Christocentric nature of Paul's gospel. As Harris notes, Paul's claim that

---

61. Philo, *Alleg. Interp.* 1.43. For a negative analysis of the influence of Wis. 7.25-26 on this portion of Paul's argument see Gordon D. Fee, *Pauline Christology: An Exegetical-Theological Study* (Peabody, Mass.: Hendrickson, 2007), 186-87, 601-2.

62. See especially Lorenzen, *Das paulinische Eikon-Konzept*, 139-256; cf. V. Henry T. Nguyen, *Christian Identity in Corinth: A Comparative Study of 2 Corinthians, Epictetus and Valerius Maximus* (WUNT 2/243; Tübingen: Mohr Siebeck, 2008), 176-79; Savage, *Power Through Weakness*, 148-52. For the alternative analysis that the emphasis is on Christ's divinity, see Fee, *Pauline Christology*, 519-20.

63. Thrall, *Second Corinthians*, 1:311.

he preaches Jesus as Lord represents a further explanation of what it meant in Paul's view for Jesus to be the embodiment of God's glory.⁶⁴ The strict dichotomy that Paul makes between himself and Christ as objects of his proclamation may reflect either evidence for previous criticism leveled against Paul or simply the apostle's desire to clarify the shape of his ministry.⁶⁵ In spite of the possible motives behind Paul's formulation at this point, the distinction itself seems to be a restatement of his previous claims concerning the source and object of his ministry. In other words, to proclaim Christ and not himself functions as the antithesis to the negative ministerial characteristics discussed in 2 Cor. 4.1-2. This connection with the preceding argument may also be manifest in Paul's unusual description of himself in the latter portion of 2 Cor. 4.5 as a slave of the Corinthians (δούλους ὑμῶν).⁶⁶ Savage posits a close connection at this point with Paul's claim in 1 Cor. 1.23 that his proclamation centres on the crucified Christ (κηρύσσομεν Χριστὸν ἐσταυρωμένον), with the structural similarity between the two assertions suggesting 'that in Paul's mind there is a unity between preaching Jesus as *Lord* and proclaiming Christ as *crucified*'.⁶⁷ The apostle's preceding description of his ministerial character (2 Cor. 4.1-2) and the subsequent *Peristasenkatalog* (2 Cor. 4.7-12), therefore, may imply that Paul considers his ministry to be an extension of this thematic connection between glory and weakness. Consequently, his perceived lack of sufficiency or ministerial effect was merely a misconception of the content of his gospel and the necessary weakness and humility derived from preaching Christ (διὰ Ἰησοῦν). In other words, Paul does not view the cruciform shape of his ministry as a mark against its validity; rather, he presents it as confirmation that both he and his message are transformed by the image of Christ and conformed to it (cf. 2 Cor. 3.18; 4.4).

64. Harris, *Second Corinthians*, 331.
65. See Thrall, *Second Corinthians*, 1:312-13, for a list of proposals that attempt to reconstruct the historical situation.
66. Although Paul frequently uses the term δοῦλος and its cognates to describe the relationship between Christ and either himself, his co-workers, or Christians in general (e.g. Rom. 1.1; 6.16; 1 Cor. 7.22-23; Gal. 1.10; Phil. 1.1; Col. 1.7; 4.7, 12), this is the only instance in which he refers to himself as a slave to others (note, however, the related concept in 1 Cor. 9.19: πᾶσιν ἐμαυτὸν ἐδούλωσα). For a concise discussion of Paul's slave language as an aspect of his ministerial identity, see Clarke, *Pauline Theology*, 96-102, 149-51.
67. Savage, *Power Through Weakness*, 153. Original emphasis. Cf. Garland, *2 Corinthians*, 315-16.

Potentially the most important aspect of Paul's argument for the present discussion is the apostle's assertion in 2 Cor. 4.6 that he has received illuminated knowledge of the glory of God. The assertion appears to function both as an explanation of the Christological nature of his proclamation (cf. ὅτι) and the conclusion to the preceding material concerning the shape of his apostolic ministry.[68] The significant issue at this point is the way in which Paul formulates the discussion concerning the illumination he received. The first portion of 2 Cor. 4.6, ὅτι ὁ θεὸς ὁ εἰπών· ἐκ σκότους φῶς λάμψει, locates Paul's argument within the broader biblical tradition. There is, however, no precise verbal overlap at this point between Paul's statement and any particular Old Testament text. Nevertheless, in light of the unique introductory formula (ὅτι ὁ θεὸς ὁ εἰπών), Paul's scriptural allusion has nearly universally been understood by commentators as having its primary referent in the creation narrative of Genesis 1–2, with specific connections being drawn between Paul's statement and the divine creation of light in Gen. 1.3 (καὶ εἶπεν ὁ θεός, Γενηθήτω φῶς).[69] The possible reference to the creation narrative in 2 Cor. 4.4 (i.e. εἰκὼν τοῦ θεοῦ) may also point to the likelihood that this section of the argument contains an allusion to the material in Genesis. In general terms, the import of the Genesis narrative is to see Paul's present argument as correlating with the later material in 2 Corinthians 5–7 that deals more explicitly with the theme of new creation.[70] In other words, the event of Paul's call is viewed as a parallel to (or possibly an extension of) the initial creative act.[71] The God of creation is consequently placed in stark contrast with ὁ θεὸς τοῦ αἰῶνος τούτου (2 Cor. 4.4)

---

68. Thrall, *Second Corinthians*, 1:314.
69. See, e.g., E.B. Allo, *Saint Paul: Seconde épître aux Corinthiens* (2d ed.; Ébib; Paris: Gabalda, 1956), 103; Barnett, *Second Corinthians*, 225; Barrett, *Second Corinthians*, 135; Rudolf Bultmann, *The Second Letter to the Corinthians* (trans. Roy A. Harrisville; Minneapolis: Fortress, 1985); Furnish, *II Corinthians*, 251; Henry L. Goudge, *The Second Epistle to the Corinthians* (WC; London: Methuen, 1927), 38; Grässer, *2 Korintherbrief*, 157-58; Harris, *Second Corinthians*, 334-35; Lambrecht, *Second Corinthians*, 69; Lietzmann, *An die Korinther*, 115; Allan Menzies, *The Second Epistle of the Apostle Paul to the Corinthians* (CGTC; Cambridge: Cambridge University Press, 1912), 29; Alfred Plummer, *A Critical and Exegetical Commentary on the Second Epistle of St. Paul to the Corinthians* (ICC 34; Edinburgh: T. & T. Clark, 1915), 120; R.H. Strachan, *The Second Epistle of Paul to the Corinthians* (MNTC; London: Hodder & Stoughton, 1935), 92; Thrall, *Second Corinthians*, 1:314-16; Heinz-Dietrich Wendland, *Die Briefe an die Korinther* (13th ed.; NTD 7; Göttingen: Vandenhoeck & Ruprecht, 1972), 163; Hans Windisch, *Der zweite Korintherbrief* (9th ed.; KEK 6; Göttingen: Vandenhoeck & Ruprecht, 1924), 139-40.
70. Cf. Beale, 'Old Testament Background', passim.
71. Thrall, *Second Corinthians*, 1:315-16.

in light of the different results produced by each figure.⁷² The broad scope of Paul's argument in 2 Cor. 4.1-6, therefore, is seen to be an affirmation that his apostolic ministry is rooted solely in the creative activity of God and pertains particularly to the embodiment of God's glory in Christ (ἐν προσώπῳ Ἰησοῦ Χριστοῦ), who is specifically connected with the theme of new creation in 2 Cor. 5.17.

However, in spite of the general thematic connections brought forth through the notions of divine discourse and the creation of light, there is little semantic overlap between the material in Genesis and 2 Corinthians. The change in lexeme, tense, and mood exhibited in the transition from γενηθήτω to λάμψει, as well as the strict contrast between darkness and light in 2 Corinthians 4, make it difficult to identify a direct correlation between the two passages. The significance of these changes has led to questions concerning the viability of the creation narrative as the background for Paul's discourse at this point. Collange's seminal argument, for example, questions the feasibility of a presumably well-known text such as Genesis 1 succumbing to such dramatic textual modifications.⁷³ Although it is likely going too far to follow Collange in abandoning the Genesis narrative entirely as a potential background for Paul's discourse, the lack of strict correlation between the two passages makes it reasonable to assume that multiple *Vorlagen* shape Paul's argument at this point (e.g. Gen. 1.1-3; LXX 2 Kgdms 22.29; Job 37.15; Pss. 18.28 [17.29 LXX]; 112.4 [111.4 LXX]; Isa. 9.1 [9.2 LXX]). Indeed, the lack of precise verbal overlap between any passage in either the Hebrew or Greek tradition and the content of 2 Cor. 4.6 likely serves to establish that Paul's material is a textually imprecise allusion, irrespective of the perceived status of its potential Old Testament background.⁷⁴

In addition to the material in Genesis, the two texts most frequently put forth as possible sources for Paul's argument are Job 37.15 and Isa. 9.1 (9.2 LXX). The connection with Job 37.15 stems from a lexically similar discussion of light coming out of darkness (φῶς ποιήσας ἐκ σκότους). Despite the verbal similarities, however, there is little contextual evidence to connect the material in Job with Paul's argument in 2 Corinthians. The

---

72. E.g. George W. MacRae, 'Anti-Dualist Polemic in 2 Cor. 4,6?', in *The New Testament Scriptures* (vol. 4.1 of *Studia Evangelica*; ed. F.L. Cross; TUGAL 102; Berlin: Akademie-Verlag, 1968), 423. MacRae's specific argument that Paul's rhetoric is here influenced by Gnostic categories, however, cannot be sustained.

73. J.-F. Collange, *Énigmes de la deuxième épître de Paul aux Corinthiens: Étude exégétique de 2 Cor. 2:14–7:4* (SNTSMS 18; Cambridge: Cambridge University Press, 1972), 138-39.

74. Stanley, *Paul and the Language of Scripture*, 215-16.

material in Job 37.15 stands within the broader context of the speeches of Elihu (Job 36–37) and the actual textual correspondence is embedded in the rhetorically charged material in the section comprised of Job 37.14-20, in which Elihu makes his final challenge to Job. Within this context the statement that potentially parallels Paul's material refers specifically to God's comprehensive control of the created order.[75] It may be possible, therefore, to see some level of rhetorical overlap between the passages with respect to their potential association with the theme of creation. However, the lack of extensive correlation between the material in 2 Corinthians and that of the larger context of Job 37 makes it difficult to discern anything beyond a tangential connection between the two texts.

In terms of verbal similarities the most likely background for Paul's scriptural framework may be Isa. 9.1 (9.2 LXX), which is the only passage within the Old Testament where the exact phrase φῶς λάμψει occurs.[76] An allusion to Isaiah at this point, however, has normally been relegated to secondary status due to the perceived creational aspects of Paul's argument and the fact that the phrase φῶς λάμψει in Isa. 9.2 (LXX) is not expressed directly through divine speech.[77] Complaints have also been raised that perceived connections with Isaiah are built on an inappropriate desire to link the ministry of Paul with that of the Isaianic servant, whose mission is described in part in Isa. 42.6-7 and 49.6 as being a light to the nations (εἰς φῶς ἐθνῶν).[78] Despite these perceived difficulties, it may still be possible to argue for a primary connection between Isaiah and Paul at this point if it can be shown that the close verbal correspondence is evidence of a more significant conceptual association between the two passages.

---

75. Cf. Robert L. Alden, *Job* (NAC 11; Nashville: Broadman & Holman, 1993), 362-63; Norman C. Habel, *The Book of Job* (OTL; London: SCM, 1985), 514; John Hartley, *The Book of Job* (NICOT; Grand Rapids: Eerdmans, 1988), 482. Although the MT and LXX versions of Job differ widely at this point, both texts emphasize the Lord's control over creation (cf. Wilk, *Die Bedeutung des Jesjabuches*, 270).

76. So Collange, *Énigmes*, 138-39; Martin, *2 Corinthians*, 80; Jones, 'Apostle Paul', 102-8; C.M. Martini, 'Alcuni temi letterari di 2 Cor. 4:6 e i racconti della conversione di San Paolo negli Atti', in *Studiorum Paulinorum Congressus Internationalis Catholicus 1961* (2 vols.; AnBib 17-18; Rome: Pontifical Biblical Institute, 1963), 1:471-72; Derk William Oostendorp, *Another Jesus: A Gospel of Jewish-Christian Superiority in II Corinthians* (Kampen: Kok, 1967), 48; Richard, 'Polemics, Old Testament, and Theology', 359-60; Savage, *Power Through Weakness*, 112-27.

77. E.g. Harris, *Second Corinthians*, 334-35.

78. E.g. Sandnes, *Paul—One of the Prophets?*, 144; Thrall, *Second Corinthians*, 1:315 n. 865. Contra Collange, *Énigmes*, 138-39; Webb, *Returning Home*, 95-101.

5. *Paul's Prophetic Rhetoric in 2 Corinthians*     207

In order to examine the potential influence of the Isaianic narrative on Paul's rhetoric at this point, it will be helpful to provide a brief analysis of the parallel context in Isaiah. The material in Isaiah 9 stands within the narrative movement of Isaiah 1–12, which broadly concerns Israel's political situation during the reign of Ahaz and Isaiah's attempt to prevent the nation from entering into a political alliance that the prophet deemed unnecessary.[79] The people's persistent refusal to listen to the Lord's message through Isaiah and their continued desire to form a foreign coalition are consequently presented as the primary catalysts for the Assyrian exile in Isa. 8.1-10. The poetic material in Isaiah 9 closely follows this proclamation of divine judgment and provides a level of assurance concerning the future hope of restoration detailed more explicitly in Isaiah 10–11.[80] Isaiah 9 itself progresses from the dramatic announcement of the coming light in Isa. 9.1 (9.2 LXX) to the specific reasons for the transition from darkness to light in Isa. 9.2-6 (9.3-7 LXX), culminating in the introduction of a unique and potentially messianic figure in Isa. 9.5-6 (9.6-7 LXX).[81] The description of this figure has served as the primary point of discussion with regard to the rhetorical import of Isaiah 9 in the broader narrative of Isaiah. However, apart from speculation concerning the identity, character, and function of this unspecified figure, Isa. 8.23–9.6 (9.1-7 LXX) functions primarily as a message of salvation to the people in both the MT and the LXX.[82] The LXX version of the passage in particular places a significant amount of emphasis on the future hope of the people and the fulfillment of the Lord's promises of salvation.[83] In specific terms, the transition from ראו to ἴδετε and from נגה to λάμψει in Isa. 9.2 (LXX) establish the future expectancy of the

79. Blenkinsopp, *Isaiah 1–39*, 171-74.
80. Blenkinsopp, *Prophecy*, 109. The addition of τὰ μέρη τῆς Ιουδιαίας at the end of Isa. 9.1 in the LXX, however, likely reflects a transition in the historical referent from the northern kingdom to Palestine in the Hellenistic period (so Isac Leo Seeligmann, *The Septuagint Version of Isaiah and Cognate Studies* [ed. Robert Hanhart and Hermann Spieckermann; FAT 40; Tübingen: Mohr Siebeck, 2004], 237).
81. Childs, *Isaiah*, 79.
82. For a comparative analysis of the MT and LXX versions of Isa. 9, see Johan Lust, *Messianism and the Septuagint: Collected Essays* (ed. K. Hauspie; BETL 178; Leuven: Leuven University Press, 2004), 169. In contrast to Lust's conclusions regarding the significance of Isa. 9, see Joachim Schaper, 'Messianism in the Septuagint of Isaiah and Messianic Intertextuality in the Greek Bible', in *The Septuagint and Messianism* (ed. Michael A. Knibb; BETL 195; Leuven: Leuven University Press, 2006), 372-75.
83. Arie van der Kooij, 'The Septuagint of Isaiah and the Mode of Reading Prophecies in Early Judaism: Some Comments on LXX Isaiah 8–9', in Karrer and Kraus (eds.), *Die Septuaginta*, 606.

subsequent material. The following material in Isa. 9.4-5 (LXX) then describes a promised change in the socio-economic condition of the people that centres primarily on the Lord's work in re-establishing their financial status. These hopeful expectations are then drawn to a dramatic conclusion in the extensive description of the potentially messianic figure in Isa. 9.6-7 (LXX). In its entirety, therefore, the message of Isa. 9.1-7 (LXX) focuses on the hope 'centred on the expectation of an upright Davidic ruler supposed to have Israel restored through the announcement of the μεγάλη βουλή of the Lord'.[84]

With regard to Paul's particular statement in 2 Cor. 4.6 that ἐκ σκότους φῶς λάμψει, the essential portion of Isaiah 9 is the reversal of the condition of the people in Isa. 9.2 (LXX), where they are first described as both walking in darkness (πορευόμενος ἐν σκότει) and living in death, and are then subsequently called to see a great light (ἴδετε φῶς μέγα) and identified as those upon whom light will shine (φῶς λάμψει). Within the overall context of Isaiah 9 the particular theme of light at this point seemingly refers to God's expected work of salvation.[85] This understanding correlates well with the larger narrative of Isaiah in which the theme of light refers to a wide variety of concepts closely associated with YHWH's identity and work (e.g. Isa. 2.5; 4.5; 26.9; 30.26; 42.16; 45.7; 51.4-5; 53.11; 60.1-3, 19-20). The significance of the concept of light in Isa. 9.2 (LXX) for Paul's argument, however, may develop more specifically from the way in which it forms an intertextual bridge with the material in Isaiah 40–66. Of particular importance at this point are the potential connections made between the material in Isaiah 9 and that in Isa. 50.10 and 53.11.

The LXX version of Isa. 50.10 consists of an interpretation of the third servant song (Isa. 50.4-9) as a call to listen to the speech of the servant (ἀκουσάτω) and as an exhortation for the audience to trust (πεποίθατε) in the name of the Lord. The specific correlation between Isa. 50.10 and Isa. 9.2 (LXX) stems from the LXX's rendition of the singular phrase הלך חשכים with the plural οἱ πορευόμενοι ἐν σκότει, wording that closely resembles the collective notion behind ὁ λαὸς ὁ πορευόμενος ἐν σκότει in Isa. 9.2 (LXX). Though not particularly unusual, the LXX also renders the noun נגה in Isa. 50.10 with the term φῶς, thereby increasing the verbal similarities between the two passages.[86] In light of these grammatical and

---

84. Schaper, 'Messianism', 374.
85. Cf. Oswalt, *Isaiah*, 1:242.
86. Ekblad, *Isaiah's Servant Poems*, 158. The noun נגה is also translated as φῶς in Isa. 4.5 and 62.1. The term, however, could also be rendered as αὐγὴν ἐν ἀωρίᾳ (Isa. 59.9), λαμπρότητι (Isa. 60.3), or ἀνατολή (Isa. 60.19).

verbal changes it may also be possible to detect a conceptual link between the contexts of Isaiah 9 and 50. More specifically, the introduction of imperatives in both contexts (ἴδετε in Isa. 9.2 [LXX] and πεποίθατε in Isa. 50.10) may reflect the notion that the addressees are being called to decide how they will respond to the light: '[t]hey are invited to either trust in the Lord's name or walk in the light of their own fire' (Isa. 50.11).[87] In this way, the distinction between light and darkness becomes the means by which the LXX describes the potential state of those who follow after the servant and those who do not.[88] It may be reasonable to argue, therefore, that the introduction of light in Isaiah 9 is a textual catalyst for the development of an association between the concept of light and the work of the servant.

This connection between the servant tradition and Isaiah 9 in the LXX is made more explicit in the context of the fourth servant song (Isa. 52.13–53.12). The specific correlation between the two themes arises specifically in the LXX version of Isa. 53.10-12, which consists of 'a thoroughly impressive presentation of the Lord's dealing with and through his Servant'.[89] The broad differences between the two textual traditions at this point likely stem from a variety of textual and theological decisions made by the LXX translator(s). Of primary importance for the present argument, however, is the LXX's translation of יראה in Isa. 53.11 as δεῖξαι αὐτῷ φῶς. The use of the infinitive δεῖξαι to render יראה probably suggests that the translator(s) read the Hebrew *qal* form (יִרְאֶה) as a *hiphil* (יַרְאֶה), and consequently interpreted the verb in causative terms.[90] The most significant change at this point, however, likely stems from the addition of the direct object φῶς. Despite the various proposals for the textual history of the insertion,[91] there is little doubt that the term φῶς

---

87. Ekblad, *Isaiah's Servant Poems*, 158.

88. This distinction, however, is not as readily transparent in the MT due to the ambiguous grammatical relationship between the servant and the one who walks in darkness. For an extensive analysis of the interpretative possibilities in the MT, see W.A.M. Beuken, *Jesaja III* (2 vols.; POut; Nijkerk: Callenbach, 1989): 1:168-70.

89. Martin Hengel and Daniel P. Bailey, 'The Effective History of Isaiah 53 in the Pre-Christian Period', in *The Suffering Servant: Isaiah 53 in Jewish and Christian Sources* (ed. Bernd Janowski and Peter Stuhlmacher; trans. Daniel P. Bailey; Grand Rapids: Eerdmans, 2003), 128.

90. The verb δείκνυμι is used throughout the LXX version of Isaiah to translate the *hiphil* form of ראה (e.g. Isa. 30.30; 39.2 [×2]); cf. Ekblad, *Isaiah's Servant Poems*, 251; Hengel and Bailey, 'Effective History of Isaiah 53', 127; Karen H. Jobes and Moisés Silva, *Invitation to the Septuagint* (Grand Rapids: Baker, 2000), 227.

91. The variant has received extensive treatment from the perspective of both the MT (e.g. Dominique Barthélemy, *Critique textuelle de l'Ancien Testament* [2 vols.;

connects this passage with the broader function of the theme of light in Isaiah (e.g. Isa. 9.1; 42.16; 50.10-11; 60.1; 62.1).[92] In particular, it has previously been noted that the addition of φῶς in Isa. 53.11 (LXX) creates an intertextual link with the material in Isaiah 9.[93] Koenig, for example, argues extensively that the connection between the material in Isaiah 9 and 53 develops through the link already made between Isa. 9.2 (LXX) and Isa. 50.10, evidenced primarily in the notion that the concepts associated with walking in darkness correlate well with the description of the Isaianic servant's situation in Isa. 52.13–53.12.[94] The narrative movement of Isaiah 53, therefore, allows for God's activity in relation to the servant to be read through the lens of Isaiah 9. In other words, the servant becomes uniquely associated with the concept of light, which in both contexts refers primarily to notions of salvation and vindication.[95] Furthermore, the assertion in the LXX that the Lord will show light to the servant connects the present material with the servant's commission to bear light to both those who continue to walk in darkness (Isa. 9.1; 50.10) and to the nations (Isa. 42.6; 49.6).[96] Consequently, the progression in the concept of light from the material in Isaiah 9 to that in Isaiah 53 seemingly points to a close connection between the Lord's promised salvation and the work of the servant, who is uniquely identified with YHWH in the context of the fourth servant song.[97] Thus, within the

OBO 50; Göttingen: Vandenhoeck & Ruprecht, 1982], 2:403-7; Jan de Waard, *A Handbook on Isaiah* [TCT 1; Winona Lake, Ind.: Eisenbrauns, 1997], 197) and the LXX (e.g. Ekblad, *Isaiah's Servant Poems*, 250-51; Jobes and Silva, *Invitation to the Septuagint*, 127; Seeligman, *Septuagint Version of Isaiah*, 276-92). The presence of the noun אור in several of the Isaiah scrolls from Qumran (i.e. 1QIsa[a]; 1QIsa[b]; 4QIsad) may point to the notion that the LXX is here dependent on a Hebrew parent text outside of the MT tradition.

92. E.g. Ekblad, *Isaiah's Servant Poems*, 250-51; Jobes and Silva, *Invitation to the Septuagint*, 227. For the alternative view that the addition of φῶς refers to traditions external to the text of Isaiah, see Isac Leo Seeligmann, 'δεῖξαι αὐτῷ φῶς', *Textus* 21 (2002): 107-27.

93. See especially Jean Koenig, *L'herméneutique analogique du Judaïsme antique d'après les témoins textuels d'Isaïe* (VTSup 33; Leiden: Brill, 1982), 274-83; Abi T. Ngunga, 'Messianism in the Old Greek of Isaiah: An Intertextual Analysis' (Ph.D. diss., University of Aberdeen, 2010), 194-97.

94. Koenig, *L'herméneutique analogique*, 275-76.

95. Cf. John W. Olley, *'Righteousness' in the Septuagint of Isaiah: A Contextual Study* (SBLSCS 8; Missoula, Mont.: Scholars Press, 1979), 50.

96. Ekblad, *Isaiah's Servant Poems*, 74-75, 252-53; cf. Ngunga, 'Messianism', 196-97.

97. Bauckham, *Jesus and the God of Israel*, 36-37.

narrative movement of Isaiah itself there may be sufficient evidence to understand the thematic notion of light as pertaining directly to the Lord's work of restoration through the servant.

Returning to Paul's argument in 2 Corinthians 4, it may be possible to connect the discussion of divine illumination in 2 Cor. 4.6 with the conceptual progression of light in the Isaianic narrative. The close association of the concept of light and YHWH himself in Isaiah potentially offers a reasonable explanation for the unique nature of Paul's introductory formula, which portrays the biblical allusion as a divine speech-act (ὅτι ὁ θεὸς ὁ εἰπών). The actual impact of the Isaianic narrative on Paul's rhetoric at this point, however, likely becomes more concrete in the apostle's subsequent claim that it was God ὅς ἔλαμψεν ἐν ταῖς καρδίαις ἡμῶν πρὸς φωτισμὸν τῆς γνώσεως τῆς δόξης τοῦ θεοῦ ἐν προσώπῳ Ἰησοῦ Χριστοῦ. The notion that Paul's rhetoric is here dependent on the Isaianic narrative is based on three arguments: (1) the meaning and function of ἔλαμψεν, (2) the thematic import of the term δόξα, and (3) Paul's particular Christological emphasis (ἐν προσώπῳ Ἰησοῦ Χριστοῦ). First, although λάμπω is normally rendered intransitively in the present context due to the lack of an explicit direct object, Paul's preceding declaration, φῶς λάμψει, may suggest that 'light' should here be read as the implied object of ἔλαμψεν.[98] The intention of the apostle's statement, therefore, would not be to express the idea that God himself shines in Paul's heart; rather, the assertion would denote a more acutely causative notion revolving around God's activity of illumination (e.g. 'God made the light to shine').[99] On this reading Paul's language could be seen as a parallel to the activity inherent in the causative declaration in Isa. 53.11 concerning God's desire to show light to his servant. In other words, Paul would be claiming that his ministry pertains to the light of salvation promised by God himself.

Secondly, Paul's understanding of the function of the light as illuminating his heart with the knowledge of the glory of God returns to the extended discussion of glory in the preceding argument and functions as a further potential link with the Isaianic narrative. Savage argues at length that the connection Paul draws between glory and the Christocentric nature of his apostolic proclamation is thoroughly dependent on the

---

98. Contra Dautzenberg, 'Überlegungen', 327-29; Harris, *Second Corinthians*, 334-35; A. Oepke, 'λάμπω, κτλ.', *TDNT* 4:25-26.

99. See especially Hans-Josef Klauck, 'Erleuchtung und Verkündigung: Auslegungsskizze zu 2 Kor 4,1-6', in De Lorenzi (ed.), *Paolo, Ministro del Nuovo Testamento*, 290-91; cf. Furnish, *II Corinthians*, 224; Martin, *2 Corinthians*, 80.

thematic progression of δόξα in the LXX version of Isaiah.[100] Savage's argument relies particularly on the material in Isa. 60.1-3 that develops the conceptual connection between God's superlative glory and the inbreaking of the promised light (cf. Isa. 9.1).[101] This close association between glory and light within the narrative of Isaiah may provide the framework for Paul's combination of the concepts in 2 Cor. 4.1-6. In other words, it may be possible to argue that Paul's presentation of the light that radiates within his heart is bound by the conceptual progression of light in the Isaianic narrative, where it develops into the means by which YHWH finally displays the brilliancy of his glory to both the Israelites and the nations (Isa. 60.1-3). Paul's presentation of his ministry as illuminated with this particular light, therefore, would be a further declaration of the authority of his ministry, connecting it specifically with a crucial development of the preceding prophetic tradition of the Old Testament.

Thirdly, Paul's return to the Christological dimension of the glory of God (ἐν προσώπῳ Ἰησοῦ Χριστοῦ) may also hark back to the intertextual connection developed in the LXX between Isa. 9.2 and 53.11. The close connection between the material in 2 Cor. 4.4 and 4.6 seemingly establishes that Paul's emphasis on the 'face of Jesus Christ' parallels his earlier iconographic language. In light of this connection Paul's specific use of πρόσωπον may serve as an additional reference to the entire narrative of Christ's life and work.[102] It is this Christological purview of the apostle's illumination that indicates an association with the Isaianic material at this stage of Paul's argument. In particular, the connection between Paul's reference to Christ and the Isaianic narrative develops from the close relationship in both Isaiah 9 and 53 between messianic categories and the concept of light.[103] In the context of Isaiah 9 the introduction of the light functions as a precursor to the messianic figure described in Isa. 9.5-6 (9.6-7 LXX), while in Isa. 53.11 the (same) light implicitly

---

100. Savage, *Power Through Weakness*, 113-27. For the function of δόξα within the LXX version of Isaiah, see L.H. Brockington, 'The Greek Translator of Isaiah and His Interest in ΔΟΞΑ', *VT* 1 (1951): 23-32.

101. Savage, *Power Through Weakness*, 116; cf. Childs, *Isaiah*, 496.

102. Nguyen, *Christian Identity in Corinth*, 179-85; C. Kavin Rowe, 'New Testament Iconography? Situating Paul in the Absence of Material Evidence', in *Picturing the New Testament: Studies in Ancient Visual Images* (ed. Annette Weissenrieder, Friederike Wendt, and Petra von Gemünden; WUNT 2/193; Tübingen: Mohr Siebeck, 2005), 300; Thomas Stegman, *The Character of Jesus: The Linchpin to Paul's Argument in 2 Corinthians* (AnBib 158; Rome: Pontifical Biblical Institute, 2005), 237-38.

103. See Ngunga, 'Messianism', 77-89, 179-87.

denotes the Lord's larger programme of restoration through the work of the servant. Paul may be forging this same type of thematic connection in the present material. That is, Paul expresses the Isaianic movement from the concept of light to the work of the servant by correlating his spiritual illumination with Christ, who is subsequently connected with the mission and character of the servant of the Lord in 2 Cor. 5.14-21. The connection in Paul's argument between the concept of light and the Christocentric nature of his illumination, therefore, may further support the claim that Paul's rhetoric in 2 Cor. 4.1-6 is dependent on the narrative movement of the Isaianic material.

The import of the Isaianic narrative on Paul's argument at this point, however, is not to create a direct correlation between the apostle and the Isaianic servant. The notion that 2 Cor. 4.6 connects the ministry of Paul with that of the Isaianic servant is primarily dependent on understanding the phrase πρὸς φωτισμόν as a description of the purpose of Paul's apostolic commission. The thrust of Paul's argument, therefore, is seen to refer to the idea that God worked in Paul's heart (ἔλαμψεν) so that he might disseminate the light he received to others (cf. Acts 26.16-18).[104] The parallel structure of 2 Cor. 4.4 and 4.6, however, likely requires that both occurrences of φωτισμός refer to the same concept, namely an illuminated knowledge of the gospel. If this linguistic assumption is accurate, then Paul's primary emphasis at this point remains on God's activity. In other words, although there may be an implicit discussion of Paul's ministerial activity at this point, the apostle's language explicitly revolves around his own reception of the gospel.[105] In this way, the present argument is able to function as a further explication of the apostle's statement in 2 Cor. 4.1 that his ministry exists only because of divine mercy (καθὼς ἠλεήθημεν). Thus, Paul is able to defend his ministry in Corinth in terms of the prophetic light from which it originates.

Furthermore, Sandnes argues thoroughly that the connection in the present material between the concepts of light, glory, and theophany establish a connection between Paul's description of his call and the Old Testament throne visions that were uniquely, though not exclusively, connected with the prophetic tradition of the Old Testament.[106] Thus, although Paul's language does not refer specifically to the activity characteristic of his apostolic commission, his definition of his experience and the gospel with rhetoric derived from the preceding prophetic

104. E.g. Kim, *Paul's Gospel*, 9-11; Webb, *Returning Home*, 97-98.
105. For an extensive defence of the argument that 2 Cor. 4.6 refers specifically to Paul, see Thrall, *Second Corinthians*, 1:316-18.
106. Sandnes, *Paul—One of the Prophets?*, 138-44.

tradition likely functions as an implicit argument for the unique and authoritative nature of his ministry in Corinth. Indeed, if Paul's scriptural allusion is meant to evoke material from the narratives of both Genesis and Isaiah, then the apostle is seemingly placing his ministry within the broader scope of salvation history, linking it with God's activity in both creation (Gen. 1) and redemption (Isa. 9).[107] It may be possible to argue, however, that it is the narrative movement of the Isaianic material in particular that allows Paul to define his apostolic ministry as an extension of God's work in displaying his eschatological light through the embodiment of his glory in Christ.

## d. *Conclusions*

Paul's rhetoric in 2 Cor. 4.1-6 draws together a number of arguments from the preceding portion of the epistle in order to confirm the viability of his apostolic ministry in Corinth. In large part the apostle's argument attempts to establish that the effectual nature of his gospel is defined most accurately in terms of its source, character, and content rather than its reception. Paul's potential reliance on themes developed within the Isaianic narrative in the formulation of his argument seemingly functions to locate his defence within a certain portion of the preceding prophetic tradition. More specifically, the close association that Paul develops between the light that functions as the source of his spiritual illumination and the person of Christ may parallel the rhetorical progression of the concept of light in the LXX version of Isaiah, in which it develops from a broad reference to the redemptive activity of the Lord (Isa. 9) into a theme specifically associated with the work of the Isaianic servant (Isa. 53). If the existence of these conceptual connections can be maintained, then it seems reasonable to argue that Paul's rhetoric in 2 Cor. 4.1-6 concerning the nature of the gospel he proclaims is uniquely defined by the narrative movement of Isaiah.

Paul's dependence upon the rhetorical movement of the Isaianic narrative at this point, however, may stem merely from the specific context of his apostolic defence in 2 Cor. 2.14–4.6. In other words, the prophetic nature of Paul's self-presentation in 2 Corinthians 2–3 may function as the primary catalyst for the rhetorical import of the allusion to Isaiah at this point. Thus, in order to examine whether Paul's rhetorical argument in 2 Corinthians has a broader connection with elements of the preceding prophetic tradition, it will be helpful to analyse material

---

107. Hays, *Echoes of Scripture*, 152-53; cf. Meyer, *The End of the Law*, 108-9; Stockhausen, *Moses' Veil*, 158-62.

from different contexts within the epistle. The following material, therefore, will attempt to outline the potential influence of the prophetic tradition on Paul's argument in 2 Cor. 6.14–7.1 and 12.1-10.

## 4. Prophetic Exhortation in 2 Corinthians 6.14–7.1

The authorship, authenticity, and purpose of the material in 2 Cor. 6.14–7.1 have been thoroughly scrutinized by exegetes throughout the history of New Testament interpretation, with the result that its presence at this point of 2 Corinthians has been deemed an 'enigma'.[108] Although questions of the integrity of the material in 2 Cor. 6.14–7.1 have arisen on a number of fronts, the two primary concerns revolve around the interrelated issues of the placement and function of the passage in the present context. These two concerns arise jointly from the seemingly stark transition between the material in 2 Cor. 6.14–7.1 and the more personal appeals made by Paul in 2 Cor. 6.13 and 7.2 that express his desire for the Corinthians to respond to his apostolic ministry with open hearts. The apparent incongruity between these two segments has led to a variety of theories detailing the way in which the present section was either interpolated or integrated into this portion of Paul's argument.[109] Potentially the most influential of these proposals is the notion that the present material is representative of thematic concerns derived from the Qumran material.[110] In contrast to these more skeptical proposals, however, a number of more recent studies have attempted to defend both the Pauline style of the material in 2 Cor. 6.14–7.1 and the congruity, both linguistic and thematic, between the present passage and the rest of 2 Corinthians.[111] Thus, in contrast to the divergent viewpoints expressed

---

108. Furnish, *II Corinthians*, 383. For a history of research on 2 Cor. 6.14–7.1 from the Reformation to the modern era, see Webb, *Returning Home*, 16-30. See also Reimund Bieringer, '2 Korinther 6,14–7,1 im Kontext des 2. Korintherbriefes: Forschungsüberblick und Versuch eines eigenen Zugangs', in Bieringer and Lambrecht (eds.), *Studies on 2 Corinthians*, 551-70.

109. See Webb, *Returning Home*, 159-75.

110. See especially Pierre Benoit, 'Qumrân et le Nouveau Testament', *NTS* 7 (1961): 276-96; Nils Alstrup Dahl, *Studies in Paul: Theology for the Early Christian Mission* (Minneapolis: Augsburg, 1977), 62-69; Joseph A. Fitzmyer, 'Qumrân and the Interpolated Paragraph in 2 Cor 6:14–7:1', *CBQ* 23 (1961): 271-80; Joachim Gnilka, '2 Cor 6:14–7:1 in the Light of the Qumran Texts and the Testaments of the Twelve Patriarchs', in *Paul and Qumran: Studies in New Testament Exegesis* (ed. Jerome Murphy-O'Connor; London: Geoffrey Chapman, 1968), 48-68; Hans-Josef Klauck, *2 Korintherbrief* (NEchtB 8; Würzburg: Echter, 1986), 60-73.

111. E.g. Beale, 'Old Testament Context', 550-581; Michael D. Goulder, '2 Cor. 6:14–7:1 as an Integral Part of 2 Corinthians', *NovT* 36 (1994): 47-57; Albert L.A.

with regard to the textual history of the material, it may be more reasonable to argue that 2 Cor. 6.14-7.1 is representative of Paul's own rhetorical strategy in 2 Corinthians. In terms of the present work, the possibility that the material in 2 Cor. 6.14-7.1 is in fact Pauline suggests that the theological import of the passage, dependent in large part on the Old Testament material in 2 Cor. 6.16-18, may reflect the influence of the preceding prophetic tradition on Paul's rhetoric.

Apart from potential ambiguity with regard to the way in which 2 Cor. 6.14-7.1 functions in the larger unit of discourse ranging from 2 Cor. 2.14-7.4, the section itself appears to develop a consistent argument concerning the theological and ethical identity of the Corinthians. It is generally recognized that the parenetic statements in 2 Cor. 6.14 and 7.1 form a ring structure, with the subjunctive καθαρίσωμεν in 2 Cor. 7.1 recapitulating the initial exhortation μὴ γίνεσθε ἑτεροζυγοῦντες in 2 Cor. 6.14.[112] The intervening material, which consists of a series of antithetical comparisons (2 Cor. 6.14-16) and a catena of Old Testament quotations (2 Cor. 6.16-18), presents two related lines of substantiation for the parenetic material which encompasses the section.[113] In spite of the relative clarity of this structural analysis, the implications of the present material for the shape of Paul's rhetoric are seemingly dependent on the

---

Hogeterp, *Paul and God's Temple: A Historical Interpretation of Cultic Imagery in the Corinthian Correspondence* (BTS 2; Leuven: Peeters, 2006), 365-73; Gerhard Sass, 'Noch einmal: 2 Kor 6,14-7,1. Literarkritische Waffen gegen einen "unpaulinischen" Paulus?', *ZNW* 84 (1993): 36-64; Thomas Schmeller, 'Der ursprüngliche Kontext von 2 Kor 6.14-7.1 Zur Frage der Einheitlichkeit des 2. Korintherbriefs', *NTS* 52 (2006): 219-38 (though Schmeller argues that 2 Cor. 6.14-7.1 originally functioned as the rhetorical link between 2 Cor. 1-9 and 10-13); James M. Scott, 'The Use of Scripture in 2 Corinthians 6.16c-18 and Paul's Restoration Theology', *JSNT* 56 (1994): 73-99 (73-79); Webb, *Returning Home*, passim; Florian Wilk, 'Gottes Wort und Gottes Verheißungen: Zur Eigenart der Schriftverwendung in 2Kor 6,14-7,1', in Karrer and Kraus (eds.), *Die Septuaginta*, 673-96; Franz Zeilinger, 'Die Echtheit von 2 Cor 6:14-7:1', *JBL* 112 (1993): 71-80. For more recent attempts to argue against Pauline authorship, see Paul Brooks Duff, 'The Mind of the Redactor: 2 Cor. 6:14-7:1 in Its Secondary Context', *NovT* 35 (1993): 160-80; Christoph Heil, 'Die Sprache der Absonderung in 2 Kor 6,17 und bei Paulus', in Bieringer (ed.), *The Corinthian Correspondence*, 717-29; Stephen J. Hultgren, '2 Cor 6.14-7.1 and Rev 21.3-8: Evidence for the Ephesian Redaction of 2 Corinthians', *NTS* 29 (2003): 39-56; William O. Walker, '2 Corinthians 6.14-7.1 and the Chiastic Structure of 6.11-13; 7.2-3', *NTS* 48 (2002): 142-44.

112. Jan Lambrecht, 'The Fragment 2 Corinthians 6,14-7,1: A Plea for Its Authenticity', in Bieringer and Lambrecht (eds.), *Studies on 2 Corinthians*, 536; Scott, 'Use of Scripture', 75.

113. Scott, 'Use of Scripture', 75.

actual content of both the parenetic material and its logical substantiations. Of particular significance for the present argument is the way in which the scriptural material in 2 Cor. 6.16-18 functions to support the broader purpose of the section. In view of this consideration, it will be helpful to provide an extensive analysis of the argument in 2 Cor. 6.14–7.1 in order to examine the potential influence of the prophetic tradition on this portion of Paul's argument.

a. *Initial Exhortation (2 Corinthians 6.14)*
The import of the section is expressed succinctly in the initial exhortation in 2 Cor. 6.14: μὴ γίνεσθε ἑτεροζυγοῦντες ἀπίστοις. The brevity of the command, however, does not diminish its rhetorical complexity. The participle ἑτεροζυγοῦντες derives from a verb (ἑτεροζυγέω) absent from any extant Greek literature prior to the composition of the New Testament, where it occurs only in the present context.[114] The most common parallel put forth at this point to explain the meaning of Paul's term is Lev. 19.19, which uses the cognate adjective ἑτερόζυγος in the midst of a literal prohibition pertaining to the cross-breeding of animals (cf. Deut. 22.9-11).[115] As Scott notes, however, the only use of a cognate of ἑτεροζυγέω in a similarly metaphorical sense stems from the description of a political discussion regarding a request from Sparta for Athenian military support, where the term ἑτερόζυγα seemingly denotes the sense of 'ally' or

114. The large number of Pauline *hapax legomena* in this section (i.e. ἑτεροζυγέω, μετοχή, συμφώνησις, βελίαρ, συγκατάθεσις, ἐμπεριπατέω, εἰσδέχομαι, θυγάτηρ, παντοκράτωρ, and μολυσμός; cf. μέρις [Col. 1.12]; καθαρίζω [Eph. 5.26; Tit. 2.14]) has been used as an argument against Pauline authorship (e.g. Hultgren, '2 Cor 6.14-7.1', 40). The weight of this argument, however, has already been thoroughly contested by Gordon D. Fee, 'II Corinthians 6:14-7:1 and Food Offered to Idols', *NTS* 23 (1977): 144-46, who notes both Paul's proclivity to use 'a sudden influx of *hapax legomena*' (e.g. 1 Cor. 4.7-13; 2 Cor. 6.3-10) and the presence of cognates for several of these terms in the Pauline corpus (e.g. μετέχω [1 Cor. 9.10, 12; 10.17, 21, 30], μολύνω [1 Cor. 8.7], σύζυγος [Phil. 4.3], and σύμφωνος [1 Cor. 7.5]). Additionally, four of the terms (ἐμπεριπατέω, εἰσδέχομαι, θυγάτηρ, παντοκράτωρ) stem from the LXX, making them relatively irrelevant with respect to the question of authorship. The only two potentially significant *hapax legomena* with regard to Pauline style, therefore, are συγκατάθεσις and βελίαρ.
115. See especially J. Ayodeji Adewuya, *Holiness and Community in 2 Cor 6:14–7:1: Paul's View of Communal Holiness in the Corinthian Correspondence* (Studies in Biblical Literature 40; New York: Peter Lang, 2001), 91-103, who argues that the Levitical holiness code is the *crux interpretum* for Paul's argument in 2 Cor. 6.14-7.1; cf. Harris, *Second Corinthians*, 498-99; Thrall, *Second Corinthians*, 1:472-73. For the potential influence of Deut. 22.9-11 at this point, see J. Duncan Derrett, '2 Cor 6:14: A Midrash on Dt. 22:10', *Bib* 59 (1978): 231-50.

'regional counterpart' (Plutarch, *Cim.* 16.10).¹¹⁶ The linguistic associations developed from both of these contexts suggest that Paul's expression has a particularly relational dimension. In other words, the general thrust of the exhortation appears to revolve around the (theologically) incongruous nature of relationships that involved both the Corinthians and the ἄπιστοι. This distinction between two dissonant groups of people is illustrated extensively in both the rhetorical questions in 2 Cor. 6.14-16 and the subsequent catena of Old Testament material in 2 Cor. 6.16-18. Ambiguity remains, however, concerning the precise nature of Paul's command. Scholars have proposed numerous suggestions of specific forms of separation that may be in view at this point, but there is little evidence within the surrounding context to formulate any type of definitive explanation.¹¹⁷ However, to anticipate a portion of the subsequent argument, more clarity may be drawn from the parenetic material in 2 Cor. 6.17 and 7.1. In more specific terms, the structural and contextual associations between the exhortations in these three verses may point to the notion that Paul's command pertains primarily to avoiding relationships that would prevent the Corinthians from living in a way that was consonant with the character of their new covenant existence (cf. 2 Cor. 6.1-2).

The particular emphasis on their Christian existence becomes more transparent in light of Paul's specific use of the term ἄπιστοι in 2 Cor. 6.14. Although several different referents have been proposed to explain the identity of the ἄπιστοι at this point of the argument, the term most likely refers either specifically to Paul's Corinthian opponents or, more generically, to all unbelievers.¹¹⁸ If ἄπιστοι functions here as a limited reference to Paul's opponents, then some of the literary dissonance between 2 Cor. 6.13 and 6.14 may be eliminated, since the present relational prohibition would then provide a way for the Corinthians to fulfill the exhortation in 2 Cor. 6.13 to open their hearts to Paul. Likewise, if the

---

116. Scott, 'Use of Scripture', 75 n. 7.
117. Furnish, *II Corinthians*, 372; Thrall, *Second Corinthians*, 1:473. A representative example is Fee, 'II Corinthians 6:14–7:1', 140-61, who contends that the present argument is a specific extension of the prohibition concerning food offered to idols developed in 1 Cor. 8.10 and 10.14-22 in light of the linguistic and conceptual similarities between those passages and 2 Cor. 6.14–7.1 (cf. Witherington, *Conflict and Community in Corinth*, 403, 406). Fee himself notes, however, that there is no explicit reference to τὰ εἰδωλόθυτα either in the present passage or in the broader context of 2 Corinthians (161). For a survey of the various propositions, see Webb, *Returning Home*, 200-213.
118. For an extended discussion of the interpretative possibilities, see Webb, *Returning Home*, 184-99.

exhortation in 2 Cor. 6.14 refers specifically to Paul's opponents, then the extreme view of separation described in 2 Cor. 6.14-7.1 may be reconciled with the more flexible presentation derived from 1 Cor. 5.9-11. Webb's extensive analysis, however, shows that despite the structural and contextual reasons for positing that Paul is here referring specifically to his Corinthian opponents, there is little explicit evidence in this portion of the epistle to support defining the term in this way.[119] Indeed, in 2 Cor. 2.14-7.4 the only other occurrence of ἄπιστοι is found in 2 Cor. 4.4, where it functions primarily as a general reference to unbelievers. That this more general referent is intended in the present context is also supported by the dichotomy established between the πιστός and ἄπιστος in 2 Cor. 6.15, which in light of the immediately preceding contrast between Christ and Beliar ostensibly refers to a theological divide between believers and unbelievers. Furthermore, the grammar of the Isaianic exhortation to come out ἐκ μέσου αὐτῶν applied to the present situation in 2 Cor. 6.17 may suggest that the Corinthians are the smaller of the two groups in view, which would not accord with the notion that the term ἄπιστοι is here a reference to the presumably smaller group that made up the Pauline opposition in Corinth.[120] On balance, therefore, it seems most likely that Paul's exhortation pertains to a general divide between believers and unbelievers. The nature and function of Paul's imperative in the present context, however, are dependent upon both the following series of rhetorical antitheses in 2 Cor. 6.14-16 and the extended argument from Scripture in 2 Cor. 6.16-18.

b. *Rhetorical Antitheses (2 Corinthians 6.14-16)*
The five rhetorical questions posed in 2 Cor. 6.14-16 function as the first line of substantiation (cf. γάρ) for the notion of exclusivity developed inherently in the initial exhortation. The questions exhibit a number of structural similarities and, despite differences with respect to their specific content, they generally appear to function 'as simple variations

---

119. Webb, *Returning Home*, 189-97; cf. Jerome Murphy-O'Connor, 'Relating 2 Corinthians 6.14-7.1 to Its Context', *NTS* 33 (1986-1987): 272-75 (272-73). For a defence of the view that ἄπιστοι here refers to Paul's opponents, see Collange, *Énigmes*, 305-6; Bruce N. Kaye, 'Paul and His Opponents in Corinth: 2 Corinthians 6:14-7:1', in *Good News in History* (Festschrift Bo Reicke; ed. Ed. L. Miller; Atlanta: Scholars Press, 1993), 111-26; David Rensberger, '2 Corinthians 6:14-7:1—A Fresh Examination', *Studia Biblica et Theologica* 8 (1978): 25-49; James M. Scott, *2 Corinthians* (NIBCNT; Peabody, Mass.: Hendrickson, 1998), 152-53.

120. Cf. Harris, *Second Corinthians*, 507 n. 68. Harris posits that if the opponents were in view the command would more likely revolve around the notion of expulsion (cf. 1 Cor. 5.13) rather than withdrawal.

on the same theme',[121] namely the prohibition to be allied or united with unbelievers. Various attempts have been made to group the questions based either on the grammatical structure of their introductory formulas (i.e. τίς [γάρ/δέ] followed by ἤ τίς) or on the potential synonymity of the relational terms used to compare the conceptual pairs (e.g. μετοχή/μερίς and κοινωνία/συμφώνησις).[122] The result of both forms of analysis is that the first four questions are grouped together in either a chiastic or parallel construction, while the fifth question (τίς δὲ συγκατάθεσις ναῷ θεοῦ μετὰ εἰδώλων;) is set apart as a type of rhetorical climax to the preceding material.[123] Consequently, the theme of the temple is elevated to the primary position of the argument, with the assertion concerning the identity of the Corinthians as the temple of God and the subsequent Old Testament material serving as an extended explanation of the antithesis introduced at this point. Conversely, it may be more helpful to identify the assertion in 2 Cor. 6.16, ἡμεῖς γὰρ ναὸς θεοῦ ἐσμεν ζῶντος, as the balanced conclusion to the final rhetorical question. The result of this analysis would be three parallel units that focus on the transparent incongruence of the two realms being described.[124] While the grammatical and semantic variations between the three units may still function to emphasize the final antithetical expression, this structural analysis allows for a potentially more balanced reading of Paul's argument at this point, with the two occurrences of γάρ functioning as a type of modified *inclusio* for an initial argument in support of the exhortation in 2 Cor. 6.14.[125] On this reading the subsequent scriptural material functions as a separate, though thematically related, argument in support of the exhortation to avoid relational unity with unbelievers.

With regard to their actual content, the questions variously express the logical incongruity of a pair of opposing concepts in order to illustrate the (theological) incompatibility between the relational spheres developed in the initial exhortation. The specific content of the contrasts developed in 2 Cor. 6.14-16 has functioned as one of the primary catalysts for the notion that the present argument contains distinct parallels

---

121. Lambrecht, 'Fragment', 537.
122. E.g. Hans Dieter Betz, '2 Cor 6:14–7:1: An Anti-Pauline Fragment?', *JBL* 92 (1973): 88-108 (90-91); Lambrecht, 'Fragment', 536-37.
123. E.g. Fee, 'II Corinthians 6:14–7:1', 158; cf. Barnett, *Second Corinthians*, 346.
124. See the structural outline in Scott, 'Use of Scripture', 97.
125. The occurrences of γάρ in 2 Cor. 6.14 and 6.16, therefore, seem to function in slightly different ways, the first introducing the entire section comprised of the rhetorical questions and the second denoting only the logical conclusion to the antithesis between the temple of God and idols developed in the final rhetorical question (contra Harris, *Second Corinthians*, 495, 504).

to material from Qumran.¹²⁶ However, the appearance of similar conceptual material both in the larger Pauline corpus and the New Testament makes it difficult to determine the level of influence that the Qumran material may have had on the apostle's thought at this point.¹²⁷ Yet, in light of the close structural and thematic relationship between the rhetorical questions and the following catena of Old Testament quotations, examining the Pauline nature of this section is seemingly necessary in an analysis of the potential congruence between Paul's rhetorical argument and the prophetic tradition of the Old Testament in the subsequent material.

The initial dichotomy that Paul puts forth between δικαιοσύνη and ἀνομία points to an ethical divide between believers and unbelievers. The distinction relates thematically to the extended argument in Rom. 6.13-19, which revolves around the divide between righteous and wicked action in light of Christ's death and resurrection. That a similar theme exists in several documents from Qumran (e.g. 1QH 14.15-16; 16.10-11; 1QS 5.1-4; CD 20.20-21) may only prove that both the present argument and the Qumran material were influenced by the development of the ethical divide between righteousness and wickedness in the Old Testament.¹²⁸ Likewise, while the divide between notions of light and darkness is prevalent at Qumran (e.g. 1QS 1.9-11; 2.16-17; 3.3-25; 1QM 1.1-13; 13.5-16; 1QH 12.6; 4Q174 1.9), the antithesis has already functioned prominently in the argument of 2 Cor. 4.1-6, where it served as a means for Paul to contrast the blinded condition of the unbelievers with the (Isaianic) illumination representative of his own experience. Thus, the particular use of φῶς and σκότος to represent distinct groups does not necessarily detract from the Pauline character of the present material (cf. Eph. 5.8; 1 Thess. 5.5).

The third rhetorical question—τίς δὲ συμφώνησις Χριστοῦ πρὸς Βελιάρ;—reflects the closest possible connection with the Qumran material in light of the use of Βελιάρ (or Βελιάλ) as an antithesis for a member of the Godhead (e.g. 1QM 13.1-4, 11-12).¹²⁹ Although Βελιάρ does not occur as a proper name in either the MT or the LXX, it does occur frequently in later Jewish texts (e.g. *Jub.* 1.20; *T. Dan* 4.7; 5.1; *T. Iss.* 6.1; *T. Jos.* 20.2; *T. Levi* 19.1; *T. Naph.* 2.6; 3.1; *T. Reu.* 4.11; *T. Sim.* 5.3) as a functional synonym for ὁ Σατανᾶς. That the term occurs only here in

---

126. E.g. Fitzmyer, 'Qumrân', 273-78; Gnilka, '2 Cor 6:14–7:1', 53-66.
127. Cf. Harris, *Second Corinthians*, 19-20.
128. Barrett, *Second Corinthians*, 197; cf. Martin, *2 Corinthians*, 198.
129. E.g. Gnilka, '2 Cor 6:14–7:1', 54-55; cf. Hanns Walter Huppenbauer, 'Belial in den Qumrantexten', *TZ* 15 (1959): 81-89.

the New Testament may suggest that its use in the present context is meant to increase the rhetorical force of the material. It may, however, simply represent a designation known to both Paul and the Corinthians from their previous personal interaction.[130] Despite ambiguity concerning the source of the terminology, the actual import of the contrast is readily transparent. The ethical distinctions developed in the first set of rhetorical questions are here amplified by the overtly theological contrast between the representative spheres of Christ and Beliar. The theological implication of this contrast is made more explicit in the subsequent antithesis in 2 Cor. 6.15 between the πιστός and ἄπιστος.[131] Due to the close structural connection with the preceding rhetorical question, the import of the present contrast between believer and unbeliever is likely theological as opposed to ontological. In other words, the antithesis is not meant to create an insurmountable divide between the respective groups; rather, the import appears to be that the defining theological characteristics of the two groups do not lend themselves to the formation of a unified relationship. This same type of theological distinction formed the basis for Paul's argument in 2 Cor. 2.14-17 and 4.1-6. In spite of certain aspects of correspondence with the material from Qumran, therefore, there appears to be little evidence to demand a non-Pauline origin for any of the thematic material introduced up to this point.[132] Indeed, it is possible to argue that the antithetical material put forth in this section is consistent with the material in the whole of 2 Corinthians.[133]

The final antithesis between the temple of God and idols (τίς δὲ συγκατάθεσις ναῷ θεοῦ μετὰ εἰδώλων;) combines the ethical and theological concerns of the preceding rhetorical questions into a more specific

---

130. Thrall, *Second Corinthians*, 1:474-75.

131. The use of πιστός as a noun occurs elsewhere in the Pauline corpus only at 1 Tim. 4.10, 12; 5.16; 6.2. The syntactical connection with ἄπιστος, however, suggests that its present use as a substantive was a natural linguistic development (so Harris, *Second Corinthians*, 503).

132. Cf. Margaret E. Thrall, 'The Problem of II Cor. VI.14-VII.1 in Some Recent Discussion', *NTS* 24 (1977–78): 132-48 (136-38). The presence of similar themes in the writings of Philo also suggests a lack of direct influence by the Qumran material on the present argument (so Jerome Murphy-O'Connor, 'Philo and 2 Cor 6:14–7:1', *RB* 95 [1988]: 55-69). Murphy-O'Connor, however, likely goes too far in the opposite direction, over-estimating the Philonic influence on Paul's rhetoric over against the thematic parallels present in 2 Corinthians itself.

133. So David A. deSilva, 'Measuring Penultimate Against Ultimate Reality: An Investigation of the Integrity and Argument of 2 Corinthians', *JSNT* 52 (1993): 41-70 (61-62); David A. deSilva, 'Recasting the Moment of Decision: 2 Corinthians in Its Literary Context', *AUSS* 31 (1993): 3-16 (10-11).

example of the way in which the Corinthians might be inappropriately allied with unbelievers. The more specific nature of this contrast may signify that this final unit is in some sense the climax of Paul's rhetoric.[134] That the antithesis is referring particularly to the situation in Corinth is made transparent in the following statement that the Corinthians are the temple of the living God (ἡμεῖς γὰρ ναὸς θεοῦ ἐσμεν ζῶντος). The use of temple imagery seemingly introduces a number of theological nuances into Paul's argument. In light of the preceding antithetical statements, the present emphasis on the identity of the Corinthians as the temple of God is likely due to their unique relationship with Christ (2 Cor. 6.15). To be united with idols, therefore, would be a distinct contradiction to the work of Christ described in 2 Cor. 5.14-21.[135] In addition, this particular antithesis may represent a further reflection on the εἰκών language introduced in 2 Corinthians 3–4. That is, the Corinthians' status as divine image-bearers negates the possibility that they could be appropriately united with images of other deities (i.e. εἴδωλα).[136] In basic terms, the redeemed status of the Corinthians is not compatible with the religious activity associated with the pagan deities in Corinth. The intent of the final antithesis and its supporting claim, therefore, seemingly mirror the overarching emphasis of the preceding material on the incompatibility of the two theological spheres that Paul defines initially in the exhortation in 2 Cor. 6.14. Furthermore, Paul's inclusion of the temple imagery at the potential climax of the sequence of rhetorical questions likely functions as a catalyst for the influence of the temple motif in the following catena of Old Testament quotations.

c. *Scriptural Substantiation (2 Corinthians 6.16-18)*
The series of antitheses developed in 2 Cor. 6.14-16 is followed by an extended argument comprised of a number of different Old Testament texts. Despite the relatively broad contextual divergence between the various passages, the Old Testament citations are presented as a unified segment of discourse, introduced and concluded by a single set of quotation formulas (καθὼς εἶπεν ὁ θεὸς ὅτι in 2 Cor. 6.16 and λέγει κύριος παντοκράτωρ in 2 Cor. 6.18). The rhetorical unity of the catena is further established by the minor grammatical and syntactical changes made to the individual quotations that allow the material to develop a consistent line of thought.[137] In terms of the structure of the catena, the various Old

134. Cf. Harris, *Second Corinthians*, 504.
135. Hafemann, 'Paul's "Jeremiah" Ministry', 79-80.
136. Van Kooten, *Paul's Anthropology*, 203.
137. Stanley, *Paul and the Language of Scripture*, 217-30.

Testament passages form a tripartite unit in which the promise formulas of 2 Cor. 6.16 and 6.17-18 provide the rhetorical basis for the parenetic material presented in 2 Cor. 6.17.[138] In other words, the catena places a particular rhetorical emphasis on the imperatives developed in 2 Cor. 6.17, which seemingly represent a recapitulation of the theme developed in the initial exhortation in 2 Cor. 6.14. The material in 2 Cor. 6.16-18, therefore, appears to constitute a carefully constructed strand of scriptural support for the initial exhortation to avoid inappropriate alliances with unbelievers.[139] This analysis, however, stands in contrast to the generally accepted view that the scriptural material in 2 Cor. 6.16-18 functions in the first instance as an extended explanation of the assertion in 2 Cor. 6.16 that ἡμεῖς…ναὸς θεοῦ ἐσμεν ζῶντος.[140] Nevertheless, in light of the close structural association between the three sections of the catena it seems difficult to isolate the scriptural material in 2 Cor. 6.16 as the foundation for the preceding assertion concerning the temple of God. This particular nuance is supported by the notion that although the scriptural material revolves in large part around themes associated with the Old Testament temple motif, none of the promises or exhortations in 2 Cor. 6.16-18 actually provides explicit justification for the statement that the Corinthians are the temple of God.[141] In light of these arguments it may be more helpful to contend that the scriptural material develops the related concept of God dwelling with his people in order to establish the consequence of that reality for the present situation in Corinth. The scriptural material in 2 Cor. 6.16-18, therefore, provides a further theological argument for the exhortation to avoid becoming allied or united with unbelievers.

---

138. This analysis of the structural unity of the scriptural material is dependent on Scott, 'Use of Scripture', 75-78; cf. Kaye, 'Paul and His Opponents in Corinth', 113.

139. Cf. Friedrich Lang, *Die Briefe an die Korinther* (17th ed.; NTD 7; Göttingen: Vandenhoeck & Ruprecht, 1994), 309: 'In V. 16b-18 bringt der Verfasser mit kombinierten Stellen aus dem Alten Testament einen Schriftbeweis für die Gegenwart Gottes bei seinem Volk, die es erforderlich macht, daß das eschatologische Gottesvolk sich von allem Unheiligen fernhält'.

140. For a representative example of this analysis, see Furnish, *II Corinthians*, 367-68.

141. So Scott, 'Use of Scripture', 76. For a concise explanation of the function of the temple motif in the present context, see G.K. Beale, *The Temple and the Church's Mission: A Biblical Theology of the Dwelling Place of God* (NSBT 18; Downers Grove, Ill.: InterVarsity, 2004), 253-56; Edmund P. Clowney, 'The Final Temple', *WTJ* 35 (1973): 156-89 (185-87).

As with the thematic material developed in the preceding rhetorical questions, the formulation of the Old Testament catena has been used as evidence that the entirety of 2 Cor. 6.14-7.1 is representative of the Qumran tradition. The primary arguments pertain to the potential influence of the Qumran material on the style of both Paul's unique introductory formula (cf. CD 6.13; 8.9) and the actual structure of the Old Testament texts in 2 Cor. 6.16-18 (cf. 4Q175).[142] Neither of these proposed connections, however, provides a significant link with the Qumran material. Although similar, there is little actual verbal correspondence between the introductory formula καθὼς εἶπεν ὁ θεός in 2 Cor. 6.16 and the phrase אל אסר אמר attested in both CD 6.13 and 8.9. Moreover, the potentially more comparable phrase כאסר דבר אל in CD 4.13-14 is itself unique within the Qumran literature and cannot, consequently, be seen as more consistent to the community at Qumran than to Paul.[143] The second proposal, that the structure of the quotations is parallel to the scriptural *testimonia* in 4Q175, accounts neither for the syntactical unity of the present material nor its function within the present context as a rhetorical extension of the preceding material.[144] Furthermore, nearly all of the modifications made to the LXX material within the catena are characteristic of other changes made by the apostle in contexts where Pauline authorship remains uncontested.[145] There appears to be little evidence to suggest, therefore, that Paul himself did not craft the scriptural material in the catena as a necessary component of the present argument.

The first segment of the Old Testament catena in 2 Cor. 6.16 consists of a conflation of Lev. 26.11-12 and Ezek. 37.27. The verse itself presents four promises that revolve around the reciprocal relationship between God and his people. The first, ἐνοικήσω ἐν αὐτοῖς, has no direct parallel in the LXX, but most likely represents a paraphrase of the statement in Lev. 26.11 that θήσω τὴν σκηνήν μου ἐν ὑμῖν.[146] The following promise,

142. See, e.g., Fitzmyer, 'Qumrân', 278-79; cf. Joseph A. Fitzmyer, '"4Q Testimonia" and the New Testament', *TS* (1957): 513-37 (518-22).
143. James M. Scott, *Adoption as Sons of God: An Exegetical Investigation into the Background of ΥΙΟΘΕΣΙΑ in the Pauline Corpus* (WUNT 2/48; Tübingen: Mohr Siebeck, 1992), 195.
144. See especially Koch, *Die Schrift als Zeuge des Evangeliums*, 247-55.
145. Wilk, 'Gottes Wort und Gottes Verheißungen', 673-96; cf. Stanley, *Paul and the Language of Scripture*, 217.
146. Contra Webb, *Returning Home*, 35, who argues that Paul's phrase is more closely related to the cognate term ἡ κατασκήνωσις in Ezek. 37.27 (cf. Thrall, *Second Corinthians*, 1:477). Webb's decision, however, is based on reading διαθήκην in Lev. 26.11 as opposed to the more likely original reading σκήνην (see John William

ἐμπεριπατήσω, undoubtedly reflects the influence of Lev. 26.11, which contains the same terminology. Taken together both statements refer generally to God's promise to dwell with his people. This particular emphasis coordinates well with the subsequent promises taken from Ezek. 37.27, which specifically introduce the so-called covenant formula: ἔσομαι αὐτῶν θεὸς καὶ αὐτοὶ ἔσονταί μου λαός. Although arguments can be made for both Leviticus 26 and Ezekiel 37 as the primary *Vorlagen* for this portion of the catena, the notion that both passages are in view is supported by the commonality of their thematic emphasis on covenant theology. As Scott notes, the two contexts deal respectively with the related notions of Israel's historic formation and the prophetic expectation of Israel's post-exilic re-formation in which God would again dwell with his people.[147] The two passages are also connected by their emphasis on the need for restoration. The material that follows the covenant formula in Leviticus 26 depicts the consequences of the Israelites' disobedience with regard to the covenant and the subsequent need for its reaffirmation. The historical situation represented in Leviticus, therefore, was seemingly already cognizant of the potential need for the promise described in the prophetic context of Ezekiel 37.[148] Further, it may be possible to argue that the use of the covenant formula in Ezekiel 37 is meant to function as a recapitulation of the initial covenant promises represented by the material in Leviticus 26.[149] The eschatological expectation presented in Ezekiel 37, therefore, likely mirrors the function of the covenant formula in Jeremiah, where it serves both as a reference back to the covenant at Sinai (e.g. Jer. 7.23; 11.4) and as an expression of expectation for God's reestablishment of his covenant with his people (e.g. Jer. 24.7; 30.22; 31.1, 33; 32.38).[150] That is, the conflation of the two Old Testament contexts at this point may function as evidence of Paul's

---

Wevers, *Septuaginta: Vetus Testamentum Graecum Auctoritate Academiae Scientiarum Gottingensis editum II.2: Leviticus* [Göttingen: Vandenhoeck & Ruprecht, 1986]). The conceptual connection between σκήνη and ἐνοικέω as well as Paul's necessary dependence on Lev. 26.11 for the following promise, ἐμπεριπατήσω, suggest that at least the first portion of the present material is primarily dependent on Lev. 26 (cf. Harris, *Second Corinthians*, 505-6; Stanley, *Paul and the Language of Scripture*, 218-19).

147. Scott, 'Use of Scripture', 79-90.
148. Beale, 'Old Testament Background', 570.
149. E.g. Cristoph Levin, *Die Verheißung des neuen Bundes in ihrem theologiegeschichtlichen Zusammenhang ausgelegt* (FRLANT 137; Göttingen: Vandenhoeck & Ruprecht, 1985), 11-12; Rudolf Smend, *Die Mitte des Alten Testaments* (ThSt 101; Zurich: EVZ-Verlag, 1970), 49, 55.
150. Contra Webb, *Returning Home*, 38-39.

incorporation of the prophetic understanding of the new covenant as a reformulation of the initial covenant formula made at Sinai.[151] In other words, the development of the Leviticus material through the lens of the narrative in Ezekiel likely affirms the notion that Paul's argument is here defined primarily by the reality of the Corinthians' new covenant existence. This particular emphasis correlates well with both Paul's earlier discussion of his new covenant ministry in 2 Corinthians 3 and his comments with regard to the new eschatological age in 2 Cor. 6.1-2. It is this new covenant perspective that appears to form the basis for the further development of the initial exhortation in 2 Cor. 6.14 in the subsequent parenetic material.

In 2 Cor. 6.17 the catena moves from a series of promises to a three-pronged parenetic section based on the text of Isa. 52.11. Contextually, the call for separation developed in Isaiah 52 is used to reiterate the initial exhortation put forth in 2 Cor. 6.14. This distinct correlation between the present material and the earlier exhortation is highlighted primarily by Paul's reversal of the Isaianic order of the imperatives. More specifically, placing the exhortation to come out from among them (ἐξέλθατε ἐκ μέσου αὐτῶν) in the primary position functions 'to give it a parallel force and meaning with the exhortation of [2 Cor.] 6.14'.[152] Additionally, the transition from the singular pronoun αὐτῆς in Isa. 52.11 to the plural αὐτῶν in the present verse likely functions as an explicit reference back to the ἄπιστοι identified in 2 Cor. 6.14. The following two exhortations (ἀφορίσθητε and ἀκαθάρτου μὴ ἅπτεσθε) parallel the initial Isaianic imperative and form a threefold emphasis on the need for the Corinthians to separate themselves from the negative theological sphere defined in the antithetical comparisons made in 2 Cor. 6.14-16.

The function of this portion of the Old Testament catena likely develops in line with the contextual background of Isaiah 52. The narrative of Isaiah 52 is prominently shaped by themes that reflect the exodus event and specifically focuses on God's intention to redeem his people from their exilic condition. The exhortations in Isa. 52.11, therefore, pertain to the need for Israel to affirm their theological allegiance to YHWH by departing from Babylon.[153] Thus, separation from the cultic identity of the Babylonians is framed within the parallel narrative of the exodus material in an apparent attempt to develop the theme of restoration closely associated with the new covenant tradition.[154] In terms of the

151. Scott, 'Use of Scripture', 82.
152. Webb, *Returning Home*, 41.
153. Beale, 'Old Testament Background', 571.
154. Scott, 'Use of Scripture', 84; cf. Oswalt, *Isaiah*, 2:371-72.

present Corinthian context, the Isaianic material functions as the direct consequence (cf. διό) of the promises established in 2 Cor. 6.16. In this way, the emphasis on the new covenant in the preceding material serves as the basis for the present parenesis regarding the necessity of the Corinthians' separation from unbelievers. In other words, the grammatical connection between the promises in 2 Cor. 6.16 and the imperatives in 2 Cor. 6.17 points to the notion that the exhortations are the logical extension of the covenant formula developed in the combination of Leviticus 26 and Ezekiel 37. The import of the present exhortation, therefore, is not that the Corinthians must submit to these regulations in order to attain the promises described in 2 Cor. 6.16; rather, the focus appears to be on the need for the Corinthians to act in a manner that coordinates with the theological circumstances of their eschatological existence (cf. 2 Cor. 6.1-2).[155] This same rhetorical connection between God's future redemption and the activity of the redeemed seemingly plays a crucial role in the narrative of Isaiah 40–55, where the discussion of YHWH's redemptive activity is developed in line with the identification of his people as those who seek to align themselves with the work of his servant.[156] The exodus typology particularly present in Isa. 52.11-12, therefore, is likely meant to function as a reminder to the Corinthians of God's primary act in re-constituting a people for himself. In light of these connections it may be reasonable to argue that it is this divine initiative that forms the basis and defines the boundaries of the call to separate from unbelievers.

The imperatives in 2 Cor. 6.17 are followed by a second set of promises that reiterate the reciprocal relationship between God and his people expressed initially in 2 Cor. 6.16. The scriptural material in 2 Cor. 6.17-18 includes references to a number of different Old Testament contexts (i.e. 2 Samuel; Isaiah; Ezekiel). The cohesion of the material, however, is evidenced early on in the crasis manifest in the introductory κἀγώ, which likely points to an intentional merging of the initial καί in Ezek. 20.34 with the opening ἐγώ of 2 Sam. 7.14 that is omitted from the subsequent quotation in 2 Cor. 6.18.[157] As with the conflation of Lev. 26.11-12 and Ezek. 37.27 in 2 Cor. 6.16, the present plurality of Old Testament references seemingly forms a single unit of thought within the Old Testament catena that functions as the theological basis for the preceding

---

155. Scott, 'Use of Scripture', 84; cf. Fee, 'II Corinthians 6:14–7:1', 160; Harris, *Second Corinthians*, 507.

156. Childs, *Isaiah*, 403-4.

157. Harris, *Second Corinthians*, 509; Scott, 'Use of Scripture', 85-86; Webb, *Returning Home*, 46 n. 4.

parenesis.¹⁵⁸ More broadly, the scriptural material at this point functions as the final segment of a chiastic unit that centres on the imperatives derived from Isaiah 52 in 2 Cor. 6.17.

The initial quotation from Ezek. 20.34, κἀγὼ εἰσδέξομαι ὑμᾶς, functions both as the conceptual conclusion to the imperatives in 2 Cor. 6.17 and the structural parallel to the first two promises in 2 Cor. 6.16 (ἐνοικήσω ἐν αὐτοῖς καὶ ἐμπεριπατήσω). In terms of the conceptual parallel, the imperatives in 2 Cor. 6.17 are balanced helpfully by the notion of divine reception inherent to the Ezekiel passage. The broader context of Ezek. 20.32-44 extends the exodus imagery derived from Isaiah 52 through the introduction of an explicit emphasis on the divine judgment involved in YHWH's activity of restoration.¹⁵⁹ God's reception of the exiles in Ezekiel, therefore, is closely related to the theological identity of the people, as the exodus imagery introduces both the language of theological purification and covenant relationship.¹⁶⁰ In this way, the contextual correlation between the covenantal identity of the people and their relationship to the sphere of influence outside of the covenant boundaries becomes an analogy for the way in which Paul understands the Corinthians' theological identity with respect to unbelievers.

Furthermore, as with the initial promises presented in 2 Cor. 6.16, the Ezekiel quotation serves as an introduction for the subsequent material derived from 2 Sam. 7.14. That the material in this portion of the catena constitutes a structural parallel to the promises expressed in 2 Cor. 6.16 stems primarily from the thematic correlation between the covenant formula derived from Lev. 26.11-12 and Ezek. 37.27 and the adoption formula present in 2 Sam. 7.14. Scott's extensive analysis of the function of the adoption formula in the Pauline corpus develops the notion that its specific father–son relationship constitutes a logical extension of the broader relationship defined in the covenant formula.¹⁶¹ Further, he shows that the material in 2 Samuel 7 functioned within early Jewish tradition as a means to elucidate the relationship of the eschatological people of God with the re-establishment of the covenant (e.g. 4Q174 1.11; *Jub*. 1.24; *T. Jud*. 24.3).¹⁶² In line with this expansion, it seems that Paul is here applying the narrative of 2 Samuel 7 more broadly to the

158. Cf. Scott, 'Use of Scripture', 75.
159. Daniel I. Block, *Ezekiel* (2 vols.; NICOT; Grand Rapids: Eerdmans, 1997-98), 1:651.
160. Cf. Garland, *2 Corinthians*, 338-39; John W. Olley, 'A Precursor of the NRSV? "Sons and Daughters" in 2 Cor 6:18', *NTS* 44 (1998-99): 204-12 (207-8).
161. Scott, *Adoption as Sons of God*, 96-117, 209-11.
162. Scott, *Adoption as Sons of God*, 116-17.

Corinthians as a means of defining the reality of their new covenant identity, a development that in certain ways was already projected in the Old Testament prophetic tradition with the application of the adoption formula to the nation of Israel (cf. Jer. 31.9; Hos. 1.10).[163] The assertion that the adoption formula from 2 Sam. 7.14 is here meant as a specific reference to the Corinthians' theological identity is further established by Paul's modification of the formula to include both υἱούς and θυγατέρας. The transition from the singular υἱόν to the plural υἱούς and the addition of θυγατέρας may signify Paul's dependence at this point on several texts from Isaiah that combine references to both sons and daughters (e.g. Isa. 43.6; 49.22; 60.4). Importantly, all of these potential backgrounds are representative of the larger discussion of restoration that serves as one of the primary thematic backgrounds of Deutero-Isaiah.[164] In light of these contextual connections it may be possible to argue that Paul's reformulation of the Samuel narrative through the lens of the Isaianic theme of restoration places the Davidic promise within the larger framework of the prophetic tradition 'as a promise associated with the second exodus'.[165] The concepts developed within the promises in 2 Cor. 6.17-18, therefore, relate thematically to those that constitute the first portion of the catena in 2 Cor. 6.16 inasmuch as they express the new, eschatological relationship between God and his people.

The extensive material and thematic correspondence between these two portions of the catena serve as further evidence that the catena itself is a closely structured composition which centres at the parenetic material in 2 Cor. 6.17.[166] In other words, the covenantal relationships defined by the first (2 Cor. 6.16) and third (2 Cor. 6.17-18) sections of the catena form the structural and logical basis for the imperatives in 2 Cor. 6.17, which in turn function in the present context as a reiteration of the exhortation in 2 Cor. 6.14. Paul's formation of the Old Testament material, therefore, serves as the second essential argument for the separation he demands between the Corinthians and their unbelieving counterparts. Moreover, the structured content of the Old Testament material in 2 Cor. 6.16-18 points to the notion that Paul's rhetoric here

---

163. Harris, *Second Corinthians*, 510.

164. Beale, 'Old Testament Background', 571. Commentators generally agree that Isa. 43.6 is the primary text in view at this point (cf. Webb, *Returning Home*, 57-58). For an alternative analysis, however, see Olley, 'Precursor', 208-12, who proposes Deut. 32.19 as the primary referent.

165. Scott, 'Use of Scripture', 87.

166. Scott, 'Use of Scripture', 88.

positions the Corinthians within the thematic stream of eschatological restoration developed in Israel's prophetic tradition.[167] The theological and rhetorical basis for Paul's parenetic material at this point, therefore, appears to derive from his perception that the Corinthians represent the locus of God's presence in this particular stage of salvation history (cf. 2 Cor. 6.1-2).

d. *Final Exhortation (2 Corinthians 7.1)*
The final section of Paul's argument returns to the initial exhortation of 2 Cor. 6.14. More specifically, the present command (καθαρίσωμεν ἑαυτοὺς ἀπὸ παντὸς μολυσμοῦ σαρκὸς καὶ πνεύματος) reiterates the earlier negative exhortation in terms of a positive response to the scriptural material developed in 2 Cor. 6.16-18 (i.e. ταύτας...τὰς ἐπαγγελίας). As with the previous material, the parenesis in 2 Cor. 7.1 continues to centre on the theological identity of the Corinthians. The particular emphasis on cleansing at this point reflects the contextual emphasis of the final imperative in 2 Cor. 6.17 (i.e. ἀκαθάρτου μὴ ἅπτεσθε), thereby connecting this exhortation with the broader theme of separation expressed in the preceding argument. Furthermore, the conceptual background developed in the limited uses of the term μολυσμός in the LXX pertains exclusively to the theological or religious defilement associated with idolatry (Jer. 23.15; 1 Esd. 8.80; 3 Macc. 5.27).[168] This particular emphasis on the notion of cleansing is consonant with the broader themes of restoration and theological separation developed in the various contexts that form the background of the Old Testament catena.[169] In this way, the Corinthians' new covenant position functions as the basis for this jointly ethical and theological exhortation, which the apostle relates to the Corinthians' entire human existence (i.e. σαρκὸς καὶ πνεύματος).[170] The themes developed in the present exhortation, therefore, reflect the theological and relational divide inherent in the preceding material, allowing the present

---

167. Balla, '2 Corinthians', 773; Beale, 'Old Testament Background', 572-73. For an overview of Paul's restoration theology, see Scott, 'Use of Scripture', 88-93.
168. Cf. Garland, *2 Corinthians*, 342.
169. Webb, *Returning Home*, 65-66.
170. E.g. Furnish, *II Corinthians*, 365. The seemingly positive correlation of σάρξ and πνεῦμα at this point has been seen as further evidence for the non-Pauline style of 2 Cor. 6.14–7.1 in light of the pejorative sense that σάρξ has at other points in the Pauline corpus (e.g. Gal. 5.19-21). Paul's use of the term, however, is not restricted to a particular theological nuance, and he uses it more broadly as a synonym for σῶμα at several points (e.g. 2 Cor. 4.11; 10.3; Gal. 2.20). See further Martin, *2 Corinthians*, 208-10.

parenesis to function as a reiteration of the exhortations expressed in both 2 Cor. 6.14 and 7.1. The contextual synthesis between these three instances of parenesis is outlined helpfully by Harris:

> This urgent call to avoid both physical and spiritual defilement restates the earlier entreaties to repudiate unholy alliances (6:14) and to reject the pagan way of life (6:17, three imperatives). In all these cases Paul seems to have uppermost in his mind the danger that the Corinthian believers constantly faced of idolatrous associations that would jeopardize their devotion to Christ (cf. 11:3). In 7:1, however, he…expands [the exhortation] to incorporate the rejection of every possible form of defilement, idolatry or otherwise, that might harm the believer.[171]

The related admonition concerning the development of sanctification (ἐπιτελοῦντες ἁγιωσύνην ἐν φόβῳ θεοῦ) seemingly confirms the more expansive referent at this point of Paul's argument. While a specific instance or form of theological incongruity likely stands in the background of the initial exhortation in 2 Cor. 6.14 this final expression parallels the extension of the parenesis to the ethical and theological conduct of the Corinthians as the apostle locates his argument within a divine purview (ἐν φόβῳ θεοῦ).[172] This particular emphasis on the fear of God may hark back to the notion of judgment developed in the context of Ezek. 20.34 (cf. 2 Cor. 6.17). That is, the thematic emphasis on YHWH's purification of the exiles in Ezekiel 20 may function in the background of Paul's language at this point as a reminder to the Corinthians that the working out of their sanctification (cf. 2 Cor. 3.18) is an appropriate response to God's own holiness.[173] Although this connection is not explicit, it seems possible to argue that the reality of the Corinthians' covenantal existence expressed in the promises in the first (2 Cor. 6.16) and third (2 Cor. 6.17-18) sections of the catena functions as the basis for Paul's exhortations for both separation (2 Cor. 6.14) and purification (2 Cor. 7.1). The apostle's rhetoric at this point, therefore, seems to be dependent in large part on his understanding of the relationship of the prophetic promises to the current theological identity of the Christians in Corinth.

---

171. Harris, *Second Corinthians*, 512-13.
172. Cf. Adewuya, *Holiness and Community*, 119-26.
173. Cf. Mark Bonnington, 'New Temples in Corinth: Paul's Use of Temple Imagery in the Ethics of the Corinthian Correspondence', in *Heaven on Earth: The Temple in Biblical Theology* (ed. T. Desmond Alexander and Simon Gathercole; Carlisle: Paternoster, 2004), 159; David Peterson, *Possessed by God: A New Testament Theology of Sanctification and Holiness* (NSBT 1; Grand Rapids: Eerdmans, 1995), 87-88.

## e. Conclusions

The argument in 2 Cor. 6.14-7.1 consists primarily of an extended explanation of the exhortation to avoid the formation of alliances with unbelievers initially expressed in 2 Cor. 6.14. The twofold rhetorical substantiation offered by Paul for this exhortation is dependent in the first instance on the transparent divide between the two theological realms defined by the Corinthians and their unbelieving counterparts in the rhetorical antitheses of 2 Cor. 6.14-16. The second related line of substantiation focuses primarily on the notion that the existence of the covenant people of God is to be marked by a certain degree of separation. This second line of argumentation is particularly important in that the unique combination of a variety of Old Testament contexts at this point suggests that the catena represents Paul's own scriptural analysis of the Corinthians' theological identity. Consequently, it appears that at least one purpose of the catena in the present context is to mould the theological and ethical conduct of the Corinthians in light of Paul's presentation of their Christian existence as representative of the new covenant realities defined by the present eschatological age (cf. 2 Cor. 5.17; 6.1-2). If the structure and content of the catena show that Paul is here positioning the Corinthians' theological existence within the framework of the prophetic expectation of the restoration of God's people from their exilic condition, then it seems reasonable to suggest that Paul's rhetoric in 2 Cor. 6.14-7.1 is uniquely defined by the prophetic tradition of the Old Testament.

The particularly prophetic nature of the material in 2 Cor. 2.14-16, 4.1-6 and 6.14-7.1 seems to point to the development of a consistent aspect of Paul's rhetoric in 2 Corinthians. Paul's presentation of his apostolic ministry as conditioned in certain respects by the prophetic tradition, therefore, may extend beyond a correlation with specific prophetic figures toward a broader connection consisting of both personal and rhetorical dimensions. In order to support further the notion that Paul's rhetoric in 2 Corinthians is conditioned in part by the prophetic tradition in the Old Testament, the following material will attempt to sketch the potential influence of the prophetic material on Paul's argument in 2 Cor. 12.1-10.

## 5. Prophetic Ascent in 2 Corinthians 12.1-10

The material in 2 Cor. 12.1-10 constitutes part of the so-called fool's speech that forms the rhetorical background of 2 Cor. 11.1-12.13. In more specific terms, Paul's argument in 2 Cor. 12.1-10 concludes the section pertaining to the concept of boasting in weakness developed in

2 Cor. 11.23–12.10. Although the structural connection between this passage and the preceding material stems from both verbal (cf. εἰ καυχᾶσθαι δεῖ in 2 Cor. 11.30) and thematic associations,[174] the actual rhetorical function of 2 Cor. 12.1-10 within this particular literary unit is not immediately transparent due to the somewhat enigmatic nature of the apostle's argument. Difficulty arises primarily with respect to Paul's description of the ecstatic experience of an ἄνθρωπος ἐν Χριστῷ in 2 Cor. 12.2-4 and his subsequent narration of his reception of a σκόλοψ τῇ σαρκί in 2 Cor. 12.7-9. The complex nature of both of these unique narratives has generated a multitude of studies on this passage that move along a number of different axes. Of particular importance for the current argument, however, is Paul's potential reliance on certain dimensions of the prophetic tradition in the formulation of the present ascent narrative. The intention within this section, therefore, will be to provide a brief analysis of 2 Cor. 12.1-10 in order to assess the amount of influence that the Old Testament prophetic material may have on this portion of Paul's argument.

a. *Paul's Failed Heavenly Ascent*
The relatively distinct nature of the material that forms the basis of Paul's argument in 2 Cor. 12.1-10 makes it somewhat difficult to determine the internal structure of the passage. The most significant structural complexity revolves around the relationship between the ascent narrative in 2 Cor. 12.2-4 and the thorn narrative in 2 Cor. 12.7-9. Although the brevity of the material likely prevents a precise identification of the relationship between the two narratives, the strong grammatical connection between the two sections (cf. διό in 2 Cor. 12.7) seems to suggest that Paul understood the events to be related at least in terms of their rhetorical significance.[175] In light of this connection it may be reasonable to assert that Paul's narration of his experience of his σκόλοψ τῇ σαρκί in 2 Cor. 12.7-9 functions as the thematic conclusion to the preceding ascent narrative.[176] In broad terms, therefore, it may be possible to argue that the introductory material in 2 Cor. 12.1 frames Paul's discussion of the related ecstatic experiences in 2 Cor. 12.2-4 and 12.7-9, while the

---

174. Cf. Harris, *Second Corinthians*, 816; Lambrecht, *Second Corinthians*, 200. The distinction, however, that Harris makes between Paul's boasting in hardship and boasting in weakness (816-17) seems to neglect Paul's own close association of these themes in 2 Cor. 12.10.

175. See the discussion in Paula R. Gooder, *Only the Third Heaven? 2 Corinthians 12.1-10 and Heavenly Ascent* (LNTS 313; London: T&T Clark International, 2006), 170-72.

176. Cf. Harris, *Second Corinthians*, 827; Thrall, *Second Corinthians*, 2:806.

material in 2 Cor. 12.5-7 and 12.10 connects the ascent and thorn narratives to the specific theme of boasting in weakness developed in the preceding material.[177]

Paul's transition to an emphasis on ecstatic experiences in 2 Cor. 12.1 (ἐλεύσομαι δὲ εἰς ὀπτασίας καὶ ἀποκαλύψεις κυρίου) serves as an introduction to the unique narrative material that forms the basis for the rest of the argument in 2 Cor. 12.1-10. The transition itself, however, is somewhat opaque. The addition of the genitive κυρίου may suggest either that the ecstatic experiences to which Paul refers originated from the Lord (subjective genitive) or that the Lord is the actual content of the experiences (objective genitive).[178] Although the absence of any direct relation of the content of the vision in the present context appears to support the subjective reading, there is precedent in the Pauline corpus for Christ being both the source and content of the apostle's revelatory experience (cf. Gal. 1.12, 16).[179] In addition, Paul's somewhat unique combination of the terms ὀπτασίας and ἀποκαλύψεις at this point may suggest that this particular phrase originated with Paul's opponents.[180] However, it may be more reasonable to argue that Paul's vocabulary functions as a type of categorical sub-heading, so that the subsequent material is marked off as the next section within the larger context of the so-called fool's speech (2 Cor. 11.1–12.13).[181] Nevertheless, the explicitly negative assertion in 2 Cor. 12.1 that this boasting is of no real benefit (οὐ συμφέρον) may point to the notion that the opponents were in fact using certain ecstatic experiences as a means of asserting their credibility and authority in Corinth.[182] Thus, as with the preceding *Peristasenkatalog* in 2 Cor. 11.23-29 and the Damascus escape narrative in 2 Cor. 11.32-33, the material here seemingly represents a paradoxical subversion of the categories which formed the basis of the opponents' boast.

This rhetorical connection, however, is mired in the enigmatic description of the heavenly ascent that follows in 2 Cor. 12.2-4. Particular

---

177. On Paul's use of weakness language in 2 Cor. 10–13, see David Alan Black, *Paul, Apostle of Weakness: Astheneia and Its Cognates in the Pauline Literature* (New York: Peter Lang, 1984), 129-72.

178. See Thrall, *Second Corinthians*, 2:774-75.

179. Andrew T. Lincoln, '"Paul the Visionary": The Setting and Significance of the Rapture to Paradise in II Corinthians XII.1-10', *NTS* 25 (1979): 204-20 (205-6).

180. E.g. Josef Zmijewski, *Der Stil der paulinischen "Narrenrede": Analyse der Sprachgestaltung in 2 Kor 11,1–12,10 als Beitrag zu Methodik von Stiluntersuchungen neutestamentlicher Texte* (BBB 52; Cologne: Hanstein, 1978), 329.

181. So Gooder, *Only the Third Heaven?*, 207; Harris, *Second Corinthians*, 832.

182. E.g. Barnett, *Second Corinthians*, 312; Harris, *Second Corinthians*, 832; Thrall, *Second Corinthians*, 2:773.

questions arise at this point of the argument in light of the apostle's repetition of certain aspects of the event in 2 Cor. 12.2 and 12.3-4, his somewhat unusual use of the third person (οἶδα ἄνθρωπον ἐν Χριστῷ), his explicit chronological formula (πρὸ ἐτῶν δεκατεσσάρων), his lack of clarity concerning his physical state (εἴτε ἐκτὸς τοῦ σώματος οὐκ οἶδα/ εἴτε ἐν σώματι εἴτε χωρὶς τοῦ σώματος οὐκ οἶδα), his particular cosmological scheme (τρίτου οὐρανοῦ/τὸν παράδεισον), and his reception of an unspeakable revelation (ἄρρητα ῥήματα ἃ οὐκ ἐξὸν ἀνθρώπῳ).[183] Apart from these specific exegetical difficulties, there is a general consensus that the material in 2 Cor. 12.2-4 constitutes a brief narration of Paul's own heavenly rapture (ἁρπαγέντα/ἡρπάγη).[184] That is, the few precise details that Paul offers in his narrative reproduction of the event seem to support the notion that the material constitutes a reference to the apostle's own personal experience.[185] Consequently, Paul relates a unique revelatory event that occurred fourteen years previously in which he ascended as far as the third heaven (ἕως τρίτου οὐρανοῦ) and then (subsequently) into paradise (εἰς τὸν παράδεισον).[186] The somewhat ironic result of this dramatic ascent experience was the reception of an inexpressible message that Paul was not permitted to communicate (ἄρρητα ῥήματα ἃ οὐκ ἐξὸν ἀνθρώπῳ). The minimal amount of information that the apostle actually provides concerning the experience, however, renders the narrative relatively ambiguous. Indeed, Furnish notes concisely that:

---

183. For a detailed analysis of these exegetical difficulties, see Gooder, *Only the Third Heaven?*, 165-89.

184. See the analysis in Harris, *Second Corinthians*, 834. The most notable alternative reading is that of Michael D. Goulder, 'Vision and Knowledge', *JSNT* 56 (1994): 53-71 (esp. 55-57), who argues that the distinction Paul makes between himself and ὁ τοιοῦτος in 2 Cor. 12.5 negates the possibility that the apostle is the ἄνθρωπος ἐν Χριστῷ (cf. Michael D. Goulder, 'The Visionaries of Laodicea', *JSNT* 43 [1991]: 15-39 [esp. 18-20]).

185. See, e.g., Margaret E. Thrall, 'Paul's Journey to Paradise: Some Exegetical Issues in 2 Cor 12,2-4', in Bieringer (ed.), *The Corinthian Correspondence*, 347-63.

186. Both the single dating formula (πρὸ ἐτῶν δεκατεσσάρων) and the parallel structure of 2 Cor. 12.2 and 12.3-4 suggest that Paul is here presenting a single revelatory experience. The potential spatial distinction marked out by the distinct prepositions ἕως and εἰς, however, may suggest that Paul's cosmological scheme was parallel to that presented in *2 En.* 8.1, in which paradise is a location within the third heaven (cf. Gooder, *Only the Third Heaven?*, 175; Andrew T. Lincoln, *Paradise Now and Not Yet* [SNTSMS 43; Cambridge: Cambridge University Press, 1981], 79). See, however, the extensive discussion in Christopher Rowland and Christopher R.A. Morray-Jones, *The Mystery of God: Early Jewish Mysticism and the New Testament* (CRINT 12; Leiden: Brill, 2009), 390-96.

the apostle has provided his readers with very little information about this extraordinary journey, and he has had nothing to say about its possible religious significance. How, precisely, he was taken up to paradise he does not know, what he saw there he does not say, and what he heard there he must not repeat.[187]

Paul's distinctly abrupt narration of the experience may suggest that this particular revelatory event has a distinctive function in the apostle's broader rhetorical argument. Of particular importance in this respect is the relationship between the material in 2 Cor. 12.2-4 and other ascent narratives within the Jewish tradition.[188] Crucial here is the work of Gooder, who provides a detailed analysis of a number of ascent texts (e.g. *1–3 Enoch*; *3 Baruch*; *Ascension of Isaiah*; Coptic *Apocalypse of Paul*; Revelation; *Testament of Levi*) in order to determine their correlation with the material in 2 Cor. 12.1-10.[189] Gooder's extensive textual comparison demonstrates that the potential similarities between Paul's narrative and the larger Jewish ascent tradition are merely superficial.[190] She notes that several significant characteristics of ascent narratives, such as their contextual function, their inclusion of a variety of figures, their detailed description of the heavenly journey, their expansive cosmology, and their inclusion of a throne-vision, are conspicuously absent from Paul's account. Further, she points out that neither Paul's specific dating formula nor his ambiguity concerning his physical state is reflective of material in the broader heavenly ascent tradition. As a result of this analysis Gooder suggests that the narrative material in 2 Cor. 12.1-10 describes a failed ascent.[191] More specifically, she argues that Paul subverts common aspects of the ascent tradition in order to express that his own experience is distinctly different from the revelatory tradition that would have likely served as a positive basis for authority in the Corinthians' view.

The notion that Paul narrates a failed ascent in 2 Cor. 12.1-10 may support the idea that this portion of the argument reflects the same ironic tone present in the preceding portion of the so-called fool's speech in 2 Corinthians 11. The failed nature of the narrative would then reflect

---

187. Furnish, *II Corinthians*, 545; cf. Gooder, *Only the Third Heaven?*, 188; Humphrey, 'Ambivalent Apocalypse', 131-32.

188. For an introduction to this relationship, see Rowland and Morray-Jones, *The Mystery of God*, 137-41, 341-420.

189. Gooder, *Only the Third Heaven?*, passim.

190. Gooder, *Only the Third Heaven?*, 189.

191. Gooder, *Only the Third Heaven?*, 190-211; cf. Rowland and Morray-Jones, *The Mystery of God*, 138-39.

the rhetorical function of the *Peristasenkatalog* in 2 Cor. 11.23-29 and the Damascus escape narrative in 2 Cor. 11.32-33, in which the apostle seemingly offers a satirical response to the types of achievements and marks of social status that the opponents were likely using to establish their authority in Corinth.[192] Paul's narration of an ascent experience which results in the dissemination of no revelation then becomes a further expression of the paradoxical activity of boasting in weakness that constitutes the rhetorical background of 2 Cor. 11.23–12.10.[193] That the ascent narrative and the emphasis on boasting are connected is manifest in the parenthetical statements that Paul makes in 2 Cor. 12.5-6, which separate the ascent narrative and the related discussion of the σκόλοψ τῇ σαρκί in 2 Cor. 12.7-9. Within these parenthetical statements Paul begins to eliminate the rhetorical distinction that he made between himself and the ἄνθρωπος ἐν Χριστῷ in 2 Cor. 12.2-4.[194] In light of Paul's subsequent discussion of his σκόλοψ (2 Cor. 12.7-9) it becomes apparent that the enigmatic figure who ascended to heaven is the afflicted apostle, with the result that there is no real distinction between boasting ὑπὲρ τοῦ τοιούτου and ὑπερ...ἐμαυτοῦ (2 Cor. 12.5).[195] Paul's boast in his heavenly ascent, therefore, constitutes another example of the 'weakness-boasting' that allows the apostle to repudiate (φείδομαι) the type of self-promotion that would prevent the Corinthians from forming a proper assessment of his apostolic ministry based on what they see in him and hear from him (ὃ βλέπει με ἢ ἀκούει [τι] ἐξ ἐμοῦ).[196] In this way, the failed ascent narrative seemingly functions as part of the broader argument in 2 Corinthians 10–13 concerning the determination of the appropriate basis of one's

---

192. Forbes, 'Comparison', 18-20; cf. Edith Humphrey, *And I Turned to See the Voice: The Rhetoric of Vision in the New Testament* (Grand Rapids: Baker, 2007), 41-43.

193. The notion that Paul subverts the heavenly ascent tradition reflects the general sense of the thesis proposed by Betz that the material in 2 Cor. 12.2-4 constitutes a parody of the heavenly ascent tradition (see Hans Dieter Betz, *Der Apostel Paulus und die sokratische Tradition: Eine exegetische Untersuchung zu seiner Apologie 2 Korinther 10–13* [BHT 45; Tübingen: Mohr Siebeck, 1972], 84-85, 89-100). The primary difficulty with Betz's view, however, is his particular use of the technical terms irony and parody (cf. Heckel, *Kraft in Schwachheit*, 20-22). In contrast to Betz, it seems more likely that Paul here relates an actual personal experience of a failed heavenly ascent in order to support his rhetorical emphasis on boasting in weakness. For a recent analysis of the function of parody in 2 Cor. 12.1-10, see M. David Litwa, 'Paul's Mosaic Ascent: An Interpretation of 2 Corinthians 12.7-9', *NTS* 57 (2011): 238-57.

194. Cf. Martin, *2 Corinthians*, 390.

195. Gooder, *Only the Third Heaven?*, 208.

196. Lim, *'The Sufferings of Christ'*, 187; Thrall, *Second Corinthians*, 2:800.

boast. In other words, Paul's particular emphasis throughout 2 Cor. 11.23–12.10 on boasting in weakness functions as an extension of the argument in 2 Cor. 10.17-18, in which the apostle formulated his conception of boasting in terms of knowing the Lord and participating in the Lord's work.

It may be possible to argue that the Christological dimension of Paul's argument that develops in the thorn narrative in 2 Cor. 12.7-9 further establishes the connection between the failed ascent narrative and the theme of boasting in weakness. Paul's desire that the Corinthians evaluate him based on what they see and hear (2 Cor. 12.6) leads directly into the discussion of the weakness manifest in the reality of the apostle's σκόλοψ τῇ σαρκί (2 Cor. 12.7-9).[197] In spite of the enigmatic nature of the σκόλοψ, the primary intention of the thorn narrative appears to be to establish Paul's position with respect to Christ (2 Cor. 12.9-10), since it confirms the notion that his apostolic weakness is reflective of the cruciform power inherent in Christ's own ministry (cf. 2 Cor. 13.4).[198] Both the failed ascent narrative and the thorn narrative, therefore, reflect the notion that Paul's apostolic status is derived appropriately from his weakness, further elucidating the emphasis on this theme developed in 2 Cor. 11.23-33. In this way, the boast highlights the Christocentric nature of his apostolic status and mission (2 Cor. 12.10), and thereby becomes an expression of boasting in the Lord inasmuch as it involves boasting not of human achievements, but of what the Lord accomplishes in and through the apostle's weakness.[199] It remains to be examined, however, why Paul develops this aspect of his apostolic ministry through a description of a failed heavenly ascent.

b. *Paul's Prophetic Framework*
The notion that the narrative in 2 Cor. 12.1-10 relates a failed heavenly ascent may provide evidence that Paul's rhetoric is here dependent to some degree on the prophetic tradition of the Old Testament. Indeed, Gooder supports her conclusion that Paul here relates a failed ascent by noting several points of correspondence between the apostle's narrative and the Old Testament prophetic material.[200] Gooder particularly

197. On the specific identification of the thorn, see the extended summary in Harris, *Second Corinthians*, 853-59; Thrall, *Second Corinthians*, 2:809-18.
198. Horrell, *Social Ethos*, 228; Lim, 'The Sufferings of Christ', 189-93; cf. Forbes, 'Comparison', 22.
199. See especially Lim, 'The Sufferings of Christ', 158-96, who understands 2 Cor. 10.17 to be the theological principle that shapes the nature and content of Paul's boasting in 2 Cor. 11.23–12.10. Cf. Heckel, *Kraft in Schwachheit*, passim.
200. Gooder, *Only the Third Heaven?*, 202-3.

highlights the passage immediately following the influential ascent narrative in Ezekiel 1, in which God encourages Ezekiel to stand firm despite the existence of (metaphorical) briers and thorns (סרבים וסלונים) that represent Ezekiel's rebellious audience (Ezek. 2.1-8).[201] She argues that Paul's narration of his own ascent experience in 2 Cor. 12.2-4 and (consequent) reception of a σκόλοψ in 2 Cor. 12.7-9 may suggest that Ezekiel's experience of affliction was paradigmatic for Paul's own self-conception as an opposed apostle.[202] This potential association between Paul's ascent narrative and Ezekiel's affliction may provide insight into the question of why this particular revelatory experience does not appear to play a significant role in Paul's other discussions of his apostolic authority.[203] The import of the narrative is not to provide an example of an extraordinary experience so that Paul could boast of his ecstatic superiority, but to provide an additional example of Paul's ineptitude in order to reflect the theme of boasting in weakness developed in 2 Corinthians 11.[204]

The larger heavenly ascent tradition may also be instructive at this point. Halperin suggests that the Jewish ascent tradition consists of both positive and negative variations on the literary motif which relate either sympathetic narrations of the ascent experience in which the subject is viewed in heroic terms or unsympathetic accounts in which the subject is understood as a threat to the divine economy and his consequent demise or failure serves as the climax of the narrative.[205] The primary example that Halperin offers in support of the existence of the negative variation

---

201. The LXX version of Ezek. 2.6, however, eliminates the thorn imagery: διότι παροιστρήσουσι καὶ ἐπισυστήσονται ἐπὶ σὲ κύκλῳ.
202. So Gooder, *Only the Third Heaven?*, 202-3.
203. Contra James D. Tabor, *Things Unutterable: Paul's Ascent to Paradise in Its Greco-Roman, Judaic, and Early Christian Contexts* (Lanham, Md.: University Press of America, 1986), 34-45, 115-25, who argues that there is a close association between the heavenly ascent material and Paul's gospel message (cf. Christopher R.A. Morray-Jones, 'Paradise Revisited [2 Cor 12:1-12]: The Jewish Mystical Background of Paul's Apostolate', *HTR* 86 [1993]: 177-217, 256-92 [270]). If the point of the revelatory experience was to highlight his apostolic authority, it seems unusual that Paul did not turn to his Damascus experience, since that particular visionary experience seemingly functions in a similar fashion at a number of points in 2 Corinthians (e.g. 2 Cor. 4.1-6; 5.14-21). On the importance of the Damascus event for Paul's apostolic identity, see Kim, *Paul's Gospel*, passim; Kim, *Paul and the New Perspective*, passim (cf. Schnelle, *Apostle Paul*, 87-102).
204. Cf. Lim, 'The Sufferings of Christ', 186.
205. David J. Halperin, 'Ascension or Invasion: Implications of the Heavenly Journey in Ancient Judaism', *Religion* 18 (1988): 47-67; Halperin, *The Faces of the Chariot* (TSAJ 16; Tübingen: Mohr Siebeck, 1988), 319-22; cf. Gooder, *Only the Third Heaven?*, 202.

of the ascent motif is Isa. 14.12-15, which relates the demise of the 'morning star' (הילל), who wished to ascend to heaven in order to be like God. In broad terms, the poetic taunt functions in the Isaianic narrative as a rejection of the type of pride that manifests itself in an inappropriate form of self-exaltation.[206] An additional illustration in this respect may arise from the progression of Ezekiel 28 in which the king of Tyre transitions from one born ἐν τῇ τρυφῇ τοῦ παραδείσου τοῦ θεοῦ (Ezek. 28.13) to being grouped with those neighbours of Israel who are described as a σκόλοψ πικρίας καὶ ἄκανθα ὀδύνης (Ezek. 28.24). In the context of the Ezekiel narrative, the demise of the king of Tyre stems from an inappropriate form of self-exaltation that manifested itself in a desire to ascend to the throne of God (Ezek. 28.2). In somewhat similar terms, Paul's ascent resulted neither in a vision of God's throne nor in the reception of an important prophetic message, but in the acquisition of an inexpressible revelation and a σκόλοψ τῇ σαρκί.[207] To combine Halperin's dual ascent framework with Gooder's failed ascent hypothesis may suggest that the rhetorical function of Paul's abrupt description of his experience is to position this event within the negative framework of self-exaltation developed in certain examples of the ascent motif. In other words, the apostle may intentionally relate this particular visionary failure in order to undermine the notion that certain forms of ecstatic experience constitute a proper basis for the determination of one's ministerial status. Paul's narration of his heavenly ascent then would function not as a means of superior boasting, but as a demonstration of the same emphasis on weakness developed in the preceding *Peristasenkatalog* (2 Cor. 11.23-29) and escape narrative (2 Cor. 11.32-33). On this reading the material in Isaiah and Ezekiel provides a prophetic foundation for Paul's rhetorical subversion of the concept of boasting.

One potential difficulty with the notion that Paul here relates a failed ascent, however, stems from the contextual relationship between the apostle's revelatory experience in 2 Cor. 12.2-4 and the thorn narrative in 2 Cor. 12.7-9. In spite of the somewhat strained syntax of 2 Cor. 12.7 it seems that in the first instance the purpose of Paul's σκόλοψ was to prevent him from becoming inappropriately arrogant in light of the apparently extraordinary quality of his ecstatic experience (καὶ τῇ ὑπερβολῇ τῶν ἀποκαλύψεων).[208] This particular emphasis on arrogance or

206. Oswalt, *Isaiah*, 1:320-21.
207. Cf. Rowland and Morray-Jones, *The Mystery of God*, 140.
208. The strained syntax of 2 Cor. 12.7 revolves around the question of whether the phrase καὶ τῇ ὑπερβολῇ τῶν ἀποκαλύψεων relates to what precedes in 2 Cor. 12.6 or to what follows in 2 Cor. 12.7. See Harris, *Second Corinthians*, 851-53, for a summary of the various exegetical options.

conceit stems from Paul's repeated claim in 2 Cor. 12.7 that the σκόλοψ was intended to restrain him from an inappropriate form of self-exaltation (ἵνα μὴ ὑπεραίρωμαι). In basic terms, the potential pride associated with the remarkable experience of a heavenly ascent required that the apostle receive the σκόλοψ in order to remain in a position of humility.[209] Paul's specific use of the verb ὑπεραίρω, however, may suggest the need for a more nuanced understanding of the argument at this point. The only other occurrence of ὑπεραίρω in the Pauline corpus is in 2 Thess. 2.4, which pertains specifically to the activity of ὁ ἄνθρωπος τῆς ἀνομίας, who exalts himself (ὑπεραιρόμενος) so that he might sit in the temple and declare himself to be God. Although the specific identity of ὁ ἄνθρωπος τῆς ἀνομίας is continually debated, there is a general consensus that certain portions of the Old Testament prophetic tradition shape the language at this point of the Thessalonian correspondence.[210] Of particular importance for the present argument is the potential association between the description of ὁ ἄνθρωπος τῆς ἀνομίας and material in Isaiah 14 and Ezekiel 28. The import of these two potential allusions is that the lawless figure in 2 Thessalonians is defined within the same tradition marked out by the somewhat ambiguous figure portrayed in Isa. 14.12-15 and the king of Tyre in Ezekiel 28, both of whom attempt to establish themselves as superior to the Lord and are consequently relegated to destruction because of their arrogant insubordination (Isa. 14.15-20; Ezek. 28.8-10). The association of the exaltation of ὁ ἄνθρωπος τῆς ἀνομίας with these particular prophetic texts may suggest that there is a specific connection in Paul's rhetoric between the concept of self-exaltation inherent in ὑπεραίρω and opposition to God. Applying this association to the argument in 2 Corinthians, Paul's language in the thorn narrative may denote a particular allusion to the type of arrogance or conceit manifest by those who attempt to place themselves in the position of God.[211] That Paul's use of ὑπεραίρω in 2 Corinthians is reflective of its use in

209. So, for example, Barnett, *Second Corinthians*, 555; David E. Garland, 'Paul's Apostolic Authority: The Power of Christ Sustaining Weakness (2 Corinthians 10–13)', *RevExp* 86 (1989): 371-89 (380-81); Harris, *Second Corinthians*, 827, 853; John Christopher Thomas, '"An Angel from Satan": Paul's Thorn in the Flesh (2 Corinthians 12:7-10)', *JPT* 9 (1996): 39-52 (41-47).

210. See, e.g., F.F. Bruce, *1 and 2 Thessalonians* (WBC 45; Waco: Word, 1982), 168, 177; Gordon D. Fee, *The First and Second Letters to the Thessalonians* (NICNT; Grand Rapids: Eerdmans, 2009), 283-84; Gene L. Green, *The Letters to the Thessalonians* (PNTC; Grand Rapids: Eerdmans, 2002), 311; Abraham J. Malherbe, *The Letters to the Thessalonians* (AB 32B; New York: Doubleday, 2000), 431; Charles A. Wanamaker, *The Epistles to the Thessalonians* (NIGTC; Grand Rapids: Eerdmans, 1990), 247-48.

211. Cf. Rowland and Morray-Jones, *The Mystery of God*, 141.

2 Thessalonians may clarify the potential influence of both Isaiah 14 and Ezekiel 28 on the immediately preceding ascent narrative. In other words, the negative framework developed in the prophetic material may here confirm that the apostle's σκόλοψ τῇ σαρκί is the consequence of a failed heavenly ascent. On this reading Paul's description of his ascent narrative as an exceedingly great revelation (τῇ ὑπερβολῇ τῶν ἀποκαλύψεων) in 2 Cor. 12.7 is not an actual expression of the greatness of the experience, but an ironic admission of his characteristic weakness.[212] It seems reasonable to argue, therefore, that Paul develops certain aspects of the Old Testament prophetic material within both the ascent and thorn narratives in order to clarify that his apostolic status is confirmed in his embodiment of the paradoxical union of weakness and strength developed in Christ's own ministry (cf. 2 Cor. 4.11; 13.4).

c. *Conclusions*

Paul's unique narrative material in 2 Cor. 12.1-10 further elaborates the thematic emphasis on boasting in weakness developed in 2 Cor. 11.23-33. In broad terms, Paul's relatively abrupt relation of his ascent narrative in 2 Cor. 12.2-4 and his subsequent reception of a σκόλοψ τῇ σαρκί in 2 Cor. 12.7-9 suggest that the argument here constitutes the development of a failed ascent narrative that provides an additional illustration of the weakness upon which Paul's apostolic authority is based. Paul's particular use of a failed ascent narrative may provide evidence for a connection at this point of 2 Corinthians with the Old Testament prophetic tradition. In more specific terms, Paul's failed ascent experience and subsequent reception of a σκόλοψ seem to establish a rhetorical connection between certain examples of the ascent motif in Isaiah 14 and Ezekiel 28 in which the desire to ascend to the throne of God is representative of an inappropriate form of self-exaltation that results in destruction. Paul's narration of this particular negative ecstatic experience then becomes an ironic reversal of the notion that authority derives from strength as the apostle interprets his experience of weakness as the paradoxical foundation for his apostolic ministry (2 Cor. 12.10). As with the material in 2 Cor. 2.14-16, 4.1-6, and 6.14–7.1, the rhetorical development of Paul's argument in 2 Cor. 12.1-10 appears to evince a particular connection with the prophetic tradition of the Old Testament.

212. The irony implicit in the adjective ὑπερβολή in 2 Cor. 12.7 is parallel to the ironic import of ὑπερλίαν in 2 Cor. 11.5 and 12.11 (cf. Gooder, *Only the Third Heaven?*, 194). Indeed, the high frequency of ὑπέρ-compounds throughout 2 Cor. 10–13 (i.e. ὑπεραίρω [12.7 (×2)], ὑπερβαλλόντως [11.22], ὑπερβολή [12.7], ὑπερέκεινα [10.16], ὑπερεκτείνω [10.14], and ὑπερλίαν [11.5; 12.11]) may provide evidence for the ironic nature of the discourse.

## 6. Conclusion

The notion that Paul's rhetoric in 2 Corinthians is conditioned to some degree by the prophetic material of the Old Testament stems from the correlation at a variety of points within the epistle between Paul's argument and certain dimensions, both textual and conceptual, of the Old Testament prophetic literature (e.g. 2 Cor. 2.14-16; 4.1-6; 6.14–7.1; 12.1-10). Paul's apparent dependence on the prophetic material in the development of his argument seems to suggest that the apostle's rhetorical agenda in 2 Corinthians is shaped at least in part by the prophetic tradition of the Old Testament. In light of the potentially prophetic nature of Paul's self-presentation in 2 Corinthians manifest in his specific association with Moses, the Isaianic servant, and Jeremiah, it may be reasonable to argue that Paul's rhetoric in 2 Corinthians is a particular outworking of his prophetic persona. The influence of the prophetic material on the formation of Paul's argument in 2 Corinthians would then represent an extension of Paul's positioning of his ministry within the prophetic history of the Old Testament. In somewhat circular fashion, Paul's potential dependence upon the rhetorical movement of certain aspects of the prophetic material of the Old Testament may provide additional support for the notion that Paul's presentation of his apostleship in 2 Corinthians is representative of a uniquely prophetic framework. Due to both the prophetic nature of Paul's self-presentation and the influence of the prophetic literature on the course of Paul's argument, it seems plausible to argue that 2 Corinthians provides support for the notion that Paul's identity and rhetoric are rooted in the prophetic tradition of the Old Testament.

Chapter 6

CONCLUSION

1. *Summary and Implications*

The principal intent of this study has been to delineate the ways in which the material in 2 Corinthians reflects the prophetic dimensions of Paul's apostolic self-presentation and rhetoric. The primary argument established is that the material in 2 Corinthians further substantiates the notion that Paul's construction of his apostolic identity and argument is influenced by the Old Testament prophetic tradition. In the introduction to the study it was noted that there is a general, though relatively undeveloped, consensus within Pauline scholarship that Paul's apostolic ministry evinces a number of connections with the prophetic material of the Old Testament in terms of both self-understanding and textual dependence. It was observed, however, that there was a noticeable deficiency in the amount of analysis done on the material in 2 Corinthians with respect to a systematic explanation of the relationship between Paul and the Old Testament prophetic tradition. The particularly overt autobiographical nature of the material in 2 Corinthians, however, constitutes an important window through which to analyse the prophetic shape of Paul's apostolic persona and the influence of that prophetic dimension on the shape of Paul's argument. Therefore, the present study sought to contribute to the broader discussion by building on the notion that Paul is conceptually connected with the Old Testament prophets by adopting the methodological model outlined by Nicklas in analysing the influence of the prophetic tradition on both Paul's apostolic self-presentation ('Berufung und Selbstverständnis') and the formation of his rhetoric ('Argumentationsformen') in 2 Corinthians.[1]

In an attempt to define the conceptual locus within which Paul develops his prophetic persona and rhetoric, the intention within Chapter 2 was to define the boundaries of the somewhat broad phrase 'the

1. See Nicklas, 'Paulus—der Apostel als Prophet', 78.

prophetic tradition'. It was argued at that point that the prophetic material manifest in the Old Testament is an organic entity that grew and developed with particular reference to Hebrew and Israelite history. The nature of this organic development was analysed primarily through the lens of the relationship between the prophetic material developed in the Pentateuch, the Historical books, and the Prophetic literature. Moreover, it was argued that both material from the Second Temple period and that characteristic of the early Christian movement serve as evidence for the unique development of the Old Testament prophetic tradition due to their extensive reliance at a number of points on the form, function, content, and themes of the Old Testament prophetic material. Consequently, in spite of the ostensible reality that the prophetic material in the Old Testament, Second Temple Judaism, and Gospel traditions evokes a multiplicity of distinct emphases, it was established that there was continuity in the development of the prophetic material throughout Israel's history, allowing it to function as a separate entity with respect to other (e.g. Hellenistic) prophetic traditions. For this reason, the present study argued that the Old Testament prophetic material provides the most plausible background through which to analyse the prophetic nature of Paul's apostolic self-presentation and rhetoric in 2 Corinthians.

The intention within Chapter 3 was to provide a methodological precursor for the subsequent examination of the material in 2 Corinthians by providing a fresh investigation of the influence of the Old Testament prophetic tradition on both Paul's presentation of his apostolic ministry and the formulation of his rhetorical argument in 1 Corinthians. The specific purpose of this methodological development was to locate the prophetic dimensions of Paul's self-presentation and rhetoric within the broader scope of the apostle's relationship with the Corinthian community, emphasizing the importance of the material in 1 Corinthians in the development of the social and rhetorical foundation of the Corinthian correspondence. The initial portion of the analysis expounded the notion that Paul's self-presentation in 1 Cor. 9.15-18 is uniquely shaped by prophetic characteristics. In more specific terms, the study advanced the argument that Paul's description of his ministry as conditioned by divine necessity and susceptible to eschatological judgment functions to position his self-presentation within a distinctly prophetic framework. The argument then turned to an examination of the complex scriptural argument in 1 Cor. 14.20-25. This portion of the analysis sought to demonstrate the unique hypothesis that the preceding prophetic tradition, particularly the Isaianic narrative, serves as the rhetorical foundation upon which the apostle constructs his explanation of the distinct functions of prophetic speech and unarticulated tongues with respect to

## 6. Conclusion

the Corinthian community. In spite of the fact that 1 Cor. 9.15-18 and 14.20-25 constitute a relatively small sample of the material in 1 Corinthians, the present investigation emphasized that the apostle's dependence on prophetic material at both points illustrates his personal and rhetorical connection with the prophetic tradition. The intention within Chapter 3, therefore, was not to argue that the Old Testament prophetic tradition constitutes the sole entity upon which Paul constructs and explains his apostolic ministry, but that the prophetic tradition is one of the conceptual backgrounds upon which Paul forms both his self-presentation and rhetoric.

Having established the conceptual background and methodological framework for the subsequent analysis, the intention within the material in Chapters 4 and 5 was to investigate the nature and extent of the influence of the Old Testament prophetic tradition on both Paul's apostolic self-presentation and his rhetoric in 2 Corinthians. In terms of Paul's self-presentation, the present study argued in particular that the apostle's formulation of aspects of his ministry along similar lines to a number of prophetic figures represents an intentional decision by Paul to position his ministry within the actual development of the prophetic tradition. The correlations that Paul establishes between himself and Moses in terms of the origin, nature, and function of their respective ministries, for example, provide a foundation for identifying conceptual parallels between the ministries of both figures. The admitted existence of distinctions between the two figures, however, required caution in defining Paul as a specific fulfillment of a possible second Moses tradition. In light of both the parallels and distinctions that Paul communicates with respect to his own ministry and that of Moses, the present study argued that a potentially more reasonable assessment of the relationship between Paul and the Mosaic tradition is developed not along an ontological axis, but along the lines of ministerial identity. The distinct parallels between Paul and Moses, therefore, provide an initial foundation for the notion that Paul conceives of at least a general connection between his own ministry and the Old Testament prophetic material even if there are significant historical and theological distinctions between them.

Likewise, the analysis of Paul's relationship with the Isaianic servant material offered distinct insight into the relationship between the two figures primarily in terms of their authority and mission. With regard to these two foci it was argued that the Isaianic servant tradition provides a conceptual background for Paul's description of his overarching apostolic mission and his expression of his position of authority as a divine co-worker. The specific associations that Paul appears to develop between the Isaianic material and Christ, however, again required caution in assessing the nature of the relationship between Paul and the Isaianic servant. As with the material on the Mosaic tradition, the present study argued that Paul is not presenting himself as the typological embodiment of the Isaianic servant tradition, but establishing a more general connection between his own ministry and that of the Old Testament prophetic material. That Paul is able to draw parallels between himself and both the Mosaic and Isaianic traditions is an essential component of the argument that the apostle relates to elements developed within those particular traditions, but is not necessarily bound by either of them.

Further aspects of the relationship between Paul's self-presentation and the prophetic tradition were examined with respect to the apostle's potential reliance on Jeremiah in the formulation of his ministerial call, his description of his role as a minister of the new covenant, his expression of his apostolic authority as that characterized by edification and not destruction, and his evaluation of the concept of boasting. In light of these particular associations, the present study advanced the notion that Paul portrays his ministry as an extension of the new covenant framework developed particularly within the Jeremianic narrative. Consequently, Paul does not present himself as a new Jeremiah; rather, he uses the Jeremianic material to locate his ministry within the continuing development of the Old Testament prophetic tradition, emphasizing both the Jeremianic nature of certain aspects of his ministry and their distinct position with regard to salvation history. The specific insight put forth at this point of the study is that the presence of particular associations with a number of prophetic figures within the same epistle points to the notion that Paul's purpose is not to define his ministry in terms of individual prophetic figures, but to position himself within the prophetic tradition corporately. The material in 2 Corinthians, therefore, supplies substantial evidence for the notion that Paul's self-presentation is distinctly influenced by the Old Testament prophetic tradition.

In addition to the examination of the ways in which the Old Testament prophetic tradition shaped Paul's self-presentation, the intention within the material in Chapter 5 was to provide an original exegetical analysis of several distinct portions of 2 Corinthians in order to examine the influence of the prophetic material on the development of the apostle's rhetoric. The material centred initially on the triumph metaphor which Paul develops in 2 Cor. 2.14-16, positing distinctively that his self-portrait as a defeated captive constitutes an allusion to the narrative portrayal in the prophetic material of God's triumphal procession in celebration of his messianic victory. In light of this particular allusion it was argued that Paul's defensive rhetoric at this point of the epistle derives in part from the theoretical framework developed in the Old Testament prophetic tradition. Likewise, the analysis of the rhetorical movement of 2 Cor. 4.1-6 points to a specific connection between Paul's description of the effectual nature of his ministry and the conceptual framework inherent in the Old Testament prophetic tradition. In particular, the study advanced the unique idea that the connection Paul presents between the light that functions as the source of his spiritual illumination and the person of Christ parallels the rhetorical progression of the concept of light in the Isaianic narrative. The presence of this particular dependence on the Isaianic material in Paul's formation of this portion of his apostolic defence provides further support for the notion that the apostle's rhetoric is conditioned to some extent by themes established within the Old Testament prophetic material.

The particular hypothesis that the shape of Paul's rhetoric in 2 Corinthians is conditioned to some extent by the prophetic tradition was then considered with respect to the apostle's argument in 2 Cor. 6.14–7.1. At that point it was argued that the scriptural catena in 2 Cor. 6.16-18 represents Paul's own scriptural analysis of the Corinthians' theological existence. In terms of the primary thesis, the distinct suggestion within this section is that Paul's use of material associated with the prophetic expectation of the restoration of God's people to define the shape of the Corinthians' theological identity demonstrates a further connection between certain aspects of the preceding Old Testament prophetic tradition and Paul's development of his rhetorical framework. Similarly, the analysis of the material in 2 Cor. 12.1-10 contended that the unique nature of Paul's heavenly ascent narrative functions to create a rhetorical connection between the apostle's argument and certain negative dimensions of ascent narratives present in the Old Testament prophetic material. The specific insight put forth at this point of the argument is that the particularly prophetic nature of Paul's apostolic persona affected not only the particular dimensions of his self-presentation, but also the shape of certain portions of his rhetorical agenda within 2 Corinthians. In broad terms, therefore, this study sought to advance discussion on Paul's relationship with the Old Testament prophetic tradition through a systematic analysis of the material in canonical 2 Corinthians. The primary contention within the study is that the seemingly pervasive influence of the Old Testament prophetic tradition on Paul's presentation of his apostolic self-understanding and on the formation of his argument in 2 Corinthians constitutes a crucial dimension in an analysis of the ways in which Paul conceived of his apostolic identity and rhetoric.

## 2. Further Research

This study has attempted to show that the material in 2 Corinthians provides a unique window through which to view the ways in which the Old Testament prophetic tradition impacts Paul's construction, explanation, and assertion of his apostolic ministry in light of its overtly autobiographical nature. Despite Paul's relatively pervasive use of prophetic material in 2 Corinthians to develop his apostolic persona and form his rhetorical framework, the present study focused in large part on those portions of 2 Corinthians that contain certain dimensions of Paul's defence of his apostolic authority in Corinth, namely the material in 2 Cor. 2.14–7.4 and 2 Corinthians 10–13. Further research on other sections of the letter may provide additional insight into the ways in which the prophetic material shaped Paul's conceptual relationship with the Corinthians. It may be possible, for example, that Paul's emphasis on the themes of consolation and comfort in 2 Cor. 1.3-11 and his development of the notion of reciprocal generosity in 2 Corinthians 8–9 reflect an even more extensive prophetic influence on the shape of Paul's theological framework at this stage of the Corinthian correspondence.

The potential impact of the Old Testament prophetic tradition on the shape of Paul's self-presentation and rhetoric, however, need not be limited strictly to the material that constitutes canonical 2 Corinthians. In line with the research highlighted initially in the introductory chapter,[2] there remains room to extend the basic hypothesis that Paul stands among the prophets through the development of systematic explanations of the influence of the prophetic nature of Paul's apostolic persona and language upon material at other points of the Pauline corpus. Although it would likely be unhelpful to attempt to transfer unilaterally the specific emphases highlighted in the present work to other Pauline texts and communities in light of their specific development *vis-à-vis* the Corinthians, Paul's use of prophetic constructs to form his self-presentation and structure his argument at a number of points in 2 Corinthians may suggest that studies developed on similar methodological lines with respect to the other Pauline epistles and communities would prove beneficial in the development of a more vivid portrait of the prophetic nature of Paul's apostleship and in answering the undoubtedly larger question of whether or not it is possible to identify a distinctly prophetic theology within the Pauline material.

---

2. Especially Nicklas, 'Paulus—der Apostel als Prophet', and Sandnes, *Paul—One of the Prophets?*

# Bibliography

Adewuya, J. Ayodeji, *Holiness and Community in 2 Cor 6:14–7:1: Paul's View of Communal Holiness in the Corinthian Correspondence* (Studies in Biblical Literature 40; New York: Peter Lang, 2001).

Albright, William F., 'Samuel and the Beginnings of the Prophetic Movement', in *Interpreting the Prophetic Tradition: The Goldenson Lectures, 1955–1966* (ed. Harry Orlinksy; LBS; Cincinnati: Hebrew Union College Press, 1969), 149-76.

Alden, Robert L., *Job* (NAC 11; Nashville: Broadman & Holman, 1993).

Allison, Dale C., 'Elijah Must Come First', *JBL* 103 (1984): 256-58.

Allo, E.B., *Saint Paul: Seconde épître aux Corinthiens* (2d ed.; Ebib; Paris: Gabalda, 1956).

Appian, *Roman History* (trans. Horace White; 4 vols.; LCL; Cambridge, Mass.: Harvard University Press, 1912–13).

Attridge, Harold W., 'Making Scents of Paul: The Background and Sense of 2 Cor 2:14-17', in *Early Christianity and Classical Culture: Comparative Studies in Honor of Abraham J. Malherbe* (ed. John T. Fitzgerald, Thomas H. Olbricht, and L. Michael White; NovTSup 110; Leiden: Brill, 2003), 71-88.

Aune, David E., *Prophecy in Early Christianity and the Ancient Mediterranean World* (Grand Rapids: Eerdmans, 1983).

—'The Use of ΠΡΟΦΗΤΗΣ in Josephus', *JBL* 101 (1982): 419-21.

Bach, Robert, 'Bauen and Pflanzen', in *Studien zur Theologie der alttestamentlichen Überlieferungen* (Festschrift Gerhard von Rad; ed. Rolf Rendtorff and Klaus Koch; Neukirchen–Vluyn: Neukirchener Verlag, 1962), 7-32.

Baer, David A., *When We All Go Home: Translation and Theology in LXX Isaiah 56–66* (JSOTSup 318; Sheffield: Sheffield Academic, 2001).

Bain, John A., '2 Cor iv.3-4', *ExpTim* 18 (1906–1907): 380.

Baker, William R., 'Did the Glory of Moses' Face Fade? A Reexamination of καταργέω in 2 Corinthians 3:7-18', *BBR* 10 (2000): 1-15.

Balla, Peter, '2 Corinthians', in Beale and Carson (eds.), *Commentary*, 753-58.

Banks, Robert, 'The Eschatological Role of Law in Pre- and Post-Christian Jewish Thought', in *Reconciliation and Hope* (Festschrift L.L. Morris; ed. Robert Banks; Grand Rapids: Eerdmans, 1974), 173-85.

Barclay, John M.G., 'Thessalonica and Corinth: Social Contrasts in Pauline Christianity', *JSNT* 47 (1992): 49-74.

Barnett, Paul, *The Second Epistle to the Corinthians* (NICNT; Grand Rapids: Eerdmans, 1997).

Barrett, C.K., *A Commentary on the Second Epistle to the Corinthians* (BNTC; London: Black, 1973).

—*A Critical and Exegetical Commentary on the Acts of the Apostles* (2 vols.; ICC 30; Edinburgh: T. & T. Clark, 1994–98).

—*The First Epistle to the Corinthians* (2d ed.; BNTC; London: Black, 1971).

—*The Holy Spirit and the Gospel Tradition* (London: SPCK, 1947).
Barstad, Hans M., 'The Understanding of the Prophets in Deuteronomy', *SJOT* 8 (1994): 236-51.
Barthélemy, Dominique, *Critique textuelle de l'Ancien Testament* (2 vols.; OBO 50; Göttingen: Vandenhoeck & Ruprecht, 1982).
Bauckham, Richard, 'Apocalypses', in *The Complexities of Second Temple Judaism* (vol. 1 of *Justification and Variegated Nomism*; ed. D.A. Carson, Peter T. O'Brien, and Mark A. Seifrid; WUNT 2/140; Tübingen: Mohr Siebeck, 2001), 135-87.
—*Jesus and the God of Israel: God Crucified and Other Studies on the New Testament's Christology of Divine Identity* (Grand Rapids: Eerdmans, 2009).
Baumert, Norbert, *Täglich Sterben und Auferstehen: Der Literalsinn von 2 Kor 4,12–5,10* (SANT 34; Munich: Kösel, 1973).
Baur, F.C., 'Die Christuspartei in der korinthischen Gemeinde, der Gegensatz des petrinishchen und paulinischen Christentum in der ältesten Kirche, der Apostel Petrus in Rom', *TZT* 4 (1831): 61-206.
Beale, G.K., 'The Old Testament Background of Reconciliation in 2 Corinthians 5–7 and Its Bearing on the Literary Problem of 2 Corinthians 6.14–7.1', *NTS* 35 (1989): 550-81.
—*The Temple and the Church's Mission: A Biblical Theology of the Dwelling Place of God* (NSBT 18; Downers Grove, Ill.: InterVarsity, 2004).
Beale, G.K, and D.A. Carson (eds.), *Commentary on the New Testament Use of the Old Testament* (Grand Rapids: Baker, 2007).
Beard, Mary, *The Roman Triumph* (Cambridge: Belknap, 2007).
Becking, Bob, 'Jeremiah's Book of Consolation: A Textual Comparison. Notes on the Masoretic Text and the Old Greek Version of Jeremiah xxx–xxxi', *VT* 44 (1994): 145-69.
Beentjes, Pancratius C., 'Prophets and Prophecy in the Book of Ben Sira', in Floyd and Haak (eds.), *Prophets, Prophecy, and Prophetic Texts*, 135-50.
Beker, J. Christiaan, *Paul the Apostle: The Triumph of God in Life and Thought* (Edinburgh: T. & T. Clark, 1980).
Belleville, Linda L., 'A Letter of Apologetic Self-Commendation: 2 Cor. 1:8–7:16', *NovT* 31 (1989): 142-63.
—*Reflections of Glory: Paul's Polemical Use of the Moses-Doxa Tradition in 2 Corinthians 3.1-18* (JSNTSup 52; Sheffield: JSOT, 1991).
—'Tradition or Creation? Paul's Use of the Exodus 34 Tradition in 2 Corinthians 3:7-18', in *Paul and the Scriptures of Israel* (ed. Craig A. Evans and James A. Sanders; JSNTSup 83; Sheffield: JSOT, 1993), 165-86.
Bellinger, William H. Jr., and William R. Farmer (eds.), *Jesus and the Suffering Servant: Isaiah 53 and Christian Origins* (Harrisburg, Pa.: Trinity Press International, 1998).
Benoit, Pierre, 'Qumrân et le Nouveau Testament', *NTS* 7 (1961): 276-96.
Berridge, John Maclennan, *Prophet, People, and the Word of Yahweh: An Examination of Form and Content in the Proclamation of the Prophet Jeremiah* (BST 4; Zurich: EVZ-Verlag, 1970).
Betz, Hans Dieter, '2 Cor 6:14–7:1: An Anti-Pauline Fragment?', *JBL* 92 (1973): 88-108.
—*Der Apostel Paulus und die sokratische Tradition: Eine exegetische Untersuchung zu seiner Apologie 2 Korinther 10–13* (BHT 45; Tübingen: Mohr Siebeck, 1972).
Beuken, W.A.M., *Jesaja III* (2 vols.; POut; Nijkerk: Callenbach, 1989).
—'Mispat: The First Servant Song in Its Context', *VT* 22 (1972): 1-30.

Bieringer, Reimund, '2 Korinther 6,14-7,1 im Kontext des 2. Korintherbriefes: Forschungsüberblick und Versuch eines eigenen Zugangs', in Bieringer and Lambrecht (eds.), *Studies on 2 Corinthians*, 551-70.
—'Teilungshypothesen zum 2 Korintherbrief: Ein Forschungsüberblick', in Bieringer and Lambrecht (eds.), *Studies on 2 Corinthians*, 67-105.
Bieringer, Reimund (ed.), *The Corinthian Correspondence* (BETL 125; Leuven: Leuven University Press, 1996).
Bieringer, Reimund, and Jan Lambrecht (eds.), *Studies on 2 Corinthians* (BETL 112; Leuven: Leuven University Press, 1994).
Black, David Alan, *Paul, Apostle of Weakness: Astheneia and Its Cognates in the Pauline Literature* (New York: Peter Lang, 1984).
Blanton, Thomas R., IV, 'Spirit and Covenant Renewal: A Theologoumenon of Paul's Opponents in 2 Corinthians', *JBL* 129 (2010): 129-51.
Blenkinsopp, Joseph, *A History of Prophecy in Israel* (rev. and enl. ed.; Louisville: Westminster John Knox, 1996).
—*Isaiah 1-39* (AB 19; New York: Doubleday, 2000).
—'Prophecy and Priesthood in Josephus', *JJS* 25 (1974): 239-62.
Block, Daniel I., *Ezekiel* (2 vols.; NICOT; Grand Rapids: Eerdmans, 1997-98).
Bock, Darrell L., *Luke* (2 vols.; BECNT; Grand Rapids: Baker, 1994-96).
Bockmuehl, Markus N.A., *Revelation and Mystery in Ancient Judaism and Pauline Christianity* (WUNT 2/36; Tübingen: Mohr Siebeck, 1990).
Boda, Mark J., 'From Fasts to Feasts: The Literary Function of Zechariah 7-8', *CBQ* 65 (2003): 390-407.
Boers, Hendrikus, '2 Corinthians 5:14-6:2: A Fragment of Pauline Christology', *CBQ* 64 (2002): 527-47.
Bonnard, Pierre, *Jésus-Christ édifiant son Eglise: Le concept d'édification dans le Nouveau Testament* (CahT 21; Neuchâtel/Paris: Delachaux & Niestlé, 1948).
Bonnington, Mark, 'New Temples in Corinth: Paul's Use of Temple Imagery in the Ethics of the Corinthian Correspondence', in *Heaven on Earth: The Temple in Biblical Theology* (ed. T. Desmond Alexander and Simon Gathercole; Carlisle: Paternoster, 2004), 151-59.
Boring, M. Eugene, *Sayings of the Risen Jesus: Christian Prophecy in the Synoptic Tradition* (SNTSMS 46; Cambridge: Cambridge University Press, 1982).
Bowers, Paul, 'Church and Mission in Paul', *JSNT* 44 (1991): 89-111.
Bowley, James E., 'Prophets and Prophecy at Qumran', in Flint and VanderKam (eds.), *The Dead Sea Scrolls After Fifty Years*, 2:354-78.
Breytenbach, Cilliers, 'Christologie, Nachfolge/Apostolat', *BTZ* 8 (1991): 183-98.
—'Paul's Proclamation and God's "Thriambos" (Notes on 2 Corinthians 2.14-16b)', *Neot* 24 (1990): 257-71.
—*Versöhnung: Eine Studie zur paulinischen Soteriologie* (WMANT 80; Neukirchen-Vluyn: Neukirchener Verlag, 1989).
Brockington, L.H., 'The Greek Translator of Isaiah and His Interest in ΔΟΞΑ', *VT* 1 (1951): 23-32.
Brooke, George J., 'Parabiblical Prophetic Narratives', in Flint and VanderKam (eds.), *The Dead Sea Scrolls After Fifty Years*, 1:271-301.
—'Prophecy', in *Encyclopedia of the Dead Sea Scrolls* (ed. Lawrence H. Schiffman and James C. VanderKam; 2 vols.; Oxford: Oxford University Press, 2000), 2:694-700.

—'Prophecy and Prophets in the Dead Sea Scrolls: Looking Backwards and Forwards', in Floyd and Haak (eds.), *Prophets, Prophecy, and Prophetic Texts*, 151-65.
—'Thematic Commentaries on Prophetic Scriptures', in Henze (ed.), *Biblical Interpretation at Qumran*, 134-57.
—'Was the Teacher of Righteousness Considered a Prophet?', in *Prophecy After the Prophets? The Contribution of the Dead Sea Scrolls to the Understanding of Biblical and Extra-Biblical Prophecy* (ed. Kristin De Troyer and Armin Lange; CBET 52; Leuven: Peeters, 2009), 77-98.
Brown, Raymond E., *The Birth of the Messiah: A Commentary on the Infancy Narratives in Matthew and Luke* (ABRL; New York: Doubleday, 1993).
Bruce, F.F., *1 and 2 Thessalonians* (WBC 45; Waco: Word, 1982).
—*Commentary on the Book of the Acts* (NICNT; Grand Rapids: Eerdmans, 1984).
—*The Epistle to the Galatians* (NIGTC; Grand Rapids: Eerdmans, 1982).
Brueggemann, Walter, *The Prophetic Imagination* (2d ed.; Minneapolis: Fortress, 2001).
Brunt, John C., 'Love, Freedom, and Moral Responsibility: The Contribution of 1 Cor 9–10 to an Understanding of Paul's Ethical Thinking', in *SBL Seminar Papers, 1981* (ed. Kent Harold Richards; SBLSP 20; Chico, Calif.: Scholars Press, 1981), 19-33.
Bultmann, Rudolf, *The Second Letter to the Corinthians* (trans. Roy A. Harrisville; Minneapolis: Fortress, 1985).
Burkhardt, Helmut, *Die Inspiration heiliger Schriften bei Philo von Alexandrien* (Monographien und Studienbücher 340; Giessen: Brunnen Verlag, 1988).
Burrows, Millar, 'Prophecy and Prophets at Qumran', in *Israel's Prophetic Heritage: Essays in Honor of James Muilenburg* (ed. Bernhard W. Anderson and Walter Harrelson; New York: Harper, 1962), 223-32.
Burtarbutar, Robinson, *Paul and Conflict Resolution: An Exegetical Study of Paul's Apostolic Paradigm in 1 Corinthians 9* (PBM; Milton Keynes: Paternoster, 2007).
Callan, Terrance, 'Prophecy and Ecstasy in Greco-Roman Religion and in 1 Corinthians', *NovT* 27 (1985): 125-40.
Calvin, John, *The Second Epistle of Paul the Apostle to the Corinthians and the Epistles to Timothy, Titus and Philemon* (trans. T.A. Smail; CNTC 10; Grand Rapids: Eerdmans, 1964).
Campbell, William S., 'Israel', *DPL* 441-46.
Carrez, Maurice, 'Odeur de mort, odeur de vie (à propos de 2 Cor 2:16)', *RB* 64 (1984): 135-42.
Carroll, Robert P., 'The Elijah–Elisha Sagas: Some Remarks on Prophetic Succession in Ancient Israel', *VT* 19 (1969): 400-15.
—*Jeremiah* (OTL; Philadelphia: Westminster, 1986).
Carson, D.A., *The Gospel According to John* (PNTC; Grand Rapids: Eerdmans, 1991).
—Review of *Prophecy in Early Christianity and the Ancient Mediterranean World*, by David E. Aune, *JETS* 28 (1985): 236-38.
—*Showing the Spirit: A Theological Exposition of 1 Corinthians 12–14* (Grand Rapids: Baker, 1987).
Ceresko, Anthony R., *Prophets and Proverbs: More Studies in Old Testament Poetry and Biblical Religion* (Quezon City: Claretian, 2002).
Cerfaux, Lucien, 'Saint Paul et le 'serviteur de Dieu' d'Isaïe', in *Recueil Lucien Cerfaux* (3 vols.; BETL 6-7; Gembloux: Duculot, 1954), 2:439-54.
Cervelli, Innocenzo, 'Questioni Sibilline', *Studi Storici* 4 (1993): 895-1001.

Chang, Steven S.H., 'The Integrity of 2 Corinthians: 1980–2000', *Torch Trinity Journal* 5 (2002): 167-202.
Chester, Stephen J., *Conversion at Corinth: Perspectives on Conversion in Paul's Theology and the Corinthian Church* (SNTW; London: T&T Clark International, 2003).
—'Divine Madness? Speaking in Tongues in 1 Corinthians 14.23', *JSNT* 27 (2005): 417-46.
Childs, Brevard S. *Isaiah* (OTL; Louisville: Westminster John Knox, 2001).
—*Isaiah and the Assyrian Crisis* (SBT 2/3; London: SCM, 1967).
—'On Reading the Elijah Narratives', *Int* 34 (1980): 128-37.
Chow, John K., *Patronage and Power: A Study of Social Networks in Corinth* (JSNTSup 75; Sheffield: JSOT, 1992).
Ciampa, Roy E., *The Presence and Function of Scripture in Galatians 1 and 2* (WUNT 2/102; Tübingen: Mohr Siebeck, 1998).
Ciampa, Roy E., and Brian S. Rosner, '1 Corinthians', in Beale and Carson (eds.), *Commentary*, 695-752.
—*The First Letter to the Corinthians* (PNTC; Grand Rapids: Eerdmans, 2010).
Clarke, Andrew D., *A Pauline Theology of Church Leadership* (LNTS 362; London: T&T Clark International, 2008).
—*Secular and Christian Leadership in Corinth: A Socio-Historical and Exegetical Study of 1 Corinthians 1–6* (PBM; Milton Keynes: Paternoster, 2006).
Clements, Ronald E., 'Isaiah 53 and the Restoration of Israel', in Bellinger and Farmer (eds.), *Jesus and the Suffering Servant*, 39-54.
—*Old Testament Prophecy: From Oracles to Canon* (Louisville: Westminster John Knox, 1996).
—*Prophecy and Tradition* (Oxford: Basil Blackwell, 1975).
Clifford, Richard J., 'The Use of *Hôy* in the Prophets', *CBQ* 28 (1966): 458-64.
Clowney, Edmund P., 'The Final Temple', *WTJ* 35 (1973): 156-89.
Coggins, Richard, 'An Alternative Prophetic Tradition?', in Coggins, Phillips, and Knibb (eds.), *Israel's Prophetic Tradition*, 77-94.
Coggins, Richard, Anthony Phillips, and Michael Knibb (eds.), *Israel's Prophetic Tradition* (Festschrift Peter R. Ackroyd; Cambridge: Cambridge University Press, 1982).
Collange, J.-F., *Énigmes de la deuxième épître de Paul aux Corinthiens: Étude exégétique de 2 Cor. 2:14–7:4* (SNTSMS 18; Cambridge: Cambridge University Press, 1972).
Collins, John J., 'The Development of the Sibylline Tradition', *ANRW* 20.1:421-59.
—'Prophecy, Apocalypse and Eschatology: Reflections on the Proposals of Lester Grabbe', in Grabbe and Haak (eds.), *Knowing the End from the Beginning*, 44-52.
—*Seers, Sibyls and Sages in Hellenistic-Roman Judaism* (Leiden: Brill, 1997).
Collins, John N., *Diakonia: Re-interpreting the Ancient Sources* (Oxford: Oxford University Press, 1990).
Collins, Nina L., 'Observations on the Jewish Background of 2 Corinthians 3:9, 3:7-8 and 3:11', in *Paul and the Corinthians: Studies on a Community in Conflict* (Festschrift Margaret Thrall; ed. Trevor J. Burke and J. Keith Elliot; NovTSup 109; Leiden: Brill, 2003), 75-92.
Collins, Raymond F., *First Corinthians* (SP 7; Collegeville, Minn.: Liturgical, 1999).
Conzelmann, Hans, *1 Corinthians* (Hermeneia; Philadelphia: Fortress, 1975).
Cousland, J.R.C., 'Prophets and Prophecy', *DNTB* 830-35.
Croatto, J. Severino, 'Jesus, Prophet Like Elijah, and Prophet-Teacher Like Moses in Luke–Acts', *JBL* 124 (2005): 451-65.

Crone, T.M., *Early Christian Prophecy: A Study of Its Origin and Function* (Baltimore: St. Mary's University, 1973).
Cross, Frank Moore, *Canaanite Myth and Hebrew Epic: Essays in the History of the Religion of Israel* (Cambridge, Mass.: Harvard University Press, 1973).
Crossan, John Dominic, *The Historical Jesus: The Life of a Mediterranean Jewish Peasant* (San Francisco: Harper, 1991).
Dahl, Nils Alstrup, *Studies in Paul: Theology for the Early Christian Mission* (Minneapolis: Augsburg, 1977).
Danker, Frederick W., *II Corinthians* (ACNT; Minneapolis: Augsburg, 1989).
Darr, Katheryn Pfisterer, 'Literary Perspectives on Prophetic Literature', in Mays, Petersen, and Richards (eds.), *Old Testament Interpretation*, 127-43.
Das, A. Andrew, *Paul, the Law, and the Covenant* (Peabody, Mass.: Hendrickson, 2001).
Dautzenberg, Gerhard, 'Überlegungen zur Exegese und Theologie von 2 Kor 4,1-6', *Bib* 82 (2001): 325-44.
—'Der Verzicht auf das apostolische Unterhaltsrecht: Eine exegetische Untersuchung zu 1 Kor 9', *Bib* 50 (1969): 212-32.
Davies, S., 'Remarks on the Second Epistle to the Corinthians 4:3,4', *BSac* 25 (1868): 23-30.
Davies, William D., *Torah in the Messianic Age and or Age to Come* (JBLMS 7; Philadelphia: Society of Biblical Literature, 1952).
Davis, George Brown, 'True and False Boasting in 2 Cor 10–13' (Ph.D. diss., University of Cambridge, 1999).
De Lorenzi, Lorenzo (ed.), *Paolo, Ministro del Nuovo Testamento (2 Co 2,14–4,6)* (SMBen; Rome: Benedictina, 1987).
DeNeui, Mark W., 'The Body, the Building and the Field: Paul's Metaphors for the Church in 1 Corinthians in Light of Their Usage in Greco-Roman Literature' (Ph.D. diss., University of Aberdeen, 2008).
Derrett, J. Duncan, '2 Cor 6:14: A Midrash on Dt. 22:10', *Bib* 59 (1978): 231-50.
deSilva, David A., 'Measuring Penultimate Against Ultimate Reality: An Investigation of the Integrity and Argument of 2 Corinthians', *JSNT* 52 (1993): 41-70.
—'Recasting the Moment of Decision: 2 Corinthians in Its Literary Context', *AUSS* 31 (1993): 3-16.
de Waard, Jan, *A Handbook on Isaiah* (TCT 1; Winona Lake, Ind.: Eisenbrauns, 1997).
Diamond, A.R., *The Confessions of Jeremiah in Context: Scenes of Prophetic Drama* (JSOTSup 45; Sheffield: JSOT, 1987).
Didier, Georges, 'Le Salaire du Désintéressement (I Cor. ix,14-27)', *RSR* (1955): 228-51.
Dinter, Paul E., 'Paul and the Prophet Isaiah', *BTB* 13 (1983): 48-52.
Dio Cassius, *Roman History* (trans. Earnest Cary and Herbert B. Foster; 9 vols; LCL; Cambridge, Mass.: Harvard University Press, 1914–27).
Dio Chrysostom (trans. J.W. Cohoon and H. Lamar Crosby; 5 vols.; LCL; Cambridge, Mass.: Harvard University Press, 1932–51).
Doughty, Darrell J., 'The Presence and Future of Salvation in Corinth', *ZNW* 66 (1975): 61-90.
Duff, Paul B., '"Glory in the Ministry of Death": Gentile Condemnation and Letters of Recommendation in 2 Cor 3:6-18', *NovT* 46 (2004): 313-37.
—'Metaphor, Motif, and Meaning: The Rhetorical Strategy Behind the Image "Led in Triumph" in 2 Corinthians 2:14', *CBQ* 53 (1991): 79-92.

—'The Mind of the Redactor: 2 Cor. 6:14–7:1 in Its Secondary Context', *NovT* 35 (1993): 160-80.
—'Transformed "from Glory to Glory": Paul's Appeal to the Experience of His Readers in 2 Corinthians 3:18', *JBL* 127 (2008): 759-80.
Duhm, Bernhard, *Das Buch Jesaia* (HKAT; Göttingen: Vandenhoeck & Ruprecht, 1892).
Dumbrell, William J., 'The Newness of the New Covenant: The Logic of the Argument in 2 Corinthians 3', *RTR* 61 (2002): 61-84.
Dungan, David L., *The Sayings of Jesus in the Churches of Paul: The Use of the Synoptic Tradition in the Regulation of Early Church Life* (Philadelphia: Fortress, 1971).
Dunn, James D.G., *Romans* (2 vols.; WBC 38; Dallas: Word, 1988).
Durham, John I., *Exodus* (WBC 3; Nashville: Thomas Nelson, 1987).
Egan, Rory B., 'Lexical Evidence on Two Pauline Passages', *NovT* 19 (1977): 34-62.
Ehrensperger, Kathy, *Paul and the Dynamics of Power: Communication and Interaction in the Early Christ-Movement* (LNTS 325; London: T&T Clark International, 2007).
Ekblad, Eugene Robert Jr., *Isaiah's Servant Poems According to the Septuagint: An Exegetical and Theological Study* (CBET 23; Leuven: Peeters, 1999).
Eutropius, *Eutropi Breviarium ab urbe condita cum versionbus graecis et Pauli Landolfique additamentis* (ed. Hans Droysen; Munich: Monumenta Germaniae Historica, 2000).
Evans, Craig A., 'Paul and the Prophets: Prophetic Criticism in the Epistle to the Romans (with Special Reference to Romans 9–11)', in *Romans and the People of God* (Festschrift Gordon D. Fee; ed. Sven K. Soderlund and N.T. Wright; Grand Rapids: Eerdmans, 1999), 115-28.
—'Prophet, Paul as', *DPL* 762-65.
Exum, J. Cheryl, '"Who Will He Teach Knowledge?": A Literary Approach to Isaiah 28', in *Art and Meaning: Rhetoric in Biblical Literature* (ed. David J.A. Clines, David M. Gunn, and Alan J. Hauser; JSOTSup 19; Sheffield: JSOT, 1982), 108-39.
Faierstein, Morris M., 'Why Do the Scribes Say That Elijah Must Come First?' *JBL* 100 (1981): 75-86.
Fascher, Erich, *ΠΡΟΦΗΤΗΣ: Eine sprach- und religionsgeschichtliche Untersuchung* (Giessen: Töpelmann, 1927).
Fee, Gordon D., 'II Corinthians 6:14–7:1 and Food Offered to Idols', *NTS* 23 (1977): 140-61.
—*The First and Second Letters to the Thessalonians* (NICNT; Grand Rapids: Eerdmans, 2009).
—*The First Epistle to the Corinthians* (NICNT; Grand Rapids: Eerdmans, 1987).
—*God's Empowering Presence: The Holy Spirit in the Letters of Paul* (Peabody, Mass.: Hendrickson, 1994).
—*Pauline Christology: An Exegetical-Theological Study* (Peabody, Mass.: Hendrickson, 2007).
Feldman, Louis H., 'Prophets and Prophecy in Josephus', *JTS* 41 (1990): 386-422.
Fitzgerald, John T., *Cracks in an Earthen Vessel: An Examination of the Catalogues of Hardships in the Corinthian Correspondence* (SBLDS 99; Atlanta: Scholars Press, 1988).
Fitzmyer, Joseph A., '"4Q Testimonia" and the New Testament', *TS* (1957): 513-37.
—*First Corinthians* (AB 32; New Haven: Yale University Press, 2008).
—'Glory Reflected on the Face of Christ (2 Cor 3:7–4:6) and a Palestinian Jewish Motif', *TS* 42 (1981): 630-44.

—'More About Elijah Coming First', *JBL* 104 (1985): 295-96.
—'Qumrân and the Interpolated Paragraph in 2 Cor 6:14–7:1', *CBQ* 23 (1961): 271-80.
Flint, Peter W., 'The Prophet David at Qumran', in Henze (ed.), *Biblical Interpretation at Qumran*, 158-67.
Flint, Peter W., and James C. VanderKam (eds.), *The Dead Sea Scrolls After Fifty Years: A Comprehensive Assessment* (2 vols.; Leiden: Brill, 1998–99).
Floyd, Michael H., 'Introduction', in Floyd and Haak (eds.), *Prophets, Prophecy, and Prophetic Texts*, 1-25.
—'The Production of Prophetic Books in the Early Second Temple Period', in Floyd and Haak (eds.), *Prophets, Prophecy, and Prophetic Texts*, 276-97.
Floyd, Michael H., and Robert D. Haak (eds.), *Prophets, Prophecy, and Prophetic Texts in Second Temple Judaism* (LHBOTS 427; London: T&T Clark International, 2006).
Fontenrose, Joseph, *The Delphic Oracle: Its Responses and Operations* (Berkeley: University of California Press, 1978).
—*Didyma: Apollo's Oracle, Cult, and Companions* (Berkeley: University of California Press, 1988).
Forbes, Christopher, 'Comparison, Self-Praise and Irony: Paul's Boasting and the Conventions of Hellenistic Rhetoric', *NTS* 32 (1986): 1-30.
—*Prophecy and Inspired Speech in Early Christianity and Its Hellenistic Environment* (WUNT 2/75; Tübingen: Mohr Siebeck, 1995).
Fox, Robin Lane, *Pagans and Christians in the Mediterranean World from the Second Century AD to the Conversion of Constantine* (New York: Penguin, 1986).
Fritsch, Charles, 'The Concept of God in the Greek Translation of Isaiah', in *Biblical Studies in Memory of H.C. Alleman* (ed. Jacob M. Myers, O. Reimherr, and H.N. Bream; Locust Valley, N.Y.: Augustin, 1960), 155-69.
Fung, Ronald Y.K., *The Epistle to the Galatians* (NICNT; Grand Rapids: Eerdmans, 1988).
Furnish, Victor Paul, *II Corinthians* (AB 32A; New York: Doubleday, 1984).
Galitis, Georg, 'Das Wesen der Freiheit: Eine Untersuchung zu 1 Ko 9 und seinem Kontext', in *Freedom and Love: The Guide for Christian Life (1 Co 8–10; Rm 14–15)* (ed. Lorenzo De Lorenzi; SMBen 6; Rome: St. Paul's Abbey, 1981), 127-47.
García Martínez, Florentino, and Eibert J.C. Tigchelaar, *The Dead Sea Scrolls Study Edition* (2 vols.; Leiden: Brill, 1997–98).
Gardner, Paul Douglas, *The Gifts of God and the Authentication of a Christian: An Exegetical Study of 1 Corinthians 8–11:1* (Lanham, Md.: University Press of America, 1994).
Garland, David E., *1 Corinthians* (BECNT; Grand Rapids: Baker, 2003).
—*2 Corinthians* (NAC 29; Nashville: Broadman & Holman, 1999).
—'Paul's Apostolic Authority: The Power of Christ Sustaining Weakness (2 Corinthians 10–13)', *RevExp* 86 (1989): 371-89.
Garrett, Susan R., 'The God of this World and the Affliction of Paul: 2 Cor 4:1-12', in *Greeks, Romans, and Christians: Essays in Honor of Abraham J. Malherbe* (ed. David L. Balch, Everett Ferguson, and Wayne A. Meeks; Minneapolis: Fortress, 1990), 99-117.
Gelin, Albert, 'Moses im Alten Testament', in *Moses in Schrift und Überlieferung* (ed. Albert Gelin; Düsseldorf: Patmos, 1963), 31-37.
Georgi, Dieter, *The Opponents of Paul in Second Corinthians* (Philadelphia: Fortress, 1985).

Gerstenberger, Erhard, 'The Woe Oracles of the Prophets', *JBL* 81 (1962): 249-63.
Giblet, Jean, 'Prophétisme et attente d'un messie prophète dans l'ancien Judaïsme', in *L'attente d'un Messie* (ed. Lucien Cerfaux; RechBib 1; Paris: Desclée de Brouwer, 1954), 85-130.
Gignilliat, Mark, '2 Corinthians 6:2: Paul's Eschatological "Now" and Hermeneutical Invitation', *WTJ* 67 (2005): 147-61.
—*Paul and Isaiah's Servants: Paul's Theological Reading of Isaiah 40–66 in 2 Corinthians 5.14–6.10* (LNTS 330; London: T&T Clark International, 2007).
—'A Servant Follower of the Servant: Paul's Eschatological Reading of Isaiah 40–66 in 2 Corinthians 5:14–6:10', *HBT* 26 (2004): 98-124.
Gillespie, Thomas W., *The First Theologians: A Study in Early Christian Prophecy* (Grand Rapids: Eerdmans, 1994).
Gitay, Yehoshua, *Prophecy and Persuasion: A Study of Isaiah 40–48* (Bonn: Linguistica Biblica, 1981).
Gleason, Randall C., 'Paul's Covenantal Contrast in 2 Corinthians 3:1-11', *BSac* 154 (1997): 61-79.
Gnilka, Joachim, '2 Cor 6:14–7:1 in the Light of the Qumran Texts and the Testaments of the Twelve Patriarchs', in *Paul and Qumran: Studies in New Testament Exegesis* (ed. Jerome Murphy-O'Connor; London: Geoffrey Chapman, 1968), 48-68.
Gnuse, Robert K., *Dreams and Dream Reports in the Writings of Josephus: A Traditio-Critical Analysis* (AGJU 36; Leiden: Brill, 1996).
Gooder, Paula R., *Only the Third Heaven? 2 Corinthians 12.1-10 and Heavenly Ascent* (LNTS 313; London: T&T Clark International, 2006).
Goodrich, John K., 'Paul, the *Oikonomos* of God: Paul's Apostolic Metaphor in 1 Corinthians and its Graeco-Roman Context' (Ph.D. diss., Durham University, 2010).
Gordon, Robert, 'From Mari to Moses: Prophecy at Mari and in Ancient Israel', in *Of Prophets' Visions and the Wisdom of Sages* (Festschrift R. Norman Whybray; ed. Heather A. McKay and David J.A. Clines; JSOTSup 162. Sheffield: JSOT, 1993), 63-79.
Goudge, Henry L., *The Second Epistle to the Corinthians* (WC; London: Methuen, 1927).
Goulder, Michael D., '2 Cor. 6:14–7:1 as an Integral Part of 2 Corinthians', *NovT* 36 (1994): 47-57.
—'Vision and Knowledge', *JSNT* 56 (1994): 3-71.
—'The Visionaries of Laodicea', *JSNT* 43 (1991): 15-39.
Grabbe, Lester L., *Judaic Religion in the Second Temple Period: Belief and Practice from the Exile to Yavneh* (London: Routledge, 2000).
—'Poets, Scribes, or Preachers: The Reality of Prophecy in the Second Temple Period', in Grabbe and Haak (eds.), *Knowing the End from the Beginning*, 192-215.
—'Prophetic and Apocalyptic: Time for New Definitions—And New Thinking', in Grabbe and Haak (eds.), *Knowing the End from the Beginning*, 107-33.
—'Thus Spake the Prophet Josephus…: The Jewish Historian on Prophets and Prophecy', in Floyd and Haak (eds.), *Prophets, Prophecy, and Prophetic Texts*, 240-47.
Grabbe, Lester L., and Robert D. Haak (eds.), *Knowing the End from the Beginning: The Prophetic, the Apocalyptic, and Their Relationships* (JSPSup 46; London: T&T Clark International, 2003).

Grässer, Erich, 'Paulus, der Apostel des neuen Bundes (2 Kor 2,14-4,6)', in De Lorenzi (ed.), *Paolo, Ministro del Nuovo Testamento*, 7-43.
—*Der zweite Brief an die Korinther* (2 vols.; ÖTK 8; Gütersloh: Gütersloher Verlagshaus; Würzburg: Echter, 2002).
Gray, Rebecca, *Prophetic Figures in Late Second Temple Jewish Palestine: The Evidence from Josephus* (Oxford: Oxford University Press, 1993).
Green, Gene L., *The Letters to the Thessalonians* (PNTC; Grand Rapids: Eerdmans, 2002).
Greenspahn, Frederick E., 'Why Prophecy Ceased', *JBL* 108 (1989): 37-49.
Grindheim, Sigurd, 'Apostate Turned Prophet: Paul's Prophetic Self-Understanding and Prophetic Hermeneutic with Special Reference to Galatians 3.10-12', *NTS* 53 (2007): 545-65.
—*The Crux of Election: Paul's Critique of the Jewish Confidence in the Election of Israel* (WUNT 2/202; Tübingen: Mohr Siebeck, 2005).
—'The Law Kills but the Gospel Gives Life: The Letter Spirit Dualism in 2 Corinthians 3.5-18', *JSNT* 84 (2001): 97-115.
Grudem, Wayne, '1 Corinthians 14.20-25: Prophecy and Tongues as Signs of God's Attitude', *WTJ* 41 (1979): 381-96.
—*The Gift of Prophecy in 1 Corinthians* (Lanham, Md.: University Press of America, 1982).
—*The Gift of Prophecy in the New Testament and Today* (Wheaton: Crossway, 2000).
Habel, Norman C., *The Book of Job* (OTL; London: SCM, 1985).
—'The Form and Significance of the Call Narratives', *ZAW* 7 (1965): 297-323.
Hackett, Jo Ann, *The Balaam Text from Deir 'Alla* (HSM 31; Chico, Calif.: Scholars Press, 1980).
Hafemann, Scott J., *2 Corinthians* (NIVAC; Grand Rapids: Zondervan, 2000).
—*Paul, Moses, and the History of Israel: The Letter/Spirit Contrast and the Argument from Scripture in 2 Corinthians 3* (PBM; Milton Keynes: Paternoster, 2005).
—'Paul's "Jeremiah" Ministry in Reverse and the Reality of the New Covenant', in *Remapping Mission Discourse* (Festschrift George Kuruvila Chavanikamannil; ed. Simon Samuel and P.V. Joseph. Dehradum: NTC; Delhi: ISPCK, 2008), 72-83.
—'Paul's Use of the Old Testament in 2 Corinthians', *Int* 52 (1998): 246-57.
—'"Self-Commendation" and Apostolic Legitimacy in 2 Corinthians: A Pauline Dialectic?', *NTS* 36 (1990): 66-88.
—*Suffering and Ministry in the Spirit: Paul's Defense of His Ministry in II Corinthians 2:14-3:3* (Grand Rapids: Eerdmans, 1990).
—*Suffering and the Spirit: An Exegetical Study of II Cor. 2:14-3:3 within the Context of the Corinthian Correspondence* (WUNT 2/19; Tübingen: Mohr Siebeck, 1986).
Hahn, Ferdinand, 'Der Apostolat im Urchristentum: seine Eigenart und seine Voraussetzungen', *KD* 20 (1974): 54-77.
Hajjar, Youssef, 'Divinités oraculaires et rites divinatoires en Syrie et en Phénicie à l'époque Gréco-Romaine', *ANRW* 18.4:2236-320.
Hall, Winfield Scott, 'Paul as a Christian Prophet in His Interpretation of the Old Testament in Romans 9-11' (Th.D. diss., Lutheran School of Theology at Chicago, 1982).
Hallo, William W., 'Isaiah 28.9-13 and the Ugaritic Abecedaries', *JBL* 77 (1958): 324-38.
Halperin, David J., 'Ascension or Invasion: Implications of the Heavenly Journey in Ancient Judaism', *Religion* 18 (1988): 47-67.

—*The Faces of the Chariot* (TSAJ; Tübingen: Mohr Siebeck, 1988).
Hanson, Anthony T., *The Living Utterances of God: The New Testament Exegesis of the Old* (London: Darton, Longman, & Todd, 1983).
—'The Midrash in 2 Corinthians 3: A Reconsideration', *JSNT* 9 (1980): 2-28.
Hanson, John S., 'Dreams and Visions in the Graeco-Roman World and Early Christianity', *ANRW* 23.2:1395-1427.
Hanson, Paul D., *The Dawn of the Apocalyptic* (Philadelphia: Fortress, 1975).
Harris, Murray J., *The Second Epistle to the Corinthians* (NIGTC; Grand Rapids: Eerdmans, 2005).
Hartley, John E., *The Book of Job* (NICOT; Grand Rapids: Eerdmans, 1988).
Hasel, Gerhard F., *The Remnant: The History and Theology of the Remnant Idea from Genesis to Isaiah* (AUM 5; Berrien Springs, Mich.: Andrews University Press, 1982).
Hawthorne, Gerald F., 'Prophets, Prophecy', *DJG* 636-42.
Hay, David M., 'Philo's View of Himself as an Exegete: Inspired, But Not Authoritative', *SPhilo* 3 (1991): 40-52.
Hayes, John H., 'The History of the Form-Critical Study of Prophecy', in MacRae (ed.), *SBL Seminar Papers, 1973*, 1:60-99.
Hays, Richard B., 'The Conversion of the Imagination: Scripture and Eschatology in 1 Corinthians', *NTS* 45 (1999): 291-412.
—*Echoes of Scripture in the Letters of Paul* (New Haven: Yale University Press, 1989).
—*First Corinthians* (IBC; Louisville: John Knox, 1997).
Heckel, Ulrich, 'Jer 9,22f. als Schlüssel für 2 Kor 10-13: Ein Beispiel für die methodischen Probleme in der gegenwärtigen Diskussion über den Schriftgebrauch bei Paulus', in *Schriftauslegung im antiken Judentum und im Urchristentum* (ed. Martin Hengel and Hermut Löhr; WUNT 73; Tübingen: Mohr Siebeck, 1994), 206-25.
—*Kraft in Schwachheit: Untersuchungen zu 2. Kor 10-13* (WUNT 2/56; Tübingen: Mohr Siebeck, 1993).
Heil, Christoph, 'Die Sprache der Absonderung in 2 Kor 6,17 und bei Paulus', in Bieringer (ed.), *The Corinthian Correspondence*, 717-29.
Heil, John Paul, *The Rhetorical Role of Scripture in 1 Corinthians* (SBLSBL 15; Atlanta: Society of Biblical Literature, 2005).
Hengel, Martin, *Judentum und Hellenismus* (WUNT 10; Tübingen: Mohr Siebeck, 1969).
Hengel, Martin, and Daniel P. Bailey, 'The Effective History of Isaiah 53 in the Pre-Christian Period', in *The Suffering Servant: Isaiah 53 in Jewish and Christian Sources* (ed. Bernd Janowski and Peter Stuhlmacher; trans. Daniel P. Bailey; Grand Rapids: Eerdmans, 2004), 75-146.
Henze, Matthias, 'Invoking the Prophets in Zechariah and Ben Sira', in Floyd and Haak (eds.), *Prophets, Prophecy, and Prophetic Texts*, 120-34.
Henze, Matthias (ed.), *Biblical Interpretation at Qumran* (Grand Rapids: Eerdmans, 2005).
Héring, Jean, *The First Epistle of Saint Paul to the Corinthians* (trans. A.W. Heathcote and P.J. Allcock; London: Epworth, 1962).
Herodian, *History of the Empire* (trans. C.R. Whittaker; 2 vols.; LCL; Cambridge, Mass.: Harvard University Press, 1969-70).
Herodotus, (trans. A.D. Godley; 4 vols.; LCL; Cambridge, Mass.: Harvard University Press, 1920-25).

Hickling, C.J.A., 'Paul's Reading of Isaiah', in *Papers on Paul and Other New Testament Authors* (vol. 3 of *Studia Biblica 1978: Sixth International Congress on Biblical Studies, Oxford 3-7 April 1978*; ed. Elizabeth A. Livingstone; JSNTSup 3; Sheffield: JSOT, 1980), 215-23.

Hill, David, *New Testament Prophecy* (London: Marshall, Morgan & Scott, 1979).

Hock, Ronald F., 'Paul's Tentmaking and the Problem of His Social Class', *JBL* 97 (1978): 555-64.

—*The Social Context of Paul's Ministry: Tentmaking and Apostleship* (Philadelphia: Fortress, 1980).

Hoffner, Harry A. Jr., 'Ancient Views of Prophecy and Fulfillment: Mesopotamia and Asia Minor', *JETS* 30 (1987): 257-65.

Hofius, Otfried, 'Erwägungen zur Gestalt und Herkunft des paulinischen Versöhnungsgedankens', in *Paulusstudien* (2d ed.; WUNT 51; Tübingen: Mohr Siebeck, 1994), 1-14.

Hoftijzer, Jacob, and Gerrit van der Kooij (eds.), *The Balaam Text from Deir 'Alla Reevaluated: Proceedings of the International Symposium Held at Leiden, 21-24 August 1989* (Leiden: Brill, 1991).

Hogeterp, Albert L.A., *Paul and God's Temple: A Historical Interpretation of Cultic Imagery in the Corinthian Correspondence* (BTS 2; Leuven: Peeters, 2006).

Holladay, William L., 'The Background of Jeremiah's Self-Understanding: Moses, Samuel, and Psalm 22', *JBL* 83 (1964): 153-64.

—*Jeremiah* (2 vols.; Hermeneia; Philadelphia: Fortress, 1986).

—'Jeremiah and Moses: Further Observations', *JBL* 85 (1966): 17-27.

—'Prototype and Copies: A New Approach to the Poetry–Prose Problem in the Book of Jeremiah', *JBL* 79 (1960): 351-67.

Holland, Glenn, 'Speaking Like a Fool: Irony in 2 Corinthians 10–13', in Porter and Olbricht (eds.), *Rhetoric and the New Testament*, 250-64.

Holland, Tom, *Contours of Pauline Theology: A Radical New Survey of the Influences on Paul's Biblical Writings* (Fearn: Christian Focus, 2004).

Hollenbach, Paul W., 'John the Baptist', *ABD* 3:887-89.

Hooker, Morna D., 'Beyond the Things That Are Written? St. Paul's Use of Scripture', *NTS* 27 (1981): 295-309.

—*The Signs of a Prophet: The Prophetic Actions of Jesus* (Harrisburg, Pa.: Trinity Press International, 1997).

Horn, Friedrich Wilhelm, *Das Angeld des Geistes: Studien zur paulinischen Pneumatologie* (FRLANT 154; Göttingen: Vandenhoeck & Ruprecht, 1992).

Horrell, David G., '"The Lord Commanded... But I Have Not Used...": Exegetical and Hermeneutical Reflections on 1 Cor 9.14-15', *NTS* 43 (1997): 587-603.

—'Paul's Narratives or Narrative Substructure? The Significance of "Paul's Story"', in *Narrative Dynamics in Paul: A Critical Assessment* (ed. Bruce W. Longenecker; Louisville: Westminster John Knox, 2002), 157-71.

—*The Social Ethos of the Corinthian Correspondence: Interests and Ideology from 1 Corinthians to 1 Clement* (SNTW; Edinburgh: T. & T. Clark, 1996).

—'Theological Principle or Christological Praxis? Pauline Ethics in 1 Corinthians 8.1–11.1', *JSNT* 61 (1997): 83-114.

Horsley, G.H.R., S.R. Llewelyn, R.A. Kearsley, and M. Harding (eds.), *New Documents Illustrating Early Christianity* (North Ryde, N.S.W.: The Ancient History Documentary Research Centre, Macquarie University, 1981–).

Horsley, Richard A., and John S. Hanson, *Bandits, Prophets, and Messiahs: Popular Movements in the Time of Jesus* (San Francisco: Harper & Row, 1988).
Hovenden, Gerald, *Speaking in Tongues: The New Testament Evidence in Context* (Sheffield: Sheffield Academic, 2002).
Hubbard, Moyer V., *New Creation in Paul's Letters and Thought* (SNTSMS 119; Cambridge: Cambridge University Press, 2002).
—'Was Paul Out of His Mind? Re-Reading 2 Corinthians 5.13', *JSNT* 70 (1998): 39-64.
Huffmon, Herbert, 'Prophecy (ANE)', *ABD* 5:477-82.
Hugenberger, Gordon P., 'The Servant of the Lord in the "Servant-Songs" of Isaiah: A Second Moses Figure', in *The Lord's Anointed: Interpretation of Old Testament Messianic Texts* (ed. Philip E. Satterthwaite, Richard S. Hess, and Gordon J. Wenham; Grand Rapids: Baker, 1995), 105-40.
Hulmi, Sini, *Paulus und Mose: Argumentation und Polemik in 2 Kor 3* (SFEG 77; Göttingen: Vandenhoeck & Ruprecht, 1999).
Hultgren, Stephen J., '2 Cor 6.14-7.1 and Rev 21.3-8: Evidence for the Ephesian Redaction of 2 Corinthians', *NTS* 49 (2003): 39-56.
Humphrey, Edith M., 'Ambivalent Apocalypse: Apocalyptic Rhetoric and Intertextuality in 2 Corinthians', in *The Intertexture of Apocalyptic Discourse in the New Testament* (ed. Duane F. Watson; SBLSymS 14. Leiden: Brill, 2002), 113-35.
—*And I Turned to See the Voice: The Rhetoric of Vision in the New Testament* (Grand Rapids: Baker, 2007).
Huppenbauer, Hanns Walter, 'Belial in den Qumrantexten', *TZ* 15 (1959): 81-89.
Hurd, John C., *The Origin of 1 Corinthians* (London: SPCK, 1965).
Hurwitz, Marshall S., 'The Septuagint of Isaiah 36-39 in Relation to That of 1-35, 40-66', *HUCA* 28 (1957): 75-83.
Hvidt, Niels Christian, *Christian Prophecy: The Post-Biblical Tradition* (Oxford: Oxford University Press, 2007).
Ingelaere, Jean-Claude, 'L'Inspiration Prophétique dans le Judaïsme: Le Témoignage de Flavius Josèphe', *ETR* 62 (1987): 236-45.
Jackson, T. Ryan, *New Creation in Paul's Letters* (WUNT 2/272; Tübingen: Mohr Siebeck, 2010).
Janzen, Waldemar, *Mourning Cry and Woe Oracle* (BZAW 125; Berlin: de Gruyter, 1972).
Jassen, Alex P., *Meditating the Divine: Prophecy and Revelation in the Dead Sea Scrolls and Second Temple Judaism* (STDJ 68; Leiden: Brill, 2007).
Jaubert, Annie, *La notion d'alliance dans le judaïsme aux abords de l'ère chrétienne* (Patristica Sorboniensia 6; Paris: Seuil, 1963).
Jeremias, Gert, *Der Lehrer der Gerechtigkeit* (SUNT 2; Göttingen: Vandenhoeck & Ruprecht, 1963).
Jeremias, Joachim, 'Chiasmus in den Paulusbriefen', *ZNW* 49 (1958): 145-56.
—*New Testament Theology* (New York: Scribner's, 1971).
Jobes, Karen H., and Moisés Silva, *Invitation to the Septuagint* (Grand Rapids: Baker, 2000).
Johanson, Bruce C., 'Tongues, A Sign for Unbelievers? A Structural and Exegetical Study of 1 Corinthians XIV. 20-25', *NTS* 25 (1979): 180-203.
Jones, F. Stanley, *'Freiheit' in den Briefen des Apostels Paulus: Eine historische, exegetische und religionsgeschichtliche Studie* (GTA 34; Göttingen: Vandenhoeck & Ruprecht, 1987).

Jones, Peter R., 'The Apostle Paul: A Second Moses According to II Corinthians 2:14–4:7' (Ph.D. diss., Princeton Theological Seminary, 1973).
—*La deuxième épître de Paul aux Corinthiens* (CEB 14; Edifac: Vaux-sur-Seine, 1992).
—Review of *Suffering and the Spirit: An Exegetical Study of II Cor. 2:14–3:3 within the Context of the Corinthian Correspondence*, by Scott J. Hafemann, *EvQ* 59 (1987): 374.
Josephus (trans. H. St. J. Thackeray, Ralph Marcus, Allen Wikgren, and Louis H. Feldman; 13 vols.; LCL; Cambridge, Mass.: Harvard University Press, 1926–65).
Judge, E.A., 'Cultural Conformity and Innovation in Paul: Some Clues from Contemporary Documents', *TynBul* 35 (1983): 3-24.
Justin, *Epitome of the Philippic History of Pompeius Trogus* (trans. J.C. Yardley; Atlanta: Scholars Press, 1994).
Kapelrud, Arvid S., 'The Main Concern of Second Isaiah', *VT* 32 (1982): 50-58.
Karrer, Martin, and Wolfgang Kraus (eds.), *Die Septuaginta — Texte, Kontext, Lebenswelten: Internationale Fachtagung veranstaltet von Septuaginta Deutsch (LXX.D), Wuppertal 20.-23. Juli 2006* (WUNT 219; Tübingen: Mohr Siebeck, 2008).
Käsemann, Ernst, 'Die Legitimität des Apostels: Eine Untersuchung zu 2 Korinther 10–13', *ZNW* 41 (1942): 33-71.
—'A Pauline Version of the "Amor Fati"', in *New Testament Questions of Today* (London: SCM, 1969), 217-35.
Kaufmann, Yehezkel, *Toldot ha-'Emunah ha-Yis-ra'elit* (4 vols.; Jerusalem: Bialik Institute, 1955).
Kautzsch, Emil, *De Veteris Testamenti locis a Paulo Apostolo allegatis* (Leipzig: Metzger und Wittig, 1869).
Kaye, Bruce N., 'Paul and His Opponents in Corinth: 2 Corinthians 6:14–7:1', in *Good News in History* (Festschrift Bo Reicke; ed. Ed. L. Miller; Atlanta: Scholars Press, 1993), 111-26.
Kennett, R.H., *Ancient Hebrew Social Life and Custom as Indicated in Law, Narrative and Metaphor* (Oxford: Oxford University Press, 1933).
Kilian, Rudolf, *Studien zu alttestamentlichen Texten und Situationen* (ed. W. Werner and J. Werlitz; SBAB 28; Stuttgart: Katholisches Bibelwerk, 1999).
Kim, Seyoon, *The Origin of Paul's Gospel* (WUNT 2/19; Tübingen: Mohr Siebeck, 1981).
—*Paul and the New Perspective: Second Thoughts on the Origin of Paul's Gospel* (WUNT 140; Tübingen: Mohr Siebeck, 2002).
Kingsbury, Jack Dean, 'Jesus as the 'Prophetic Messiah' in Luke's Gospel', in *The Future of Christology* (Festschrift Leander E. Keck; ed. Abraham J. Malherbe and Wayne A. Meeks; Minneapolis: Fortress, 1993), 29-42.
Kistemaker, Simon J., *1 Corinthians* (Grand Rapids: Baker, 1993).
Kitzberger, Ingrid, *Bau der Gemeinde: Das paulinische Wortfeld οἰκοδομή/(ἐπ)οικοδομεῖν* (FzB 53; Würzburg: Echter, 1986).
Klauck, Hans-Josef, *2 Korintherbrief* (NEchtB 8; Würzburg: Echter, 1986).
—'Erleuchtung und Verkündigung: Auslegungsskizze zu 2 Kor 4,1-6', in De Lorenzi (ed.), *Paolo, Ministro del Nuovo Testamento*, 267-316.
Knibb, Michael A., 'Prophecy and the Emergence of the Jewish Apocalypses', in Coggins, Phillips, and Knibb (eds.), *Israel's Prophetic Tradition*, 155-80.
Knight, Jonathan M., 'Apocalyptic and Prophetic Literature', in Porter (ed.), *Handbook of Classical Rhetoric*, 467-88.

Koch, Dietrich-Alex, 'Abraham und Mose im Streit der Meinungen: Beobachtungen und Hypothesen zur Debatte zwischen Paulus und seinen Gegnern in 2 Kor 11,22-23 und 3,7-18', in Bieringer (ed.), *The Corinthian Correspondence*, 305-24.
—*Die Schrift als Zeuge des Evangeliums: Untersuchungen zur Verwendung und zum Verständnis der Schrift bei Paulus* (BHT 69; Tübingen: Mohr Siebeck, 1986).
Koenig, Jean, *L'herméneutique analogique du Judaïsme antique d'après les témoins textuels d'Isaïe* (VTSup 33; Leiden: Brill, 1982).
Kraftchick, Steven J., 'Death in Us, Life in You: The Apostolic Medium', in *1 and 2 Corinthians* (ed. David M. Hay; vol. 2 of *Pauline Theology*; ed. Jouette M. Bassler, David M. Hay, and E. Elizabeth Johnson; Minneapolis: Fortress, 1993), 156-81.
Kruse, Colin G., 'Servant, Service', *DPL* 869-71.
Kwon, Duke L., 'Obfuscation and Restoration: Paul's Use of Isaiah in 1 Corinthians 14:20-25' (Th.M. thesis, Gordon-Conwell Theological Seminary, 2004).
Laberge, Léo, 'The Woe-Oracles of Isaiah 28–33', *EgT* 13 (1982): 157-90.
Lambrecht, Jan, 'Dangerous Boasting: Paul's Self-Commendation in 2 Corinthians 10–13', in Bieringer (ed.), *The Corinthian Correspondence*, 325-46.
—'The Defeated Paul, Aroma of Christ: An Exegetical Study of 2 Corinthians 2:14-16b', *LS* 20 (1995): 170-86.
—'The Favorable Time: A Study of 2 Corinthians 6,2a in Its Context', in Bieringer and Lambrecht (eds.), *Studies on 2 Corinthians*, 515-29.
—'The Fool's Speech and Its Context: Paul's Particular Way of Arguing in 2 Cor 10–13', *Bib* 83 (2001): 305-24.
—'The Fragment 2 Corinthians 6,14–7,1: A Plea for Its Authenticity', in Bieringer and Lambrecht (eds.), *Studies on 2 Corinthians*, 531-49.
—'Paul's Appeal and the Obedience to Christ: The Line of Thought in 2 Corinthians 10,1-6', *Bib* 77 (1996): 398-416.
—'"Reconcile Yourselves…": A Reading of 2 Corinthians 5,11-21', in Bieringer and Lambrecht (eds.), *Studies on 2 Corinthians*, 363-412.
—*Second Corinthians* (SP 8; Collegeville, Minn.: Liturgical Press, 1999).
—'Structure and Line of Thought in 2 Cor 2,14–4,6', in Bieringer and Lambrecht (eds.), *Studies on 2 Corinthians*, 257-94.
Lane, William L., 'Covenant: The Key to Paul's Conflict with Corinth', *TynBul* 33 (1982): 3-29.
Lang, Friedrich, *Die Briefe an die Korinther* (17th ed.; NTD 7; Göttingen: Vandenhoeck & Ruprecht, 1994).
Lange, Armin, *Die Handschriften biblischer Bücher von Qumran und den anderen Fundorten* (vol. 1 of *Handbuch der Textfunde vom Toten Meer*; Tübingen: Mohr Siebeck, 2009).
Lanier, David E., 'With Stammering Lips and Another Tongue: 1 Cor 14:20-22 and Isa 28:11-12', *CTR* 5 (1991): 259-86.
Leiman, Sid Z., 'Josephus and the Canon of the Bible', in *Josephus, the Bible, and History* (ed. Louis H. Feldman and G. Hata; Detroit: Wayne State University Press, 1989), 50-58.
Leonhardt-Balzer, Jutta, 'The Minor Prophets in the Judaism of the Second Temple Period', in *The Minor Prophets in the New Testament* (ed. Maarten J.J. Menken and Steve Moyise; LNTS 377; London: T&T Clark International, 2009), 7-25.
—'Philo und die Septuaginta', in Karrer and Kraus (eds.), *Die Septuaginta*, 623-37.
Lévi, Israel, *L'Ecclésiastique* (2 vols.; Paris: Ernest Lerous, 1898).

Levin, Cristoph, *Die Verheißung des neuen Bundes in ihrem theologiegeschichtlichen Zusammenhang ausgelegt* (FRLANT 137; Göttingen: Vandenhoeck & Ruprecht, 1985).
Levine, Baruch A., *Numbers 1-20* (AB 4A; New York: Doubleday, 1993).
Levison, John R., 'Did the Spirit Withdraw from Israel? An Evaluation of the Earliest Jewish Data', *NTS* 43 (1997): 35-57.
—'Philo's Personal Experience and the Persistence of Prophecy', in Floyd and Haak (eds.), *Prophets, Prophecy, and Prophetic Texts*, 194-209.
Lierman, John, *The New Testament Moses* (WUNT 2/173; Tübingen: Mohr Siebeck, 2004).
Lietaert Peerbolte, L.J., *Paul the Missionary* (CBET 34; Leuven: Peeters, 2003).
Lietzmann, Hans, *An die Korinther I, II* (rev. W.G. Kümmel; HNT 9; Tübingen: Mohr Siebeck, 1969).
Lim, Kar Yong, *'The Sufferings of Christ Are Abundant in Us' (2 Corinthians 1.5): A Narrative Dynamics Investigation of Paul's Sufferings in 2 Corinthians* (LNTS 399; London: T&T Clark International, 2009).
Lincoln, Andrew T., *Paradise Now and Not Yet* (SNTSMS 43; Cambridge: Cambridge University Press, 1981).
—'"Paul the Visionary": The Setting and Significance of the Rapture to Paradise in II Corinthians XII.1-10', *NTS* 25 (1979): 204-20.
Lindblom, Johannes, *Prophecy in Ancient Israel* (Oxford: Blackwell, 1962).
Lindgård, Fredrik, *Paul's Line of Thought in 2 Corinthians 4:16–5:10* (WUNT 2/189; Tübingen: Mohr Siebeck, 2005).
Litwa, M. David, 'Paul's Mosaic Ascent: An Interpretation of 2 Corinthians 12.7-9', *NTS* 57 (2011): 238-57.
Long, Frederick J., *Ancient Rhetoric and Paul's Apology: The Compositional Unity of 2 Corinthians* (SNTSMS 131; Cambridge: Cambridge University Press, 2004).
Longenecker, Richard N., *Galatians* (WBC 41; Nashville: Thomas Nelson, 1990).
Longinus, *On the Sublime* (trans. James A. Arieti and John M. Crossett; Texts and Studies in Religion 21; New York: Edwin Mellen, 1985).
Lorenzen, Stefanie, *Das paulinische Eikon-Konzept: Semantische Analysen zur Sapientia Salomonis, zu Philo und den Paulusbriefen* (WUNT 2/250; Tübingen: Mohr Siebeck, 2008).
Lundbom, Jack R., *Jeremiah* (3 vols.; AB 21; New York: Doubleday, 1999–2004).
Lust, Johan, *Messianism and the Septuagint: Collected Essays* (ed. K. Hauspie; BETL 178; Leuven: Leuven University Press, 2004).
MacGorman, Jack W., *The Gifts of the Spirit: An Exposition of 1 Corinthians 12–14* (Nashville: Broadman & Holman, 1974).
MacRae, George W., 'Anti-Dualist Polemic in 2 Cor. 4,6?', in *The New Testament Scriptures* (vol. 4.1 of *Studia Evangelica*; ed. F.L. Cross; TUGAL 102; Berlin: Akademie-Verlag, 1968), 420-31.
MacRae, George W. (ed.), *SBL Seminar Papers, 1973* (2 vols.; SBLSP 12; Missoula, Mont.: Scholars Press, 1973).
Malamat, Abraham, 'A Forerunner of Biblical Prophecy: The Mari Documents', in *Ancient Israelite Religion* (Festschrift Frank Moore Cross; ed. Patrick D. Miller Jr., Paul D. Hanson, and S. Dean McBride; Philadelphia: Fortress, 1987), 33-52.
Malan, Francois S., 'The Use of the Old Testament in 1 Corinthians', *Neot* 14 (1981): 134-70.

Malherbe, Abraham J., 'Determinism and Free Will in Paul: The Argument of 1 Corinthians 8 and 9', in *Paul in His Hellenistic Context* (ed. Troels Engberg-Pedersen; Edinburgh: T. & T. Clark, 1994), 231-55.
—*The Letters to the Thessalonians* (AB 32B; New York: Doubleday, 2000).
Maly, Karl, *Mündige Gemeinde* (Stuttgart: Katholisches Bibelwerk, 1967).
March, W. Eugene, 'Prophecy', in *Old Testament Form Criticism* (ed. John H. Hayes; San Antonio: Trinity University Press, 1974), 141-77.
Marshall, I. Howard, 'Acts', in Beale and Carson (eds.), *Commentary*, 513-606.
—'The Meaning of "Reconciliation"', in *Unity and Diversity in New Testament Theology* (Festschrift George E. Ladd; ed. Robert A. Guelich; Grand Rapids: Eerdmans, 1978), 117-32.
Marshall, Peter, *Enmity in Corinth: Social Conventions in Paul's Relations with the Corinthians* (WUNT 2/23; Tübingen: Mohr Siebeck, 1987).
—'A Metaphor of Social Shame: ΘΡΙΑΜΒΕΥΕΙΝ in 2 Cor. 2:14', *NovT* 25 (1983): 302-17.
Martin, Dale B., *Slavery as Salvation: The Metaphor of Slavery in Pauline Christianity* (New Haven: Yale University Press, 1990).
—'Tongues of Angels and Other Status Indicators', *JAAR* 59 (1991): 547-89.
Martin, Ralph P., *2 Corinthians* (WBC 40; Nashville: Thomas Nelson, 1986).
—*Reconciliation: A Study of Paul's Theology* (Atlanta: John Knox, 1981).
—*The Spirit and the Congregation: Studies in 1 Corinthians 12–15* (Grand Rapids: Eerdmans, 1984).
Martini, C.M., 'Alcuni temi letterari di 2 Cor. 4:6 e i racconti della conversione di San Paolo negli Atti', in *Studiorum Paulinorum Congressus Internationalis Catholicus 1961* (2 vols.; AnBib 17-18; Rome: Pontifical Biblical Institute, 1963), 1:461-74.
Martyn, J. Louis, *Galatians* (AB 33A; New York: Doubleday, 1997).
Mason, Rex, 'The Prophets of the Restoration', in Coggins, Phillips, and Knibb (eds.), *Israel's Prophetic Tradition*, 137-54.
Maurer, C., 'Grund und Grenze apostolischer Freiheit', in *Antwort: Karl Barth zum siebzigsten Geburtstag am 10. Mai 1956* (ed. Ernst Wolf, Charlotte von Kirschbaum, and Rudolf Frey; Zollikon-Zurich: Evangelischer, 1956), 630-42.
Maurizio, L., 'Anthropology and Spirit Possession: A Reconsideration of the Pythia's Role at Delphi', *JHS* 115 (1995): 69-86.
Mays, James Luther, David L. Petersen, and Kent Harold Richards (eds.), *Old Testament Interpretation: Past, Present, and Future* (Festschrift Gene M. Tucker; Edinburgh: T. & T. Clark, 1995).
Mays, James Luther, and Paul J. Achtemeier (eds.), *Interpreting the Prophets* (Philadelphia: Fortress, 1987).
Menzies, Allan, *The Second Epistle of the Apostle Paul to the Corinthians* (CGTC; Cambridge: Cambridge University Press, 1912).
Menzies, Robert P., *The Development of Early Christian Pneumatology, with Special Reference to Luke–Acts* (JSNTSup 54; Sheffield: JSOT, 1991).
Merklein, Helmut, 'Die Einheitlichkeit des ersten Korintherbriefes', *ZNW* 75 (1984): 153-83.
Metzger, Bruce M., *A Textual Commentary on the Greek New Testament* (Stuttgart: Deutsche Bibelgesellschaft, 1994).
Meyer, Jason C., *The End of the Law: Mosaic Covenant in Pauline Theology* (NACSBT 6; Nashville: Broadman & Holman, 2009).

Meyers, Carol L., and Eric M. Meyers, *Zechariah 9–14* (AB 25C; New York: Doubleday, 1993).
Michel, Otto, *Paulus und seine Bibel* (Darmstadt: Wissenschaftliche Buchgesellschaft, 1972).
Miller, Patrick D., Jr., 'The World and Message of the Prophets: Biblical Prophecy in Its Context', in Mays, Petersen, and Richards (eds.), *Old Testament Interpretation*, 97-112.
Mitchell, Margaret M., *Paul and the Rhetoric of Reconciliation: An Exegetical Investigation of the Language and Composition of 1 Corinthians* (Louisville: Westminster John Knox, 1993).
Momigliano, Arnaldo, 'From the Pagan to the Christian Sibyl: Prophecy as History of Religion', in *Nono Contributo alla Storia Degli studi Classici e del Mondo Antico* (ed. Riccardo di Donato; Storia e Letteratura: Raccolta di Studi e Testi 180; Rome: Edizioni di Storia e Letteratura, 1992), 725-44.
Moo, Douglas J., *The Epistle to the Romans* (NICNT; Grand Rapids: Eerdmans, 1996).
Morray-Jones, Christopher R.A., 'Paradise Revisited (2 Cor 12:1-12): The Jewish Mystical Background of Paul's Apostolate', *HTR* 86 (1993): 177-217, 256-92.
Motyer, J. Alec, *The Prophecy of Isaiah* (Downers Grove, Ill.: InterVarsity, 1993).
Moule, C.F.D., 'Fulfilment-Words in the New Testament', *NTS* 14 (1968): 293-320.
Moyise, Steve, *Paul and Scripture* (London: SPCK, 2010).
Müller, Ulrich B., *Prophetie und Predigt im Neuen Testament, Formgeschichtliche Untersuchung zu urchristliche Prophetie* (SNT 10; Gütersloh: Gütersloher Verlagshaus, 1972).
Munck, Johannes, *Christ and Israel: An Interpretation of Romans 9–11* (trans. Ingeborg Nixon; Philadelphia: Fortress, 1967).
—*Paul and the Salvation of Mankind* (trans. Frank Clarke; London: SCM, 1959).
Murphy-O'Connor, Jerome, 'A Ministry Beyond the Letter (2 Cor 3:1-6)', in De Lorenzi (ed.), *Paolo, Ministro del Nuovo Testamento*, 105-57.
—'Philo and 2 Cor 6:14–7:1', *RB* 95 (1988): 55-69.
—'Relating 2 Corinthians 6.14–7.1 to Its Context', *NTS* 33 (1986–87): 272-75.
Myers, Jacob M., and Edwin D. Freed, 'Is Paul also among the Prophets?', *Int* 20 (1966): 40-53.
Najda, Andrzej Jacek, *Der Apostel als Prophet: Zur prophetischen Dimension des paulinischen Apostolats* (Europäische Hochschulschriften 784; Frankfurt: Peter Lang, 2004).
Nasuti, Harry P., 'The Woes of the Prophets and the Rights of the Apostle: The Internal Dynamics of 1 Corinthians 9', *CBQ* 50 (1988): 246-64.
Ngunga, Abi T., 'Messianism in the Old Greek of Isaiah: An Intertextual Analysis' (Ph.D. diss., University of Aberdeen, 2010).
Nguyen, V. Henry T., *Christian Identity in Corinth: A Comparative Study of 2 Corinthians, Epictetus and Valerius Maximus* (WUNT 2/243; Tübingen: Mohr Siebeck, 2008).
—'God's Execution of His Condemned Apostles: Paul's Imagery of the Roman Arena in 1 Cor 4:9', *ZNW* 99 (2008): 33-48.
—'The Identification of Paul's Spectacle of Death Metaphor in 1 Corinthians 4.9', *NTS* 53 (2007): 489-501.

Nicklas, Tobias, 'Paulus — der Apostel als Prophet', in *Prophets and Prophecy in Jewish and Early Christian Literature* (ed. Joseph Verheyden, Korinna Zamfir, and Tobias Nicklas; WUNT 2/286; Tübingen: Mohr Siebeck, 2010), 77-104.

Nissinen, Martti, *Prophets and Prophecy in the Ancient Near East* (ed. Peter Machinist; SBLWAW 12; Atlanta: Society of Biblical Literature, 2003).

Nolland, John, *The Gospel of Matthew* (NIGTC; Grand Rapids: Eerdmans, 2005).

Oakes, Peter, 'Moses in Paul', in *La Construction de la figure de Moïse* (ed. Thomas Römer; Supplément à Transeuphratène 13; Paris: Gabalda, 2007), 249-61.

O'Brien, Peter T., *Gospel and Mission in the Writings of Paul: An Exegetical and Theological Analysis* (Grand Rapids: Baker, 1995).

—*The Letter to the Ephesians* (PNTC; Grand Rapids: Eerdmans, 1999).

O'Connor, Kathleen M., *The Confessions of Jeremiah: Their Interpretation and Role in Chapters 1–25* (SBLDS 94; Atlanta: Scholars Press, 1984).

O'Day, Gail R., 'Jeremiah 9:22-23 and 1 Corinthians 1:26-31: A Study in Intertextuality', *JBL* 109 (1990): 259-67.

Olley, John W., 'A Precursor of the NRSV? "Sons and Daughters" in 2 Cor 6.18', *NTS* 44 (1998–99): 204-12.

—*'Righteousness' in the Septuagint of Isaiah: A Contextual Study* (SBLSCS 8; Missoula, Mont.: Scholars Press, 1979).

Omanson, Roger L., 'Some Comments About Style and Meaning: 1 Corinthians 9:15 and 7:10', *BT* 34 (1983): 135-39.

Oostendorp, Derk William, *Another Jesus: A Gospel of Jewish-Christian Superiority in II Corinthians* (Kampen: Kok, 1967).

Origen, *Philocalia* (Cambridge: Cambridge University Press, 1893).

Oswalt, John N., *The Book of Isaiah* (2 vols.; NICOT; Grand Rapids: Eerdmans, 1986).

Parke, H.W., *Sibyls and Sibylline Prophecy in Classical Antiquity* (ed. B.C. McGing; London: Routledge, 1988).

Parke, H.W., and D.E.W. Wormell, *The Delphic Oracle I: The History* (Oxford: Blackwell, 1956).

Parker, Simon B., 'Official Attitudes Toward Prophecy at Mari and in Israel', *VT* 43 (1993): 50-68.

Parpola, Simo, *Assyrian Prophecies* (SAA 9; Helsinki: Helsinki University Press, 1997).

Patrick, Dale, and Allen Scult, *Rhetoric and Biblical Interpretation* (JSOTSup 82; Sheffield: Almond, 1990).

Pausanias, *Description of Greece* (trans. W.H.S Jones, H.A. Ormerod, and R.E. Whycherley; 5 vols.; LCL; Cambridge, Mass.: Harvard University Press, 1918–35).

Petersen, David L., *Late Israelite Prophecy: Studies in Deutero-Prophetic Literature and in Chronicles* (SBLMS 23; Missoula, Mont.: Scholars Press, 1977).

—*Possessed by God: A New Testament Theology of Sanctification and Holiness* (NSBT 1; Grand Rapids: Eerdmans, 1995).

—*The Prophetic Literature: An Introduction* (Louisville: Westminster John Knox, 2002).

Petersen, David L. (ed.), *Prophecy in Israel: Search for an Identity* (IRT 10; Philadelphia: Fortress, 1987).

Peterson, David, *Engaging with God: A Biblical Theology of Worship* (Leicester: Apollos, 1992).

Pfammatter, Josef, *Die Kirche als Bau: Eine exegetisch-theologische Studie zur Ekklesiologie der Paulusbriefe* (Analecta Gregoriana 110; Rome: Gregorian University Press, 1960).

Phillips, J.B., *The New Testament in Modern English* (New York: Macmillan, 1960).
Philo (trans. F.H. Colson, Ralph Marcus, and G.H. Whitaker; 12 vols.; LCL; Cambridge, Mass.: Harvard University Press, 1929-62).
Phua, Richard Liong-Seng, *Idolatry and Authority: A Study of 1 Corinthians 8.1-11.1 in the Light of the Jewish Diaspora* (LNTS 299; London: T&T Clark International, 2005).
Plato (trans. R.G. Bury, Harold North Fowler, W.R.M. Lamb, and Paul Shorey; 12 vols.; LCL; Cambridge, Mass.: Harvard University Press, 1914-35).
Plummer, Alfred, *A Critical and Exegetical Commentary on the Second Epistle of St. Paul to the Corinthians* (ICC 34; Edinburgh: T. & T. Clark, 1915).
Plutarch (trans. Frank Cole Babbitt, Harold Cherniss, P.A. Clement, Phillip H. de Lacy, Benedict Einarson, Harold North Fowler, W.C. Helmbold, H.B. Hoffleit, Edwin L. Minar Jr., Edward N. O'Neil, Lionel Pearson, Bernadotte Perrin, and F.H. Sandbach; 28 vols.; LCL; Cambridge, Mass.: Harvard University Press, 1914-2004).
Polk, Timothy, *The Prophetic Persona: Jeremiah and the Language of the Self* (JSOTSup 32; Sheffield: JSOT, 1984).
Polybius, *The Histories* (trans. W.R. Paton; rev. F.W. Walbank; 6 vols.; LCL; Cambridge, Mass.: Harvard University Press, 1922-2010).
Porter, J.R., 'The Origins of Prophecy in Israel', in Coggins, Phillips, and Knibb (eds.), *Israel's Prophetic Tradition*, 12-31.
Porter, Stanley E., 'Allusions and Echoes', in *As It Is Written: Studying Paul's Use of Scripture* (ed. Stanley E. Porter and Christopher D. Stanley; SBLSymS 50; Atlanta: Society of Biblical Literature, 2008), 29-40.
—*Καταλλάσσω in Ancient Greek Literature, with Reference to the Pauline Writings* (Cordoba: El Almendro, 1994).
Porter, Stanley E. (ed.), *Handbook of Classical Rhetoric in the Hellenistic Period (330 B.C.-A.D. 400)* (Leiden: Brill, 1997).
Porter, Stanley E., and Thomas H. Olbricht (eds.), *Rhetoric and the New Testament: Essays from the 1992 Heidelberg Conference* (JSNTSup 90. Sheffield: JSOT, 1993).
Potter, David, *Prophets and Emperors: Human and Divine Authority from Augustus to Theodosius* (Cambridge, Mass.: Harvard University Press, 1994).
Preisendanz, K., and A. Vogliano, 'Laminetta Magica Siciliana', *Acme* 1 (1948): 73-85.
Price, Simon, 'Delphi and Divination', in *Greek Religion and Society* (ed. P.E. Easterling and J.V. Muir; Cambridge: Cambridge University Press, 1985), 128-54.
Provence, Thomas E., '"Who Is Sufficient for These Things?" An Exegesis of 2 Corinthians 2:15-3:18', *NovT* 24 (1982): 54-81.
Pseudo-Philo, *Liber Antiquitatum Biblicarum* (trans. M.R. James; LBS; New York: KTAV, 1971).
Qimron, Elisha, 'Le-Pišrah šel Rešimat Nevi'e ha-Šeqer', *Tarbiz* 63 (1993): 273-75.
Quintillian, *The Orator's Education* (trans. Donald A. Russell; LCL; 5 vols.; Cambridge, Mass.: Harvard University Press, 2002).
Rad, Gerhard von, *Old Testament Theology* (trans. D.M.G. Stalker; 2 vols.; San Francisco: Harper & Row, 1965).
Radl, Walter, 'Alle Mühe umsonst? Paulus und der Gottesknecht', in *L'Apôtre Paul: Personnalité, style et conception du ministère* (ed. Albert Vanhoye; BETL 73; Leuven: Leuven University Press, 1986), 144-49.
Räisänen, Heikki, *Paul and the Law* (WUNT 29; Tübingen: Mohr Siebeck, 1983).
Redditt, Paul L., *Introduction to the Prophets* (Grand Rapids: Eerdmans, 2008).

Reiling, Jannes, 'The Use of ΨΕΥΔΟΠΡΟΦΗΤΗΣ in the Septuagint, Philo and Josephus', *NovT* 13 (1971): 147-56.
Rensberger, David, '2 Corinthians 6:14–7:1—A Fresh Examination', *Studia Biblica et Theologica* 8 (1978): 25-49.
Renwick, David A., *Paul, the Temple and the Presence of God* (BJS; 224; Atlanta: Scholars Press, 1991).
Reumann, John, 'Οἰκονομία = "Covenant"; Terms for *Heilsgeschichte* in Early Christian Usage', *NovT* 3 (1959): 282-92.
—'Οἰκονομία-Terms in Paul in Comparison with Lucan *Heilsgeschichte*', *NTS* 13 (1967): 147-67.
Richard, Earl, 'Polemics, Old Testament, and Theology: A Study of II Cor. III,1-IV,6', *RB* 88 (1981): 340-67.
Ringgren, Helmer, 'Prophecy in the Ancient Near East', in Coggins, Phillips, and Knibb (eds.), *Israel's Prophetic Tradition*, 1-11.
Rissi, Mathias, *Studien zum zweiten Korintherbrief: Der alte Bund-Der Prediger-Der Tod* (ATANT 56; Zurich: Zwingli, 1969).
Robbins, Vernon K., *The Tapestry of Early Christian Discourse: Rhetoric, Society, and Ideology* (London: Routledge, 1996).
Robertson, A.T., and Alfred Plummer, *A Critical and Exegetical Commentary on the First Epistle of St Paul to the Corinthians* (2d ed.; ICC 34; Edinburgh: T. & T. Clark, 1914).
Robertson, O. Palmer, 'Tongues: Sign of Covenantal Curse and Blessing', *WTJ* 38 (1975): 43-53.
Rochester, Kathleen, 'Prophetic Ministry in Jeremiah and Ezekiel' (Ph.D. diss., Durham University, 2009).
Rofé, Alexander, 'The Classification of the Prophetical Stories', *JBL* 89 (1970): 427-40.
Roloff, Jürgen, *Apostolat-Verkündigung-Kirche: Ursprung, Inhalt und Funktion des kirchlichen Apostelamtes nach Paulus, Lukas und den Pastoralbriefen* (Gütersloh: Gütersloher, 1965).
Rowe, C. Kavin, 'New Testament Iconography? Situation Paul in the Absence of Material Evidence', in *Picturing the New Testament: Studies in Ancient Visual Images* (ed. Annette Weissenrieder, Friederike Wendt, and Petra von Gemünden; WUNT 2/193; Tübingen: Mohr Siebeck, 2005), 289-312.
Rowland, Christopher, and Christopher R.A. Morray-Jones, *The Mystery of God: Early Jewish Mysticism and the New Testament* (CRINT 12; Leiden: Brill, 2009).
Sandnes, Karl Olav, *Paul — One of the Prophets? A Contribution to the Apostle's Self-Understanding* (WUNT 2/43; Tübingen: Mohr Siebeck, 1991).
—'Prophecy — A Sign for Believers (1 Cor 14,20-25)', *Bib* 77 (1996): 1-15.
Sass, Gerhard, 'Noch einmal: 2 Kor 6,14–7,1. Literarkritische Waffen gegen einen "unpaulinischen" Paulus?', *ZNW* 84 (1993): 36-64.
Savage, Timothy B., *Power Through Weakness: Paul's Understanding of the Christian Ministry in 2 Corinthians* (SNTSMS 86; Cambridge: Cambridge University Press, 1996).
Sawyer, John, *The Fifth Gospel: Isaiah in the History of Christianity* (Cambridge: Cambridge University Press, 1996).
Schaper, Joachim, 'Messianism in the Septuagint of Isaiah and Messianic Intertextuality in the Greek Bible', in *The Septuagint and Messianism* (ed. Michael A. Knibb; BETL 195; Leuven: Leuven University Press, 2006), 371-80.

Schille, Gottfried, *Die Apostelgeschichte des Lukas* (THKNT 5; Berlin: Evangelische Verlagsanstalt, 1983).
Schlatter, Adolf, *Paulus, Der Bote Jesu, Eine Deutung seiner Briefe an die Korinther* (Stuttgart: Calwer, 1969).
Schmeller, Thomas, 'Der ursprüngliche Kontext von 2 Kor 6.14–7.1 Zur Frage der Einheitlichkeit des 2. Korintherbriefs', *NTS* 52 (2006): 219-38.
—*Der zweite Brief an die Korinther (2Kor 1,1–7,4)* (EKKNT 8/1; Neukirchen–Vluyn: Neukirchener Verlage; Ostfildern: Patmos-Verlag, 2010).
Schmithals, Walter, *Gnosticism in Corinth* (trans. John E. Steely; Nashville: Abingdon, 1971).
Schnabel, Eckhard J., *Der erste Brief des Paulus an die Korinther* (HTA; Wuppertal: Brockhaus, 2006).
—*Law and Wisdom from Ben Sira to Paul: A Tradition-Historical Enquiry into the Relation of Law, Wisdom, and Ethics* (WUNT 2/16; Tübingen: Mohr Siebeck, 1985).
Schnelle, Udo, *Apostle Paul: His Life and Theology* (trans. M. Eugene Boring; Grand Rapids: Baker, 2005).
Schrage, Wolfgang, *Der erste Brief an die Korinther* (4 vols.; EKKNT 7/1-4; Zurich: Benziger; Neukirchen–Vluyn: Neukirchener Verlag, 1991–2001).
Schreckenberg, Heinz, *Ananke: Untersuchungen zur Geschichte des Wortgebrauchs* (Zetemata 36; Munich: Beck, 1964).
Schreiner, Josef, 'Jeremia 9,22.23 als Hintergrund des paulinischen "Sich-Rühmens"', in *Neues Testament und Kirche* (Festschrift Rudofl Schnackenburg; ed. Joachim Gnilka; Freiburg: Herder, 1974), 530-42.
Schreiner, Thomas R., *Paul, Apostle of God's Glory in Christ: A Pauline Theology* (Downers Grove, Ill.: InterVarsity, 2001).
—*Romans* (BECNT; Grand Rapids: Baker, 1998).
Schulz, Siegfried, 'Die Decke des Moses: Untersuchungen zu einer vorpaulinischen Überlieferung in II Cor. 3.7-18', *ZNW* 49 (1958): 1-30.
Schütz, John Howard, *Paul and the Anatomy of Apostolic Authority* (SNTSMS 26; Cambridge: Cambridge University Press, 1975).
Scott, James M., *2 Corinthians* (NIBCT; Peabody, Mass.: Hendrickson, 1998).
—*Adoption as Sons of God: An Exegetical Investigation into the Background of ΥΙΟΘΕΣΙΑ in the Pauline Corpus* (WUNT 2/48; Tübingen: Mohr Siebeck, 1992).
—'The Triumph of God in 2 Cor 2:14: Additional Evidence of Merkabah Mysticism in Paul', *NTS* 42 (1996): 260-81.
—'The Use of Scripture in 2 Corinthians 6.16c-18 and Paul's Restoration Theology', *JSNT* 56 (1994): 73-99.
Seeligmann, Isac Leo, 'δεῖξαι αὐτῷ φῶς', *Textus* 21 (2002): 107-27.
—*The Septuagint Version of Isaiah and Cognate Studies* (ed. Robert Hanhart and Hermann Spieckermann; FAT 40; Tübingen: Mohr Siebeck, 2004).
Seitz, Christopher R., 'How Is the Prophet Isaiah Present in the Latter Half of the Book? The Logic of Chapters 40–66', *JBL* 115 (1996): 219-40.
—'Isaiah 40–66', in *Introduction to Prophetic Literature, Isaiah, Jeremiah, Baruch, Letter of Jeremiah, Lamentations, Ezekiel* (vol. 6 of *The New Interpreter's Bible*; ed. Leander E. Keck; Nashville: Abingdon, 2001), 307-552.
—'On the Question of Divisions Internal to the Book of Isaiah', in *SBL Seminar Papers, 1993* (ed. Eugene H. Lovering, Jr.; SBLSP 32; Atlanta: Scholars Press, 1993), 260-66.

—*Prophecy and Hermeneutics: Toward a New Introduction to the Prophets* (Grand Rapids: Baker, 2007).
—'The Prophet Moses and the Canonical Shape of Jeremiah', *ZAW* 101 (1989): 3-27.
—'"You Are My Servant, You Are the Israel in Whom I Will Be Glorified": The Servant Songs and the Effect of Literary Context in Isaiah', *CTJ* 39 (2004): 117-34.
Senft, Christophe, *La première épître de saint Paul aux Corinthiens* (CNT 7; Neuchâtel: Delachaux & Niestlé, 1979).
Shanor, Jay, 'Paul as Master Builder: Construction Terms in First Corinthians', *NTS* 34 (1988): 461-71.
Sloan, Robert B., '2 Corinthians 2:14–4:6 and "New Covenant Hermeneutics"—A Response to Richard Hays', *BBR* 5 (1995): 129-54.
Smend, Rudolf, *Die Mitte des Alten Testaments* (ThSt 101; Zurich: EVZ-Verlag, 1970).
Smit, Joop, 'Argument and Genre of 1 Corinthians 12–14', in Porter and Olbricht (eds.), *Rhetoric and the New Testament*, 211-30.
—'The Rhetorical Disposition of First Corinthians 8:7–9:27', *CBQ* 59 (1997): 476-91.
—'Tongues and Prophecy: Deciphering 1 Cor 14,22', *Bib* 75 (1994): 175-90.
Smith, D. Moody, 'The Pauline Literature', in *It Is Written: Scripture Citing Scripture* (Festschrift Barnabas Lindars; ed. D.A. Carson and H.G.M. Williamson; Cambridge: Cambridge University Press, 1998), 265-91.
Smith, Morton, *Palestinian Parties and Politics that Shaped the Old Testament* (New York: Columbia University Press, 1971).
Sommer, Benjamin D., 'Did Prophecy Cease? Evaluating a Reevaluation', *JBL* 115 (1996): 31-47.
Stanley, Christopher D., *Arguing with Scripture: The Rhetoric of Quotations in the Letters of Paul* (London: T&T Clark International, 2004).
—*Paul and the Language of Scripture: Citation Technique in the Pauline Epistles and Contemporary Literature* (SNTSMS 74; Cambridge: Cambridge University Press, 1992).
Stanley, David M., 'The Theme of the Servant of Yahweh in Primitive Christian Soteriology, and Its Transposition by St. Paul', *CBQ* 16 (1954): 385-425.
Steck, Odil Hannes, *The Prophetic Books and Their Theological Witness* (trans. James D. Nogalski; St. Louis: Chalice, 2000).
Stegman, Thomas, *The Character of Jesus: The Linchpin to Paul's Argument in 2 Corinthians* (AnBib 158; Rome: Pontifical Biblical Institute, 2005).
Stendahl, Krister, *Paul Among Jews and Gentiles* (Philadelphia: Fortress, 1976).
Still, Todd D., 'Did Paul Loathe Manual Labor? Revisiting the Work of Ronald F. Hock on the Apostle's Tentmaking and Social Class', *JBL* 125 (2006): 781-95.
Stockhausen, Carol Kern, *Moses' Veil and the Glory of the New Covenant* (AnBib 116; Rome: Pontifical Biblical Institute, 1989).
Strabo, *Geography* (trans. Horace Leonard Jones; 8 vols.; LCL; Cambridge, Mass.: Harvard University Press, 1917–32).
Strachan, R.H., *The Second Epistle of Paul to the Corinthians* (MNTC; London: Hodder & Stoughton, 1935).
Strange, James F., '2 Corinthians 10:13-16 Illuminated by a Recently Published Inscription', *BA* 46 (1983): 167-68.
Stuart, Douglas, *Hosea–Jonah* (WBC 31; Waco: Word, 1987).
Stuhlmacher, Peter, *Das paulinische Evangelium* (FRLANT 95; Göttingen: Vandenhoeck & Ruprecht, 1968).

—'Das paulinische Evangelium', in *Das Evangelium und die Evangelien: Vorträge vom Tübinger Symposium 1982* (ed. Peter Stuhlmacher; WUNT 28; Tübingen: Mohr Siebeck, 1983), 157-82.

Suetonius (trans. J.C. Rolfe; 2 vols.; LCL; Cambridge, Mass.: Harvard University Press, 1914).

Sumney, Jerry L., *Identifying Paul's Opponents: The Question of Method in 2 Corinthians* (JSNTSup 40; Sheffield: JSOT, 1990).

Tabor, James D., *Things Unutterable: Paul's Ascent to Paradise in Its Greco-Roman, Judaic, and Early Christian Contexts* (Lanham, Md.: University Press of America, 1986).

Tacitus (trans. John Jackson, M. Hutton, Clifford H. Moore, and W. Peterson; rev. R.M. Ogilvie, E.H. Warmington, and Michael Winterbottom; 5 vols.; LCL; Cambridge, Mass.: Harvard University Press, 1914–37).

Teeple, Howard M., *The Mosaic Eschatological Prophet* (JBLMS 10; Philadelphia: Society of Biblical Literature, 1957).

Thielman, Frank, *From Plight to Solution: A Jewish Framework of Understanding Paul's View of the Law* (NovTSup 61; Leiden: Brill, 1989).

Thiselton, Anthony C., *The First Epistle to the Corinthians* (NIGTC; Grand Rapids: Eerdmans, 2000).

—'The "Interpretation" of Tongues: A New Suggestion in the Light of Greek Usage in Philo and Josephus', *JTS* 30 (1979): 15-36.

Thomas, John Christopher, '"An Angel from Satan": Paul's Thorn in the Flesh (2 Corinthians 12:7-10)', *JPT* 9 (1996): 39-52.

Thompson, John Arthur, *The Book of Jeremiah* (NICOT; Grand Rapids: Eerdmans, 1980).

Thrall, Margaret E., 'Conversion to the Lord: The Interpretation of Exodus 34 in II Cor. 3:14b-18', in De Lorenzi (ed.), *Paolo, Ministro del Nuovo Testamento*, 197-232.

—*A Critical and Exegetical Commentary on the Second Epistle to the Corinthians* (2 vols.; ICC 34; Edinburgh: T. & T. Clark, 1994).

—*Greek Particles in the New Testament: Linguistic and Exegetical Studies* (NTTS 3; Leiden: Brill, 1962).

—'The Pauline Use of ΣΥΝΕΙΔΗΣΙΣ', *NTS* 14 (1967–68): 118-25.

—'Paul's Journey to Paradise: Some Exegetical Issues in 2 Cor 12,2-4', in Bieringer (ed.), *The Corinthian Correspondence*, 347-63.

—'The Problem of II Cor. VI.14-VII.1 in Some Recent Discussion', *NTS* 24 (1977–78): 132-48.

Tiemeyer, Lena-Sofia, *For the Comfort of Zion: The Geographical and Theological Location of Isaiah 40–55* (VTSup 139; Leiden: Brill, 2010).

Tucker, Gene M., *Form Criticism of the Old Testament* (GBS; Philadelphia: Fortress, 1971).

—'Prophecy and the Prophetic Literature', in *The Hebrew Bible and Its Modern Interpreters* (ed. Douglas A. Knight and Gene M. Tucker; Chico, Calif.: Scholars Press, 1985), 325-68.

—'Prophetic Speech', *Int* 32 (1978): 31-45.

Turner, Max, *The Holy Spirit and Spiritual Gifts: Then and Now* (Carlisle: Paternoster, 1996).

Uddin, Mohan, 'Paul, the Devil and "Unbelief" in Israel (with Particular Reference to 2 Corinthians 3–4 and Romans 9–11)', *TynBul* 50 (1999): 265-80.

Urbach, Ephraim E., 'Matai Pasqa ha-Nevuah?', *Tarbiz* 17 (1945–46): 2-3, 9-11.
Utzschneider, Helmut, 'Flourishing Bones: The Minor Prophets in the New Testament', in *Septuagint Research: Issues and Challenges in the Study of the Greek Jewish Scriptures* (ed. Wolfgang Kraus and R. Glenn Wooden; SBLSCS 53; Atlanta: Society of Biblical Literature, 2006), 273-92.
VanderKam, James C. *The Dead Sea Scrolls Today* (Grand Rapids: Eerdmans, 1994).
—'The Prophetic-Sapiential Origins of Apocalyptic Thought', in *A Word in Season: Essays in Honour of William McKane* (Festschrift William McKane; ed. James D. Martin and Philip R. Davies; JSOTSup 42; Sheffield: JSOT, 1986), 163-76.
van der Kooij, Arie, 'The Septuagint of Isaiah and the Mode of Reading Prophecies in Early Judaism: Some Comments on LXX Isaiah 8–9', in Karrer and Kraus (eds.), *Die Septuaginta*, 597-611.
VanGemeren, Willem A., *Interpreting the Prophetic Word: An Introduction to the Prophetic Literature of the Old Testament* (Grand Rapids: Zondervan, 1990).
van Kooten, George H., *Paul's Anthropology in Context: The Image of God, Assimilation to God, and Tripartitie Man in Ancient Judaism, Ancient Philosophy and Early Christianity* (WUNT 232; Tübingen: Mohr Siebeck, 2008).
van Unnik, Willem Cornelis, '"With Unveiled Face": An Exegesis of 2 Corinthians iii 12-18', *NovT* 6 (1963): 153-69.
Versnel, H.S., *Triumphus: An Inquiry into the Origin, Development and Meaning of the Roman Triumph* (Leiden: Brill, 1970).
Vielhauer, Philipp, 'Oikodome: Das Bild vom Bau in der christlichen Literatur vom Neuen Testament bis Clemens Alexandrinus', in *Oikodome: Aufsätze zum Neuen Testament* (ed. Günter von Klein; TBü 65; Munich: Kaiser, 1979), 1-168.
Vieweger, Dieter, *Die Spezifik der Berufungsberichte Jeremias und Ezechiels im Umfeld ähnlicher Einheiten des Alten Testaments* (BEATAJ 6; Frankfurt: Peter Lang, 1986).
Wagner, J. Ross, 'The Heralds of Isaiah and the Mission of Paul: An Investigation of Paul's Use of Isaiah 51–55 in Romans', in Bellinger and Farmer (eds.), *Jesus and the Suffering Servant*, 193-222.
Walker, William O., '2 Corinthians 6.14–7.1 and the Chiastic Structure of 6.11-13; 7.2-3', *NTS* 48 (2002): 142-44.
Wallace, Daniel B., *Greek Grammar Beyond the Basics: An Exegetical Syntax of the New Testament* (Grand Rapids: Zondervan, 1996).
Wanamaker, Charles A., *The Epistles to the Thessalonians* (NIGTC; Grand Rapids: Eerdmans, 1990).
Wanke, Gunter, 'אוי und הוי', *ZAW* 78 (1966): 215-18.
Watson, Duane F., 'Paul and Boasting', in *Paul in the Greco-Roman World: A Handbook* (ed. J. Paul Sampley; Harrisburg, Pa.: Trinity Press International, 2003), 77-100.
—'Paul's Boasting in 2 Corinthians 10–13 as Defense of His Honor: A Socio-Rhetorical Analysis', in *Rhetorical Argumentation in Biblical Texts: Essays from the Lund 2000 Conference* (ed. Anders Eriksson, Thomas H. Olbricht, and Walter Übelacker; ESEC 8; Harrisburg, Pa.: Trinity Press International, 2002), 260-75.
Watson, Francis, *Paul and the Hermeneutics of Faith* (London: T&T Clark International, 2004).
Webb, Robert L., 'John the Baptist and His Relationship to Jesus', in *Studying the Historical Jesus: Evaluations of the State of Current Research* (ed. Bruce Chilton and Craig A. Evans; NTTS 19; Leiden: Brill, 1994), 179-229.

—*John the Baptizer and Prophet: A Socio-Historical Study* (JSNTSup 62; Sheffield: JSOT, 1991).
Webb, William J., *Returning Home: New Covenant and Second Exodus as the Context for 2 Corinthians 6.14–7.1* (JSNTSup 85; Sheffield: JSOT, 1993).
Weiss, Johannes, *Der erste Korintherbrief* (9th ed.; KEK 5; Göttingen: Vandenhoeck & Ruprecht, 1910).
Wellhausen, Julius, *Prolegomena to the History of Israel* (Atlanta: Scholars Press, 1994; repr. of *Prolegomena to the History of Israel*; trans. J. Sutherland Black and Allan Enzies, with preface by W. Robertson Smith; Edinburgh: Black, 1885; trans. *Prolegomena zur Geschichte Israels*; 2d ed.; Berlin: Reimer, 1883).
Wendland, Heinz-Dietrich, *Die Briefe an die Korinther* (13th ed.; NTD 7; Göttingen: Vandenhoeck & Ruprecht, 1972).
Westermann, Claus, *Basic Forms of Prophetic Speech* (trans. Hugh Clayton White; Philadelphia: Westminster, 1967).
—*Isaiah 40–66* (OTL; London: SCM, 1969).
Wevers, John William, *Septuaginta: Vetus Testamentum Graecum Auctoritate Academiae Scientiarum Gottingensis editum II.2: Leviticus* (Göttingen: Vandenhoeck & Ruprecht, 1986).
Wilcox, Peter, and David Paton-Williams, 'The Servant Songs in Deutero-Isaiah', *JSOT* 42 (1988): 79-102.
Wiles, Gordon P., *Paul's Intercessory Prayers: The Significance of the Intercessory Prayer Passages in the Letters of Paul* (SNTSMS 24; Cambridge: Cambridge University Press, 1974).
Wilk, Florian, *Die Bedeutung des Jesajabuches für Paulus* (FRLANT 179; Göttingen: Vandenhoeck & Ruprecht, 1998).
—'Gottes Wort und Gottes Verheißungen: Zur Eigenart der Schriftverwendung in 2Kor 6,14–7,1', in Karrer and Kraus (ed.), *Die Septuaginta*, 673-96.
—'Isaiah in 1 and 2 Corinthians', in *Isaiah in the New Testament* (ed. Steve Moyise and Maarten J.J. Menken; London: T&T Clark International, 2005), 133-58.
—'Paulus als Interpret der prophetischen Schriften', *KD* 45 (1999): 284-306.
Williams, James G., 'The Alas-Oracles of the Eighth Century Prophets', *HUCA* 38 (1967): 75-91.
Williamson, Lamar, 'Led in Triumph: Paul's Use of *Thriambeuō*', *Int* 22 (1968): 317-32.
Willis, Wendell, 'An Apostolic Apologia? The Form and Function of 1 Corinthians 9', *JSNT* 24 (1985): 33-48.
Wilson, Robert R., 'Early Israelite Prophecy', in Mays and Achtemeier (eds.), *Interpreting the Prophets*, 1-13.
—'Form-Critical Investigation of the Prophetic Literature: The Present Situation', in MacRae (ed.), *SBL Seminar Papers, 1973*, 1:100-27.
—'The Former Prophets: Reading the Book of Kings', in Mays, Petersen, and Richards (eds.), *Old Testament Interpretation*, 83-96.
—*Prophecy and Society in Ancient Israel* (Philadelphia: Fortress, 1980).
Windisch, Hans, *Paulus und Christus: Eine biblisch-religionsgeschichtlicher Vergleich.* (UNT 24; Leipzig: J.C. Hinrichs, 1934).
—*Der zweite Korintherbrief* (9th ed.; KEK 6; Göttingen: Vandenhoeck & Ruprecht, 1924).
Winston, David, 'Two Types of Mosaic Prophecy According to Philo', *JSP* 2 (1989): 49-67.

Winter, Bruce W., *Seek the Welfare of the City: Christians as Benefactors and Citizens* (vol. 1 of *First Century Christians in the Graeco-Roman World*; ed. Andrew D. Clarke; Grand Rapids: Eerdmans, 1994).

Wire, Antoinette Clark, *The Corinthian Women Prophets: A Reconstruction Through Paul's Rhetoric* (Minneapolis: Fortress, 1990).

Witherington, Ben, III, *Conflict and Community in Corinth: A Socio-Rhetorical Commentary on 1 and 2 Corinthians* (Grand Rapids: Eerdmans, 1995).

—*Grace in Galatia: A Commentary on St Paul's Letter to the Galatians* (Grand Rapids: Eerdmans, 1998).

—*Jesus the Seer: The Progress of Prophecy* (Peabody, Mass.: Hendrickson, 1999).

—'John the Baptist', *DJG* 383-91.

Wolff, Christian, *Jeremia im Frühjudentum und Urchristentum* (TUGAL 118; Berlin: Akademie-Verlag, 1976).

Wolff, Hans Walter, *Confrontations with Prophets: Discovering the Old Testament's New and Contemporary Significance* (Philadelphia: Fortress, 1983).

—'Prophecy from the Eighth Through the Fifth Century', in Mays and Achtemeier (eds.), *Interpreting the Prophets*, 14-26.

Wong, Kasper Ho-yee, *Boasting and Foolishness: A Study of 2 Cor 10,12-18 and 11,1a* (JDDS 5; Hong Kong: Alliance Bible Seminary, 1998).

Wright, Benjamin G., *No Small Differences: Sirach's Relationship to Its Parent Text* (SBLSCS 26; Atlanta: Scholars Press, 1989).

Wright, N.T., *The Climax of the Covenant: Christ and the Law in Pauline Theology* (Minneapolis: Fortress, 1992).

—*Jesus and the Victory of God* (Christian Origins and the Question of God 2; London: SPCK, 1996).

Xenophon (trans. W. Miller, C.L. Brownson, E.C. Marchant, O.J. Todd, and G.W. Bowersock; 7 vols.; LCL; Cambridge, Mass.: Harvard University Press, 1968–84).

Yates, John W., *The Spirit and Creation in Paul* (WUNT 2/251; Tübingen: Mohr Siebeck, 2008).

Young, Frances, and David F. Ford, *Meaning and Truth in 2 Corinthians* (BFT; London: SPCK, 1987).

Zeilinger, Franz, 'Die Echtheit von 2 Cor 6:14–7:1', *JBL* 112 (1993): 71-80.

Zimmerli, Walther, *Ezekiel 1* (Hermeneia; Philadelphia: Fortress, 1979).

Zmijewski, Josef, *Der Stil der paulinischen "Narrenrede": Analyse der Sprachgestaltung in 2 Kor 11,1–12,10 als Beitrag zu Methodik von Stiluntersuchungen neutestamentlicher Texte* (BBB 52; Cologne: Hanstein, 1978).

# INDEXES

## INDEX OF REFERENCES

| HEBREW BIBLE/ | | 32.33-34 | 132 | 22.9-11 | 217 |
|---|---|---|---|---|---|
| OLD TESTAMENT | | 34.1 | 163 | 32.19 | 230 |
| *Genesis* | | | | 34.10-12 | 12 |
| 1–2 | 202, 204 | *Leviticus* | | 34.10 | 26 |
| 1 | 214 | 1.9 LXX | 191 | | |
| 1.1-3 | 205 | 19.19 | 217 | *Joshua* | |
| 1.3 | 204 | 26 | 226, 228 | 12.22 | 55 |
| 1.27 | 202 | 26.11-12 | 225, 228, | | |
| 8.21 LXX | 191 | | 229 | *Judges* | |
| 20.7 | 11 | 26.11 | 225, 226 | 4.4 | 11 |
| 24.14 | 141 | | | 6.11-24 | 117 |
| 28.10-12 | 14 | *Numbers* | | 16.17 LXX | 159 |
| 35.7-11 | 14 | 11.12 | 132 | | |
| 40.1-23 | 14 | 12 | 11, 12 | *1 Samuel* | |
| 41.1-40 | 14 | 12.6 | 11 | 2.10 LXX | 175 |
| | | 12.7-8 | 26 | 2.18-21 | 17 |
| *Exodus* | | 12.8 | 11 | 3.1 | 33 |
| 3–4 | 82, 116, | 22–24 | 13, 14, 40 | 3.19-20 | 17 |
| | 117, 144 | 22.1-7 | 14, 60 | 6.2 | 55 |
| 3.14 | 122 | | | 9.11-14 | 17 |
| 4 | 160 | *Deuteronomy* | | 10.17-27 | 16 |
| 4.10-12 | 156 | 4.7 | 108 | 12.1-25 | 16 |
| 4.10 LXX | 118, 160 | 4.34-35 | 104 | 13.1-4 | 16 |
| 7.1 | 11 | 6.10-11 | 168 | 15.22-26 | 16 |
| 10.1-2 | 104 | 6.22 | 104 | 19.18-24 | 16 |
| 11.9-10 | 104 | 7.19 | 104 | | |
| 15.20 | 11 | 13 | 40 | *2 Samuel* | |
| 19–31 | 122 | 13.1-2 | 13 | 3.18 | 141 |
| 24 | 17 | 13.2-6 | 40 | 5.17-25 | 97 |
| 24.12 | 163 | 18.10-13 | 14, 60 | 7 | 229 |
| 29.18 LXX | 191 | 18.14-22 | 12 | 7.14 | 228-30 |
| 31.18 | 163 | 18.15-18 | 120, 125- | 22.29 LXX | 205 |
| 32–34 | 121, 122, | | 28, 144, | | |
| | 132, 199 | | 160 | *1 Kings* | |
| 32.15-16 | 163 | 18.18-22 | 40 | 11.29-40 | 69 |
| 32.31-34 | 144 | 18.18 | 160 | 11.29-39 | 17 |
| 32.31-32 | 132 | 20.5-6 | 168 | 11.31 | 22 |

## Index of References

| | | | | | |
|---|---|---|---|---|---|
| 13 | 18 | 106.6 LXX | 79 | 28–35 | 94, 97, 102, 107 |
| 13.11-31 | 40 | 106.13 LXX | 80 | | |
| 14.1-18 | 18 | 111.4 LXX | 205 | 28 | 93-95, 97, 100-108 |
| 16.1-4 | 18 | 112.4 | 205 | | |
| 18.16-29 | 19 | 113.1 | 141 | 28.1-7 | 99 |
| 18.16-19 | 16 | | | 28.1-6 | 94 |
| 18.20-40 | 13 | *Isaiah* | | 28.1-4 | 95 |
| 18.21 | 18 | 1–39 | 136 | 28.5-6 | 95 |
| 18.39 | 108 | 1–12 | 207 | 28.7-13 | 94-96 |
| 19 | 17 | 1.19 | 101 | 28.7-9 LXX | 100 |
| 19.11-13 | 18 | 1.20 | 101 | 28.7-8 | 95 |
| 21.17-19 | 22 | 2.5 | 208 | 28.9-10 | 95, 96 |
| 22 | 18 | 3.12 | 22 | 28.10 | 96 |
| 22.1-28 | 40 | 4.5 | 208 | 28.11-13 | 96 |
| 22.2 LXX | 79 | 6 | 26, 153 | 28.11-12 | 91, 93, 94, 97, 98, 101, 108 |
| 22.19-23 | 26 | 6.1-13 | 17 | | |
| | | 6.1-3 | 117 | | |
| *2 Kings* | | 6.1 | 143 | 28.11 | 96, 99 |
| 1.3-4 | 22 | 6.5 | 83 | 28.12 | 96, 99-101 |
| 1.6 | 22 | 7 | 104 | 28.13 | 95-98, 100, 101 |
| 20.5-6 | 22 | 7.16 | 104 | | |
| 21.1-6 | 14, 60 | 7.17 | 104 | 28.14-22 | 94, 96 |
| | | 8.1-10 | 207 | 28.16-17 | 97 |
| *2 Chronicles* | | 8.1-4 | 69 | 28.21 | 97 |
| 33.1-6 | 14, 60 | 8.11 | 82 | 28.23-29 | 94, 97 |
| | | 8.14-15 | 97 | 28.29 | 97 |
| *Ezra* | | 8.23–9.6 | 207 | 29.13-14 | 22 |
| 5.1-2 | 17 | 9 | 207-10, 212, 214 | 30.9 | 101 |
| | | | | 30.15 | 101 |
| *Nehemiah* | | 9.1-7 LXX | 207, 208 | 30.26 | 208 |
| 9.10 | 104 | 9.1 | 205-207, 210, 212 | 30.30 | 209 |
| | | | | 33.19 | 97 |
| *Job* | | 9.1 LXX | 207 | 39.2 | 209 |
| 1.21 LXX | 159 | 9.2-6 | 207 | 40–66 | 136, 139-41, 144, 149, 151, 208 |
| 5.19 LXX | 79 | 9.2 | 205-10, 212 | | |
| 15.24 LXX | 79 | | | | |
| 36–37 | 206 | 9.3-7 LXX | 207 | | |
| 37 | 206 | 9.4-5 LXX | 208 | 40–55 | 140, 145, 147, 155 |
| 37.14-20 | 206 | 9.5-6 | 212 | | |
| 37.15 | 205, 206 | 9.6-7 LXX | 208, 212 | 40.1-10 | 192, 193 |
| | | 10–11 | 207 | 40.1 | 63 |
| *Psalms* | | 14 | 242, 243 | 40.3-5 | 144 |
| 17.29 LXX | 205 | 14.12-15 | 241, 242 | 40.9 | 63 |
| 18.28 | 205 | 14.15-20 | 242 | 40.27 | 141 |
| 21.10 LXX | 159 | 20.3 | 141 | 41.8 | 141 |
| 24.17 LXX | 79 | 26.9 | 208 | 41.17-20 | 144 |
| 74.9 | 29, 30 | 26.16–27.6 | 193 | 42.1-4 | 136, 141 |

| Isaiah (cont.) | | 50.4-9 | 136, 142, | 60.1-3 | 208, 212 |
|---|---|---|---|---|---|
| 42.1 | 141 | | 208 | 60.1 | 210 |
| 42.6-7 | 206 | 50.4 | 156 | 60.3 | 208 |
| 42.6 | 210 | 50.6 | 143 | 60.4-7 | 194 |
| 42.7 | 136 | 50.10-11 | 210 | 60.4 | 230 |
| 42.13 | 193 | 50.10 | 208-10 | 60.19-20 | 208 |
| 42.14-16 | 144 | 50.10 LXX | 208 | 60.19 | 208 |
| 42.16 | 208, 210 | 50.11 | 209 | 61.1-4 | 155 |
| 42.18-25 | 149 | 51.3 | 63 | 61.2 | 63 |
| 42.18-19 | 142 | 51.4-11 | 193 | 62.1 | 208, 210 |
| 42.23 | 101 | 51.4-5 | 208 | 63.1-6 | 193 |
| 42.24 | 101 | 51.9-10 | 144, 193 | 63.4 | 63 |
| 43.1-9 | 141 | 52 | 227, 229 | 63.11-12 | 13 |
| 43.1-3 | 144 | 52.7 | 137, 155 | 65.7-8 | 23 |
| 43.6 | 230 | 52.9 | 63 | 65.13-15 | 23 |
| 43.14-21 | 144 | 52.10-12 | 140 | 65.16-17 | 141 |
| 43.18-19 | 141 | 52.10 | 148 | | |
| 43.24 | 149 | 52.11-12 | 144, 228 | *Jeremiah* | |
| 44–46 | 108 | 52.11 | 227 | 1.1 | 17 |
| 44.24-26 | 14, 60 | 52.13–53.12 | 136, 143, | 1.4-10 | 117, 174 |
| 45 | 108, 110 | | 144, 148, | 1.5 | 136, 159 |
| 45.1 | 140 | | 209 | 1.6 | 160 |
| 45.7 | 208 | 52.13 | 143 | 1.7 | 160 |
| 45.14 | 108-10 | 52.15 | 138 | 1.9 | 160 |
| 45.20-25 | 109 | 53 | 143, 210, | 1.10 | 166, 167, |
| 45.22-25 | 109 | | 212, 214 | | 174 |
| 47.13-15 | 14 | 53.1 | 137, 155 | 1.10 LXX | 166 |
| 48.8 | 142 | 53.5-6 | 149 | 1.13-19 | 168 |
| 49 | 156 | 53.10-12 LXX | 209 | 4.13 | 83 |
| 49.1-6 | 136, 142, | 53.10 | 149, 155 | 4.31 | 83 |
| | 144, 148 | 53.11 | 208, 211, | 5.4-5 | 181 |
| 49.1 | 137, 159 | | 212 | 6.4 | 83 |
| 49.2 | 156 | 53.11 LXX | 209, 210 | 7.23 | 226 |
| 49.3 | 87, 142 | 53.12 | 149 | 7.24 | 101 |
| 49.4 | 138 | 55.12-13 | 144 | 7.25 | 23 |
| 49.5-6 | 142 | 56–66 | 140, 154, | 7.26 | 101 |
| 49.5 | 87 | | 155 | 9 | 181, 182 |
| 49.6 | 135, 206, | 56.7 | 194 | 9.15 LXX | 80 |
| | 210 | 56.12–57.1 | 23 | 9.22-23 LXX | 158, 175, |
| 49.7 | 87 | 57.1 | 155 | | 181, 183 |
| 49.8-12 | 144 | 57.2 | 155 | 10.19 | 83 |
| 49.8 | 140, 151, | 57.14 | 192 | 11.4 | 226 |
| | 152, 155, | 57.15 | 143 | 11.7 | 23 |
| | 156 | 57.18 | 63 | 11.18–12.6 | 177 |
| 49.13 | 63 | 59 | 155 | 11.20 | 173 |
| 49.22 | 230 | 59.9 | 208 | 12.1-10 | 186 |
| 50 | 209 | 59.15-20 | 193 | 12.1-3 | 173 |

| | | | | | | |
|---|---|---|---|---|---|---|
| 12.14-17 | 166, 167 | 30.22 | 226 | 28.2 | 241 | |
| 12.14 LXX | 167 | 31 | 129, 158, | 28.8-10 | 242 | |
| 12.15 LXX | 167 | | 174 | 28.13 | 241 | |
| 12.17 | 167 | 31.1 | 226 | 28.24 | 241 | |
| 12.17 LXX | 167 | 31.4-5 | 166 | 36 | 129 | |
| 13.11 | 101 | 31.9 | 230 | 36.8 | 55 | |
| 15.1 | 13, 15 | 31.27-40 | 174 | 36.26-27 | 165 | |
| 15.10-21 | 177 | 31.27-28 | 166, 167 | 36.26 | 163, 165 | |
| 15.10 | 83 | 31.28 | 167 | 36.36 | 168 | |
| 15.15 | 173 | 31.33 | 226 | 37 | 226, 228 | |
| 16.11-13 | 22 | 32.37 | 23 | 37.1 | 82 | |
| 17.12-18 | 177 | 32.38 | 226 | 37.27 | 225, 226, | |
| 17.18 | 173 | 33.6 | 23 | | 228, 229 | |
| 18.7-11 | 166, 167 | 34.5 | 83 | | | |
| 18.7 | 167 | 35.7 | 166 | *Daniel* | | |
| 18.7 LXX | 167 | 36.8 | 55 | 2 | 14 | |
| 18.18-23 | 177 | 38 | 162, 163, | 2.46-47 | 108 | |
| 18.21-23 | 173 | | 165, 183 | 4 | 14 | |
| 19.1-13 | 69 | 38 LXX | 165 | 7–12 | 14 | |
| 20.7-18 | 84, 177 | 38.28 LXX | 167 | 8–12 | 34 | |
| 20.7-10 | 82 | 38.31 LXX | 163 | | | |
| 20.11 | 159 | 38.33 LXX | 164 | *Hosea* | | |
| 20.14-18 | 83 | 42.10 | 166, 167, | 1.9 | 24 | |
| 21.8-10 | 168 | | 174 | 1.10 | 230 | |
| 22.18 | 83 | 45.2 | 83 | 2.14-15 | 24 | |
| 23.15 | 231 | 45.3 | 83 | 3.4-5 | 24 | |
| 23.16-22 | 26 | 45.4 | 166, 167 | 4.6 | 24 | |
| 23.18-22 | 159 | 49.10 LXX | 166 | 5.7 | 24 | |
| 24.6 | 166, 167, | 49.10 | 167 | 5.14 | 24 | |
| | 174 | 51.35 LXX | 167 | 6.5 | 23 | |
| 24.7 | 226 | | | 7.16 | 24 | |
| 25.4-11 | 173 | *Ezekiel* | | 8.13-14 | 24 | |
| 25.7 | 101 | 1 | 240 | 9.3 | 24 | |
| 26.15 | 159 | 1.1–3.11 | 117 | 9.7-8 | 23 | |
| 27.9 | 22 | 1.1 | 17 | 9.17 | 24 | |
| 27.16 | 22 | 2.1-8 | 240 | 10.15 | 24 | |
| 28 | 24, 40 | 2.6 LXX | 240 | 11.5-6 | 24 | |
| 28.2-4 | 22 | 3.14-19 | 82 | 12.10 | 23 | |
| 28.5-17 | 159 | 4–5 | 69 | 12.13 | 23 | |
| 29.5 | 166, 167 | 11.19 | 163 | | | |
| 29.10-11 | 23 | 13.9 | 29, 30 | *Joel* | | |
| 29.21-24 | 40 | 20 | 232 | 1.1–2.27 | 24 | |
| 29.24-32 | 40 | 20.32-44 | 229 | 2.11 | 118 | |
| 29.26-27 | 17 | 20.34 | 228, 232 | | | |
| 29.28 | 166 | 20.41 | 191, 194 | *Amos* | | |
| 30.3-22 | 174 | 20.41 LXX | 191 | 2.6-8 | 23 | |
| 30.10 | 141 | 28 | 241-43 | 2.11-12 | 23 | |

## Index of References

| Amos (cont.) | | New Testament | | Luke | |
|---|---|---|---|---|---|
| 3.2 | 23 | Matthew | | 1.41 | 62 |
| 3.7-8 | 82, 87 | 3.1-12 | 66 | 1.67 | 62 |
| 4.1-2 | 23 | 3.1-6 | 64 | 1.68-79 | 62 |
| 6.11-12 | 23 | 3.7-10 | 64 | 2.25-35 | 63 |
| 7 | 24 | 5.17 | 170 | 2.25 | 63 |
| 7.10-13 | 17 | 9.36 | 66 | 2.26 | 63 |
| 7.14 | 24 | 11.2-6 | 65 | 2.29-32 | 63 |
| 7.15 | 24 | 11.9 | 64, 127 | 2.29 | 63 |
| 7.16-17 | 23 | 11.14 | 127 | 2.32 | 135, 136 |
| 8.4-8 | 23 | 12.28 | 180 | 2.34-35 | 63 |
| 9.14 | 168 | 12.38-42 | 66 | 2.36 | 63 |
| | | 13.57 | 65 | 3.1-20 | 66 |
| Obadiah | | 17.5 | 127 | 3.2 | 64 |
| 1–21 | 24 | 17.12 | 127 | 3.3 | 64 |
| | | 21.11 | 65 | 3.21-22 | 68 |
| Jonah | | 21.12 | 66 | 3.30-35 | 68 |
| 1 | 82 | 21.23-27 | 64 | 4.16-30 | 68 |
| | | 21.46 | 65 | 4.16-21 | 65 |
| Micah | | 23.38 | 66 | 7.11-17 | 66 |
| 3.7 | 55 | 24.2 | 170 | 7.16 | 65 |
| 3.9-12 | 23 | 26.28 | 163 | 7.18-23 | 65 |
| 5.5 | 101 | 26.61 | 170 | 7.26 | 64 |
| 6.4 | 13 | | | 9.12 | 170 |
| 7.13 | 23 | Mark | | 9.19-20 | 68 |
| | | 1.2-8 | 66 | 9.35 | 68 |
| Zephaniah | | 1.4-8 | 63 | 10.13-15 | 66 |
| 1.13 | 168 | 1.4 | 64 | 11.29-32 | 66 |
| | | 1.7-8 | 65 | 11.32 | 66 |
| Zechariah | | 1.14-15 | 66 | 13.3-5 | 66 |
| 1–8 | 30 | 6.4 | 65 | 13.31-33 | 65 |
| 1.4-6 | 24 | 6.12 | 66 | 13.35 | 66 |
| 1.4 | 101 | 6.14-16 | 65 | 19.7 | 170 |
| 7.3 | 55 | 6.15 | 127 | 19.45-48 | 66 |
| 7.4-12 | 24 | 6.17-29 | 64 | 20.6 | 64 |
| 7.13 | 101 | 6.18 | 64 | 21.6 | 170 |
| 8 | 110 | 6.34 | 66 | 22.20 | 163 |
| 8.9 | 24 | 8.28 | 65, 127 | 23.2 | 170 |
| 8.23 | 108 | 9.7 | 127 | 24.19 | 65 |
| 9–14 | 30, 34 | 11.15-19 | 66 | 24.27 | 127 |
| 10.2 | 55 | 11.32 | 64 | | |
| 13.1-6 | 30 | 13.2 | 170 | John | |
| 13.2-3 | 29 | 14.24 | 163 | 1.19-28 | 64 |
| | | 14.58 | 170 | 1.21 | 127 |
| Malachi | | 15.29 | 170 | 1.25 | 127 |
| 3.1 | 192 | | | | |
| 4.4 | 13 | | | | |

| | | | | | |
|---|---|---|---|---|---|
| 1.45 | 127 | 6.17 | 190 | 3.14 | 88, 169, 171 |
| 4.19 | 65 | 7.25 | 190 | | |
| 5.33-36 | 64 | 9.3 | 132, 147 | 3.18 | 200 |
| 5.46 | 127 | 9.5 | 147 | 4.1 | 86 |
| 6.14 | 127 | 9.27 | 101 | 4.7-13 | 217 |
| 7.40 | 127 | 9.31 | 180 | 4.9 | 189 |
| 7.52 | 65 | 9.33 | 101 | 5.9-11 | 219 |
| 9.17 | 65 | 10.6-8 | 101 | 5.13 | 219 |
| 10.20 | 105 | 10.9 | 202 | 6.6 | 201 |
| 10.34 | 93 | 10.14-18 | 4 | 7.5 | 217 |
| 12.33 | 69 | 10.14 | 137 | 7.12-15 | 201 |
| 18.32 | 69 | 10.15-16 | 137 | 7.22-23 | 203 |
| 21.19 | 69 | 10.16 | 133 | 7.26 | 79 |
| | | 10.20 | 133 | 7.31 | 89 |
| Acts | | 11.8 | 101 | 7.37 | 79 |
| 2.4 | 99 | 11.25-36 | 4 | 8 | 73 |
| 3.22 | 65, 127 | 11.33 | 190 | 8.1–11.1 | 73-75, 79, 89 |
| 5.38 | 170 | 12.2 | 200 | | |
| 5.39 | 170 | 12.3 | 178 | 8.1 | 169, 171 |
| 6.14 | 170 | 13.5 | 79, 81 | 8.7 | 217 |
| 7.37 | 127 | 14.19 | 169, 170 | 8.10 | 169, 171, 218 |
| 9.1-19 | 118 | 14.20 | 170 | | |
| 11.27 | 69 | 15.2 | 169, 170 | 8.13 | 74 |
| 11.28 | 69 | 15.12 | 133 | 9 | 73-76 |
| 11.29 | 69 | 15.19 | 103 | 9.1-14 | 75 |
| 13.1 | 6 | 15.21 | 138 | 9.3 | 74 |
| 13.47 | 135 | 16.1-2 | 162 | 9.4-14 | 75, 76, 85 |
| 18.1-4 | 122 | | | 9.10 | 217 |
| 21.10-11 | 69 | 1 Corinthians | | 9.12 | 76, 78, 85, 88, 217 |
| 22.2-16 | 118 | 1 | 175 | | |
| 25.27 | 69 | 1.10-17 | 74 | 9.14 | 78 |
| 26 | 136 | 1.20 | 200 | 9.15-18 | 1, 4, 72, 73, 76, 89, 112, 246, 247 |
| 26.9-18 | 118 | 1.22 | 103 | | |
| 26.16-18 | 213 | 1.23 | 201, 203 | | |
| 26.17-18 | 136 | 1.26-31 | 182 | | |
| 26.24-25 | 105 | 1.26 | 147, 181 | 9.15-17 | 87-89 |
| | | 1.27-30 | 181 | 9.15 | 74, 76-78, 85, 88 |
| Romans | | 1.31 | 158, 175 | | |
| 1.1-5 | 4 | 2.6-16 | 4 | 9.16-18 | 78 |
| 1.1 | 203 | 2.6 | 200 | 9.16-17 | 78-81, 85-87 |
| 1.3 | 147 | 2.8 | 200 | | |
| 3.19 | 93 | 3 | 171 | 9.16 | 78-80, 83, 84 |
| 4.1 | 147 | 3.8 | 88 | | |
| 4.11 | 103 | 3.9-15 | 172 | 9.17 | 80, 84-88 |
| 6.13-19 | 221 | 3.9-10 | 169, 171 | 9.18 | 85-88 |
| 6.16 | 203 | 3.12 | 169, 171 | 9.19-27 | 76 |

| 1 Corinthians (cont.) | | 14.24-25 | 102, 105, | 3.1-11 | 124 |
|---|---|---|---|---|---|
| 9.19 | 85, 88, 203 | 14.24 | 107 105, 109 | 3.1-6 | 2, 116, 124, 129, 132 |
| 9.24-27 | 88 | 14.25 | 108, 109 | | |
| 10 | 73 | 14.26 | 169, 171 | 3.1-5 | 161 |
| 10.14-22 | 218 | 14.29-33 | 111 | 3.1-3 | 145, 161 |
| 10.17 | 217 | 15.9-10 | 119 | 3.1 | 119, 162 |
| 10.18 | 147 | 15.57 | 190 | 3.2-3 | 181, 183 |
| 10.21 | 217 | | | 3.2 | 131, 162, 199 |
| 10.23 | 169, 171 | 2 Corinthians | | | |
| 10.27 | 201 | 1–9 | 216 | 3.3 | 162, 163, 165 |
| 10.30 | 217 | 1.3-11 | 250 | | |
| 11.1 | 75 | 2–3 | 196, 214 | 3.4-6 | 158, 163, 197 |
| 11.25 | 163 | 2.14–7.4 | 1, 113, 145, 186, 216, 219, 250 | 3.4 | 119, 129 |
| 12–14 | 61, 90, 100, 171 | | | 3.5 | 118, 119 |
| 12.2 | 106 | | | 3.6 | 114, 118, 119, 123, 124, 131, 161-65, 183 |
| 12.3 | 202 | 2.14–4.6 | 123, 125, 186, 195, 214 | | |
| 12.10 | 105 | | | | |
| 13 | 92 | | | | |
| 13.9-12 | 91 | 2.14–3.18 | 117, 195, 196 | | |
| 13.11 | 92 | | | 3.7-18 | 114, 120, 121, 132, 133, 163, 165, 195, 196 |
| 14 | 91, 106 | 2.14–3.6 | 195 | | |
| 14.1-19 | 90, 91 | 2.14-17 | 195, 222 | | |
| 14.1-5 | 107 | 2.14-16 | 2, 132, 133, 186, 192, 195, 233, 243, 244, 248 | | |
| 14.3 | 169, 171 | | | | |
| 14.6-19 | 92 | | | 3.7-11 | 121, 123, 124, 128, 129, 165, 201 |
| 14.11 | 99 | | | | |
| 14.12 | 169, 171 | | | | |
| 14.13-17 | 93 | 2.14-15 | 186, 192, 194 | | |
| 14.17 | 99 | | | 3.7 | 121, 123, 198, 201 |
| 14.19 | 107 | 2.14 | 152, 187-94 | | |
| 14.20-25 | 1, 72, 90-92, 109-12, 246, 247 | | | 3.8 | 121, 165 |
| | | 2.15-16 | 187, 194, 199-201 | 3.9 | 121 |
| | | | | 3.10 | 121, 122 |
| | | 2.15 | 187, 190, 191 | 3.11 | 121, 123 |
| 14.20 | 91-93 | | | 3.12-18 | 124 |
| 14.21 | 91, 93, 94, 100-102, 106-108 | 2.16–3.18 | 2 | 3.12-13 | 129 |
| | | 2.16-17 | 162 | 3.13 | 124, 129, 198, 201 |
| | | 2.16 | 118, 119, 129, 160, 187, 191, 197, 200 | | |
| 14.22-25 | 100, 102 | | | 3.14-16 | 199 |
| 14.22-24 | 201 | | | 3.14-15 | 124 |
| 14.22 | 91, 94, 102, 104, 106, 107 | | | 3.14 | 199 |
| | | 2.17 | 118 | 3.16-18 | 124 |
| | | 3–4 | 114, 223 | 3.18 | 121, 196, 198, 199, 203, 232, 205, 211 |
| 14.23-25 | 91, 94, 102 | 3 | 122, 141, 192, 199, 201 | | |
| 14.23 | 105 | | | 4 | |

| | | | | | | |
|---|---|---|---|---|---|---|
| 4.1-6 | 2, 186, 195, 196, 205, 212-14, 221, 222, 233, 240, 243, 244, 249 | 5.15 | 145, 146 | 6.16 | 220, 223-25, 228-30 |
| | | 5.16-17 | 146 | | |
| | | 5.16 | 147 | 6.17-18 | 224, 228, 230, 232 |
| | | 5.17 | 7, 147, 193, 205, 233 | 6.17 | 193, 218, 219, 224, 227-32 |
| | | 5.18-21 | 147, 148 | | |
| 4.1-2 | 196, 197, 203 | 5.20 | 150 | 6.18 | 223, 228 |
| | | 5.21 | 146, 149 | 7.1 | 216, 218, 231, 232 |
| 4.1 | 213 | 6 | 149, 156 | | |
| 4.2 | 198 | 6.1-2 | 145, 149, 157, 194, 218, 227, 228, 231, 233 | 7.2 | 215 |
| 4.3-4 | 196, 199, 200 | | | 7.6 | 7 |
| | | | | 8–9 | 250 |
| 4.3 | 199 | | | 8.16-24 | 162 |
| 4.4 | 198-201, 203, 204, 212, 213, 219 | 6.1 | 150-52, 157, 175, 183 | 8.16 | 190 |
| | | | | 9.10 | 7 |
| | | | | 9.15 | 190 |
| | | | | 9.17 | 79 |
| 4.5-6 | 196, 202 | 6.2 | 7, 139, 148, 150-52, 154, 155, 193 | 10 | 169, 176 |
| 4.5 | 201-203 | | | 10–13 | 1, 113, 118, 166, 174, 216, 235, 238, 243, 250 |
| 4.6 | 4, 6, 7, 190, 193, 196, 200, 201, 204, 205, 208, 211-13 | | | | |
| | | 6.3-10 | 152-54, 217 | | |
| | | 6.3 | 79 | 10.1-11 | 169, 175 |
| | | 6.4 | 79, 131 | 10.1 | 177 |
| 4.7-15 | 154 | 6.11-13 | 157 | 10.3-6 | 173 |
| 4.7-12 | 191, 203 | 6.13 | 215, 218 | 10.3-5 | 169, 173 |
| 4.8-10 | 154 | 6.14–7.1 | 2, 186, 195, 215-19, 225, 231, 233, 243, 244, 249 | 10.3 | 231 |
| 4.11 | 7, 231, 243 | | | 10.5 | 173, 190 |
| | | | | 10.6 | 169, 173 |
| 4.18 | 198 | | | 10.7-11 | 176 |
| 5–7 | 145, 204 | | | 10.7-8 | 169 |
| 5.1 | 170 | | | 10.8 | 2, 158, 166, 169-72, 174-76, 182, 183 |
| 5.11–6.10 | 134, 139, 145 | 6.14-16 | 218-20, 223, 227, 233 | | |
| 5.11-13 | 145 | | | | |
| 5.13 | 86 | 6.14-15 | 201 | | |
| 5.14–6.10 | 152, 154, 155, 157 | 6.14 | 216-20, 223, 227, 230-33 | 10.10-11 | 177 |
| | | | | 10.11 | 169 |
| 5.14–6.2 | 2 | | | 10.12-18 | 175, 176, 182 |
| 5.14-21 | 145, 149, 150, 152, 153, 155, 157, 213, 223, 240 | 6.15 | 219, 222, 223 | 10.12-16 | 181 |
| | | 6.16-18 | 216-19, 223-25, 230, 231, 249 | 10.12 | 176, 177 |
| | | | | 10.13-18 | 178 |
| | | | | 10.13 | 178, 180, 182 |
| 5.14-15 | 145-47 | | | | |
| 5.14 | 146 | | | 10.14-16 | 180, 182 |

| 2 Corinthians (cont.) | | 12.11 | 243 | 2.11 | 202 |
|---|---|---|---|---|---|
| 10.14 | 180, 243 | 12.12 | 103 | 2.16 | 138, 151 |
| 10.15 | 178, 180 | 13 | 169 | 2.19-23 | 162 |
| 10.16-17 | 180 | 13.1-4 | 169 | 3.16 | 180 |
| 10.16 | 243 | 13.2-4 | 173 | 3.19 | 200 |
| 10.17-18 | 239 | 13.4 | 132, 169, 239, 243 | 4.3 | 217 |
| 10.17 | 2, 158, 182, 183, 239 | 13.5-10 | 173 | Colossians | |
| | | 13.5 | 169 | 1.7 | 203 |
| 10.18 | 182 | 13.10 | 2, 158, 166, 169-74, 183 | 1.12 | 217 |
| 11 | 237, 240 | | | 1.15-19 | 201 |
| 11.1–12.13 | 233, 235 | | | 2.15 | 189 |
| 11.3 | 232 | | | 4.7-9 | 162 |
| 11.5 | 243 | Galatians | | 4.7 | 203 |
| 11.22 | 243 | 1 | 161 | 4.12 | 203 |
| 11.23–12.10 | 234, 238, 239 | 1.4 | 200 | | |
| | | 1.10 | 203 | 1 Thessalonians | |
| 11.23-33 | 239, 243 | 1.12 | 235 | 2.3-8 | 4 |
| 11.23-29 | 154, 235, 238, 241 | 1.15-16 | 3, 9, 82, 137, 183 | 2.16 | 180 |
| | | | | 3.5 | 138, 151 |
| 11.23 | 131 | 1.15 | 136, 138, 159, 161 | 3.7 | 79 |
| 11.30 | 80, 234 | | | 5.5 | 221 |
| 11.32-33 | 235, 238, 241 | 1.16 | 161, 235 | 5.11 | 169 |
| | | 2.2 | 138, 151 | | |
| 12.1-10 | 2, 195, 215, 233-35, 237-39, 243, 244, 249 | 2.6 | 77 | 2 Thessalonians | |
| | | 2.18 | 170 | 2.4 | 242 |
| | | 2.20 | 231 | 2.9 | 103 |
| | | 4.9 | 190 | 3.17 | 103 |
| | | 5.19-21 | 231 | | |
| 12.1 | 234, 235 | | | 1 Timothy | |
| 12.2-4 | 234-38, 240, 241, 243 | Ephesians | | 1.13 | 197 |
| | | 1.21 | 200 | 4.10 | 222 |
| | | 2.19–3.7 | 4 | 4.12 | 222 |
| 12.2 | 236 | 2.21 | 169 | 5.8 | 201 |
| 12.3-4 | 236 | 4.7 | 178 | 5.16 | 222 |
| 12.5-7 | 235 | 4.12-13 | 169 | 6.2 | 222 |
| 12.5-6 | 238 | 4.12 | 170 | | |
| 12.5 | 236, 238 | 4.13 | 178 | Titus | |
| 12.6 | 239, 241 | 4.16 | 169, 170, 178 | 1.15 | 201 |
| 12.7-9 | 234, 238-41, 243 | | | 2.14 | 217 |
| | | 4.29 | 169 | | |
| 12.7 | 234, 241-43 | 5.8 | 221 | Philemon | |
| | | 5.26 | 217 | 14 | 79 |
| 12.9-10 | 154, 239 | | | | |
| 12.10 | 79, 132, 234, 235, 239, 243 | Philippians | | Revelation | |
| | | 1.1 | 203 | 1.1 | 69 |
| | | 2.6 | 201 | | |

# Index of References

| Apocrypha/Deutero-Canonical Works | | 2 Enoch | | Qumran | |
|---|---|---|---|---|---|
| | | 8.1 | 236 | 1QH | |
| 1 Esdras | | | | 12.6 | 221 |
| 8.80 | 231 | 4 Maccabees | | 14.15-16 | 221 |
| | | 7.5 LXX | 105 | 16.10-11 | 221 |
| Wisdom of Solomon | | 8.5 LXX | 105 | | |
| 7.24-26 | 202 | 10.13 LXX | 105 | 1QH$^a$ | |
| 7.25-26 | 202 | | | 4.26 | 38 |
| 7.26 | 202 | Jubilees | | 6.25 | 38 |
| 14.28 | 105 | 1.20 | 221 | 9.21 | 38 |
| | | 1.24 | 229 | 10–17 | 38 |
| Sirach | | | | 10.10-18 | 37 |
| 24.32-34 | 49 | Liber antiquitatum biblicarum | | 12.5-17 | 37-39 |
| 24.32-33 | 50 | | | 12.16 | 37, 39 |
| 24.32 | 50 | 9.7-8 | 119 | 12.23 | 38 |
| 24.33 | 50 | | | 12.27-28 | 37 |
| 36.20-21 | 49 | Testament of Dan | | 15.26-27 | 37 |
| 38.34–39.3 | 49 | 4.7 | 221 | 16.16-19 | 37 |
| 44.1–50.24 | 49 | 5.1 | 221 | 17.32 | 38 |
| 44.3 | 49 | | | 23.10-14 | 37 |
| 45.2 | 122 | Testament of Issachar | | | |
| 46.20 | 49 | 6.1 | 221 | 1QM | |
| 47.1 | 49 | | | 1.1-13 | 221 |
| | | Testament of Joseph | | 13.1-4 | 221 |
| Baruch | | 20.2 | 221 | 13.5-16 | 221 |
| 1.21 | 29 | | | 13.11-12 | 221 |
| | | Testament of Judah | | | |
| Prayer of Azariah | | 24.3 | 229 | 1QS | |
| 15 | 29 | | | 1.2-3 | 37 |
| | | Testament of Levi | | 1.9-11 | 221 |
| 1 Maccabees | | 19.1 | 221 | 2.16-17 | 221 |
| 4.44-46 | 31 | | | 3.3-25 | 221 |
| 4.46 | 29, 125 | Testament of Naphthali | | 3.6-7 | 38 |
| 9.27 | 29, 31 | 2.6 | 221 | 5.1-4 | 221 |
| 14.41 | 29, 31, 125 | 3.1 | 221 | 8.15-16 | 37 |
| | | | | 9.3-4 | 38 |
| | | Testament of Reuben | | 9.11 | 37 |
| 2 Maccabees | | 4.11 | 221 | | |
| 5.27 | 231 | | | 1QpHab | |
| | | Testament of Simeon | | 2.8-9 | 37 |
| Pseudepigrapha | | 5.3 | 221 | 4.3-8 | 38 |
| Assumption of Moses | | | | 7.4-5 | 41 |
| 11.6 | 122 | Testament of Moses | | | |
| | | 1.14 | 119 | 3Q4 | |
| 2 Baruch | | 11.16 | 119 | 3 | 37 |
| 85.1 | 29 | 12.6-7 | 119 | | |
| 85.3 | 29 | | | | |

| 4Q165 | | | 11Q5 | | | 8.418 | 43 |
|---|---|---|---|---|---|---|---|
| 1-2.1 | | 37 | 27.11 | | 37 | 9.35 | 43 |
| | | | | | | 9.276 | 43 |
| 4Q174 | | | 11Q19 | | | 9.280 | 43 |
| 1.9 | | 221 | 54.8-19 | | 40 | 10.245-49 | 43 |
| 1.11 | | 229 | 54.8-18 | | 39, 40 | 10.267-69 | 43 |
| | | | | | | 10.267-68 | 44 |
| 4Q175 | | | CD | | | 10.267 | 43 |
| 1.5 | | 37 | 1.10-12 | | 126 | 10.275 | 46 |
| | | | 4.13-14 | | 225 | 10.277 | 43 |
| 4Q248 | | | 4.13 | | 37 | 10.280 | 43 |
| 1.5 | | 38 | 5.20–6.2 | | 39 | 10.78 | 43 |
| | | | 6.1 | | 37, 39 | 10.79 | 43, 46 |
| 4Q286 | | | 6.3 | | 126 | 10.92 | 44 |
| 1.ii.1-8 | | 39 | 6.13 | | 225 | 11.322 | 43 |
| | | | 7.17 | | 37 | 13.299-300 | 44 |
| 4Q300 | | | 8.9 | | 225 | 13.300 | 44 |
| 1.ii.3 | | 39 | 20.20-21 | | 221 | 13.311-13 | 45 |
| | | | | | | 15.373-79 | 39 |
| 4Q301 | | | PAM | | | 18.116-19 | 64 |
| 1.1 | | 38 | 44.102 66 4 | | 37 | 18.118 | 64 |
| | | | | | | 20.169 | 44, 45 |
| 4Q339 | | | Rabbinic Texts and | | | 20.97 | 45 |
| — | | 39 | Other Jewish | | | | |
| | | | Literature | | | Against Apion | |
| 4Q370 | | | Josephus | | | 1.1 | 43 |
| — | | 38 | Jewish Antiquities | | | 1.37-41 | 44 |
| | | | 1.5 | | 43 | 1.37-40 | 32 |
| 4Q375 | | | 1.240 | | 45, 46 | 1.41 | 29, 32, 33, |
| — | | 39 | 2.327 | | 43 | | 42, 45 |
| | | | 3.180 | | 122 | 1.312 | 45 |
| 4Q385 | | | 4.104 | | 46 | | |
| — | | 37 | 4.112 | | 46 | Life | |
| | | | 4.320 | | 44 | 424-25 | 44 |
| 4Q386 | | | 4.329 | | 43 | | |
| — | | 37 | 5.341 | | 43 | Jewish War | |
| | | | 6.50 | | 69 | 1.18 | 46 |
| 4Q399 | | | 6.56 | | 43 | 1.68-69 | 44 |
| — | | 39 | 6.76 | | 43 | 1.78-80 | 45 |
| | | | 6.344 | | 44 | 1.78 | 39 |
| 4Q417 | | | 7.91 | | 43 | 2.113 | 39 |
| 1.7-10 | | 39 | 7.334 | | 44 | 2.159 | 39 |
| 2.i.16 | | 39 | 8.236-42 | | 44 | 2.261 | 45 |
| | | | 8.319-62 | | 43 | 3.340 | 46 |
| 4Q458 | | | 8.346 | | 43 | 3.351-53 | 46 |
| 15.2 | | 37 | 8.352 | | 43 | 3.399-408 | 46 |
| | | | 8.409 | | 69 | 4.388 | 43 |

## Index of References

| | | | | | |
|---|---|---|---|---|---|
| 6.285-87 | 44-46 | *Sanhedrin* | | Eutropius | |
| 7.132-57 | 188 | 90a | 33 | *Breviarium* | |
| 7.438 | 44 | | | 1.11 | 189 |
| | | *Soṭa* | | | |
| PHILO | | 48b | 33 | Herodian | |
| *Allegorical Interpretation* | | | | *History* | |
| 1.43 | 202 | *Yoma* | | 1.6.6 | 189 |
| | | 9b | 33 | | |
| *Cherubim* | | | | Herodotus | |
| 27–29 | 48 | JERUSALEM TALMUD | | *Historiae* | |
| | | *Soṭa* | | 7.111 | 53 |
| *On Dreams* | | 9.13 | 33 | 8.36-37 | 53 |
| 2.252 | 48 | | | 8.135 | 53 |
| | | TOSEFTA TALMUD | | 9.93 | 53 |
| *On the Life of Moses* | | *Soṭa* | | | |
| 2.187 | 44, 47, 49 | 13.2 | 33 | Justin | |
| 2.188-90 | 48 | 13.2b-4 | 33 | *Epitome* | |
| 2.188-89 | 47 | | | 36.2.11-6 | 122 |
| 2.264-269 | 48 | MIDRASH | | | |
| | | *Canticles Rabbah* | | Longinus | |
| *On the Migration of* | | 8.11 | 33 | *De sublimitate* | |
| *Abraham* | | | | 9.9 | 122 |
| 34–35 | 48 | *Sifre on Deuteronomy* | | | |
| | | 33.21 | 125 | Origen | |
| *On the Special Laws* | | | | *Philocalia* | |
| 1.65 | 47, 48 | GREEK/ROMAN/ | | 9.2 | 98 |
| 4.49 | 48 | CLASSICAL WORKS | | | |
| | | *1 Clement* | | Pausanius | |
| *Questions and Answers* | | 41.1 | 179 | *Graeciae description* | |
| *on Genesis* | | | | 9.23-6 | 53 |
| 3.9 | 48 | Appian | | | |
| | | *Bella civilian* | | Plato | |
| *Who is the Heir?* | | 2.15.101-102 | 188 | *Alcibiades major* | |
| 259-66 | 47 | | | II.148d-150b | 53 |
| 259-60 | 49 | *Historia romana* | | | |
| 264-65 | 48 | 8.9.66 | 188, 191 | *Charmides* | |
| | | 12.11.77 | 189 | 173c | 53 |
| MISHNAH | | | | | |
| *Sanhedrin* | | Dio Cassius | | *Phaedrus* | |
| 1.5 | 33 | *Historiae* | | 244B-C | 56 |
| 11.1 | 33 | 6.23 | 188 | | |
| | | | | *Philebus* | |
| BABYLONIAN TALMUD | | Dio Chrysotom | | 28b | 53 |
| *Berakot* | | *Oratio* | | | |
| 55b | 33 | 7.101 | 54 | *Timaeus* | |
| | | 36.42 | 54 | 71e-72b | 53 |
| | | 48.14 | 171 | | |

Plutarch
*Aemilius Paullus*
32.1–36.6    188

*Aratus*
54.3    189

*Aristides*
19.1-2    53

*Cimon*
16.10    218

*Comparatio Thesei
et Romuli*
4.2    189

*Moralia*
201E    189
318B    189
397B    54
405C    56
407B    56
412A    53
792F    54

Polybius
*Historiae*
4.19.10    197

Quintilian
*Institutio oratoria*
3.7.21    122

Strabo
*Geographica*
12.3.35    189
16.2.39    122
9.3.5    56

Suetonius
Nero 25.2    191

Tacitus
*Historiae*
5.4-5    122

Xenophon
*Memorabilia*
4.4.16-17    171

## INDEX OF AUTHORS

Adewuya, J.A.  217, 232
Albright, W.F.  11
Alden, R.L.  206
Allison, D.C.  65
Allo, E.B.  204
Attridge, H.W.  190, 191
Aune, D.E.  14, 16, 17, 19-23, 31, 33, 34, 42, 45, 46, 52, 53, 55, 58, 62, 65, 67, 70

Bach, R.  168
Baer, D.A.  100
Bailey, D.P.  209
Bain, J.A.  200
Baker, W.R.  114
Balla, P.  152, 231
Banks, R.  125-27
Barclay, J.M.G.  106
Barnett, P.  113, 118, 119, 121, 151, 178, 204, 220, 235, 242
Barrett, C.K.  28, 69, 91, 92, 107, 122, 136, 178, 188, 204, 221
Barstad, H.M.  12
Barthélemy, D.  209, 210
Bauckham, R.  34, 59, 60, 143, 210
Baumert, N.  197
Baur, F.C.  113
Beale, G.K.  134, 139, 147, 149, 152, 153, 204, 215, 224, 226, 227, 230, 231
Beard, M.  188, 189
Becking, B.  167
Beentjes, P.C.  49, 50
Beker, J.C.  159, 185
Belleville, L.L.  114, 198
Benoit, P.  215
Berridge, J.M.  177
Betz, H.D.  104, 220, 238
Beuken, W.A.M.  136, 209
Beyer, H.W.  178, 179
Bieringer, R.  2, 215
Black, D.A.  235
Blanton, T.R.  164

Blenkinsopp, J.  16, 23, 42, 95, 96, 207
Block, D.I.  229
Bock, D.L.  62, 63, 68
Bockmuehl, M.N.A.  43, 45, 46, 48
Boda, M.J.  102
Boers, H.  145
Bonnard, P.  170
Bonnington, M.  232
Boring, M.E.  54
Bowers, P.  74
Bowley, J.E.  37, 38
Breytenbach, C.  148, 188, 189, 191
Brockington, L.H.  212
Brooke, G.J.  38, 39, 41, 42
Brown, C.  103
Brown, R.E.  63
Bruce, F.F.  127, 136, 137, 242
Brueggemann, W.  12, 19
Brunt, J.C.  73
Bultmann, R.  204
Burkhardt, H.  48
Burrows, M.  39
Burtarbutar, R.  73, 75, 79

Callan, T.  54
Calvin, J.  188
Campbell, W.S.  134, 137
Carrez, M.  187
Carroll, R.P.  17, 164
Carson, D.A.  19, 67, 104
Ceresko, A.R.  50
Cerfaux, L.  134, 153
Cervelli, I.  59
Chang, S.S.H.  2
Chester, S.J.  92, 105, 106, 109
Childs, B.S.  18, 94-97, 103, 104, 108, 109, 135, 136, 140-43, 207, 212, 228
Chow, J.K.  75
Ciampa, R.E.  77, 82, 88, 110, 111, 137
Clarke, A.D.  86, 130, 172, 182, 203
Clements, R.E.  20, 21, 24, 25, 144

Clifford, R.J.  83
Clowney, E.P.  224
Coggins, R.  12
Collange, J.-F.  205, 206, 219
Collins, J.J.  35, 58, 59
Collins, J.N.  130
Collins, N.L.  114
Collins, R.F.  108
Conzelmann, H.  73, 82, 99
Cousland, J.R.C.  56
Croatto, J.S.  68
Crone, T.M.  9, 55
Cross, F.M.  11, 28
Crossan, J.D.  66

Dahl, N.A.  215
Danker, F.W.  189
Darr, K.P.  22
Das, A.A.  124
Dautzenberg, G.  74, 196, 211
Davies, S.  200
Davies, W.D.  125
Davis, G.B.  177, 181
Deissner, K.  178
DeNeui, M.W.  170-72
Derrett, J.D.  217
deSilva, D.A.  222
de Waard, J.  210
Diamond, A.R.  177
Didier, G.  85
Dinter, P.E.  134
Doughty, D.J.  88
Duff, P.B.  114, 115, 192, 216
Duhm, B.  136
Dumbrell, W.J.  115, 121, 124
Dungan, D.L.  75, 76, 88
Dunn, J.D.G.  170
Durham, J.I.  116, 132

Egan, R.B.  188
Ehrensperger, K.  159, 185, 219
Ekblad, E.R., Jr.  142, 208-10
Evans, C.A.  4, 134
Exum, J.C.  95, 96

Faierstein, M.M.  65
Fascher, E.  9

Fee, G.D.  29, 74, 76, 78, 87, 88, 90, 91, 93, 98, 99, 102-4, 108, 110, 111, 123, 202, 217, 218, 220, 228, 242
Feldman, L.H.  32, 42-44, 46
Fitzgerald, J.T.  92, 93, 153
Fitzmyer, J.A.  65, 73, 87, 90, 115, 215, 221, 225
Flint, P.W.  37
Floyd, M.H.  30, 34
Fontenrose, J.  54, 57
Forbes, C.  9, 47, 49, 53, 55, 58, 60, 90, 105, 111, 176-78, 238, 239
Ford, D.F.  184, 200
Fox, R.L.  70
Freed, E.D.  3
Fritsch, C.  100
Fung, R.Y.K.  137, 161
Furnish, V.P.  148, 149, 179, 187, 198, 204, 211, 215, 218, 224, 231, 237

Galitis, G.  73
García Martínez, F.  40
Gardner, P.D.  73, 78, 84, 88
Garland, D.E.  78, 82, 90, 93, 98, 103, 104, 106, 129, 182, 200, 203, 229, 231, 242
Garrett, S.R.  197, 200
Gelin, A.  132
Georgi, D.  113
Gerstenberger, E.  83
Giblet, J.  28
Gignilliat, M.  4, 139, 142-44, 146, 148, 149, 151, 154, 155
Gillespie, T.W.  93, 174
Gitay, Y.  108
Gleason, R.C.  115, 164
Gnilka, J.  215, 221
Gnuse, R.K.  42
Goetzmann, J.  171
Gooder, P.R.  234-40, 243
Goodrich, J.K.  85
Gordon, R.  14
Goudge, H.L.  204
Goulder, M.D.  215, 236
Grabbe, L.L.  29-32, 34, 35, 42, 44, 46-48
Grässer, E.  162, 199, 204
Gray, R.  32, 33, 39, 42, 44-46
Green, G.L.  242

Greenspahn, F.E. 31-33
Grindheim, S. 4, 6, 115, 164
Grudem, W. 70, 90, 96, 101, 103, 104, 107, 109, 111
Grundmann, W. 80, 81

Habel, N.C. 160, 206
Hackett, J.A. 13
Hafemann, S.J. 3, 4, 80, 88, 114-19, 121, 123, 124, 127-29, 131, 132, 160, 162, 163, 165, 169, 174, 176-83, 185, 187, 188, 190, 191, 195, 198, 199, 201, 223
Hahn, F. 137
Hajjar, Y. 56
Hall, W.S. 4
Hallo, W.W. 96
Halperin, D.J. 240
Hanson, A.T. 115, 134
Hanson, J.S. 39, 52, 56, 64
Hanson, P.D. 28
Harris, M.J. 119, 123, 145-47, 150, 166, 169, 173, 174, 176, 177, 179, 180, 187, 189-91, 196-98, 200, 201, 203, 204, 206, 211, 217, 219-23, 226, 228, 230, 232, 234-36, 239, 241, 242
Hartley, J.E. 206
Hasel, G.F. 94
Hauck, F. 80
Hawthorne, G.F. 61
Hay, D.M. 47
Hayes, J.H. 22
Hays, R.B. 91, 107, 108, 110, 115, 162, 181, 214
Heckel, U. 118, 175, 238, 239
Heil, C. 216
Heil, J.P. 73
Hengel, M. 49, 209
Henze, M. 30, 50
Héring, J. 73, 92
Hickling, C.J.A. 134
Hill, D. 28
Hock, R.F. 172
Hoffner, H.A., Jr. 13, 14
Hofius, O. 103, 148, 149
Hoftijzer, J. 13
Hogeterp, A.L.A. 216
Holladay, W.L. 158, 160, 167, 177
Holland, G. 183

Holland, T. 134
Hollenbach, P.W. 64
Hooker, M.D. 66, 68, 162
Horn, F.W. 28
Horrell, D.G. 3, 73, 75, 76, 239
Horsley, G.H.R. 64
Horsley, R.A. 39
Hovenden, G. 104
Hubbard, M.V. 86, 146, 147, 185
Huffmon, H. 13
Hugenberger, G.P. 144
Hulmi, S. 115
Hultgren, S.J. 216, 217
Humphrey, E.M. 116, 120, 237, 238
Huppenbauer, H.W. 221
Hurd, J.C. 74
Hurwitz, M.S. 100
Hvidt, N.C. 12, 65

Ingelaere, J.-C. 43

Jackson, T.R. 147, 154
Janzen, W. 83
Jassen, A.P. 29, 31, 37-40, 42, 43, 45, 50
Jaubert, A. 164
Jeremias, G. 37, 38, 74
Jeremias, J. 28
Jobes, K.H. 209, 210
Johanson, B.C. 91
Jones, F.S. 74
Jones, P.R. 115, 125-28, 156, 206
Judge, E.A. 174, 179

Kapelrud, A.S. 140
Käsemann, E. 81, 83, 113
Kaufmann, Y. 28
Kautzsch, E. 98
Kaye, B.N. 219, 224
Kennett, R.H. 96
Kilian, R. 117
Kim, S. 134, 137, 153, 156, 157, 197, 213, 240
Kingsbury, J.D. 68
Kistemaker, S.J. 92
Kitzberger, I. 170, 171
Klauck, H.-J. 211, 215
Knibb, M. 34
Knight, J.M. 34

Koch, D.-A. 115, 158, 163, 225
Koenig, J. 210
Kooij, G. van der 13, 207
Kraftchick, S.J. 191
Krämer, H. 8, 53
Kruger, P.A. 103
Kruse, C.G. 153
Kwon, D.L. 96, 98-101, 104, 108

Laberge, L. 94
Lambrecht, J. 123, 145, 146, 151, 154, 163, 166, 169, 173, 177, 181, 188, 189, 195, 196, 204, 216, 220, 234
Lane, W.L. 156, 165, 166, 175
Lang, F. 224
Lange, A. 98
Lanier, D.E. 100, 104
Leiman, S.Z. 43, 45
Leonhardt-Balzer, J. 38, 49, 127
Lévi, I. 49
Levin, C. 226
Levine, B.A. 11
Levison, J.R. 33, 47-49
Lierman, J. 120, 121
Lietaert Peerbolte, L.J. 159, 161
Lietzmann, H. 73, 204
Lim, K.Y. 134, 138, 140, 150-54, 181-83, 187, 189-94, 238, 239
Lincoln, A.T. 235, 236
Lindblom, J. 11, 15, 19, 21, 22, 24
Lindgård, F. 2
Litwa, M.D. 238
Long, F.J. 2
Longenecker, R.N. 137
Lorenzen, S. 201, 202
Lundbom, J.R. 82, 167, 168, 174, 181
Lust, J. 207

MacGorman, J.W. 92
MacRae, G.W. 205
Malamat, A. 15
Malan, F.S. 108
Malherbe, A.J. 81, 85, 242
Maly, K. 171
March, W.E. 22
Marshall, I.H. 136, 148
Marshall, P. 162, 192

Martin, D.B. 73, 75, 86, 105, 106
Martin, R.P. 91, 134, 146, 147, 194, 200, 206, 221, 231, 238
Martini, C.M. 206
Martyn, J.L. 137
Mason, R. 28
Maurer, C. 80
Maurizio, L. 57
Menzies, A. 204
Menzies, R.P. 62
Merklein, H. 73
Metzger, B.M. 77
Meyer, J.C. 121-24, 164, 165, 214
Meyers, C.L. 30
Meyers, E.M. 30
Michel, O. 100, 170, 175
Miller, P.D., Jr. 20, 26
Mitchell, M.M. 73-75, 77, 171
Momigliano, A. 59
Moo, D.J. 132, 137, 170
Morgenthaler, R. 81
Morray-Jones, C.R.A. 236, 237, 240-42
Motyer, J.A. 97
Moule, C.F.D. 129
Moyise, S. 122
Müller, U.B. 4
Munck, J. 3, 132, 134
Murphy-O'Connor, J. 164, 219, 222
Myers, J.M. 3

Najda, A.J. 4
Nasuti, H.P. 77-80, 83, 88
Ngunga, A.T. 210, 212
Nguyen, V.H.T. 189, 202, 212
Nicklas, T. 5, 6, 82, 137, 245, 250
Nissinen, M. 13, 14
Nolland, J. 67

O'Brien, P.T. 137, 170
O'Connor, K.M. 177
O'Day, G.R. 181
Oakes, P. 115, 128
Oepke, A. 211
Olley, J.W. 210, 229, 230
Omanson, R.L. 77
Oostendorp, D.W. 206
Oswalt, J.N. 95, 96, 133, 141, 208, 227, 241

Parke, H.W. 56, 58, 59
Parker, S.B. 14
Parpola, S. 13
Paton-Williams, D. 142, 143
Patrick, D. 6
Petersen, D.L. 8, 10-12, 14-16, 20, 23, 38, 232
Peterson, D. 170
Pfammatter, J. 170
Phillips, J.B. 91
Phua, R.L.-S. 73, 74
Plummer, A. 82, 204
Polk, T. 177
Porter, J.R. 13, 18
Porter, S.E. 7, 52, 148
Potter, D. 52
Preisendanz, K. 122
Price, S. 57
Provence, T.E. 115

Qimron, E. 40

Rad, G. von 144
Radl, W. 134
Räisänen, H. 163
Redditt, P.L. 15
Reiling, J. 45, 55
Rengstorff, K.H. 103, 104
Rensberger, D. 219
Renwick, D.A. 191
Reumann, J. 80, 85, 86
Richard, E. 162, 206
Ringgren, H. 15, 27
Rissi, M. 164
Robbins, V.K. 85
Robertson, A.T. 82
Robertson, O.P. 103
Rochester, K. 117, 161
Rofé, A. 22
Roloff, J. 156
Rosner, B.S. 77, 82, 88, 110, 111
Rowe, C.K. 212
Rowland, C. 236, 237, 241, 242

Sandnes, K.O. 3, 4, 6, 78, 80-82, 86-89, 100, 102-4, 111, 128, 129, 156, 157, 159, 161, 184, 206, 213

Sass, G. 216
Savage, T.B. 114, 118, 122, 134, 202, 203, 206, 212
Sawyer, J. 143
Schaper, J. 207, 208
Schille, G. 69
Schlatter, A. 179
Schmeller, T. 119, 145, 165, 188, 196, 200, 216
Schmithals, W. 113
Schnabel, E.J. 50, 84, 88, 93, 99, 104, 110
Schneider, C. 173
Schnelle, U. 2, 137
Schrage, W. 76, 82, 84, 88, 105
Schreckenberg, H. 79
Schreiner, J. 134, 175, 176, 183
Schreiner, T.R. 138, 170
Schulz, S. 115
Schütz, J.H. 175
Scott, J.M. 190, 192, 216, 218-20, 224-31
Scult, A. 6
Seeligmann, I.L. 207, 210
Seitz, C.R. 8, 21, 25, 120, 133, 136, 140, 142, 160
Senft, C. 77
Shanor, J. 172
Silva, M. 209, 210
Sjøberg, E. 28
Sloan, R.B. 162
Smend, R. 226
Smit, J. 74, 90, 102
Smith, D.M. 185
Smith, M. 18
Sommer, B.D. 29, 33, 46
Stanley, C.D. 94, 98, 101, 152, 185, 205, 223, 225, 226
Stanley, D.M. 134, 135, 137
Steck, O.H. 21, 23, 25, 26
Stegman, T. 212
Stendahl, K. 103
Still, T.D. 172
Stockhausen, C.K. 115, 116, 163, 214
Strachan, R.H. 204
Strange, J.F. 179
Stuart, D. 23, 24
Stuhlmacher, P. 3, 83, 84
Sumney, J.L. 113

Tabor, J.D. 240
Teeple, H.M. 39
Thielman, F. 4
Thiselton, A.C. 74-77, 82, 84, 89-92, 104-6, 109-11, 172
Thomas, J.C. 242
Thompson, J.A. 82, 164, 173
Thrall, M.E. 115, 129, 150, 151, 164, 166, 169, 172, 173, 178-80, 187, 190, 193, 197-200, 202-4, 206, 213, 217, 218, 222, 225, 234-36, 238, 239
Tiemeyer, L.-S. 140
Tigchelaar, E.J.C. 40
Tucker, G.M. 15, 22
Turner, M. 62

Uddin, M. 200
Urbach, E.E. 33
Utzschneider, H. 158

VanderKam, J.C. 34, 41
VanGemeren, W.A. 12, 15, 16, 18, 20, 23, 24, 30, 102, 120
van Kooten, G.H. 201, 223
van Unnik, W.C. 115
Versnel, H.S. 188
Vielhauer, P. 170, 172
Vieweger, D. 117
Vogliano, A. 122

Wagner, J.R. 138
Walker, W.O. 216
Wallace, D.B. 85
Wanamaker, C.A. 242
Wanke, G. 83
Watson, D.F. 176

Watson, F. 115, 123
Webb, R.L. 63-66
Webb, W.J. 135, 139, 156, 192, 193, 206, 213, 215, 216, 218, 219, 225-28, 230, 231
Weiss, J. 73, 85, 88, 104
Wellhausen, J. 28
Wendland, H.-D. 204
Westermann, C. 22, 135, 140, 142
Wevers, J.W. 226
Wilcox, P. 142, 143
Wiles, G.P. 132
Wilk, F. 4, 5, 7, 108, 152, 206, 216, 225
Williams, J.G. 83
Williamson, L. 188
Willis, W. 74, 75
Wilson, R.R. 10, 11, 16-19, 22, 25, 28
Windisch, H. 3, 204
Winston, D. 47
Winter, B.W. 172
Wire, A.C. 104
Witherington, B., III 34, 59, 64, 66-69, 74, 107, 124, 137, 218
Wolff, C. 158
Wolff, H.W. 8, 164
Wong, K. H.-Y. 176, 177, 180, 181
Wormell, D.E.W. 56
Wright, B.G. 49
Wright, N.T. 65-67, 115, 125

Yates, J.W. 163
Young, F. 184, 200

Zeilinger, F. 216
Zimmerli, W. 117
Zmijewski, J. 235